CONNEC

DARLING, I WANT TO REPEAT "SOFT-SCRIBE PODCAST" OVER & OVER SO THAT IT LOSES ALL MEANING!
THEN DO IT!

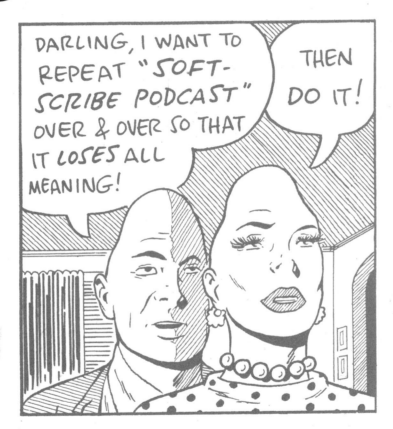

Zippy

CONNECT THE POLKA DOTS

December 2005 — August 2006

Bill Griffith

FANTAGRAPHICS BOOKS

ZIPPY / Connect The Polka Dots
Zippy Annual – Volume 7
Copyright © 2005, 2006 Bill Griffith

FANTAGRAPHICS BOOKS

7563 Lake City Way NE, Seattle WA 98115
www.fantagraphics.com
Call 1-800-657-1100 for a full color catalog of fine comics publications.
First Edition: November 2006
Designed by Bill Griffith
Production managed by Kim Thompson
Production by Paul Baresh
Cover production by Paul Baresh
Published by Gary Groth and Kim Thompson

Printed in Malaysia
ISBN-13: 978-1-56097-777-3
ISBN-10: 1-56097-777-9

The comic strips in this book have appeared in newspapers in the
United States and abroad, distributed by King Features Syndicate, 300
W. 57th St., New York NY 10019.
www.kingfeatures.com

For more on Zippy (and many added features, including the Zippy
Storefront, Zippy Strip Search and extensive Zippy Archives), visit:
www.zippythepinhead.com

Thanks and a tip o' th' pin to: Jay Kennedy, American Color, Gary
Groth, Kim Thompson, Jon Buller, Kristin Griffin and all the roadside
field researchers who continue to send in Zip-worthy photos and
location information.

Books by Bill Griffith:
Zippy Stories • *Nation of Pinheads* • *Pointed Behavior* • *Pindemonium*
Are We Having Fun Yet? • *Kingpin* • *Pinhead's Progress* • *Get Me A*
Table Without Flies, Harry • *From A To Zippy* • *Zippy's House Of Fun*
Griffith Observatory • *Zippy Annual #1* • *Zippy Annual 2001*
Zippy Annual 2002 • *Zippy Annual 2003* • ZIPPY: *From Here To*
Absurdity • ZIPPY: *Type Z Personality*

To contact Bill Griffith:
Pinhead Productions, LLC, P.O. Box 88, Hadlyme CT 06439
Griffy@zippythepinhead.com

Dedicated to Diane Noomin.

Zippy & Griffy 6

Zippy Solo 26

Zippy & Co. 44

Dinerama 58

Sunday Color & More 70

Roadside Attractions 94

Selected Shorts 120

Pindex 140

Zippy & Griffy

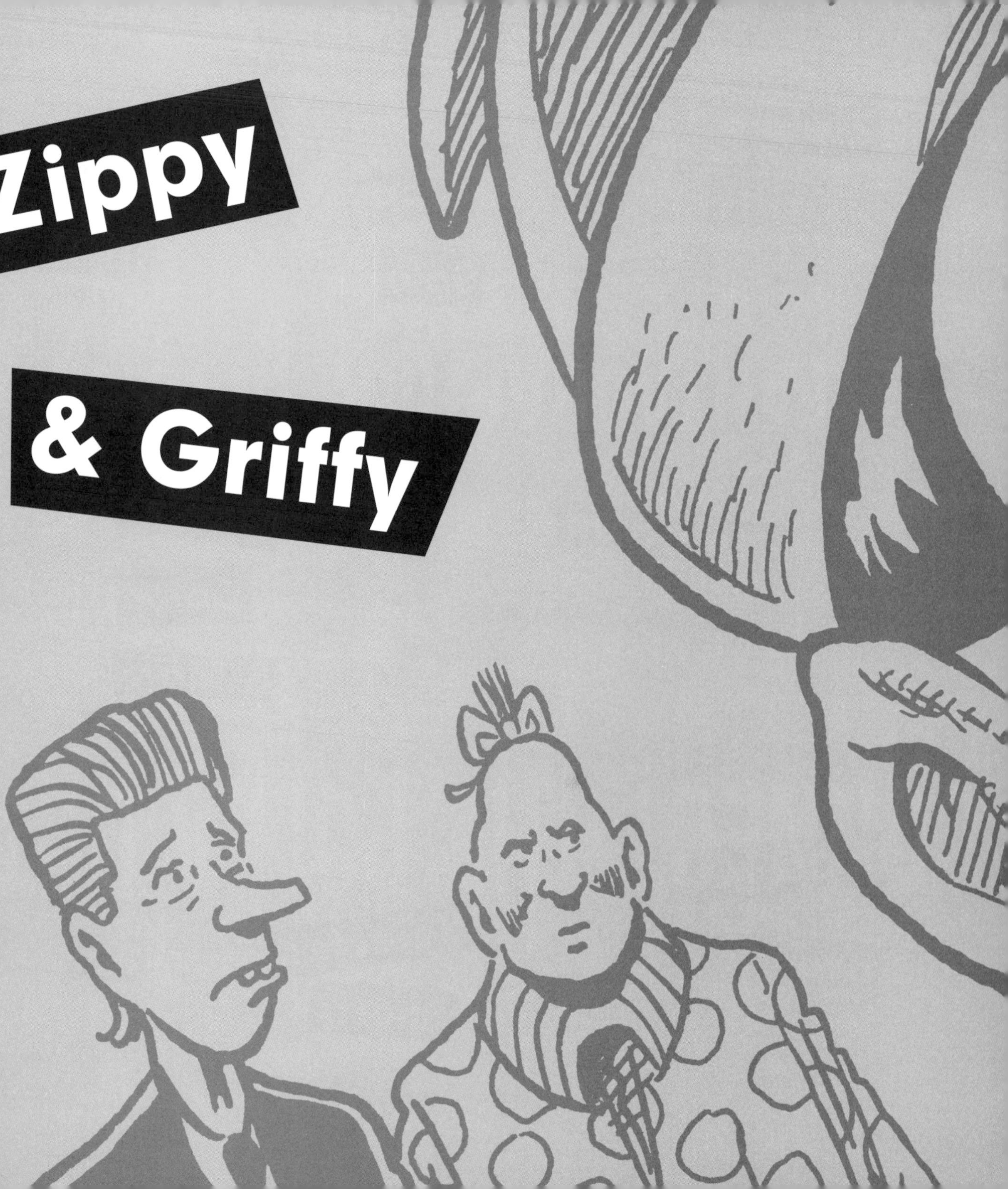

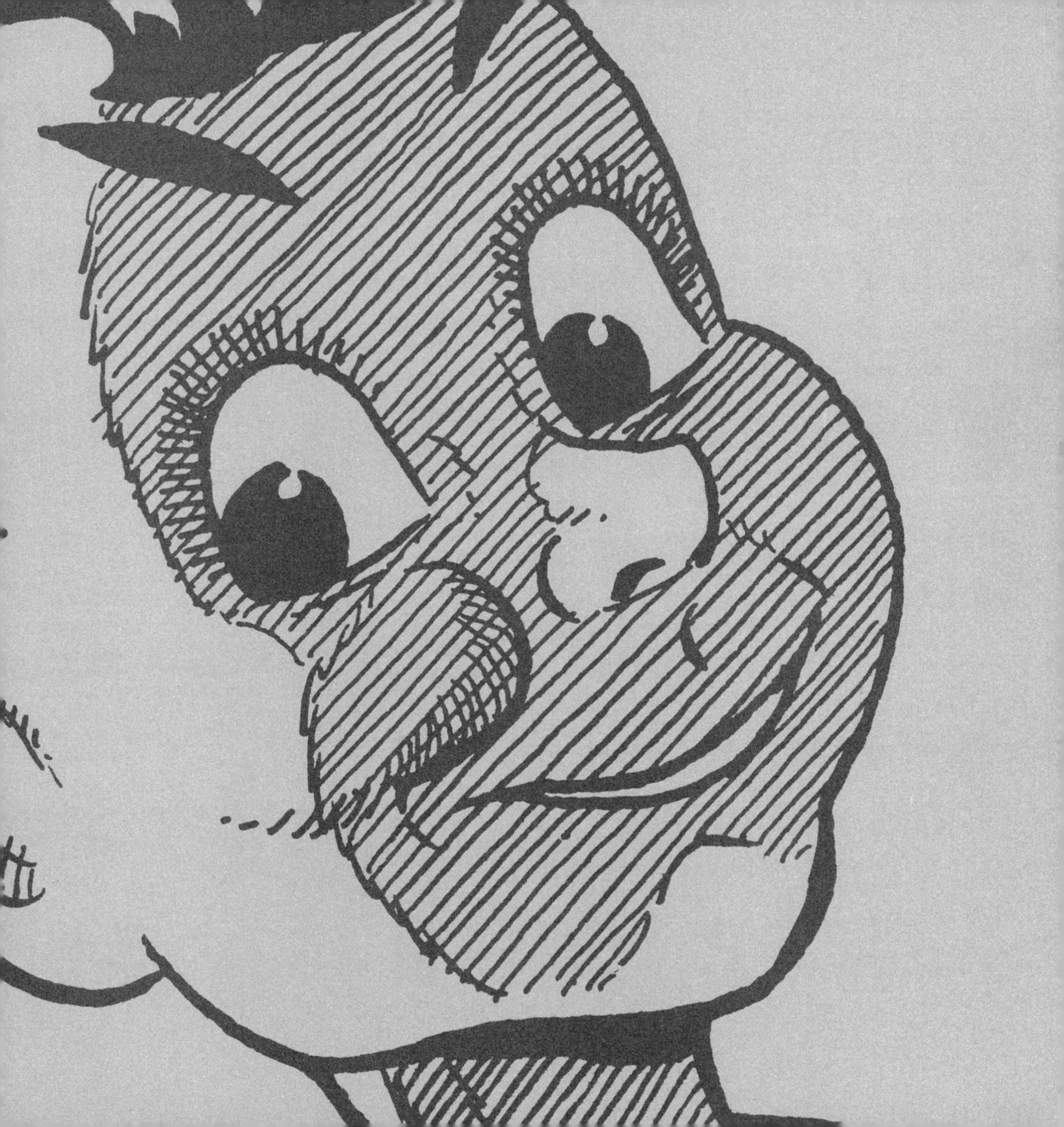

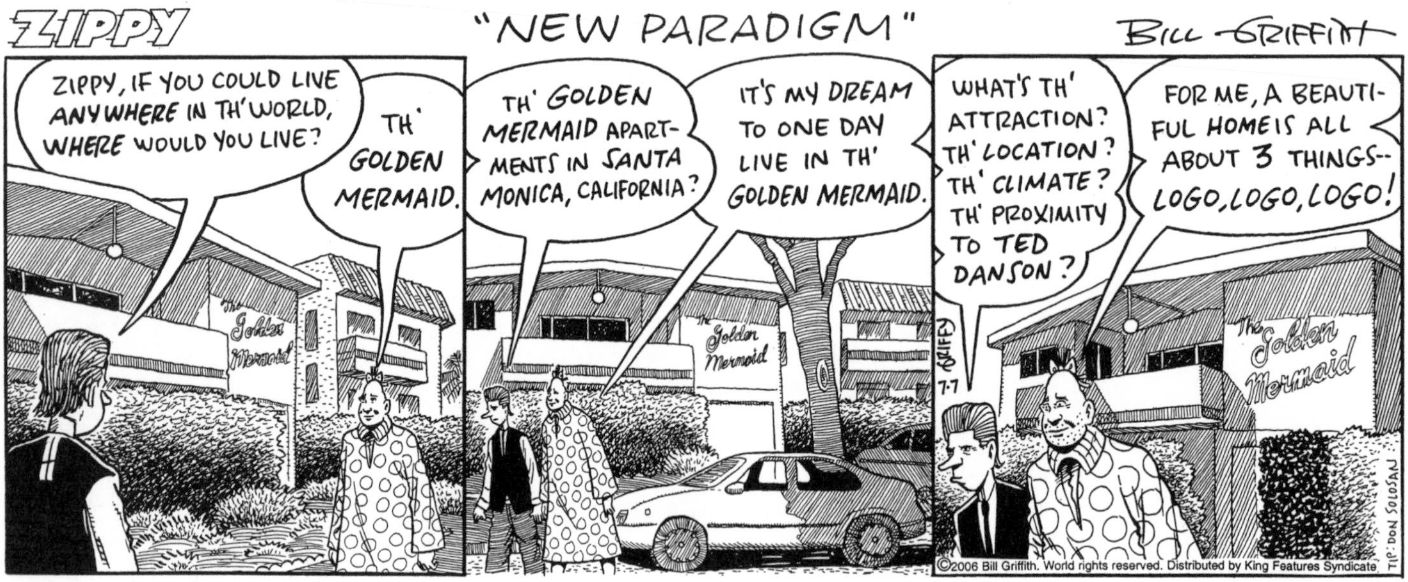
ZIPPY
"NEW PARADIGM"
BILL GRIFFITH
ZIPPY, IF YOU COULD LIVE ANYWHERE IN TH' WORLD, WHERE WOULD YOU LIVE?
TH' GOLDEN MERMAID.
The Golden Mermaid
TH' GOLDEN MERMAID APARTMENTS IN SANTA MONICA, CALIFORNIA?
IT'S MY DREAM TO ONE DAY LIVE IN TH' GOLDEN MERMAID.
The Golden Mermaid
WHAT'S TH' ATTRACTION? TH' LOCATION? TH' CLIMATE? TH' PROXIMITY TO TED DANSON?
FOR ME, A BEAUTIFUL HOME IS ALL ABOUT 3 THINGS-- LOGO, LOGO, LOGO!
The Golden Mermaid
GRIFFY 7-7
TIP: DON SOLOSAN
©2006 Bill Griffith. World rights reserved. Distributed by King Features Syndicate

1

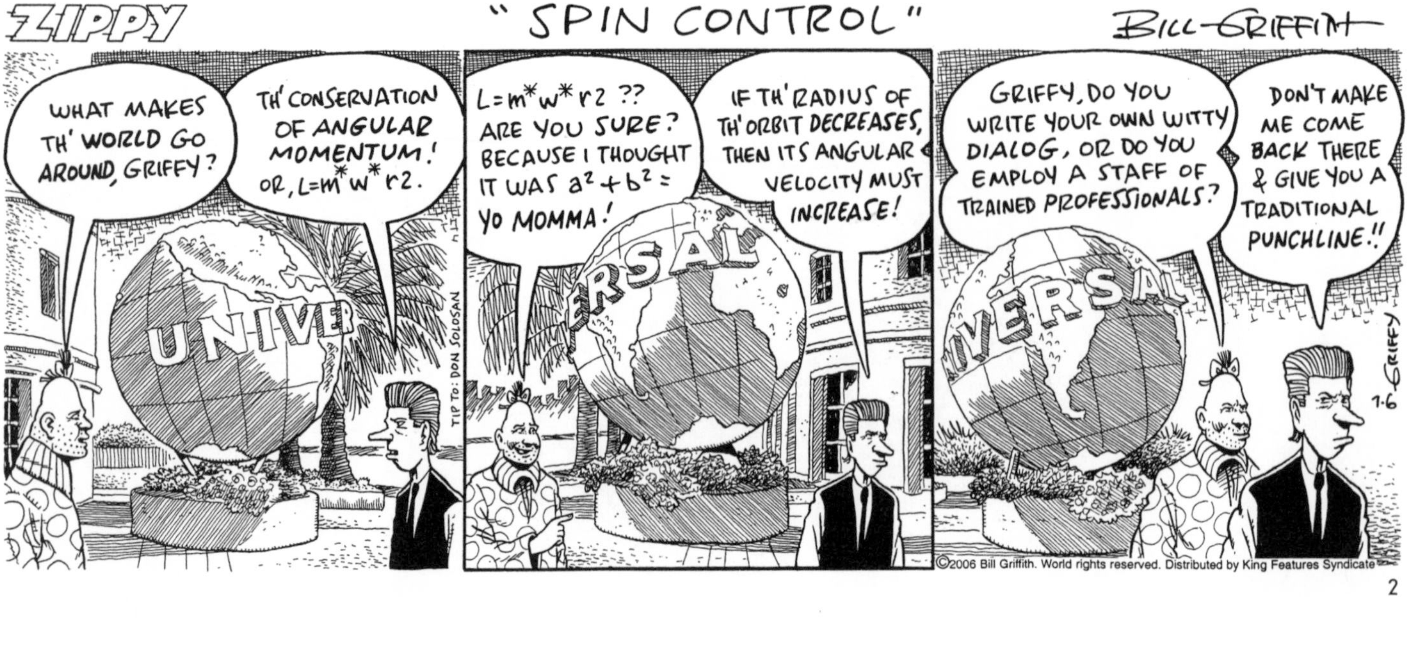
ZIPPY
"SPIN CONTROL"
BILL GRIFFITH
WHAT MAKES TH' WORLD GO AROUND, GRIFFY?
TH' CONSERVATION OF ANGULAR MOMENTUM! OR, L=m*w*r2.
UNIVER
TIP TO: DON SOLOSAN
L=m*w*r2 ?? ARE YOU SURE? BECAUSE I THOUGHT IT WAS $a^2 + b^2$ = YO MOMMA!
IF TH' RADIUS OF TH' ORBIT DECREASES, THEN ITS ANGULAR VELOCITY MUST INCREASE!
ERSAL
GRIFFY, DO YOU WRITE YOUR OWN WITTY DIALOG, OR DO YOU EMPLOY A STAFF OF TRAINED PROFESSIONALS?
DON'T MAKE ME COME BACK THERE & GIVE YOU A TRADITIONAL PUNCHLINE!!
IVERSAL
GRIFFY 1-6
©2006 Bill Griffith. World rights reserved. Distributed by King Features Syndicate

2

ZIPPY "QUITE A SPREAD" BILL GRIFFITH

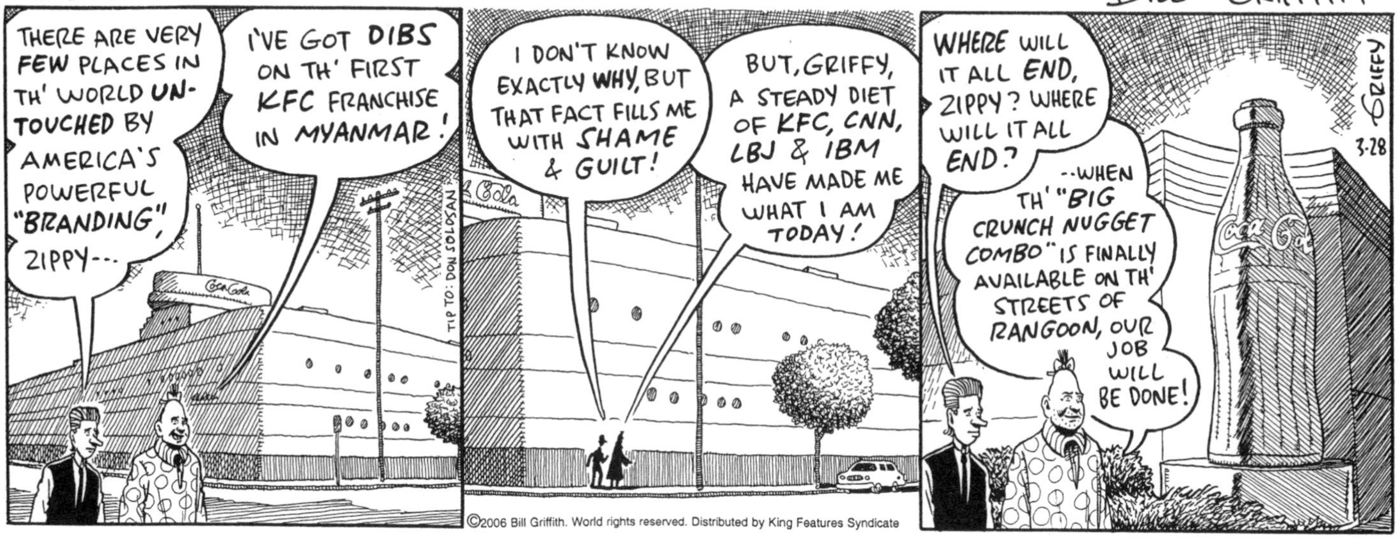
THERE ARE VERY FEW PLACES IN TH' WORLD UN-TOUCHED BY AMERICA'S POWERFUL "BRANDING", ZIPPY---
I'VE GOT DIBS ON TH' FIRST KFC FRANCHISE IN MYANMAR!
TIP TO: DON SOLOSAN
I DON'T KNOW EXACTLY WHY, BUT THAT FACT FILLS ME WITH SHAME & GUILT!
BUT, GRIFFY, A STEADY DIET OF KFC, CNN, LBJ & IBM HAVE MADE ME WHAT I AM TODAY!
©2006 Bill Griffith. World rights reserved. Distributed by King Features Syndicate
WHERE WILL IT ALL END, ZIPPY? WHERE WILL IT ALL END?
--WHEN TH' "BIG CRUNCH NUGGET COMBO" IS FINALLY AVAILABLE ON TH' STREETS OF RANGOON, OUR JOB WILL BE DONE!
GRIFFY 3-28

3

ZIPPY "CHOOSING THE DELUXE PACKAGE" BILL GRIFFITH

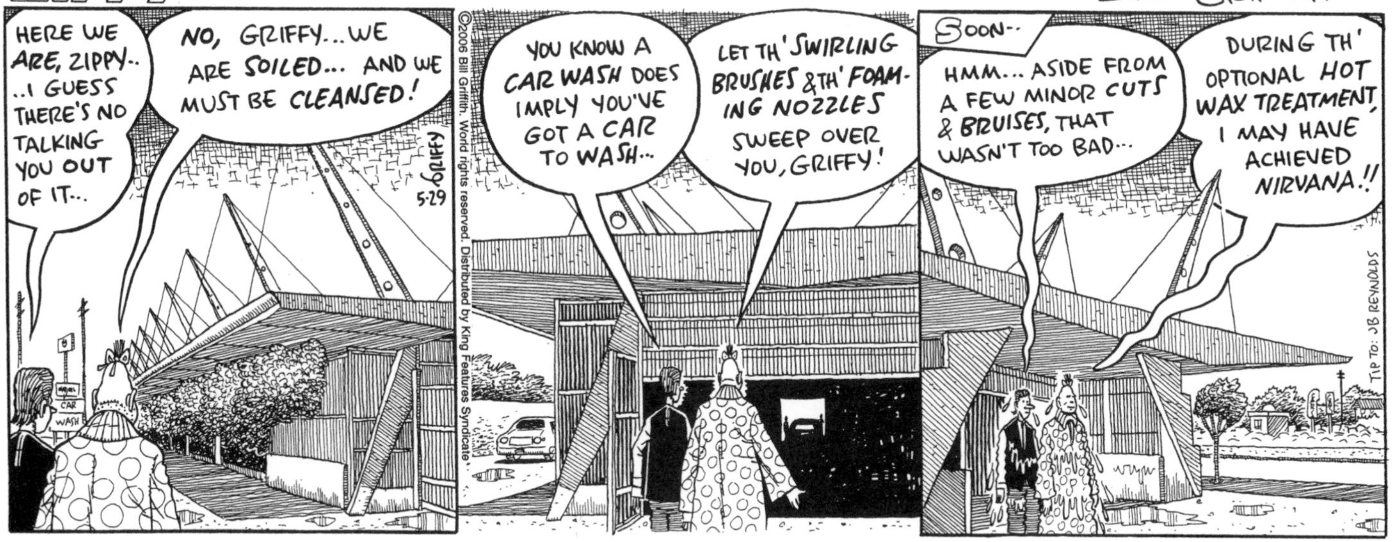
HERE WE ARE, ZIPPY.. ..I GUESS THERE'S NO TALKING YOU OUT OF IT..
NO, GRIFFY...WE ARE SOILED... AND WE MUST BE CLEANSED!
GRIFFY 5-29
CAR WASH
©2006 Bill Griffith. World rights reserved. Distributed by King Features Syndicate
YOU KNOW A CAR WASH DOES IMPLY YOU'VE GOT A CAR TO WASH..
LET TH' SWIRLING BRUSHES & TH' FOAMING NOZZLES SWEEP OVER YOU, GRIFFY!
SOON--
HMM... ASIDE FROM A FEW MINOR CUTS & BRUISES, THAT WASN'T TOO BAD...
DURING TH' OPTIONAL HOT WAX TREATMENT, I MAY HAVE ACHIEVED NIRVANA!!
TIP TO: JB REYNOLDS

4

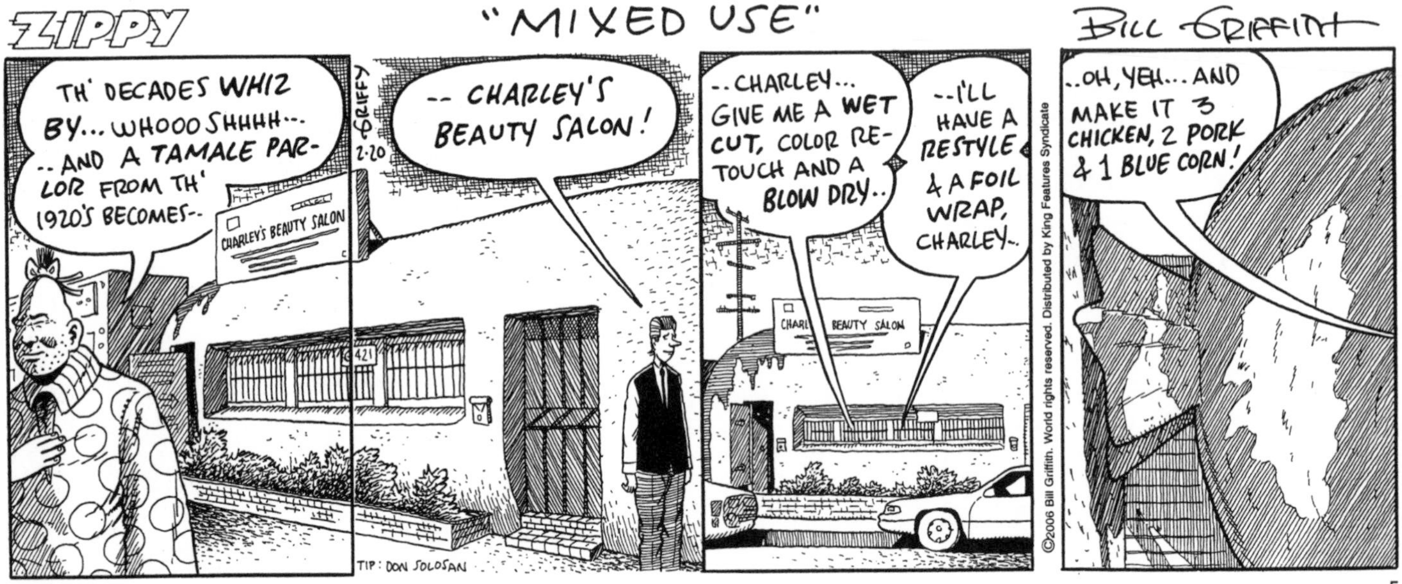
ZIPPY
"MIXED USE"
BILL GRIFFITH
TH' DECADES WHIZ BY... WHOOOSHHHH--- ..AND A TAMALE PARLOR FROM TH' 1920'S BECOMES--
CHARLEY'S BEAUTY SALON
GRIFFY 2-20
-- CHARLEY'S BEAUTY SALON!
TIP: DON SOLOSAN
..CHARLEY... GIVE ME A WET CUT, COLOR RE-TOUCH AND A BLOW DRY..
--I'LL HAVE A RESTYLE & A FOIL WRAP, CHARLEY..
BEAUTY SALON
©2006 Bill Griffith. World rights reserved. Distributed by King Features Syndicate
..OH, YEH... AND MAKE IT 3 CHICKEN, 2 PORK & 1 BLUE CORN!

5

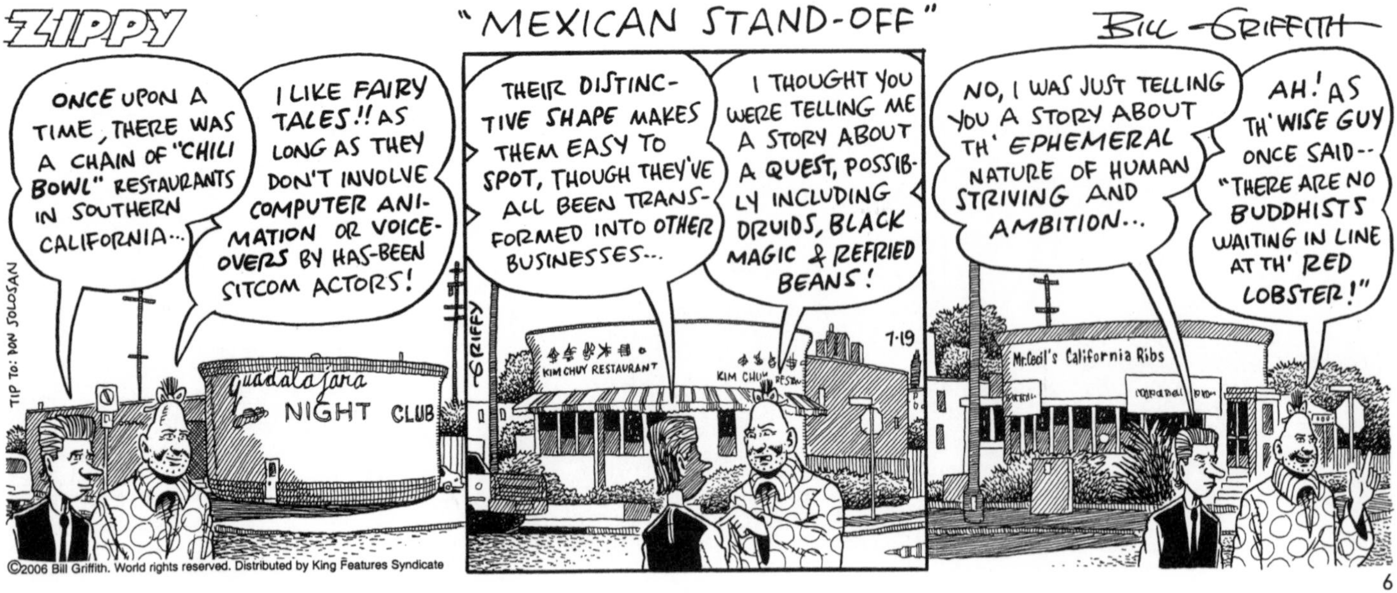
ZIPPY
"MEXICAN STAND-OFF"
BILL GRIFFITH
ONCE UPON A TIME, THERE WAS A CHAIN OF "CHILI BOWL" RESTAURANTS IN SOUTHERN CALIFORNIA...
I LIKE FAIRY TALES!! AS LONG AS THEY DON'T INVOLVE COMPUTER ANIMATION OR VOICE-OVERS BY HAS-BEEN SITCOM ACTORS!
TIP TO: DON SOLOSAN
Guadalajara NIGHT CLUB
©2006 Bill Griffith. World rights reserved. Distributed by King Features Syndicate
THEIR DISTINCTIVE SHAPE MAKES THEM EASY TO SPOT, THOUGH THEY'VE ALL BEEN TRANSFORMED INTO OTHER BUSINESSES...
I THOUGHT YOU WERE TELLING ME A STORY ABOUT A QUEST, POSSIBLY INCLUDING DRUIDS, BLACK MAGIC & REFRIED BEANS!
GRIFFY 7-19
KIM CHUY RESTAURANT
NO, I WAS JUST TELLING YOU A STORY ABOUT TH' EPHEMERAL NATURE OF HUMAN STRIVING AND AMBITION...
AH! AS TH' WISE GUY ONCE SAID-- "THERE ARE NO BUDDHISTS WAITING IN LINE AT TH' RED LOBSTER!"
Mr. Cecil's California Ribs

6

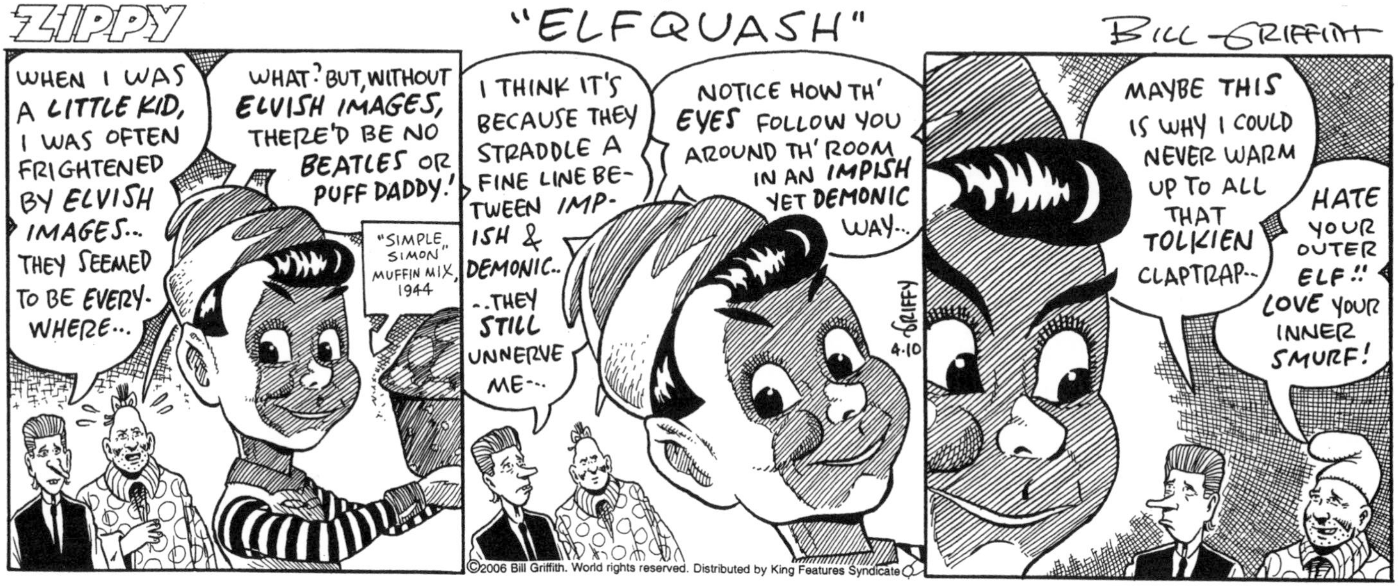
ZIPPY
"ELFQUASH"
BILL GRIFFITH
WHEN I WAS A LITTLE KID, I WAS OFTEN FRIGHTENED BY ELVISH IMAGES... THEY SEEMED TO BE EVERYWHERE...
WHAT? BUT, WITHOUT ELVISH IMAGES, THERE'D BE NO BEATLES OR PUFF DADDY!
"SIMPLE SIMON" MUFFIN MIX, 1944
I THINK IT'S BECAUSE THEY STRADDLE A FINE LINE BETWEEN IMPISH & DEMONIC.. ..THEY STILL UNNERVE ME...
NOTICE HOW TH' EYES FOLLOW YOU AROUND TH' ROOM IN AN IMPISH YET DEMONIC WAY...
GRIFFY 4-10
©2006 Bill Griffith. World rights reserved. Distributed by King Features Syndicate
MAYBE THIS IS WHY I COULD NEVER WARM UP TO ALL THAT TOLKIEN CLAPTRAP...
HATE YOUR OUTER ELF!! LOVE YOUR INNER SMURF!

7

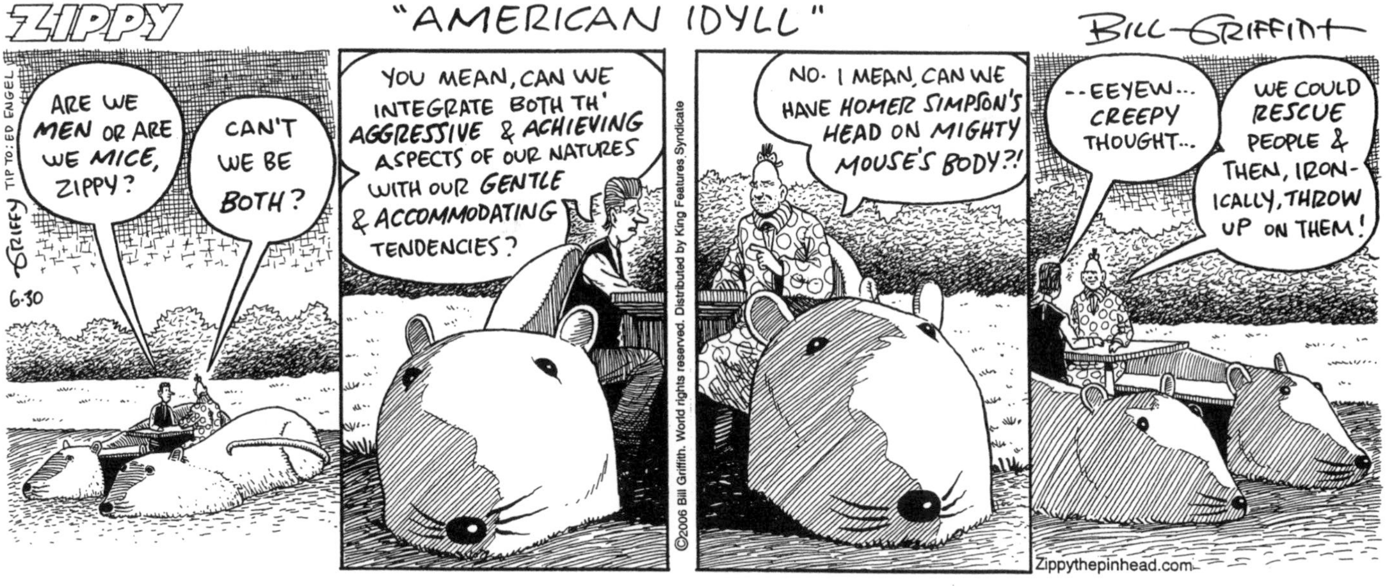
ZIPPY
"AMERICAN IDYLL"
BILL GRIFFITH
GRIFFY TIP TO: ED ENGEL 6-30
ARE WE MEN OR ARE WE MICE, ZIPPY?
CAN'T WE BE BOTH?
YOU MEAN, CAN WE INTEGRATE BOTH TH' AGGRESSIVE & ACHIEVING ASPECTS OF OUR NATURES WITH OUR GENTLE & ACCOMMODATING TENDENCIES?
©2006 Bill Griffith. World rights reserved. Distributed by King Features Syndicate
NO. I MEAN, CAN WE HAVE HOMER SIMPSON'S HEAD ON MIGHTY MOUSE'S BODY?!
--EEYEW... CREEPY THOUGHT...
WE COULD RESCUE PEOPLE & THEN, IRONICALLY, THROW UP ON THEM!
Zippythepinhead.com

8

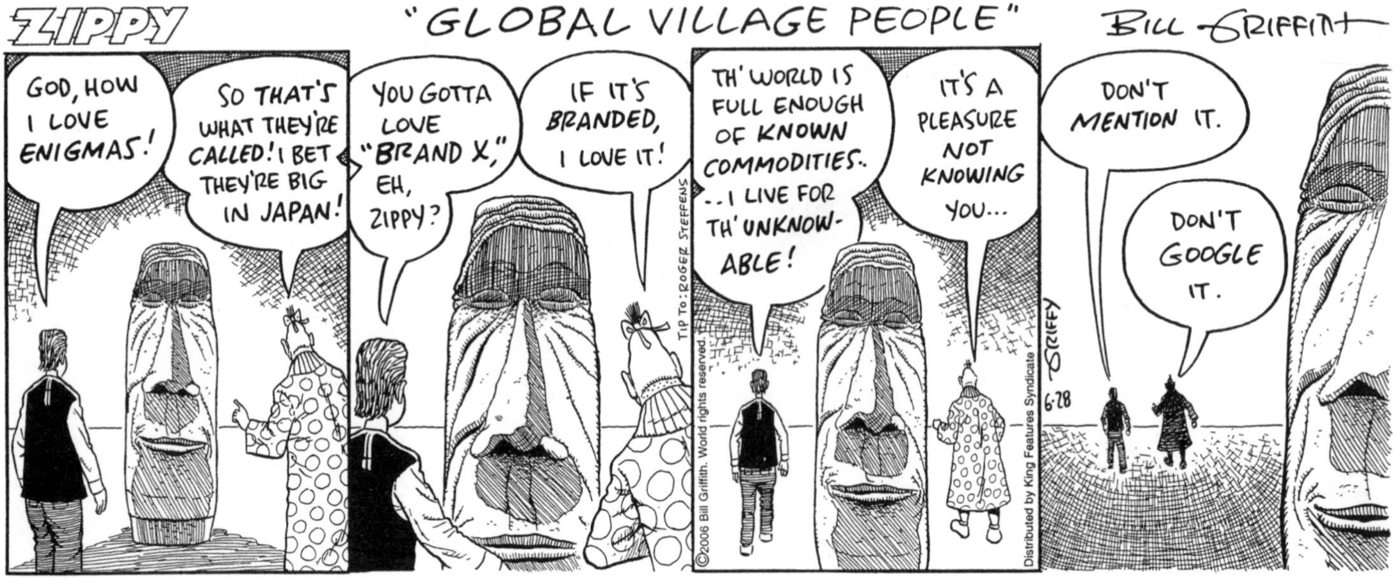
ZIPPY
"GLOBAL VILLAGE PEOPLE"
BILL GRIFFITH
GOD, HOW I LOVE ENIGMAS!
SO THAT'S WHAT THEY'RE CALLED! I BET THEY'RE BIG IN JAPAN!
YOU GOTTA LOVE "BRAND X," EH, ZIPPY?
IF IT'S BRANDED, I LOVE IT!
TIP TO: ROGER STEFFENS
©2006 Bill Griffith. World rights reserved.
TH' WORLD IS FULL ENOUGH OF KNOWN COMMODITIES.. ..I LIVE FOR TH' UNKNOWABLE!
IT'S A PLEASURE NOT KNOWING YOU...
GRIFFY
6-28
Distributed by King Features Syndicate
DON'T MENTION IT.
DON'T GOOGLE IT.

9

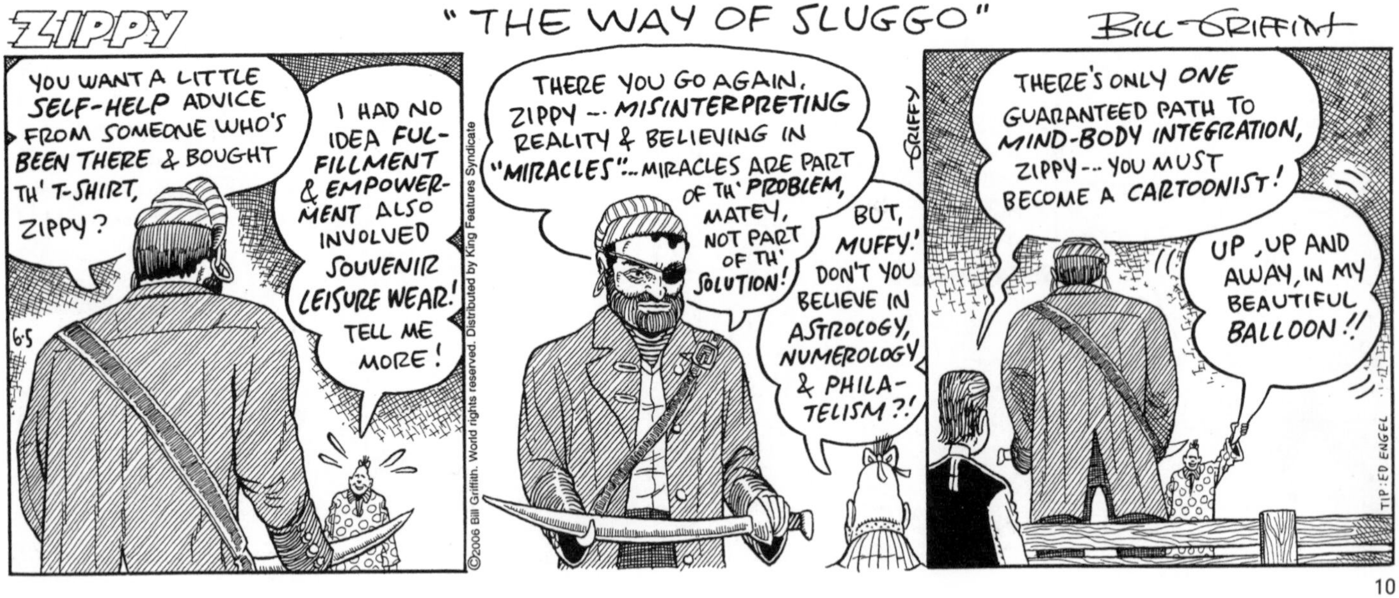
ZIPPY
"THE WAY OF SLUGGO"
BILL GRIFFITH
YOU WANT A LITTLE SELF-HELP ADVICE FROM SOMEONE WHO'S BEEN THERE & BOUGHT TH' T-SHIRT, ZIPPY?
I HAD NO IDEA FULFILLMENT & EMPOWERMENT ALSO INVOLVED SOUVENIR LEISURE WEAR! TELL ME MORE!
6-5
©2006 Bill Griffith. World rights reserved. Distributed by King Features Syndicate
THERE YOU GO AGAIN, ZIPPY -- MISINTERPRETING REALITY & BELIEVING IN "MIRACLES"... MIRACLES ARE PART OF TH' PROBLEM, MATEY, NOT PART OF TH' SOLUTION!
BUT, MUFFY! DON'T YOU BELIEVE IN ASTROLOGY, NUMEROLOGY & PHILATELISM?!
GRIFFY
THERE'S ONLY ONE GUARANTEED PATH TO MIND-BODY INTEGRATION, ZIPPY -- YOU MUST BECOME A CARTOONIST!
UP, UP AND AWAY, IN MY BEAUTIFUL BALLOON!!
TIP: ED ENGEL

10

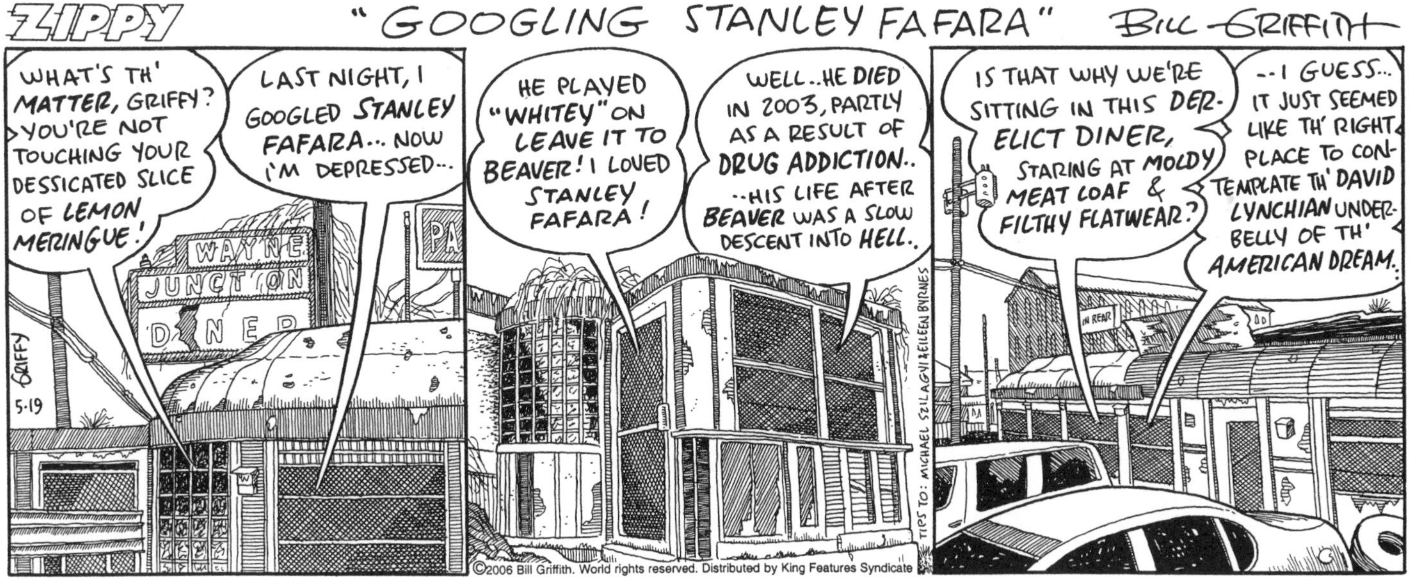
ZIPPY
"GOOGLING STANLEY FAFARA"
BILL GRIFFITH
WHAT'S TH' MATTER, GRIFFY? YOU'RE NOT TOUCHING YOUR DESSICATED SLICE OF LEMON MERINGUE!
LAST NIGHT, I GOOGLED STANLEY FAFARA... NOW I'M DEPRESSED...
WAYNE JUNCTION DINER
GRIFFY
5-19
HE PLAYED "WHITEY" ON LEAVE IT TO BEAVER! I LOVED STANLEY FAFARA!
WELL.. HE DIED IN 2003, PARTLY AS A RESULT OF DRUG ADDICTION.. ..HIS LIFE AFTER BEAVER WAS A SLOW DESCENT INTO HELL..
TIPS TO: MICHAEL SZILAGYI & EILEEN BYRNES
©2006 Bill Griffith. World rights reserved. Distributed by King Features Syndicate
IS THAT WHY WE'RE SITTING IN THIS DERELICT DINER, STARING AT MOLDY MEAT LOAF & FILTHY FLATWEAR?
--I GUESS... IT JUST SEEMED LIKE TH' RIGHT PLACE TO CONTEMPLATE TH' DAVID LYNCHIAN UNDERBELLY OF TH' AMERICAN DREAM..
IN REAR

11

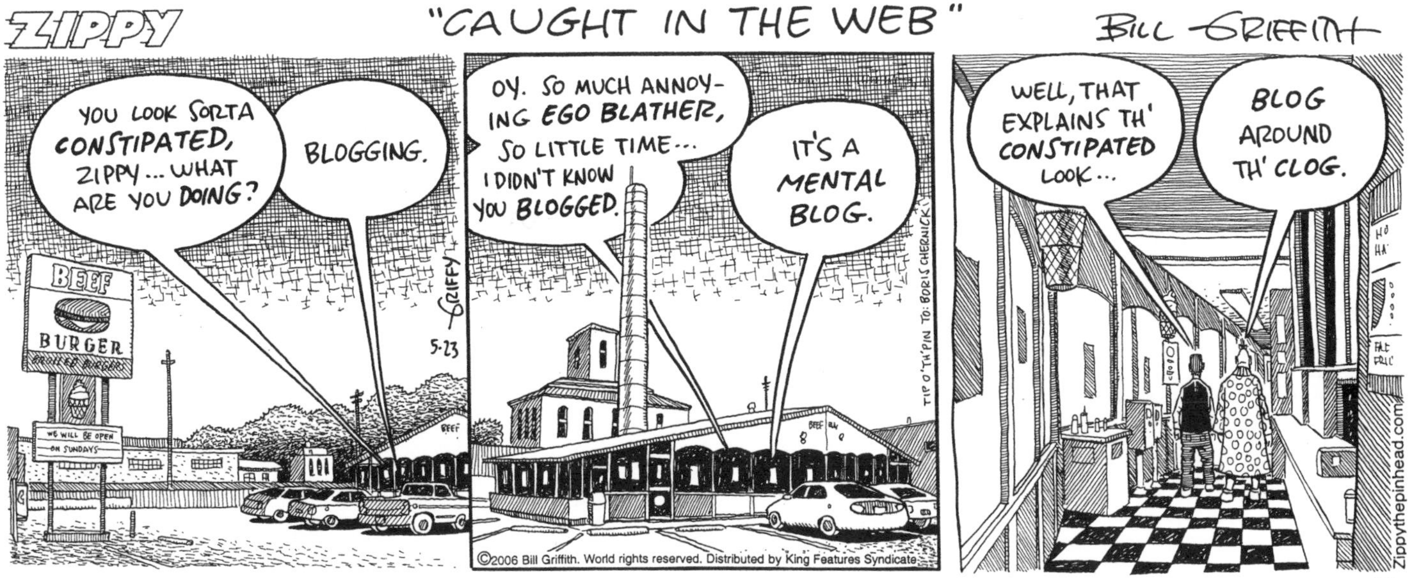
ZIPPY
"CAUGHT IN THE WEB"
BILL GRIFFITH
YOU LOOK SORTA CONSTIPATED, ZIPPY... WHAT ARE YOU DOING?
BLOGGING.
BEEF BURGER
WE WILL BE OPEN ON SUNDAYS
GRIFFY
5-23
OY. SO MUCH ANNOYING EGO BLATHER, SO LITTLE TIME... I DIDN'T KNOW YOU BLOGGED.
IT'S A MENTAL BLOG.
TIP O' TH' PIN TO: BORIS CHERNICK
©2006 Bill Griffith. World rights reserved. Distributed by King Features Syndicate
WELL, THAT EXPLAINS TH' CONSTIPATED LOOK...
BLOG AROUND TH' CLOG.
Zippythepinhead.com

12

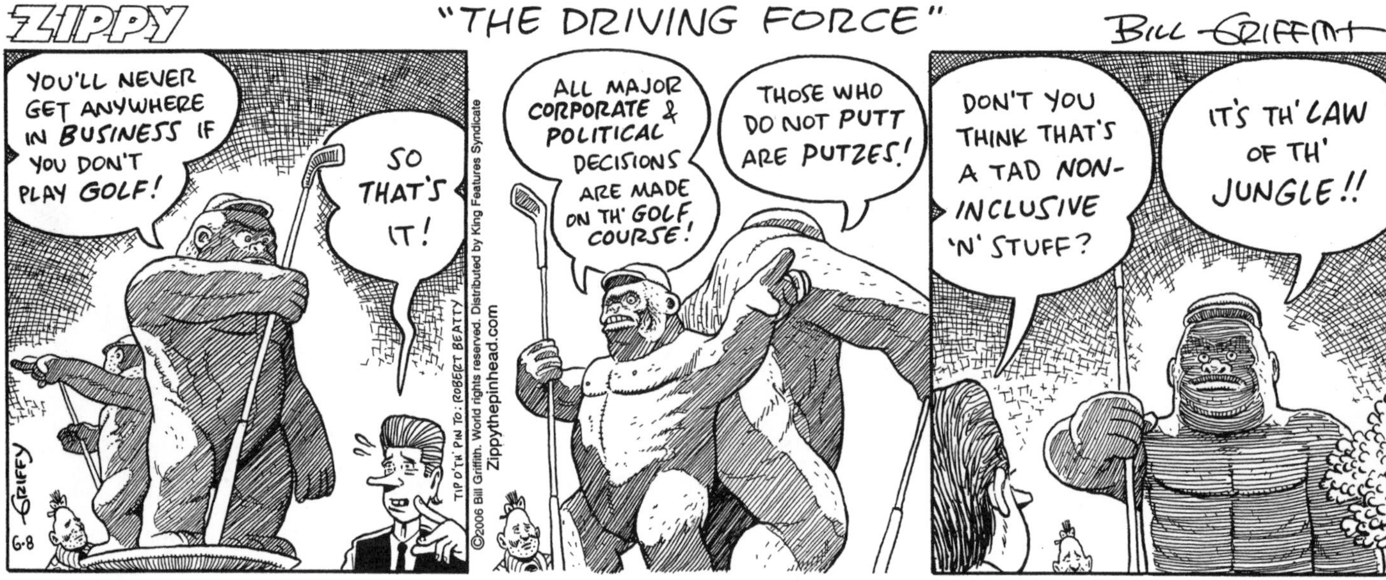
ZIPPY
"THE DRIVING FORCE"
BILL GRIFFITH
YOU'LL NEVER GET ANYWHERE IN BUSINESS IF YOU DON'T PLAY GOLF!
SO THAT'S IT!
GRIFFY
6·8
TIP O'TH' PIN TO: ROBERT BEATTY
©2006 Bill Griffith. World rights reserved. Distributed by King Features Syndicate
Zippythepinhead.com
ALL MAJOR CORPORATE & POLITICAL DECISIONS ARE MADE ON TH' GOLF COURSE!
THOSE WHO DO NOT PUTT ARE PUTZES!
DON'T YOU THINK THAT'S A TAD NON-INCLUSIVE 'N' STUFF?
IT'S TH' LAW OF TH' JUNGLE!!

13

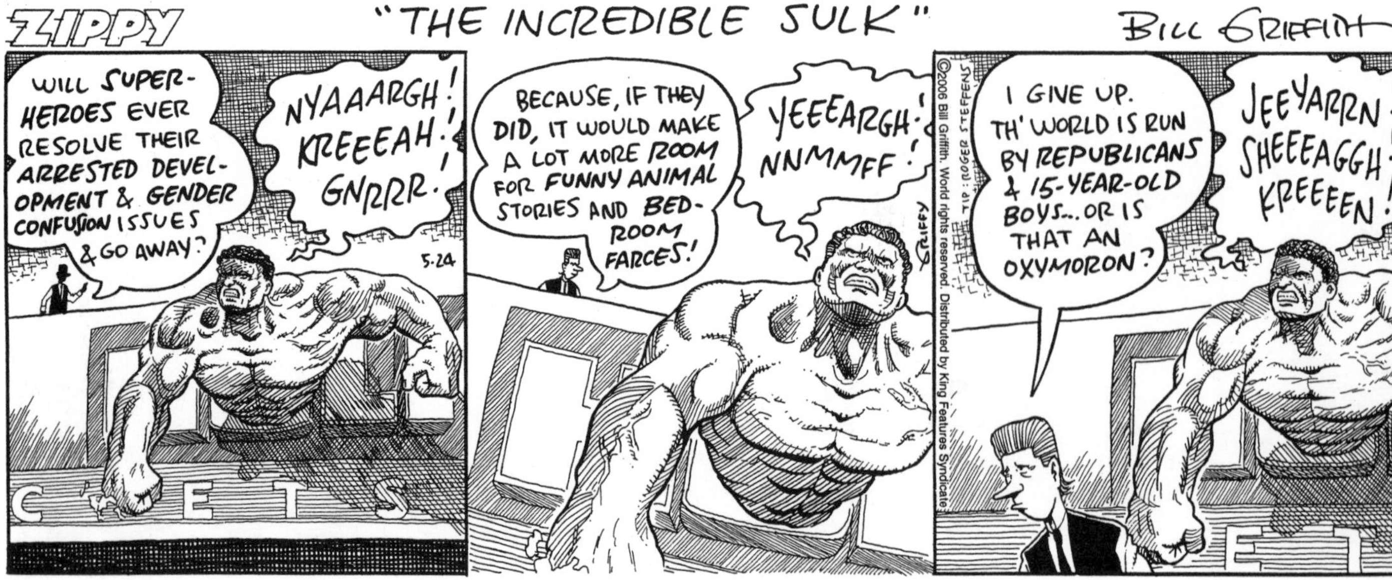
ZIPPY
"THE INCREDIBLE SULK"
BILL GRIFFITH
WILL SUPER-HEROES EVER RESOLVE THEIR ARRESTED DEVEL-OPMENT & GENDER CONFUSION ISSUES & GO AWAY?
NYAAARGH! KREEEAH! GNRRR.
5·24
C E T S
BECAUSE, IF THEY DID, IT WOULD MAKE A LOT MORE ROOM FOR FUNNY ANIMAL STORIES AND BED-ROOM FARCES!
YEEEARGH! NNMMFF!
GRIFFY
©2006 Bill Griffith. World rights reserved. Distributed by King Features Syndicate
I GIVE UP. TH' WORLD IS RUN BY REPUBLICANS & 15-YEAR-OLD BOYS...OR IS THAT AN OXYMORON?
JEEYARRN! SHEEEAGGH! KREEEEN!
E T

14

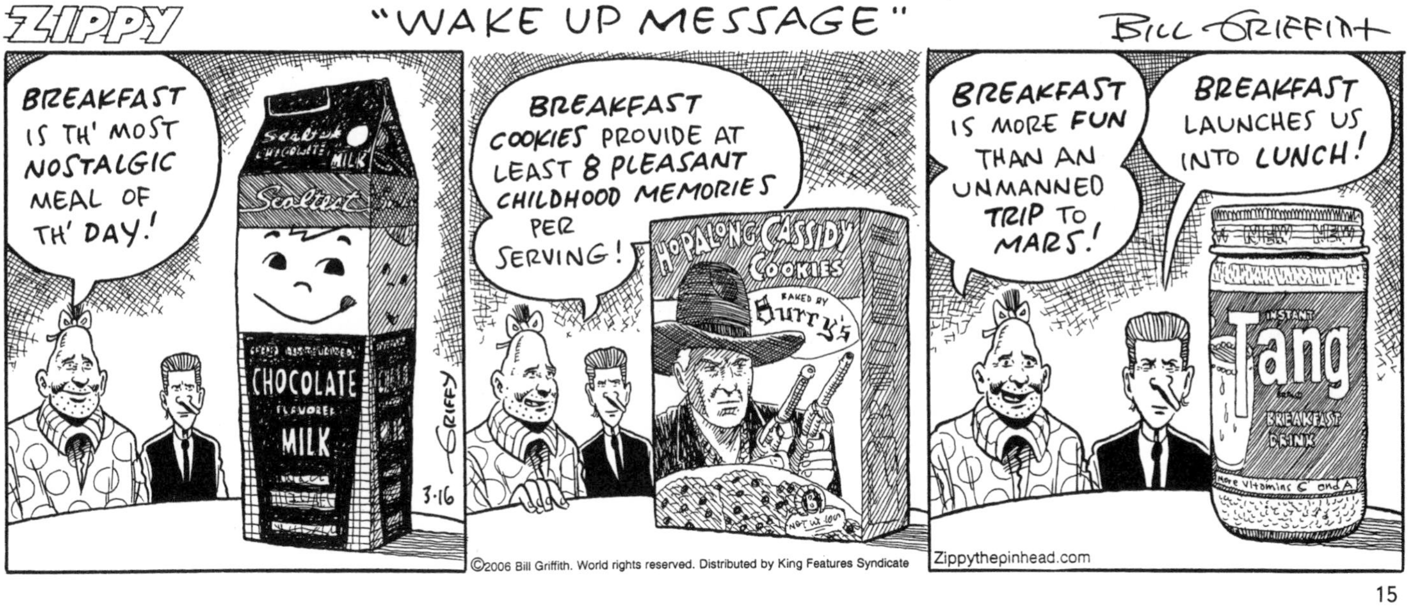
ZIPPY
"WAKE UP MESSAGE"
BILL GRIFFITH
BREAKFAST IS TH' MOST NOSTALGIC MEAL OF TH' DAY!
CHOCOLATE FLAVORED MILK
GRIFFY
3-16
BREAKFAST COOKIES PROVIDE AT LEAST 8 PLEASANT CHILDHOOD MEMORIES PER SERVING!
HOPALONG CASSIDY COOKIES
BREAKFAST IS MORE FUN THAN AN UNMANNED TRIP TO MARS!
BREAKFAST LAUNCHES US INTO LUNCH!
INSTANT
Tang
BREAKFAST DRINK
More Vitamins C and A
©2006 Bill Griffith. World rights reserved. Distributed by King Features Syndicate
Zippythepinhead.com
15

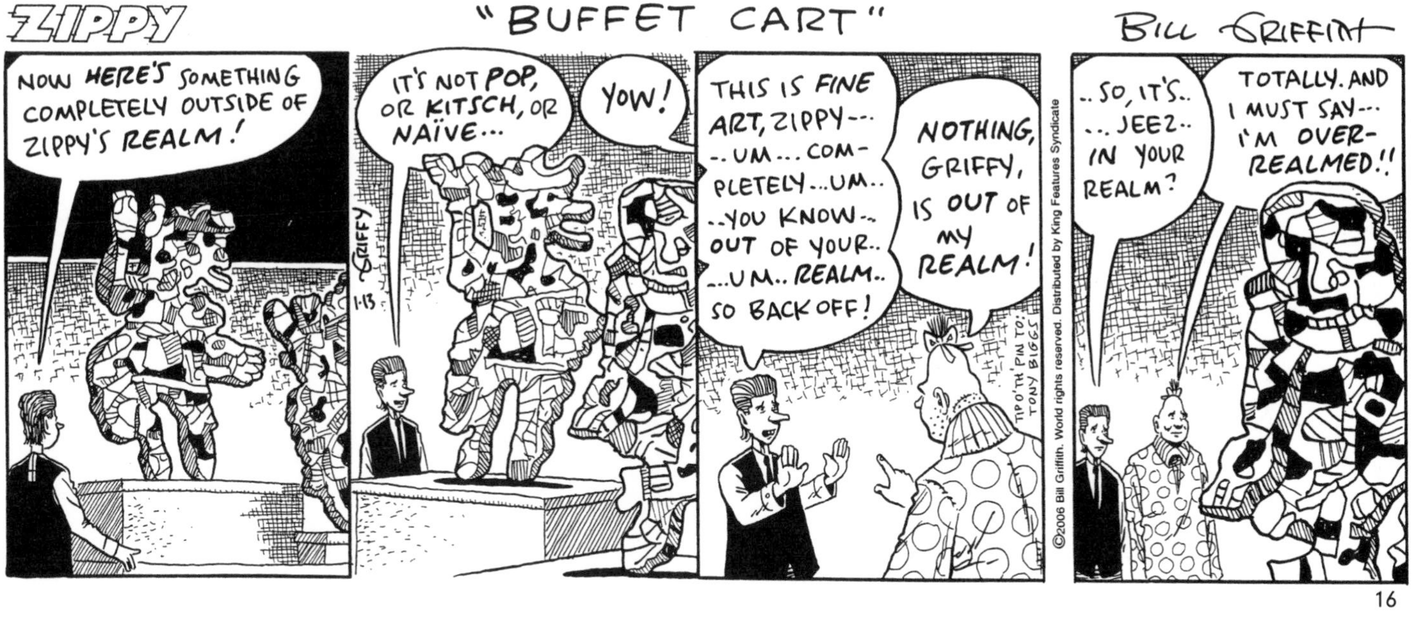
ZIPPY
"BUFFET CART"
BILL GRIFFITH
NOW HERE'S SOMETHING COMPLETELY OUTSIDE OF ZIPPY'S REALM!
GRIFFY
1-13
IT'S NOT POP, OR KITSCH, OR NAÏVE...
YOW!
THIS IS FINE ART, ZIPPY-- --UM... COM-PLETELY...UM.. ..YOU KNOW.. OUT OF YOUR.. ..UM.. REALM.. SO BACK OFF!
NOTHING, GRIFFY, IS OUT OF MY REALM!
TIP O'TH' PIN TO: TONY BIGGS
©2006 Bill Griffith. World rights reserved. Distributed by King Features Syndicate
..SO, IT'S.. ...JEEZ.. IN YOUR REALM?
TOTALLY. AND I MUST SAY--- I'M OVER-REALMED!!
16

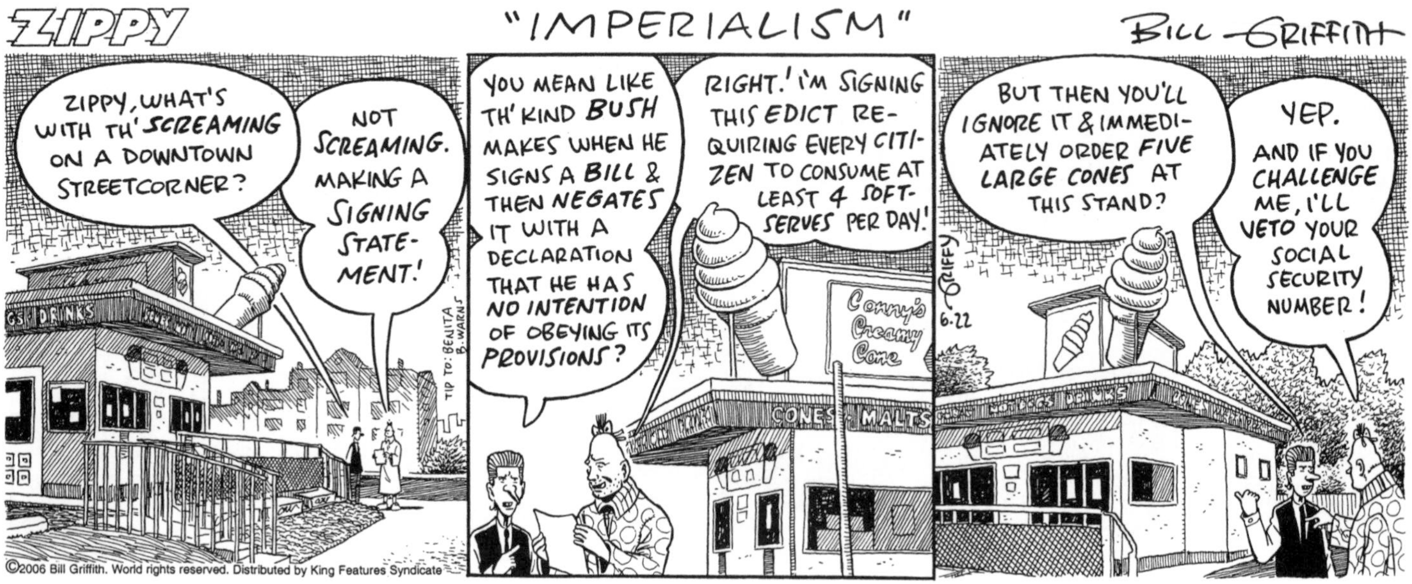
ZIPPY
"IMPERIALISM"
BILL GRIFFITH
ZIPPY, WHAT'S WITH TH' SCREAMING ON A DOWNTOWN STREETCORNER?
NOT SCREAMING. MAKING A SIGNING STATEMENT!
TIP TO: BENITA B. WARNS
YOU MEAN LIKE TH' KIND BUSH MAKES WHEN HE SIGNS A BILL & THEN NEGATES IT WITH A DECLARATION THAT HE HAS NO INTENTION OF OBEYING ITS PROVISIONS?
RIGHT! I'M SIGNING THIS EDICT REQUIRING EVERY CITIZEN TO CONSUME AT LEAST 4 SOFT-SERVES PER DAY!
Conny's Creamy Cone
CONES MALTS
GRIFFY 6.22
BUT THEN YOU'LL IGNORE IT & IMMEDIATELY ORDER FIVE LARGE CONES AT THIS STAND?
YEP. AND IF YOU CHALLENGE ME, I'LL VETO YOUR SOCIAL SECURITY NUMBER!
©2006 Bill Griffith. World rights reserved. Distributed by King Features Syndicate

17

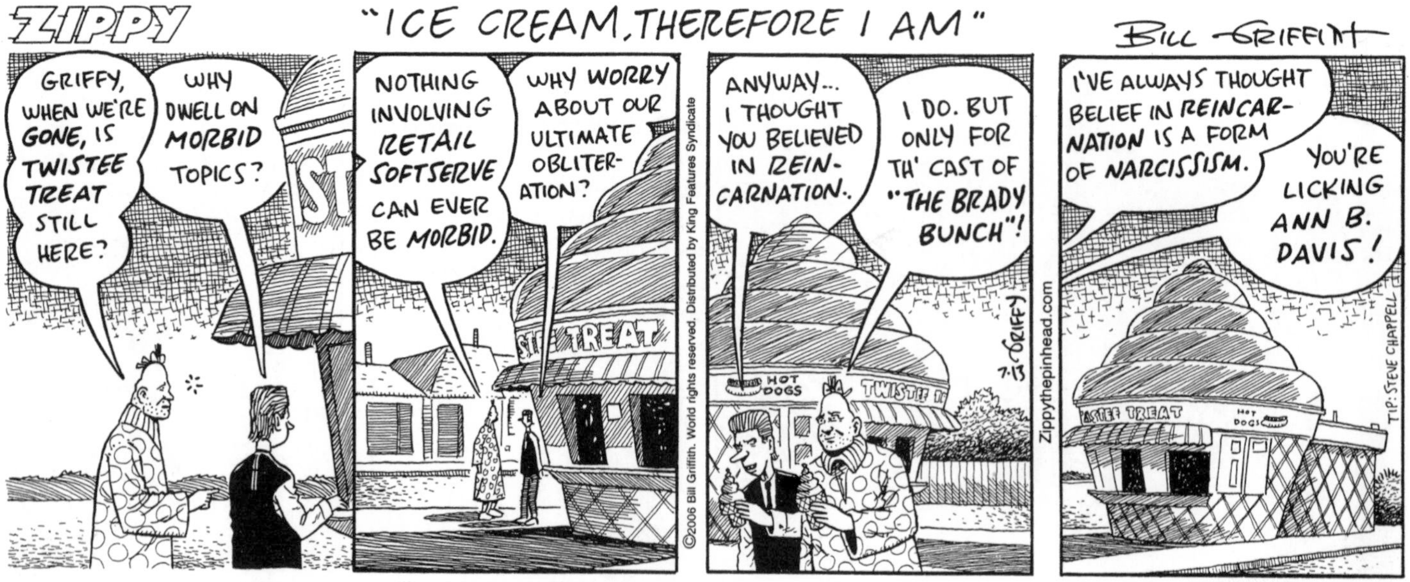
ZIPPY
"ICE CREAM, THEREFORE I AM"
BILL GRIFFITH
GRIFFY, WHEN WE'RE GONE, IS TWISTEE TREAT STILL HERE?
WHY DWELL ON MORBID TOPICS?
NOTHING INVOLVING RETAIL SOFTSERVE CAN EVER BE MORBID.
WHY WORRY ABOUT OUR ULTIMATE OBLITERATION?
TREAT
©2006 Bill Griffith. World rights reserved. Distributed by King Features Syndicate
ANYWAY... I THOUGHT YOU BELIEVED IN REINCARNATION..
I DO. BUT ONLY FOR TH' CAST OF "THE BRADY BUNCH"!
HOT DOGS
TWISTEE
GRIFFY 7.13
Zippythepinhead.com
I'VE ALWAYS THOUGHT BELIEF IN REINCARNATION IS A FORM OF NARCISSISM.
YOU'RE LICKING ANN B. DAVIS!
TIP: STEVE CHAPPELL

18

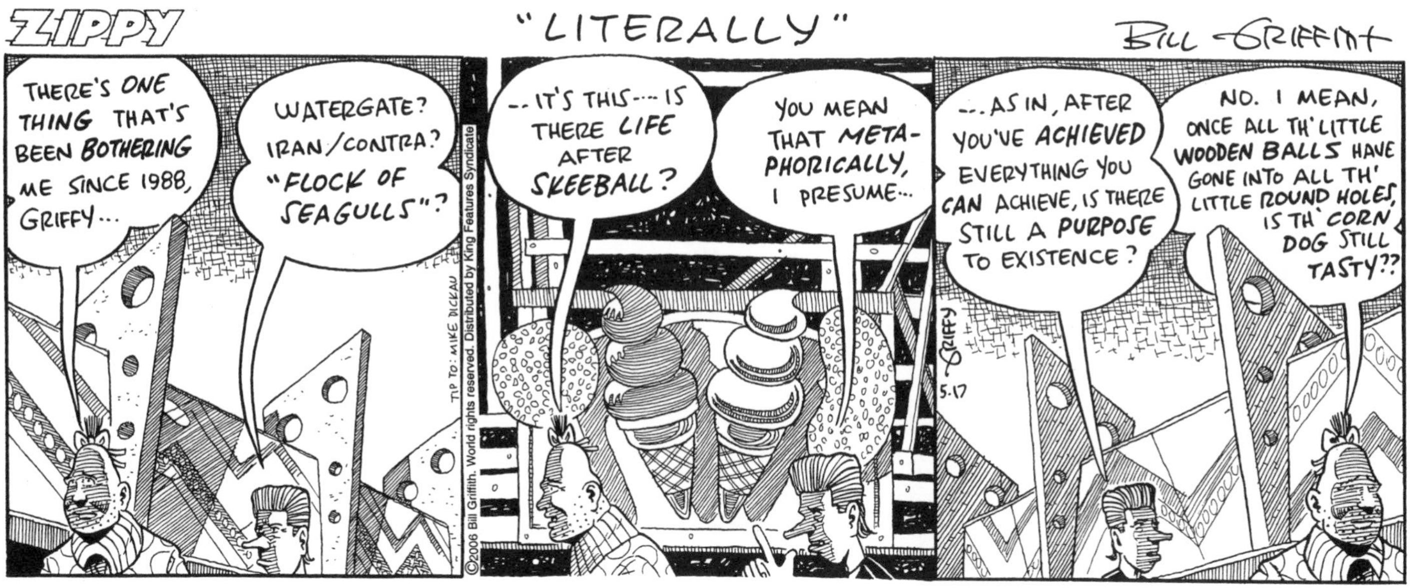
ZIPPY
"LITERALLY"
BILL GRIFFITH
THERE'S ONE THING THAT'S BEEN BOTHERING ME SINCE 1988, GRIFFY...
WATERGATE? IRAN/CONTRA? "FLOCK OF SEAGULLS"?
TIP TO: MIKE DICKAU
©2006 Bill Griffith. World rights reserved. Distributed by King Features Syndicate
--IT'S THIS--- IS THERE LIFE AFTER SKEEBALL?
YOU MEAN THAT META-PHORICALLY, I PRESUME...
GRIFFY 5.17
--.AS IN, AFTER YOU'VE ACHIEVED EVERYTHING YOU CAN ACHIEVE, IS THERE STILL A PURPOSE TO EXISTENCE?
NO. I MEAN, ONCE ALL TH' LITTLE WOODEN BALLS HAVE GONE INTO ALL TH' LITTLE ROUND HOLES, IS TH' CORN DOG STILL TASTY??

19

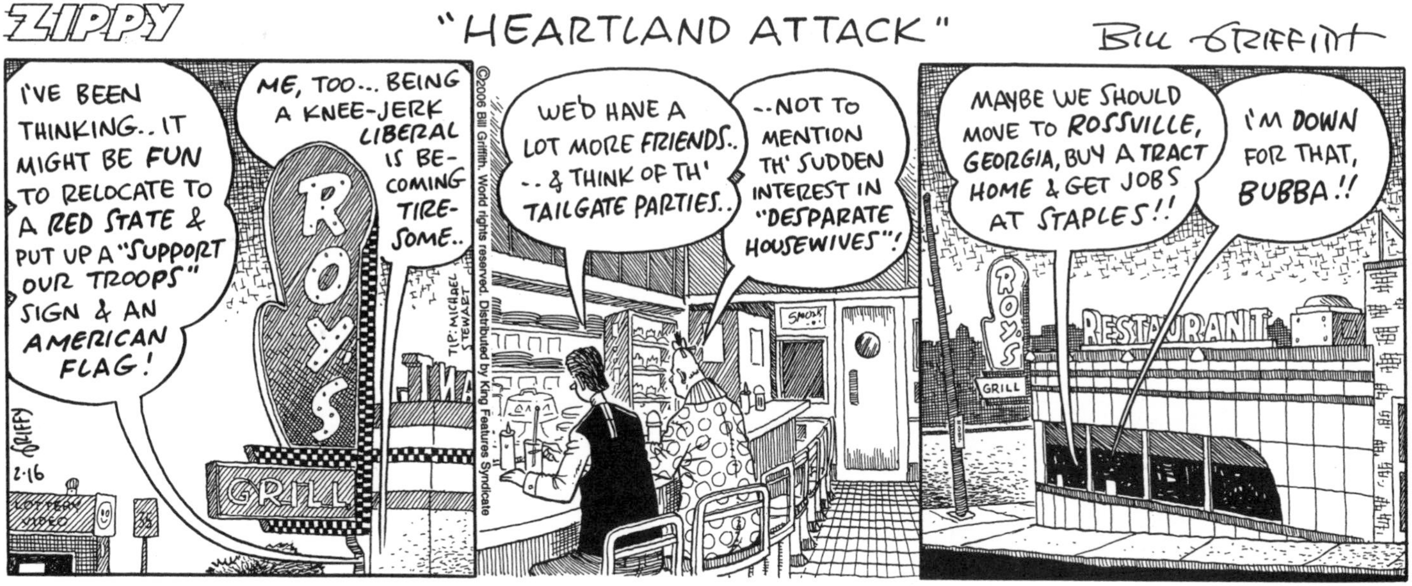
ZIPPY
"HEARTLAND ATTACK"
BILL GRIFFITH
I'VE BEEN THINKING.. IT MIGHT BE FUN TO RELOCATE TO A RED STATE & PUT UP A "SUPPORT OUR TROOPS" SIGN & AN AMERICAN FLAG!
ME, TOO... BEING A KNEE-JERK LIBERAL IS BE-COMING TIRE-SOME..
ROY'S
GRILL
GRIFFY 2.16
TIP: MICHAEL STEWART
©2006 Bill Griffith. World rights reserved. Distributed by King Features Syndicate
WE'D HAVE A LOT MORE FRIENDS.. -- & THINK OF TH' TAILGATE PARTIES..
--NOT TO MENTION TH' SUDDEN INTEREST IN "DESPARATE HOUSEWIVES"!
MAYBE WE SHOULD MOVE TO ROSSVILLE, GEORGIA, BUY A TRACT HOME & GET JOBS AT STAPLES!!
I'M DOWN FOR THAT, BUBBA!!
ROY'S
GRILL
RESTAURANT

20

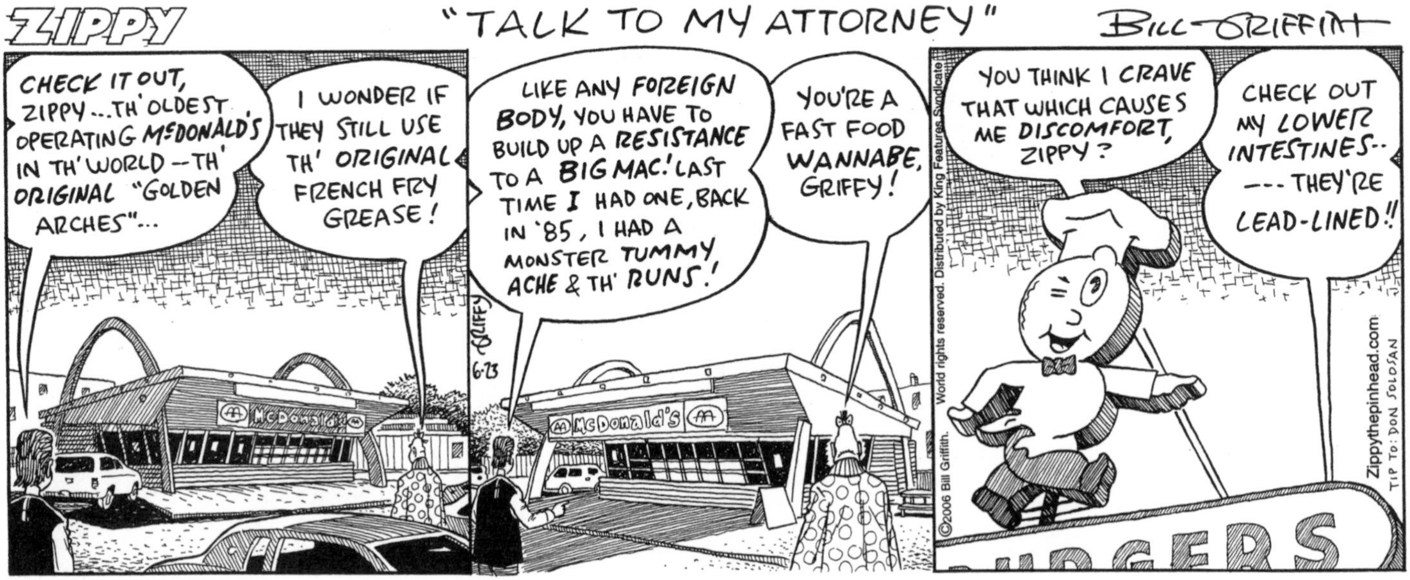
ZIPPY
"TALK TO MY ATTORNEY"
BILL GRIFFITH
CHECK IT OUT, ZIPPY...TH' OLDEST OPERATING McDONALD'S IN TH' WORLD -- TH' ORIGINAL "GOLDEN ARCHES"...
I WONDER IF THEY STILL USE TH' ORIGINAL FRENCH FRY GREASE!
LIKE ANY FOREIGN BODY, YOU HAVE TO BUILD UP A RESISTANCE TO A BIG MAC! LAST TIME I HAD ONE, BACK IN '85, I HAD A MONSTER TUMMY ACHE & TH' RUNS!
YOU'RE A FAST FOOD WANNABE, GRIFFY!
YOU THINK I CRAVE THAT WHICH CAUSES ME DISCOMFORT, ZIPPY?
CHECK OUT MY LOWER INTESTINES-- --- THEY'RE LEAD-LINED!!
McDonald's
©2006 Bill Griffith. World rights reserved. Distributed by King Features Syndicate
Zippythepinhead.com
TIP TO: DON SOLOSAN

21

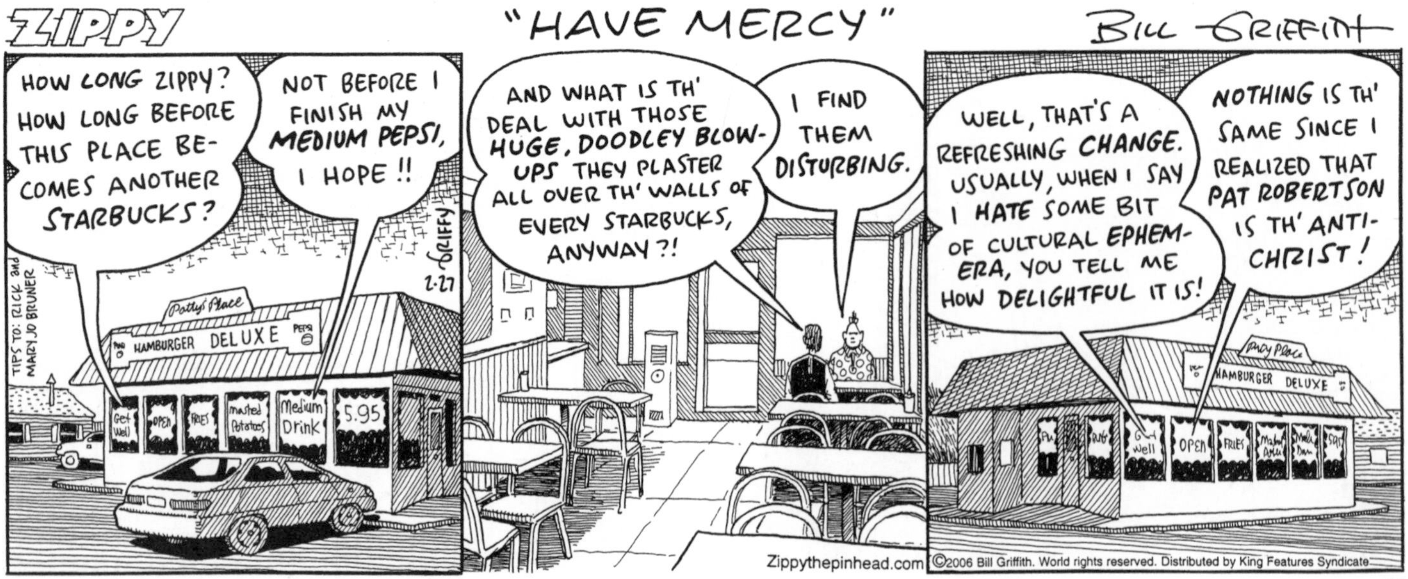
ZIPPY
"HAVE MERCY"
BILL GRIFFITH
HOW LONG ZIPPY? HOW LONG BEFORE THIS PLACE BECOMES ANOTHER STARBUCKS?
NOT BEFORE I FINISH MY MEDIUM PEPSI, I HOPE!!
AND WHAT IS TH' DEAL WITH THOSE HUGE, DOODLEY BLOW-UPS THEY PLASTER ALL OVER TH' WALLS OF EVERY STARBUCKS, ANYWAY?!
I FIND THEM DISTURBING.
WELL, THAT'S A REFRESHING CHANGE. USUALLY, WHEN I SAY I HATE SOME BIT OF CULTURAL EPHEMERA, YOU TELL ME HOW DELIGHTFUL IT IS!
NOTHING IS TH' SAME SINCE I REALIZED THAT PAT ROBERTSON IS TH' ANTI-CHRIST!
TIPS TO: RICK and MARY JO BRUNER
Patty's Place
HAMBURGER DELUXE
Get Well
OPEN
FRIES
mashed Potatoes
Medium Drink
5.95
Zippythepinhead.com
©2006 Bill Griffith. World rights reserved. Distributed by King Features Syndicate

22

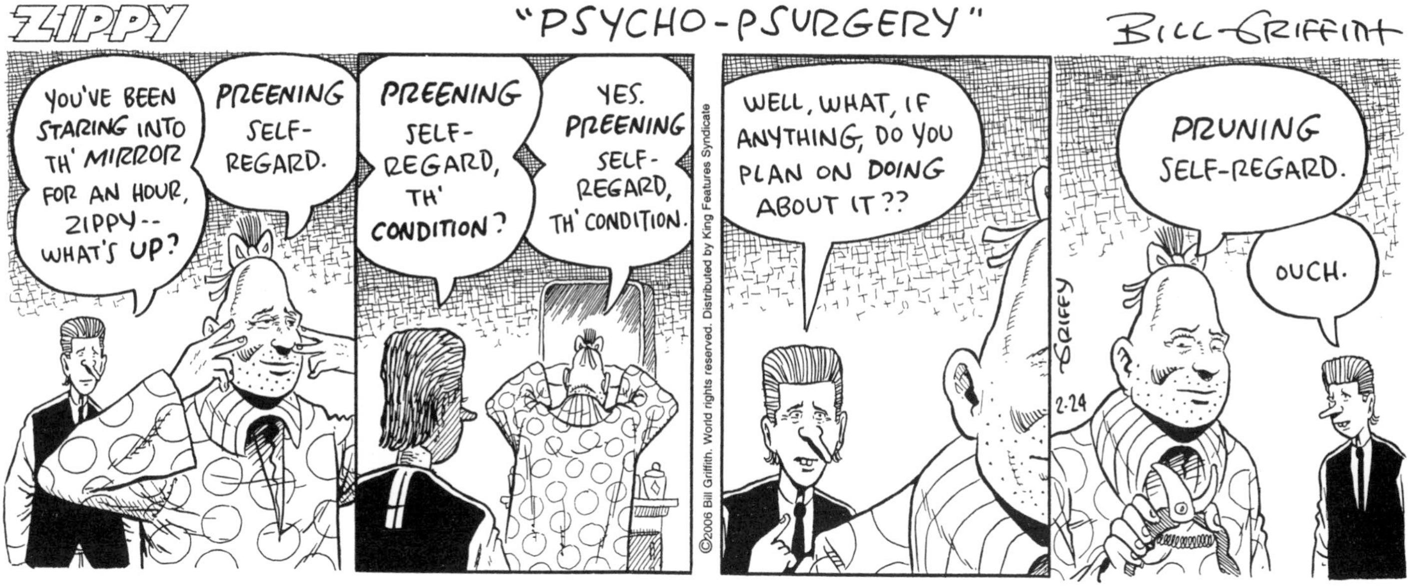
ZIPPY
"PSYCHO-PSURGERY"
BILL GRIFFITH
YOU'VE BEEN STARING INTO TH' MIRROR FOR AN HOUR, ZIPPY-- WHAT'S UP?
PREENING SELF-REGARD.
PREENING SELF-REGARD, TH' CONDITION?
YES. PREENING SELF-REGARD, TH' CONDITION.
©2006 Bill Griffith. World rights reserved. Distributed by King Features Syndicate
WELL, WHAT, IF ANYTHING, DO YOU PLAN ON DOING ABOUT IT??
GRIFFY 2·24
PRUNING SELF-REGARD.
OUCH.

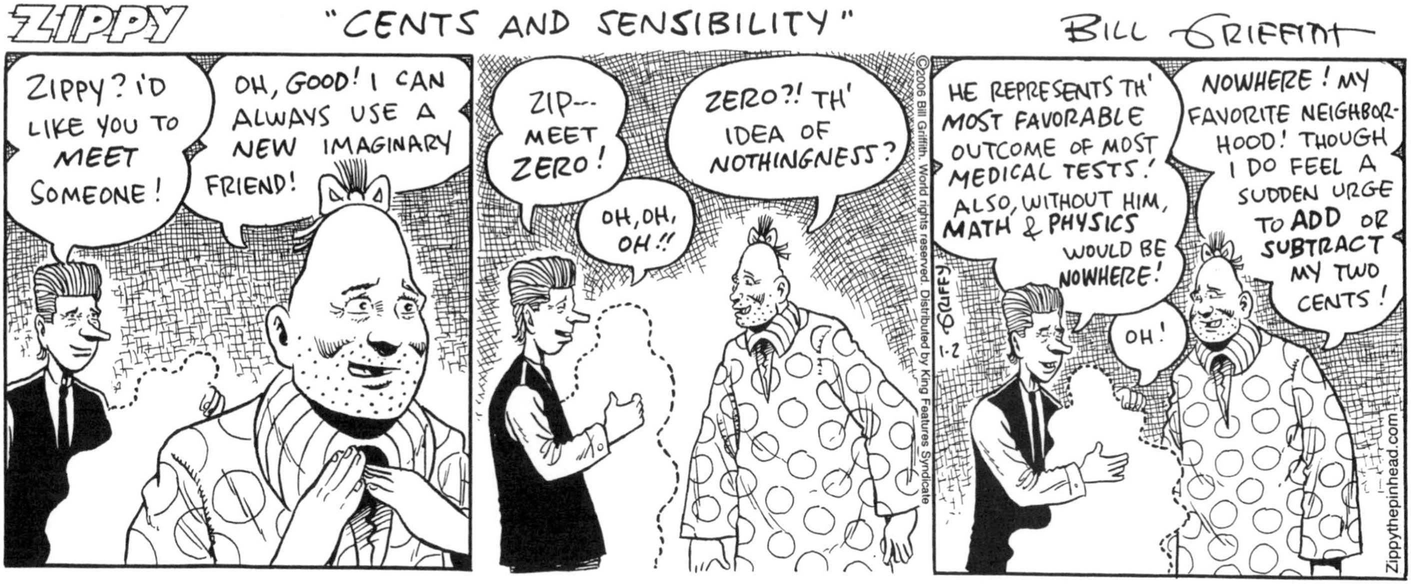
ZIPPY
"CENTS AND SENSIBILITY"
BILL GRIFFITH
ZIPPY? I'D LIKE YOU TO MEET SOMEONE!
OH, GOOD! I CAN ALWAYS USE A NEW IMAGINARY FRIEND!
ZIP--- MEET ZERO!
OH, OH, OH!!
ZERO?! TH' IDEA OF NOTHINGNESS?
©2006 Bill Griffith. World rights reserved. Distributed by King Features Syndicate
GRIFFY 1·2
HE REPRESENTS TH' MOST FAVORABLE OUTCOME OF MOST MEDICAL TESTS! ALSO, WITHOUT HIM, MATH & PHYSICS WOULD BE NOWHERE!
OH!
NOWHERE! MY FAVORITE NEIGHBORHOOD! THOUGH I DO FEEL A SUDDEN URGE TO ADD OR SUBTRACT MY TWO CENTS!
Zippythepinhead.com

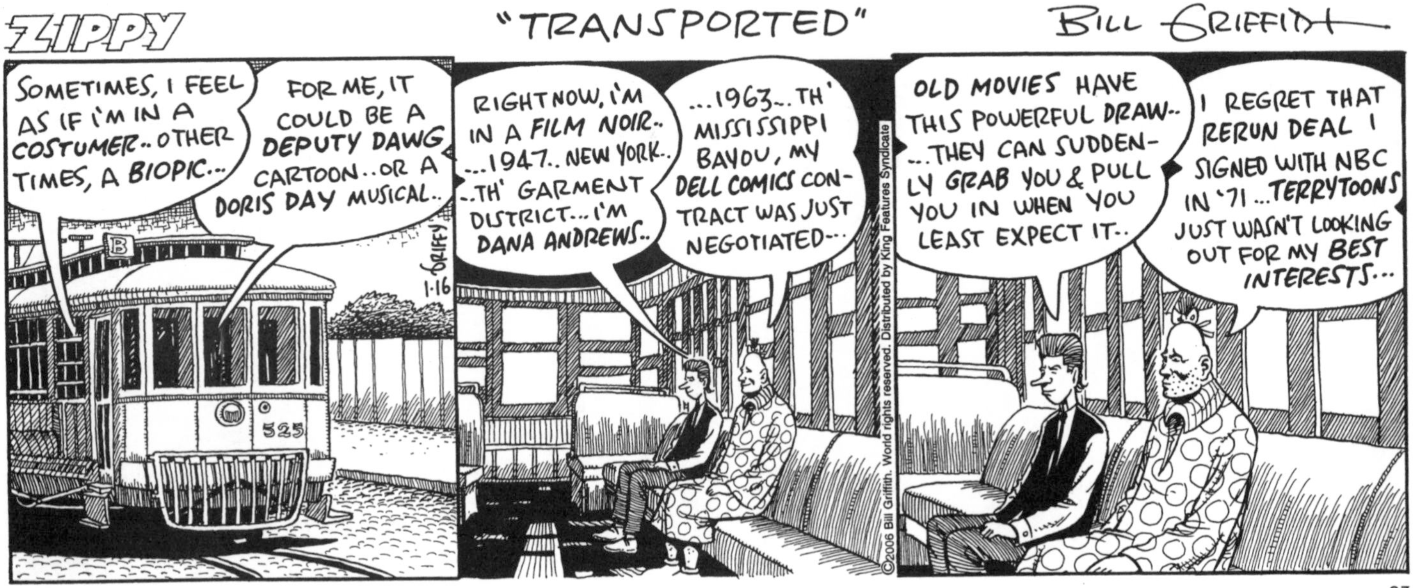
ZIPPY
"TRANSPORTED"
BILL GRIFFITH
SOMETIMES, I FEEL AS IF I'M IN A COSTUMER.. OTHER TIMES, A BIOPIC...
FOR ME, IT COULD BE A DEPUTY DAWG CARTOON.. OR A DORIS DAY MUSICAL..
B
525
GRIFFY 1·16
RIGHT NOW, I'M IN A FILM NOIR.. ..1947.. NEW YORK.. ..TH' GARMENT DISTRICT... I'M DANA ANDREWS..
...1963... TH' MISSISSIPPI BAYOU, MY DELL COMICS CONTRACT WAS JUST NEGOTIATED...
©2006 Bill Griffith. World rights reserved. Distributed by King Features Syndicate
OLD MOVIES HAVE THIS POWERFUL DRAW.. ...THEY CAN SUDDENLY GRAB YOU & PULL YOU IN WHEN YOU LEAST EXPECT IT..
I REGRET THAT RERUN DEAL I SIGNED WITH NBC IN '71... TERRYTOONS JUST WASN'T LOOKING OUT FOR MY BEST INTERESTS...

23

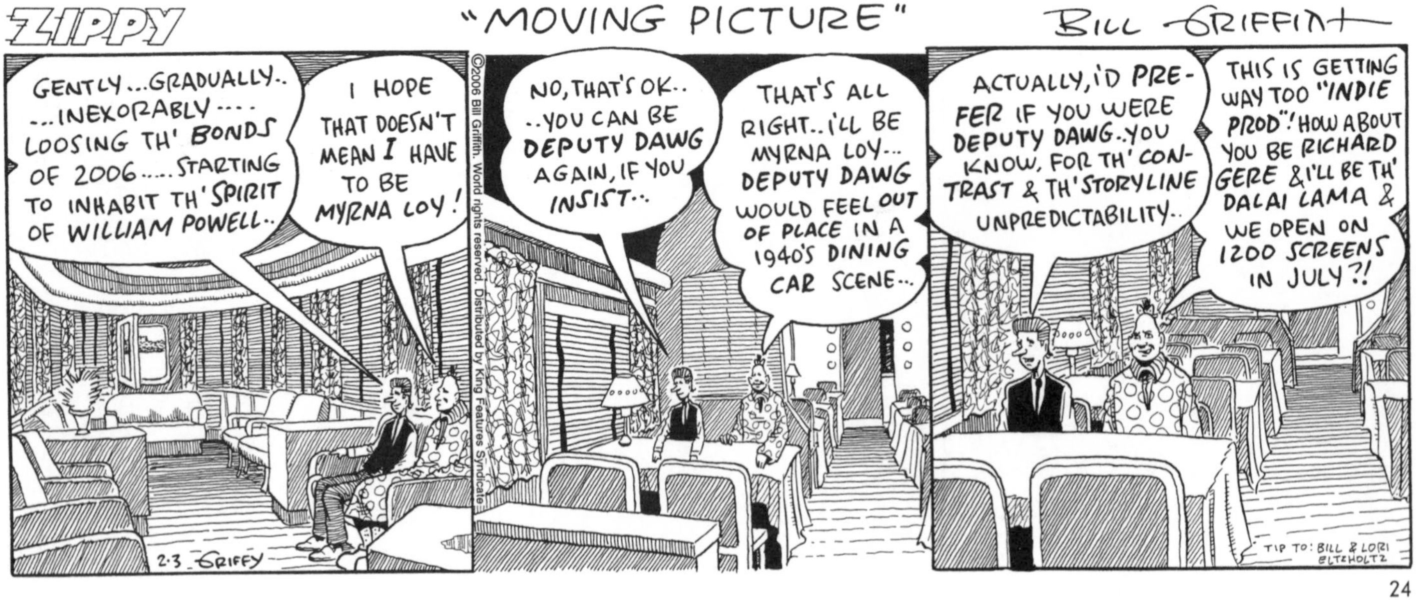
ZIPPY
"MOVING PICTURE"
BILL GRIFFITH
GENTLY... GRADUALLY.. ...INEXORABLY.... ..LOOSING TH' BONDS OF 2006..... STARTING TO INHABIT TH' SPIRIT OF WILLIAM POWELL..
I HOPE THAT DOESN'T MEAN I HAVE TO BE MYRNA LOY!
2·3 GRIFFY
©2006 Bill Griffith. World rights reserved. Distributed by King Features Syndicate
NO, THAT'S OK.. ..YOU CAN BE DEPUTY DAWG AGAIN, IF YOU INSIST..
THAT'S ALL RIGHT.. I'LL BE MYRNA LOY... DEPUTY DAWG WOULD FEEL OUT OF PLACE IN A 1940'S DINING CAR SCENE...
ACTUALLY, I'D PREFER IF YOU WERE DEPUTY DAWG.. YOU KNOW, FOR TH' CONTRAST & TH' STORYLINE UNPREDICTABILITY..
THIS IS GETTING WAY TOO "INDIE PROD"! HOW ABOUT YOU BE RICHARD GERE & I'LL BE TH' DALAI LAMA & WE OPEN ON 1200 SCREENS IN JULY?!
TIP TO: BILL & LORI ELTZHOLTZ

24

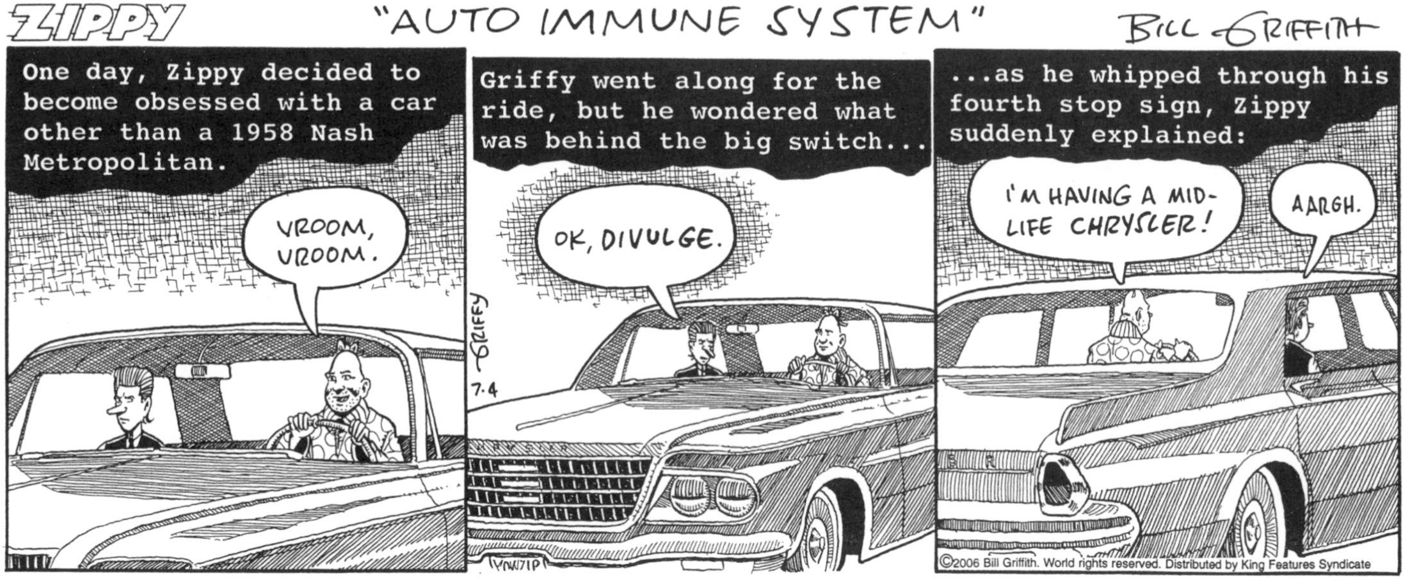
ZIPPY
"AUTO IMMUNE SYSTEM"
BILL GRIFFITH
One day, Zippy decided to become obsessed with a car other than a 1958 Nash Metropolitan.
VROOM, VROOM.
Griffy went along for the ride, but he wondered what was behind the big switch...
OK, DIVULGE.
GRIFFY 7.4
...as he whipped through his fourth stop sign, Zippy suddenly explained:
I'M HAVING A MID-LIFE CHRYSLER!
AARGH.
©2006 Bill Griffith. World rights reserved. Distributed by King Features Syndicate

25

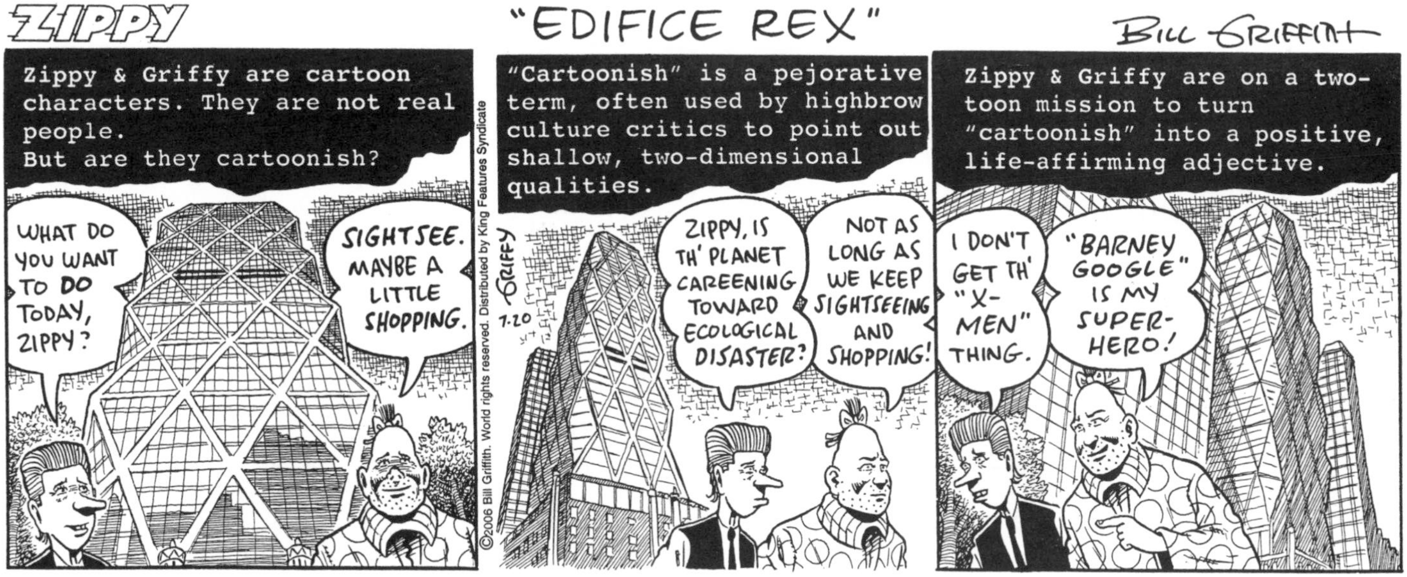
ZIPPY
"EDIFICE REX"
BILL GRIFFITH
Zippy & Griffy are cartoon characters. They are not real people.
But are they cartoonish?
WHAT DO YOU WANT TO DO TODAY, ZIPPY?
SIGHTSEE. MAYBE A LITTLE SHOPPING.
©2006 Bill Griffith. World rights reserved. Distributed by King Features Syndicate
"Cartoonish" is a pejorative term, often used by highbrow culture critics to point out shallow, two-dimensional qualities.
GRIFFY 7.20
ZIPPY, IS TH' PLANET CAREENING TOWARD ECOLOGICAL DISASTER?
NOT AS LONG AS WE KEEP SIGHTSEEING AND SHOPPING!
Zippy & Griffy are on a two-toon mission to turn "cartoonish" into a positive, life-affirming adjective.
I DON'T GET TH' "X-MEN" THING.
"BARNEY GOOGLE" IS MY SUPER-HERO!

26

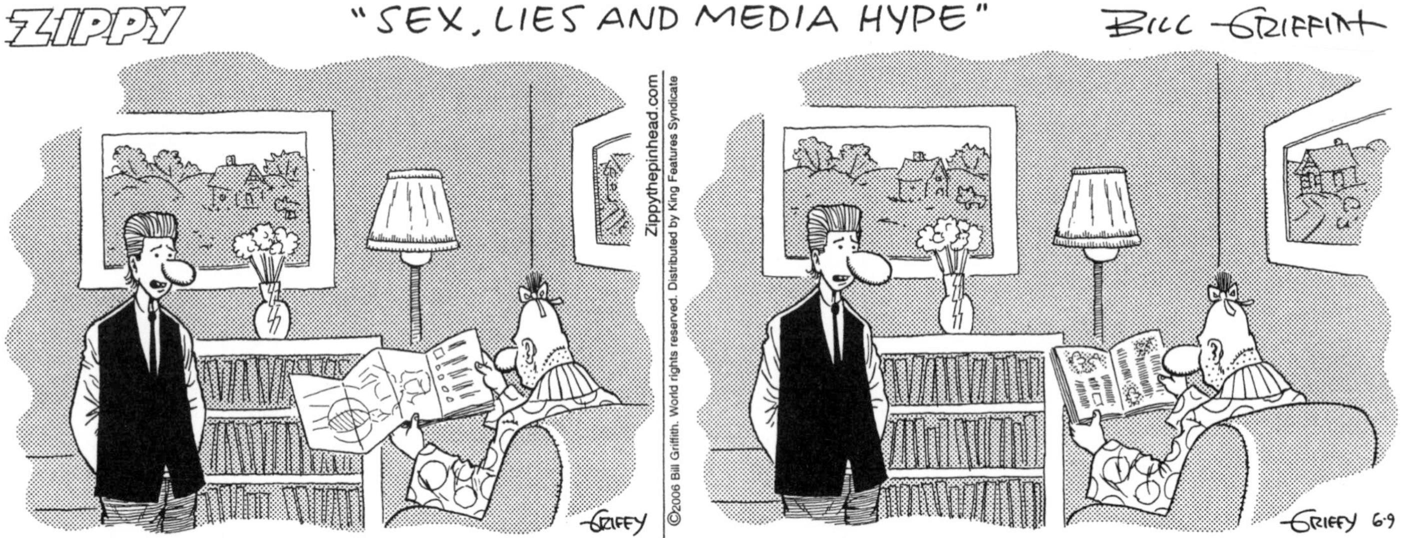
ZIPPY
"SEX, LIES AND MEDIA HYPE"
BILL GRIFFITH
Zippythepinhead.com
©2006 Bill Griffith. World rights reserved. Distributed by King Features Syndicate
GRIFFY
GRIFFY 6-9

"Why do you read Playboy, Zippy?" "For the articles!" "Why do you read The New Yorker, Zippy?" "For the articles!"

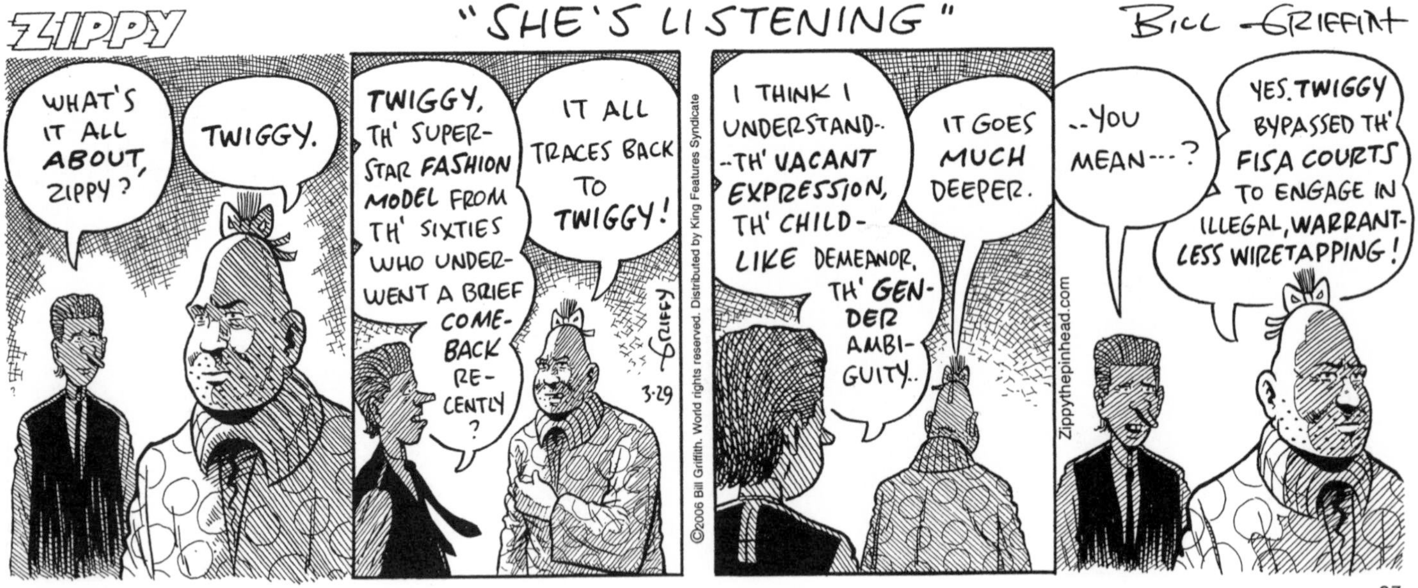
ZIPPY
"SHE'S LISTENING"
BILL GRIFFITH
WHAT'S IT ALL ABOUT, ZIPPY?
TWIGGY.
TWIGGY, TH' SUPER-STAR FASHION MODEL FROM TH' SIXTIES WHO UNDER-WENT A BRIEF COME-BACK RE-CENTLY?
IT ALL TRACES BACK TO TWIGGY!
GRIFFY
3-29
©2006 Bill Griffith. World rights reserved. Distributed by King Features Syndicate
I THINK I UNDERSTAND-- --TH' VACANT EXPRESSION, TH' CHILD-LIKE DEMEANOR, TH' GEN-DER AMBI-GUITY..
IT GOES MUCH DEEPER.
Zippythepinhead.com
--YOU MEAN---?
YES. TWIGGY BYPASSED TH' FISA COURTS TO ENGAGE IN ILLEGAL, WARRANT-LESS WIRETAPPING!

27

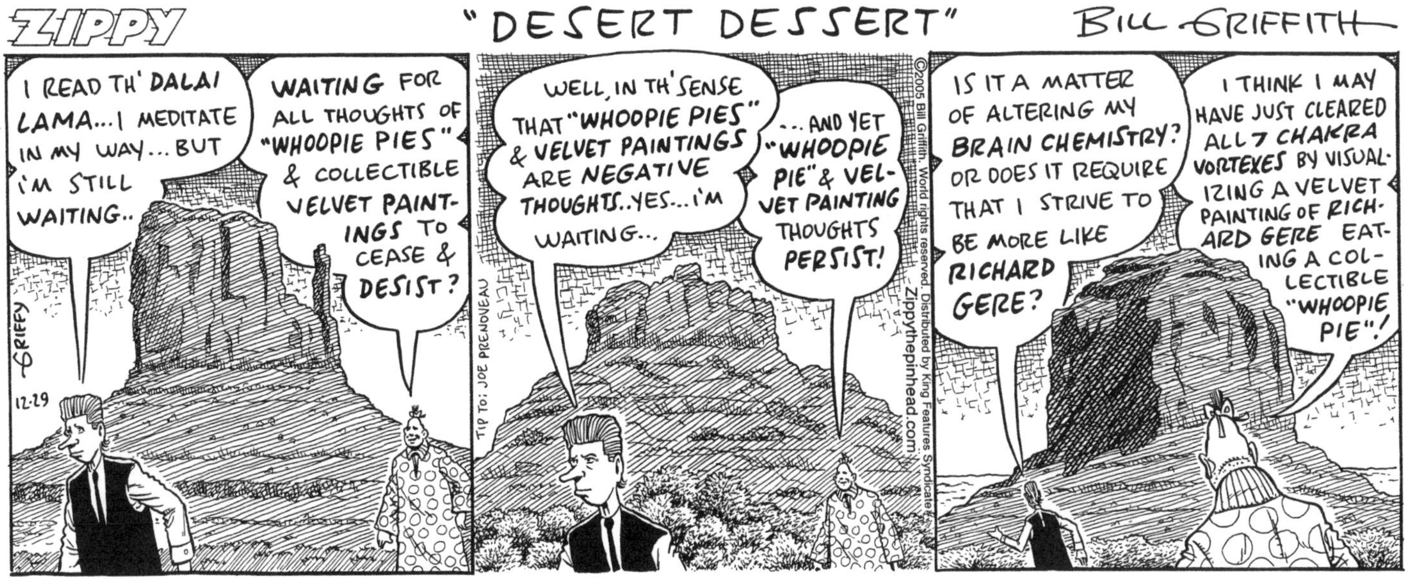
ZIPPY
"DESERT DESSERT"
BILL GRIFFITH
I READ TH' DALAI LAMA...I MEDITATE IN MY WAY...BUT I'M STILL WAITING..
WAITING FOR ALL THOUGHTS OF "WHOOPIE PIES" & COLLECTIBLE VELVET PAINTINGS TO CEASE & DESIST?
GRIFFY 12-29
TIP TO: JOE PRENOVEAU
WELL, IN TH' SENSE THAT "WHOOPIE PIES" & VELVET PAINTINGS ARE NEGATIVE THOUGHTS..YES...I'M WAITING...
...AND YET "WHOOPIE PIE" & VELVET PAINTING THOUGHTS PERSIST!
©2005 Bill Griffith. World rights reserved. Distributed by King Features Syndicate
Zippythepinhead.com
IS IT A MATTER OF ALTERING MY BRAIN CHEMISTRY? OR DOES IT REQUIRE THAT I STRIVE TO BE MORE LIKE RICHARD GERE?
I THINK I MAY HAVE JUST CLEARED ALL 7 CHAKRA VORTEXES BY VISUALIZING A VELVET PAINTING OF RICHARD GERE EATING A COLLECTIBLE "WHOOPIE PIE"!

28

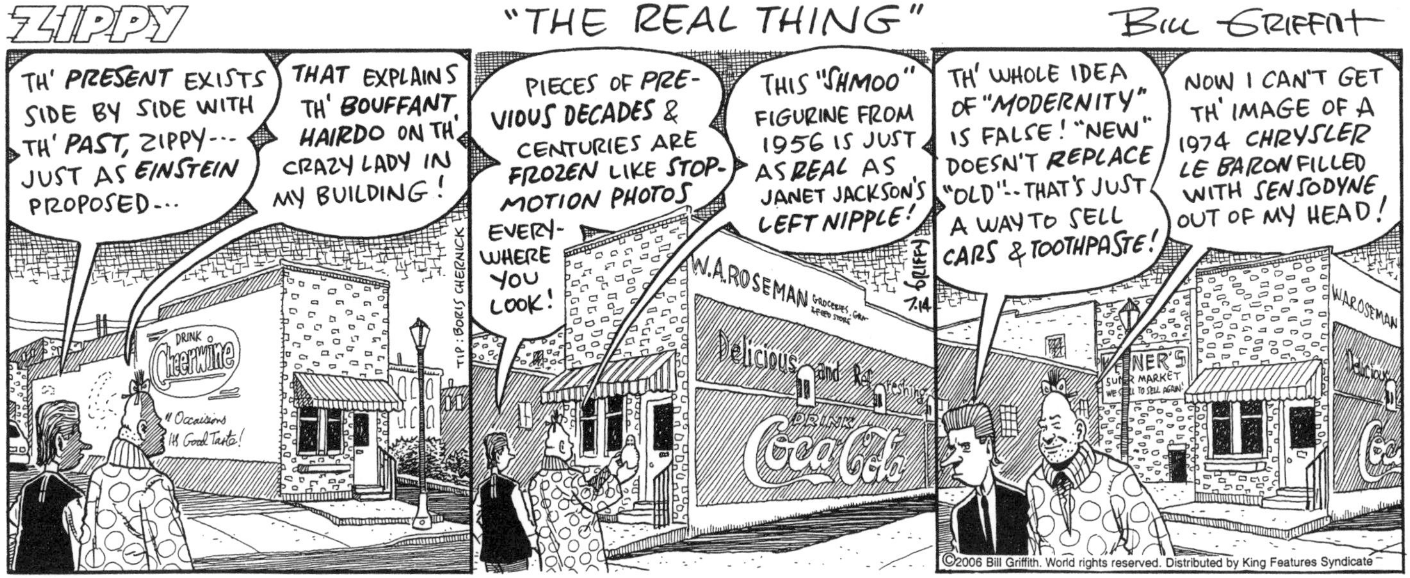
ZIPPY
"THE REAL THING"
BILL GRIFFITH
TH' PRESENT EXISTS SIDE BY SIDE WITH TH' PAST, ZIPPY--- JUST AS EINSTEIN PROPOSED...
THAT EXPLAINS TH' BOUFFANT HAIRDO ON TH' CRAZY LADY IN MY BUILDING!
DRINK Cheerwine
TIP: BORIS CHERNICK
PIECES OF PREVIOUS DECADES & CENTURIES ARE FROZEN LIKE STOP-MOTION PHOTOS EVERYWHERE YOU LOOK!
THIS "SHMOO" FIGURINE FROM 1956 IS JUST AS REAL AS JANET JACKSON'S LEFT NIPPLE!
GRIFFY 7-14
W.A. ROSEMAN
Delicious and Refreshing
DRINK Coca-Cola
TH' WHOLE IDEA OF "MODERNITY" IS FALSE! "NEW" DOESN'T REPLACE "OLD"!--THAT'S JUST A WAY TO SELL CARS & TOOTHPASTE!
NOW I CAN'T GET TH' IMAGE OF A 1974 CHRYSLER LE BARON FILLED WITH SENSODYNE OUT OF MY HEAD!
©2006 Bill Griffith. World rights reserved. Distributed by King Features Syndicate

29

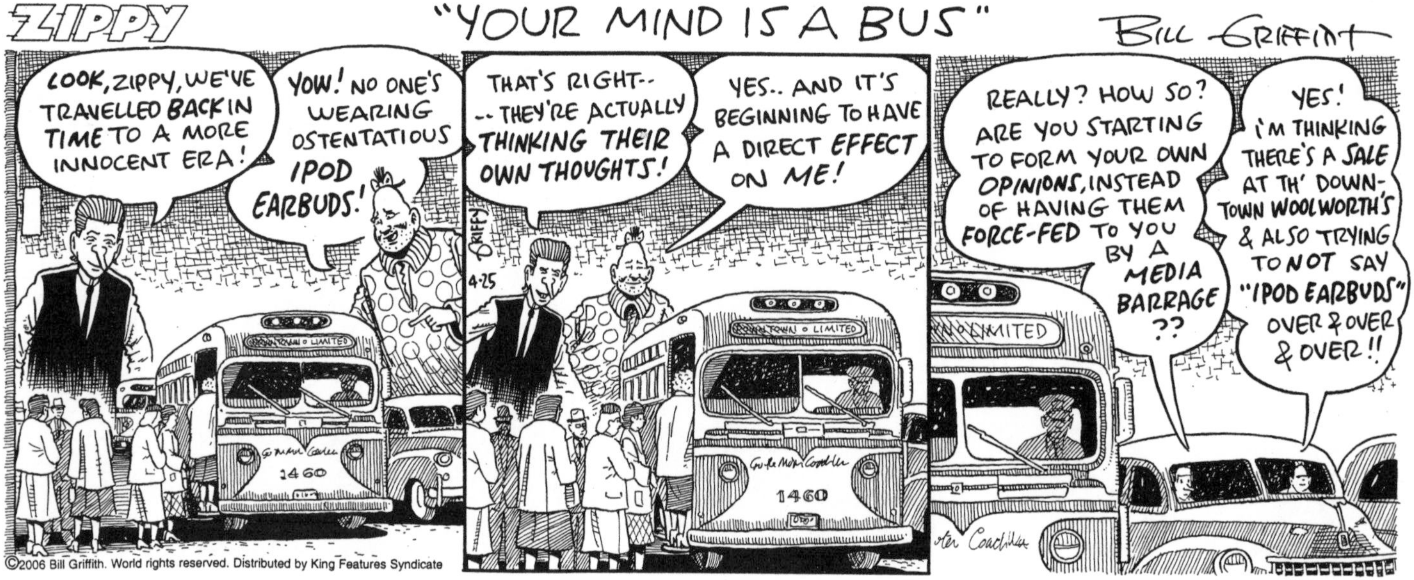
ZIPPY
"YOUR MIND IS A BUS"
BILL GRIFFITH
LOOK, ZIPPY, WE'VE TRAVELLED BACK IN TIME TO A MORE INNOCENT ERA!
YOW! NO ONE'S WEARING OSTENTATIOUS IPOD EARBUDS!
THAT'S RIGHT-- --THEY'RE ACTUALLY THINKING THEIR OWN THOUGHTS!
YES.. AND IT'S BEGINNING TO HAVE A DIRECT EFFECT ON ME!
REALLY? HOW SO? ARE YOU STARTING TO FORM YOUR OWN OPINIONS, INSTEAD OF HAVING THEM FORCE-FED TO YOU BY A MEDIA BARRAGE??
YES! I'M THINKING THERE'S A SALE AT TH' DOWNTOWN WOOLWORTH'S & ALSO TRYING TO NOT SAY "IPOD EARBUDS" OVER & OVER & OVER!!
LIMITED
1460
GRIFFY
4-25
©2006 Bill Griffith. World rights reserved. Distributed by King Features Syndicate

30

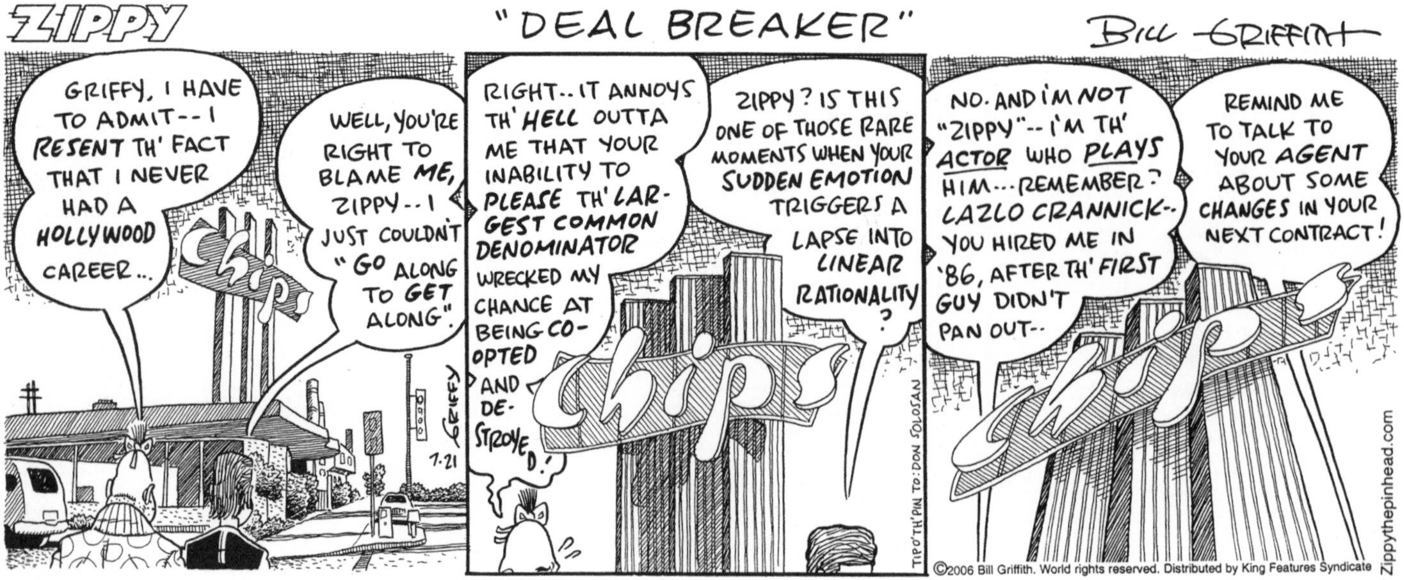
ZIPPY
"DEAL BREAKER"
BILL GRIFFITH
GRIFFY, I HAVE TO ADMIT-- I RESENT TH' FACT THAT I NEVER HAD A HOLLYWOOD CAREER...
WELL, YOU'RE RIGHT TO BLAME ME, ZIPPY-- I JUST COULDN'T "GO ALONG TO GET ALONG".
RIGHT.. IT ANNOYS TH' HELL OUTTA ME THAT YOUR INABILITY TO PLEASE TH' LARGEST COMMON DENOMINATOR WRECKED MY CHANCE AT BEING CO-OPTED AND DE-STROYED!
ZIPPY? IS THIS ONE OF THOSE RARE MOMENTS WHEN YOUR SUDDEN EMOTION TRIGGERS A LAPSE INTO LINEAR RATIONALITY?
NO. AND I'M NOT "ZIPPY"-- I'M TH' ACTOR WHO PLAYS HIM... REMEMBER? LAZLO CRANNICK-- YOU HIRED ME IN '86, AFTER TH' FIRST GUY DIDN'T PAN OUT--
REMIND ME TO TALK TO YOUR AGENT ABOUT SOME CHANGES IN YOUR NEXT CONTRACT!
Chips
GRIFFY
7-21
TIP O' TH' PIN TO: DON SOLOSAN
©2006 Bill Griffith. World rights reserved. Distributed by King Features Syndicate
Zippythepinhead.com

31

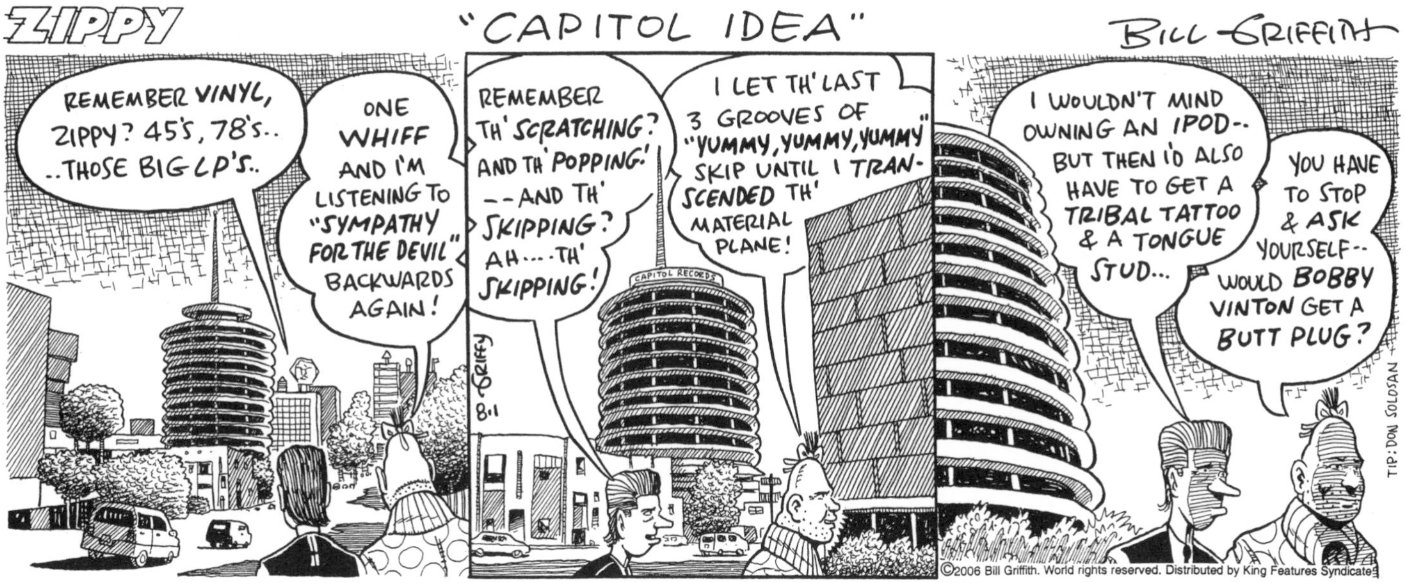
ZIPPY
"CAPITOL IDEA"
BILL GRIFFITH
REMEMBER VINYL, ZIPPY? 45'S, 78'S.. ..THOSE BIG LP'S..
ONE WHIFF AND I'M LISTENING TO "SYMPATHY FOR THE DEVIL" BACKWARDS AGAIN!
REMEMBER TH' SCRATCHING? AND TH' POPPING! --AND TH' SKIPPING? AH.... TH' SKIPPING!
I LET TH' LAST 3 GROOVES OF "YUMMY, YUMMY, YUMMY" SKIP UNTIL I TRANSCENDED TH' MATERIAL PLANE!
CAPITOL RECORDS
GRIFFY 8-1
I WOULDN'T MIND OWNING AN IPOD-- BUT THEN I'D ALSO HAVE TO GET A TRIBAL TATTOO & A TONGUE STUD...
YOU HAVE TO STOP & ASK YOURSELF-- WOULD BOBBY VINTON GET A BUTT PLUG?
TIP: DON SOLOSAN
©2006 Bill Griffith. World rights reserved. Distributed by King Features Syndicate

32

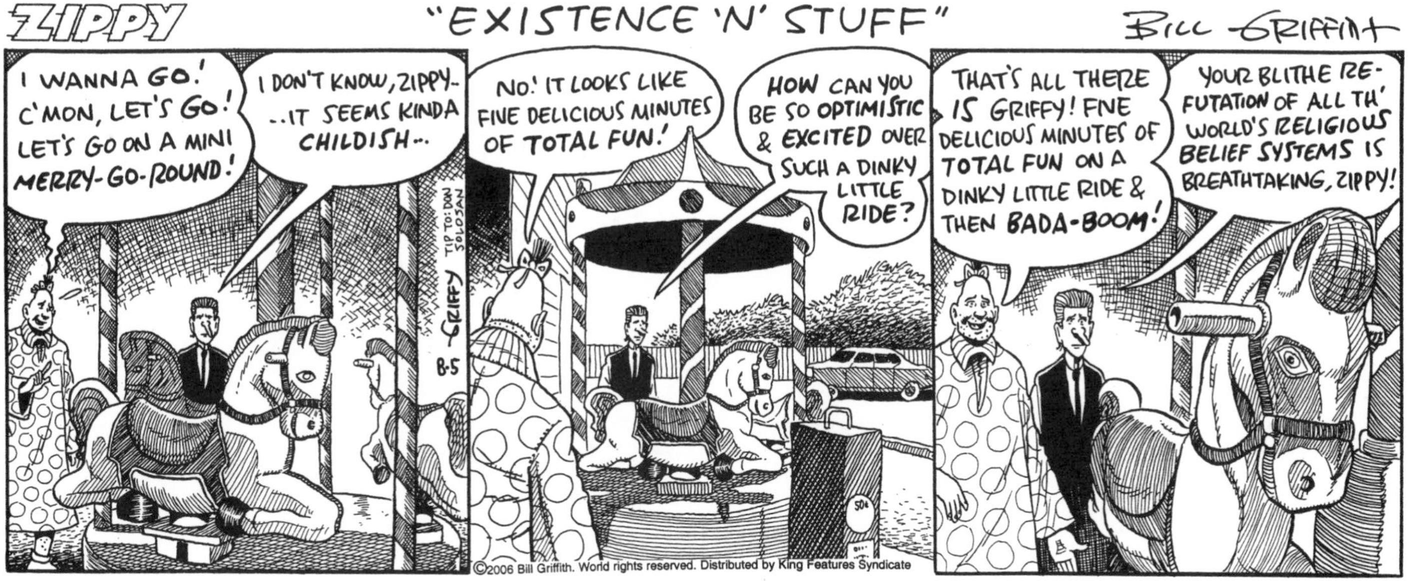
ZIPPY
"EXISTENCE 'N' STUFF"
BILL GRIFFITH
I WANNA GO! C'MON, LET'S GO! LET'S GO ON A MINI MERRY-GO-ROUND!
I DON'T KNOW, ZIPPY-- ..IT SEEMS KINDA CHILDISH--
TIP TO: DON SOLOSAN
GRIFFY 8-5
NO! IT LOOKS LIKE FIVE DELICIOUS MINUTES OF TOTAL FUN!
HOW CAN YOU BE SO OPTIMISTIC & EXCITED OVER SUCH A DINKY LITTLE RIDE?
THAT'S ALL THERE IS GRIFFY! FIVE DELICIOUS MINUTES OF TOTAL FUN ON A DINKY LITTLE RIDE & THEN BADA-BOOM!
YOUR BLITHE REFUTATION OF ALL TH' WORLD'S RELIGIOUS BELIEF SYSTEMS IS BREATHTAKING, ZIPPY!
©2006 Bill Griffith. World rights reserved. Distributed by King Features Syndicate

33

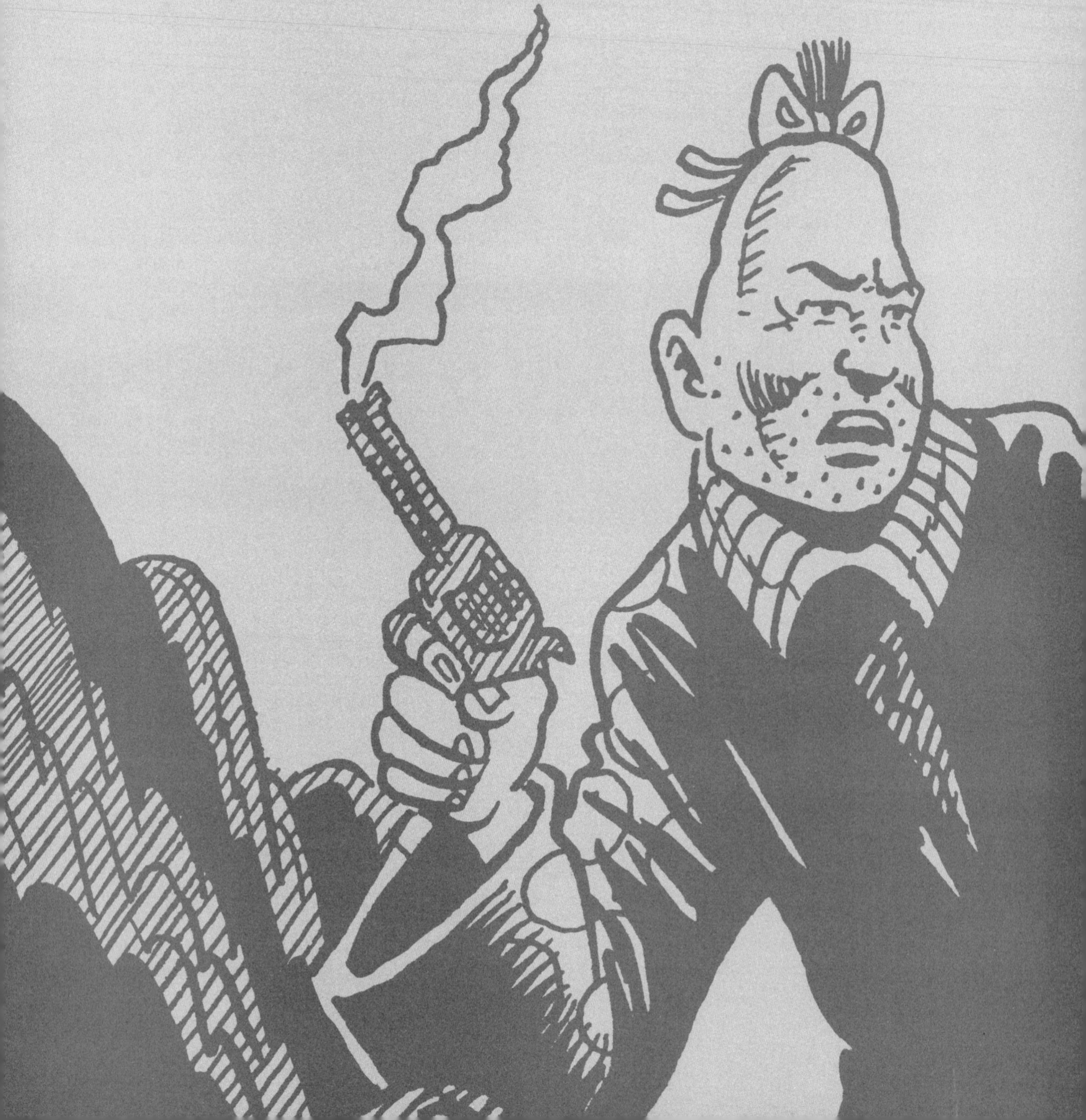

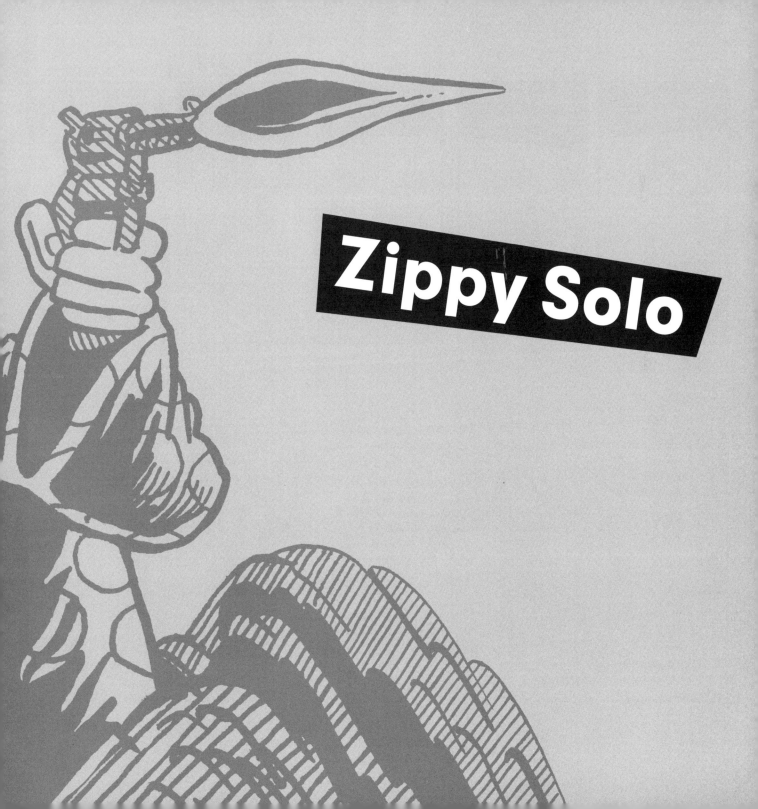

Zippy Solo

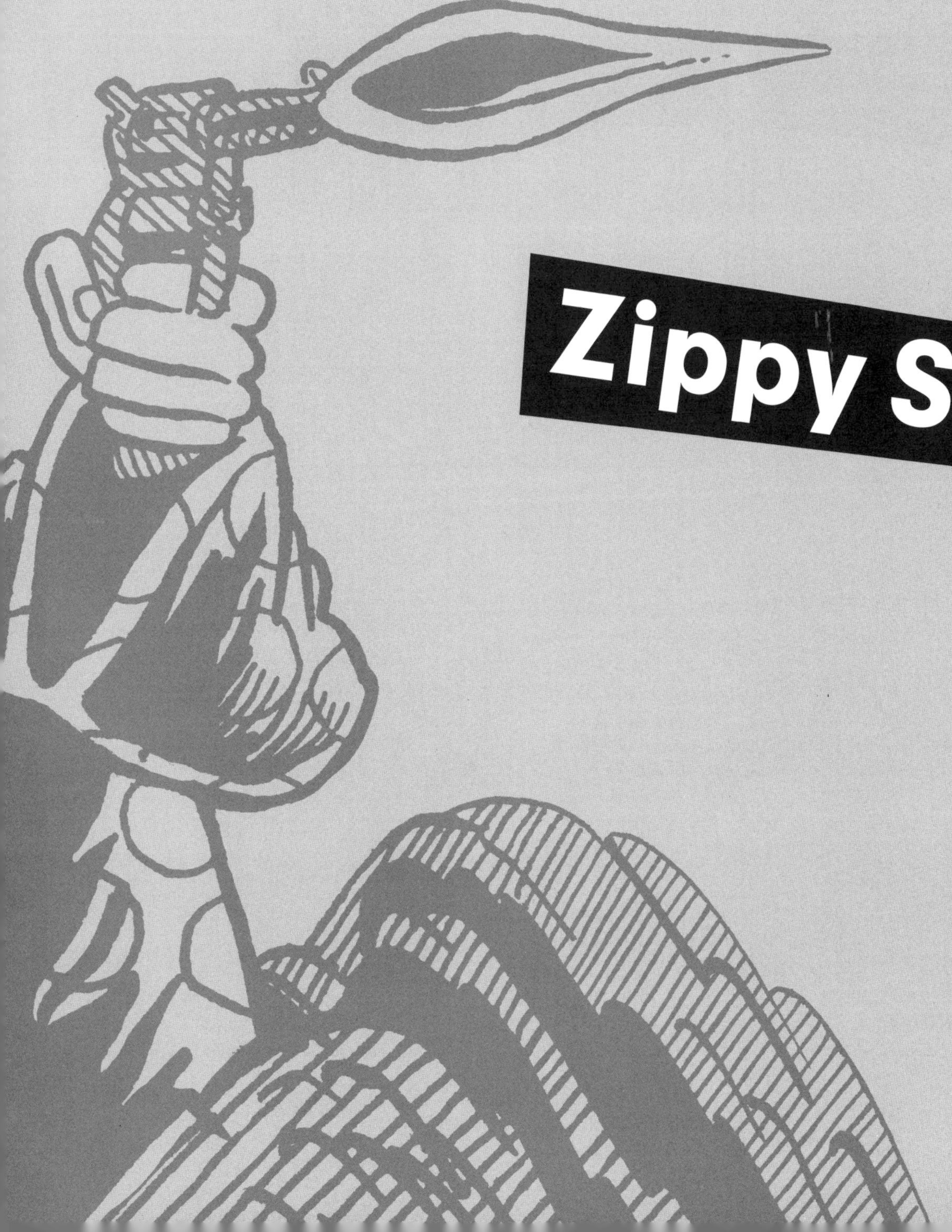

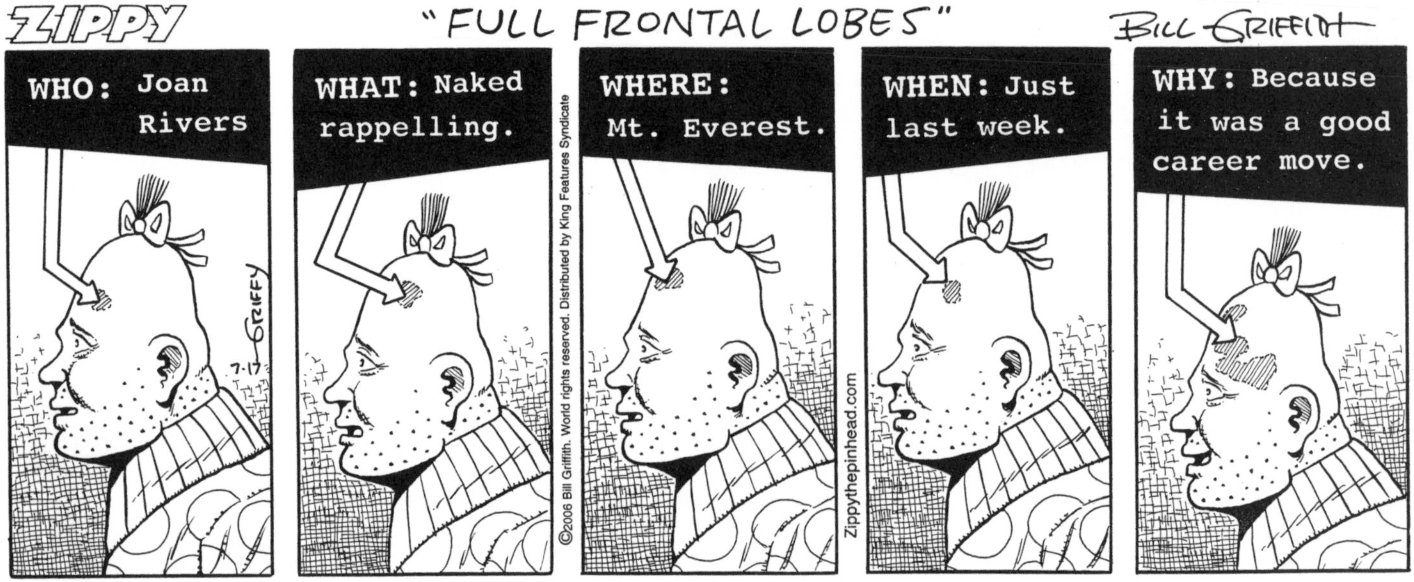
ZIPPY
"FULL FRONTAL LOBES"
BILL GRIFFITH
WHO: Joan Rivers
WHAT: Naked rappelling.
©2006 Bill Griffith. World rights reserved. Distributed by King Features Syndicate
WHERE: Mt. Everest.
Zippythepinhead.com
WHEN: Just last week.
WHY: Because it was a good career move.
GRIFFY 7-17

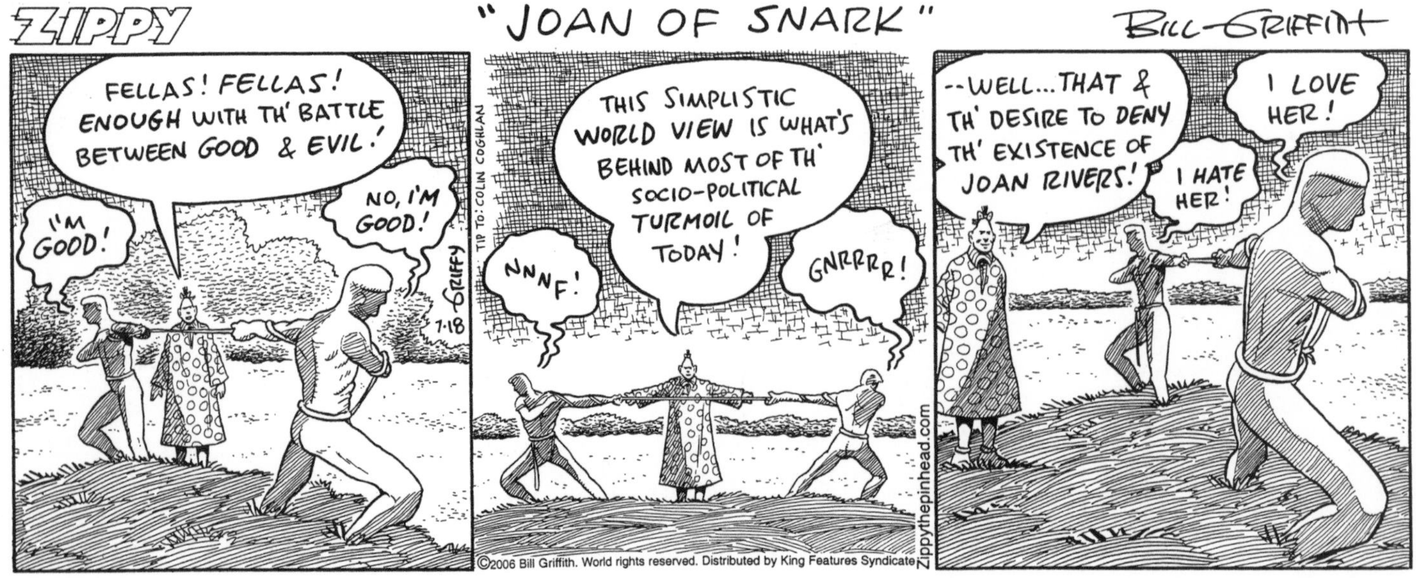
ZIPPY
"JOAN OF SNARK"
BILL GRIFFITH
FELLAS! FELLAS! ENOUGH WITH TH' BATTLE BETWEEN GOOD & EVIL!
I'M GOOD!
NO, I'M GOOD!
GRIFFY 7-18
TIP TO: COLIN COGHLAN
THIS SIMPLISTIC WORLD VIEW IS WHAT'S BEHIND MOST OF TH' SOCIO-POLITICAL TURMOIL OF TODAY!
NNNF!
GNRRRR!
©2006 Bill Griffith. World rights reserved. Distributed by King Features Syndicate
Zippythepinhead.com
--WELL...THAT & TH' DESIRE TO DENY TH' EXISTENCE OF JOAN RIVERS!
I LOVE HER!
I HATE HER!

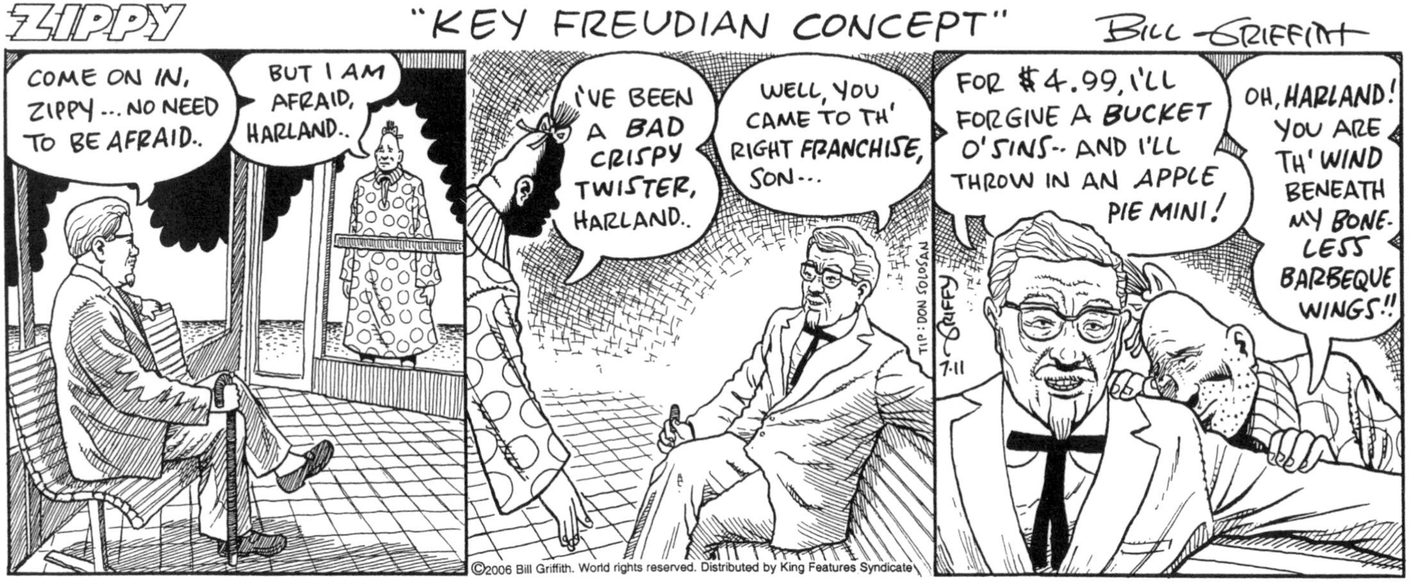
ZIPPY
"KEY FREUDIAN CONCEPT"
BILL GRIFFITH
COME ON IN, ZIPPY... NO NEED TO BE AFRAID..
BUT I AM AFRAID, HARLAND..
I'VE BEEN A BAD CRISPY TWISTER, HARLAND..
WELL, YOU CAME TO TH' RIGHT FRANCHISE, SON...
TIP: DON SOLOSAN
GRIFFY 7·11
FOR $4.99, I'LL FORGIVE A BUCKET O' SINS-- AND I'LL THROW IN AN APPLE PIE MINI!
OH, HARLAND! YOU ARE TH' WIND BENEATH MY BONE-LESS BARBEQUE WINGS!!
©2006 Bill Griffith. World rights reserved. Distributed by King Features Syndicate

35

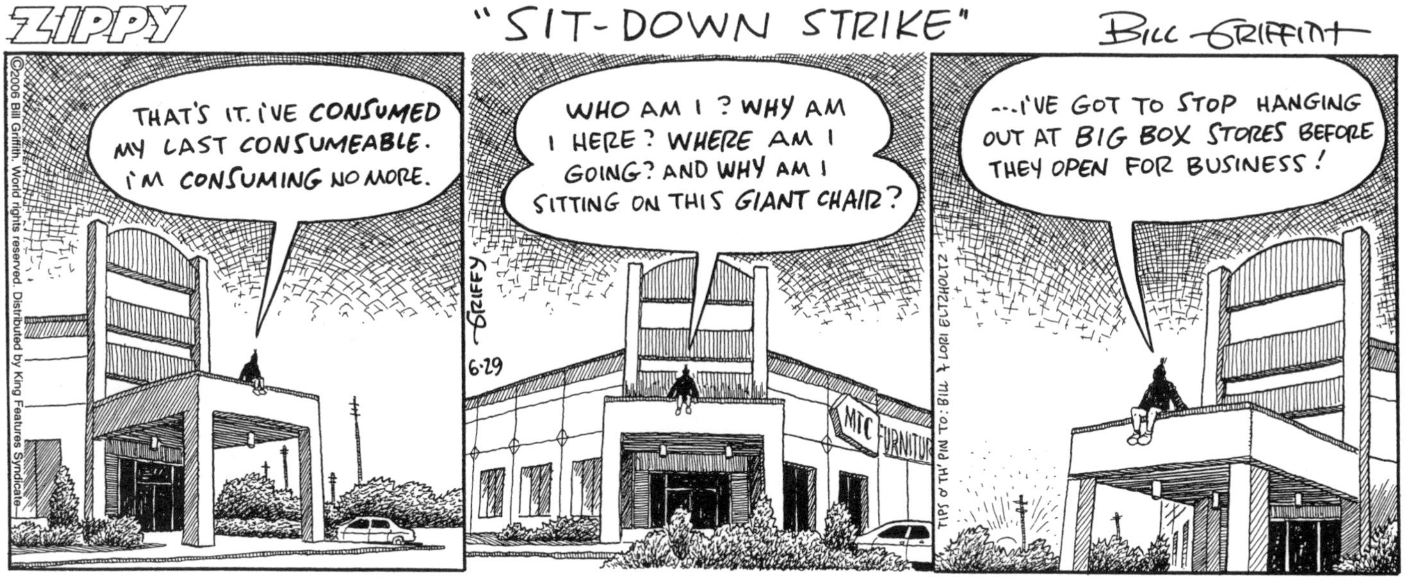
ZIPPY
"SIT-DOWN STRIKE"
BILL GRIFFITH
©2006 Bill Griffith. World rights reserved. Distributed by King Features Syndicate
THAT'S IT. I'VE CONSUMED MY LAST CONSUMEABLE. I'M CONSUMING NO MORE.
GRIFFY 6·29
WHO AM I? WHY AM I HERE? WHERE AM I GOING? AND WHY AM I SITTING ON THIS GIANT CHAIR?
MTC FURNITUR
TIPS O' TH' PIN TO: BILL & LORI ELTZHOLTZ
...I'VE GOT TO STOP HANGING OUT AT BIG BOX STORES BEFORE THEY OPEN FOR BUSINESS!

36

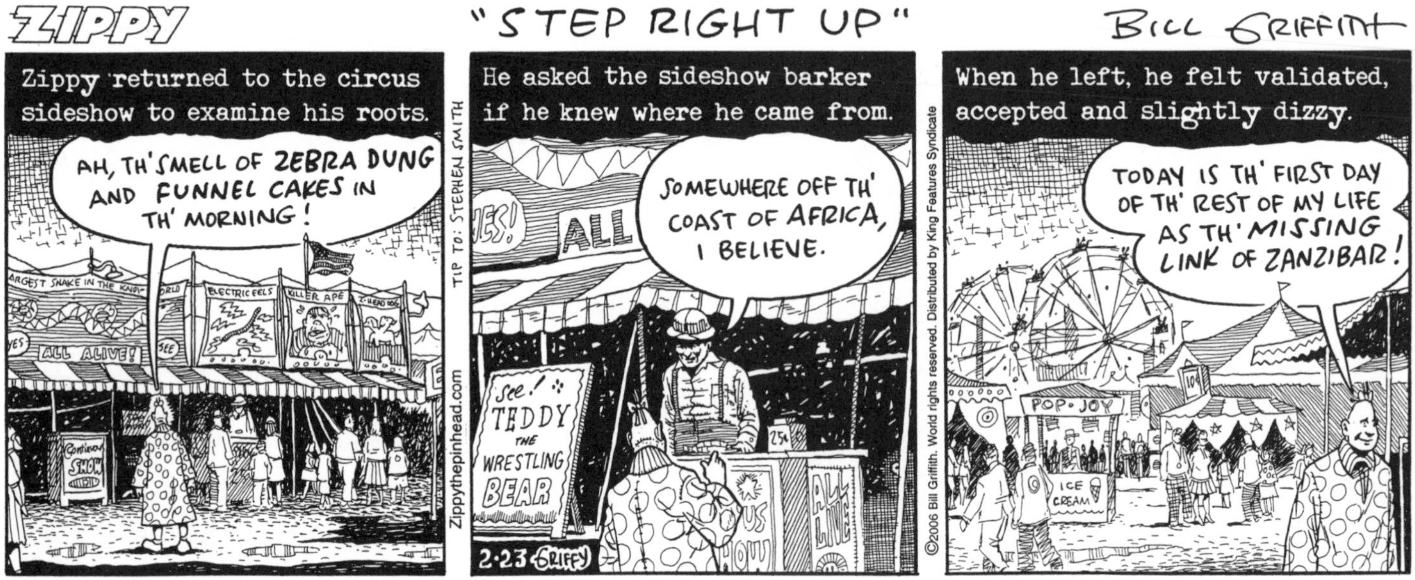
ZIPPY
"STEP RIGHT UP"
BILL GRIFFITH
Zippy returned to the circus sideshow to examine his roots.
AH, TH' SMELL OF ZEBRA DUNG AND FUNNEL CAKES IN TH' MORNING!
ELECTRIC EELS
KILLER APE
ALL ALIVE!
TIP TO: STEPHEN SMITH
Zippythepinhead.com
He asked the sideshow barker if he knew where he came from.
SOMEWHERE OFF TH' COAST OF AFRICA, I BELIEVE.
ALL
See! TEDDY THE WRESTLING BEAR
2·23 GRIFFY
©2006 Bill Griffith. World rights reserved. Distributed by King Features Syndicate
When he left, he felt validated, accepted and slightly dizzy.
TODAY IS TH' FIRST DAY OF TH' REST OF MY LIFE AS TH' MISSING LINK OF ZANZIBAR!
POP·JOY
ICE CREAM

37

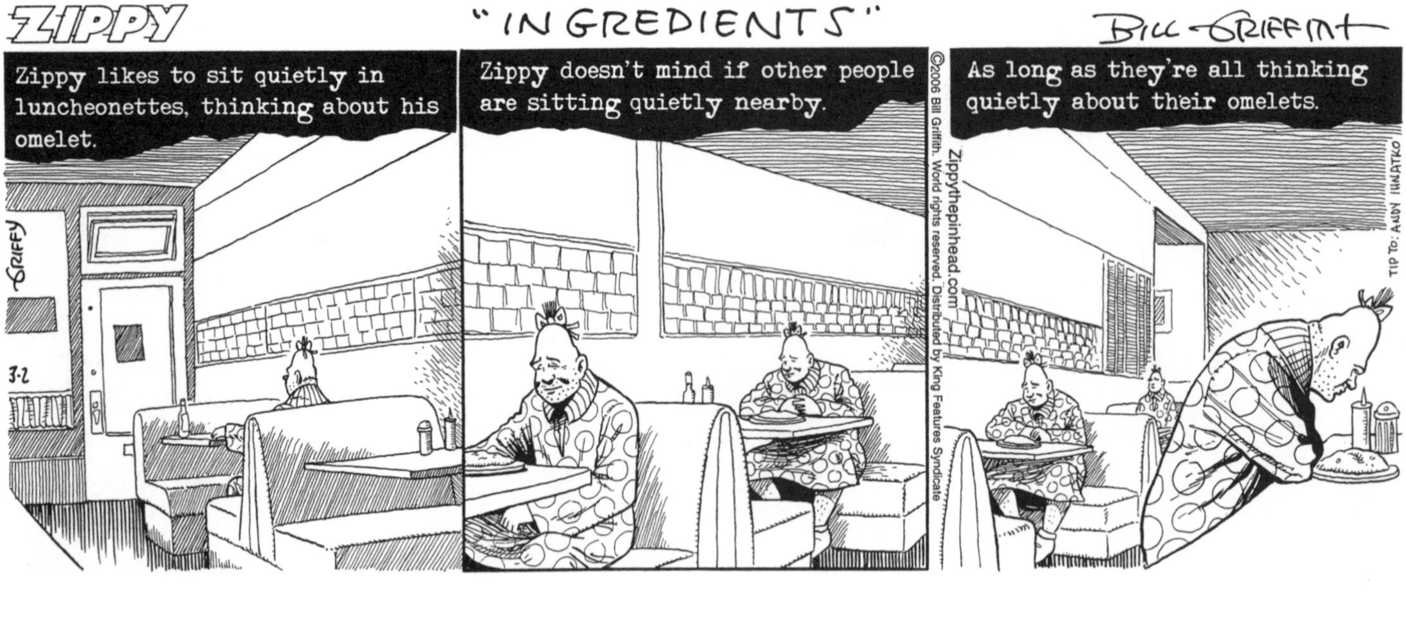
ZIPPY
"INGREDIENTS"
BILL GRIFFITH
Zippy likes to sit quietly in luncheonettes, thinking about his omelet.
GRIFFY
3-2
Zippy doesn't mind if other people are sitting quietly nearby.
©2006 Bill Griffith. World rights reserved. Distributed by King Features Syndicate
Zippythepinhead.com
As long as they're all thinking quietly about their omelets.
TIP TO: ANDY IWATKO

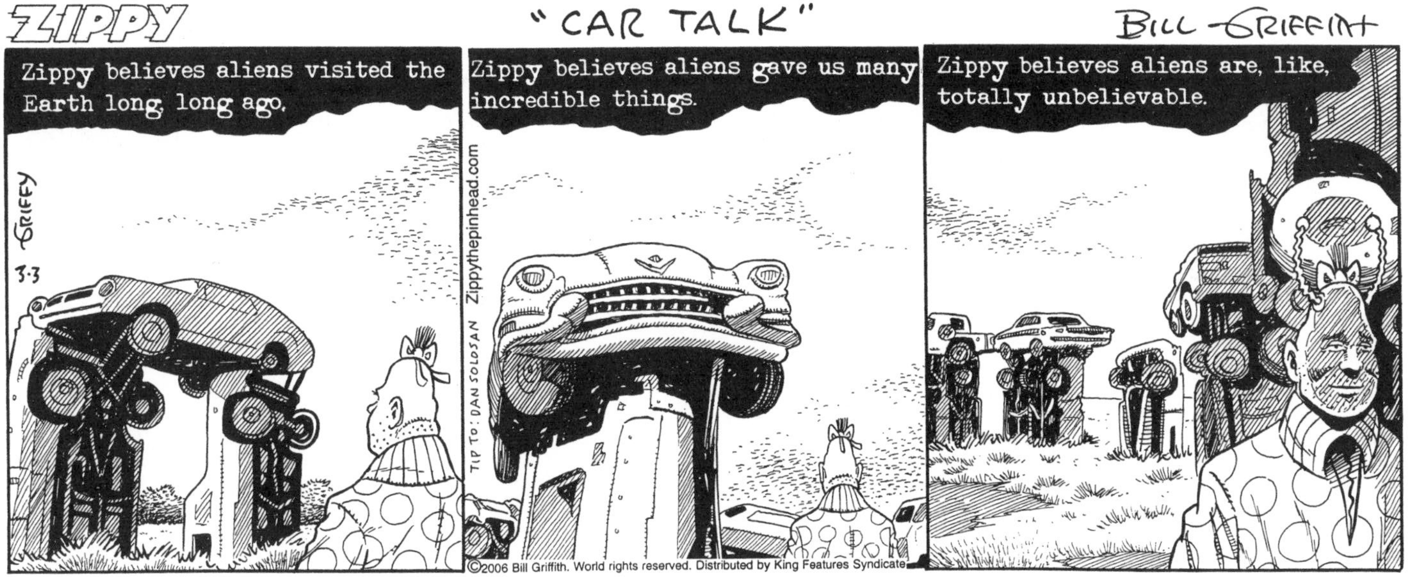
ZIPPY
"CAR TALK"
BILL GRIFFITH
Zippy believes aliens visited the Earth long, long ago.
GRIFFY
3·3
Zippy believes aliens gave us many incredible things.
TIP TO: DAN SOLDSAN
Zippythepinhead.com
©2006 Bill Griffith. World rights reserved. Distributed by King Features Syndicate
Zippy believes aliens are, like, totally unbelievable.

38

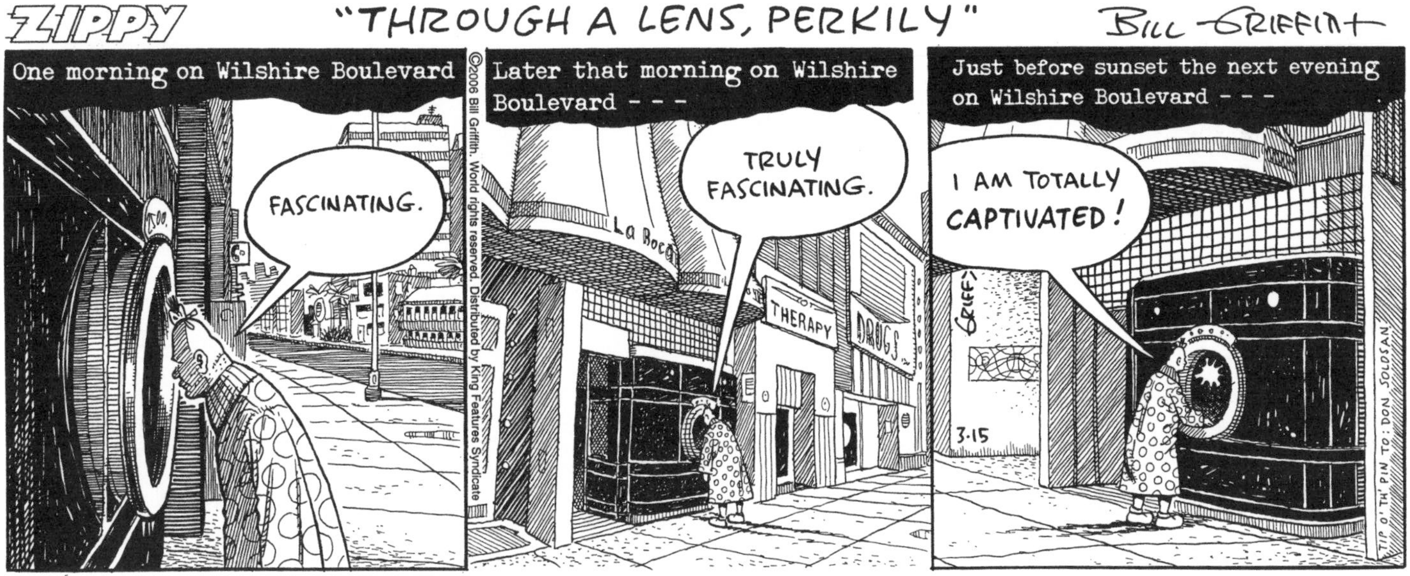
ZIPPY
"THROUGH A LENS, PERKILY"
BILL GRIFFITH
One morning on Wilshire Boulevard
FASCINATING.
©2006 Bill Griffith. World rights reserved. Distributed by King Features Syndicate
Later that morning on Wilshire Boulevard - - -
TRULY FASCINATING.
La Boca
THERAPY
DRUGS
Just before sunset the next evening on Wilshire Boulevard - - -
I AM TOTALLY CAPTIVATED!
GRIFFY
3·15
TIP O' TH' PIN TO: DON SOLDSAN

39

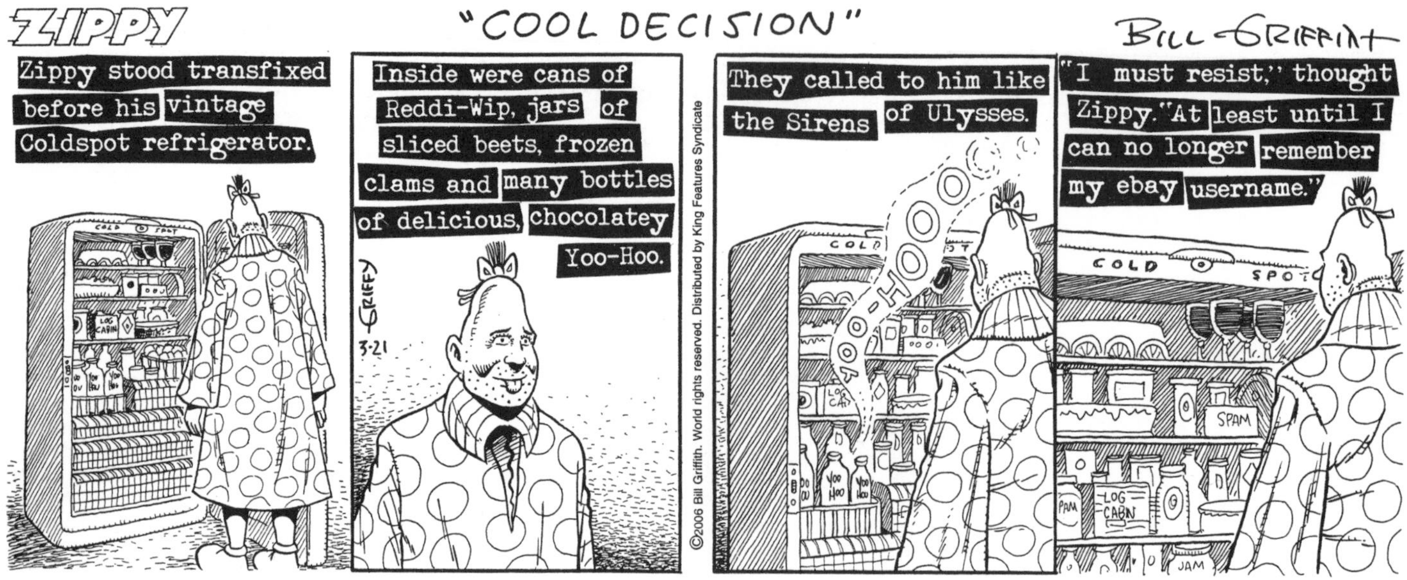
ZIPPY
"COOL DECISION"
BILL GRIFFITH
Zippy stood transfixed before his vintage Coldspot refrigerator.
Inside were cans of Reddi-Wip, jars of sliced beets, frozen clams and many bottles of delicious, chocolatey Yoo-Hoo.
They called to him like the Sirens of Ulysses.
YOO-HOO
"I must resist," thought Zippy. "At least until I can no longer remember my ebay username."
©2006 Bill Griffith. World rights reserved. Distributed by King Features Syndicate
SPAM
LOG CABIN
JAM

40

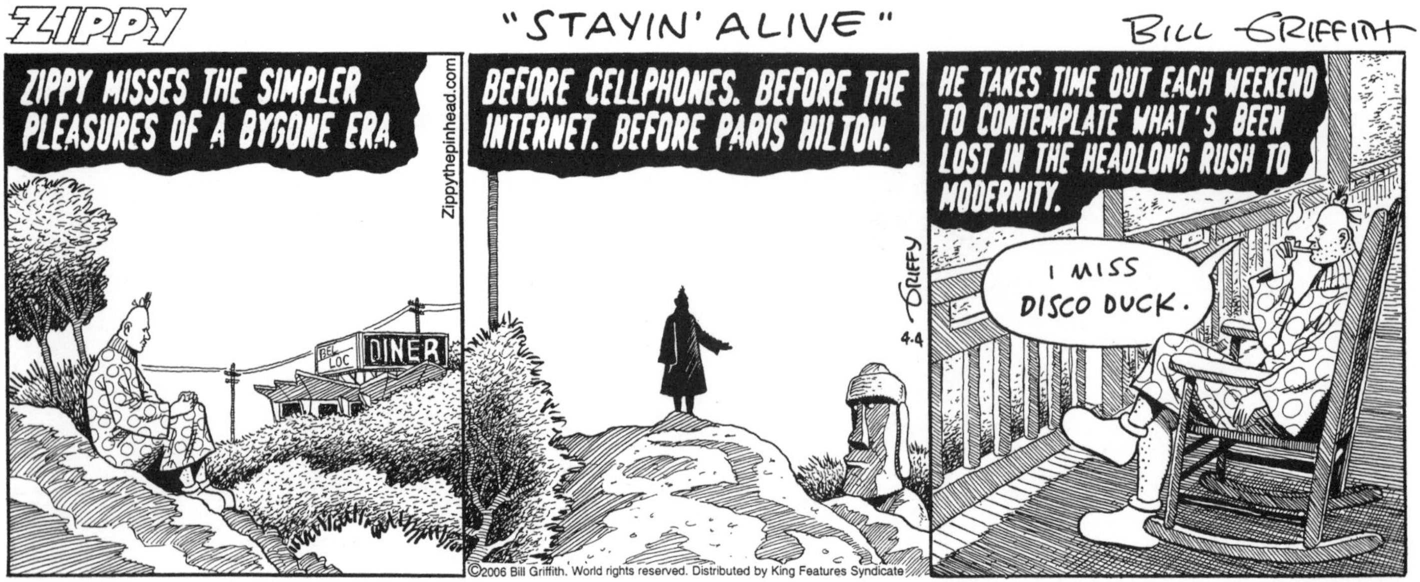
ZIPPY
"STAYIN' ALIVE"
BILL GRIFFITH
ZIPPY MISSES THE SIMPLER PLEASURES OF A BYGONE ERA.
Zippythepinhead.com
DINER
BEFORE CELLPHONES. BEFORE THE INTERNET. BEFORE PARIS HILTON.
HE TAKES TIME OUT EACH WEEKEND TO CONTEMPLATE WHAT'S BEEN LOST IN THE HEADLONG RUSH TO MODERNITY.
I MISS DISCO DUCK.
©2006 Bill Griffith. World rights reserved. Distributed by King Features Syndicate

41

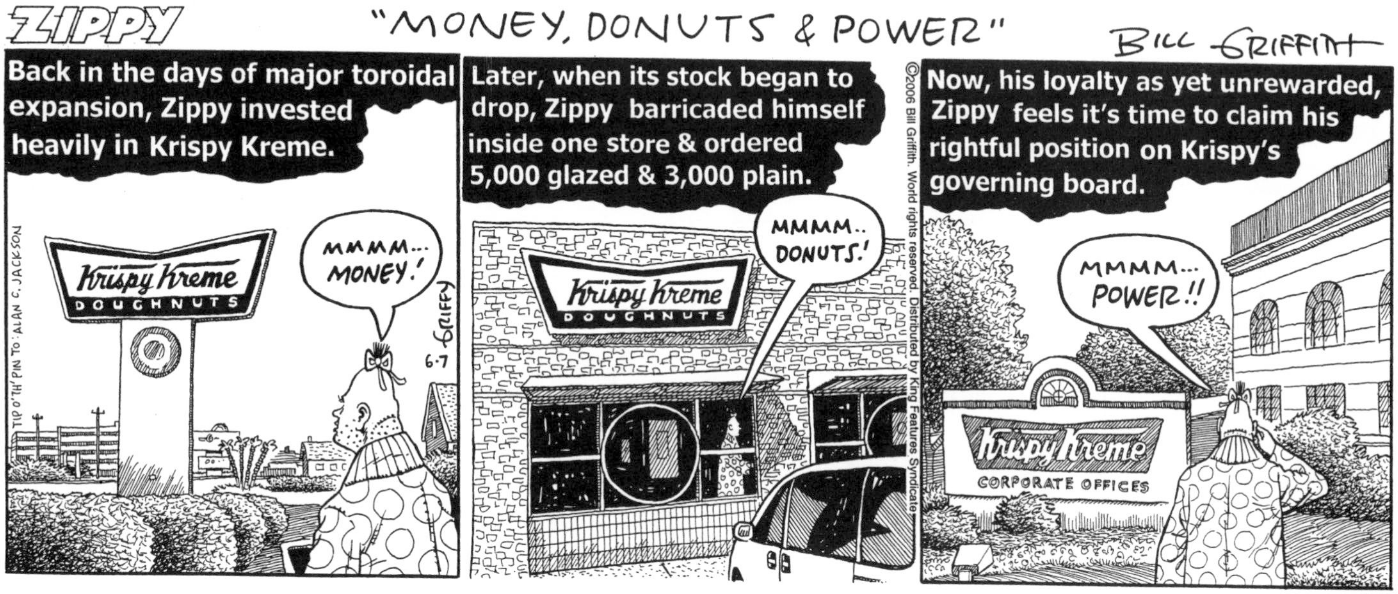
ZIPPY
"MONEY, DONUTS & POWER"
BILL GRIFFITH
Back in the days of major toroidal expansion, Zippy invested heavily in Krispy Kreme.
Krispy Kreme DOUGHNUTS
MMMM... MONEY!
TIP O'TH' PIN TO: ALAN C. JACKSON
GRIFFY 6-7
Later, when its stock began to drop, Zippy barricaded himself inside one store & ordered 5,000 glazed & 3,000 plain.
Krispy Kreme DOUGHNUTS
MMMM.. DONUTS!
©2006 Bill Griffith. World rights reserved. Distributed by King Features Syndicate
Now, his loyalty as yet unrewarded, Zippy feels it's time to claim his rightful position on Krispy's governing board.
MMMM... POWER!!
Krispy Kreme
CORPORATE OFFICES

42

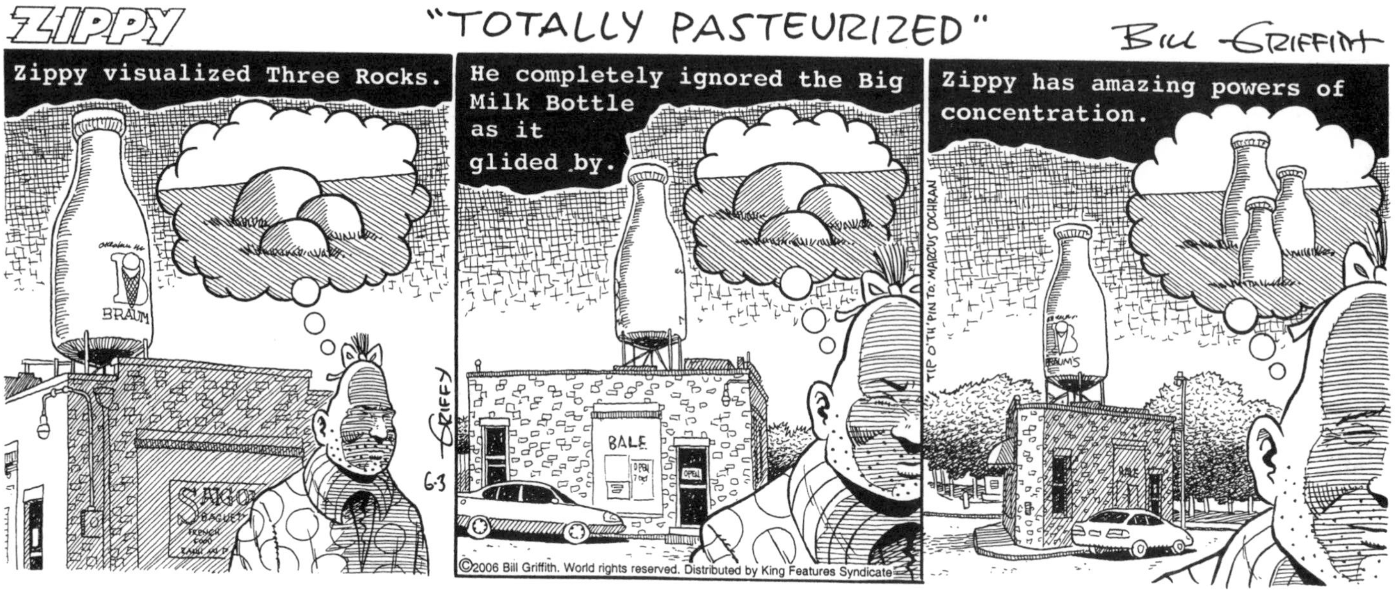
ZIPPY
"TOTALLY PASTEURIZED"
BILL GRIFFITH
Zippy visualized Three Rocks.
BRAUM
GRIFFY 6-3
He completely ignored the Big Milk Bottle as it glided by.
BALE
OPEN
©2006 Bill Griffith. World rights reserved. Distributed by King Features Syndicate
Zippy has amazing powers of concentration.
TIP O'TH' PIN TO: MARCUS OCHRAN

43

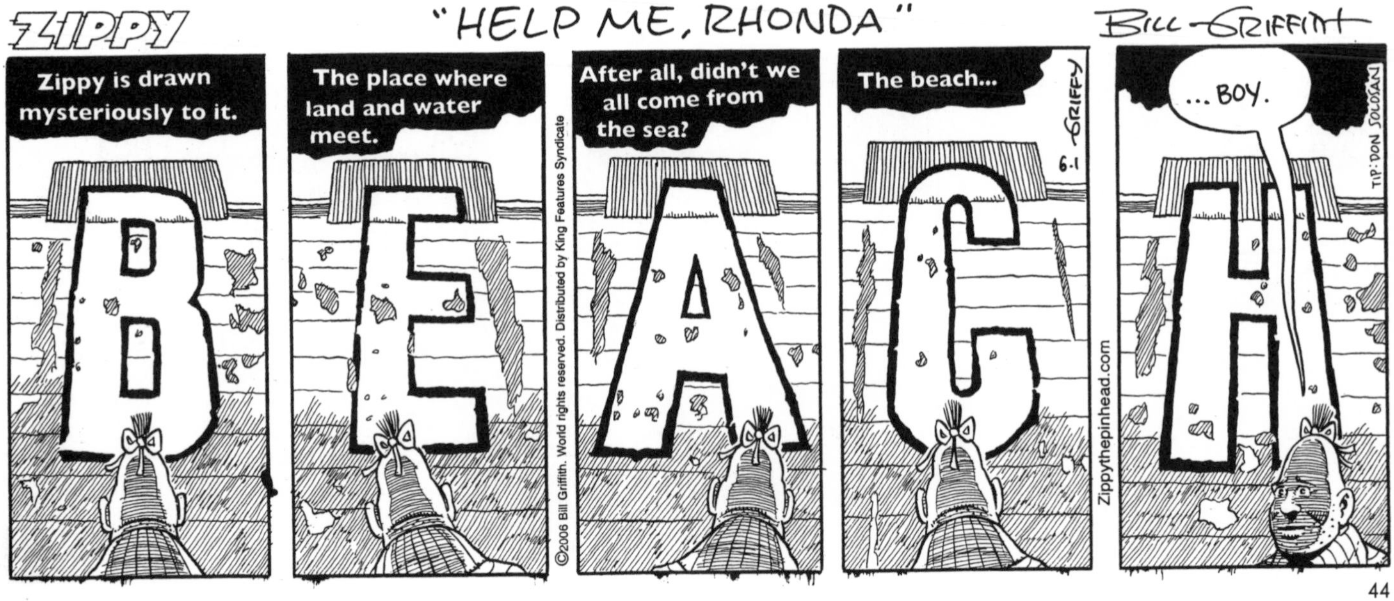
ZIPPY
"HELP ME, RHONDA"
BILL GRIFFITH
Zippy is drawn mysteriously to it.
The place where land and water meet.
©2006 Bill Griffith. World rights reserved. Distributed by King Features Syndicate
After all, didn't we all come from the sea?
The beach...
GRIFFY 6-1
Zippythepinhead.com
...BOY.
TIP: DON SOLOSAN

44

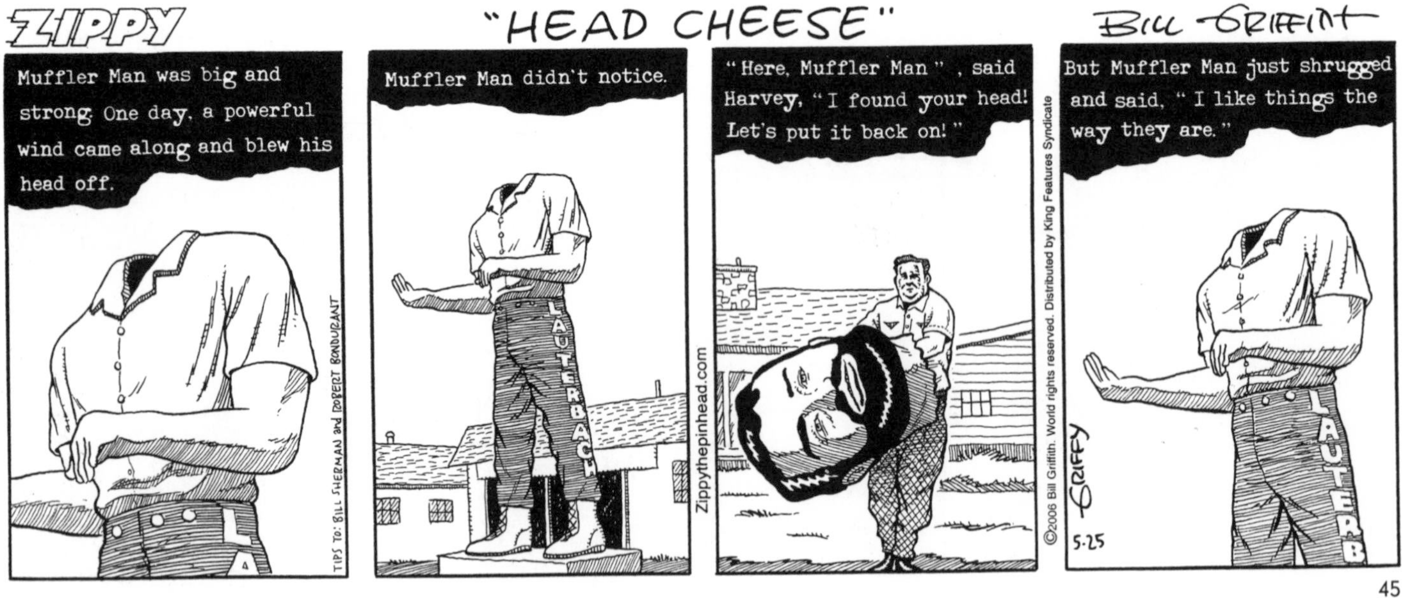
ZIPPY
"HEAD CHEESE"
BILL GRIFFITH
Muffler Man was big and strong. One day, a powerful wind came along and blew his head off.
TIPS TO: BILL SHERMAN and ROBERT BONDURANT
Muffler Man didn't notice.
LAUTERBACH
Zippythepinhead.com
"Here, Muffler Man", said Harvey, "I found your head! Let's put it back on!"
©2006 Bill Griffith. World rights reserved. Distributed by King Features Syndicate
GRIFFY 5-25
But Muffler Man just shrugged and said, "I like things the way they are."
LAUTERB

45

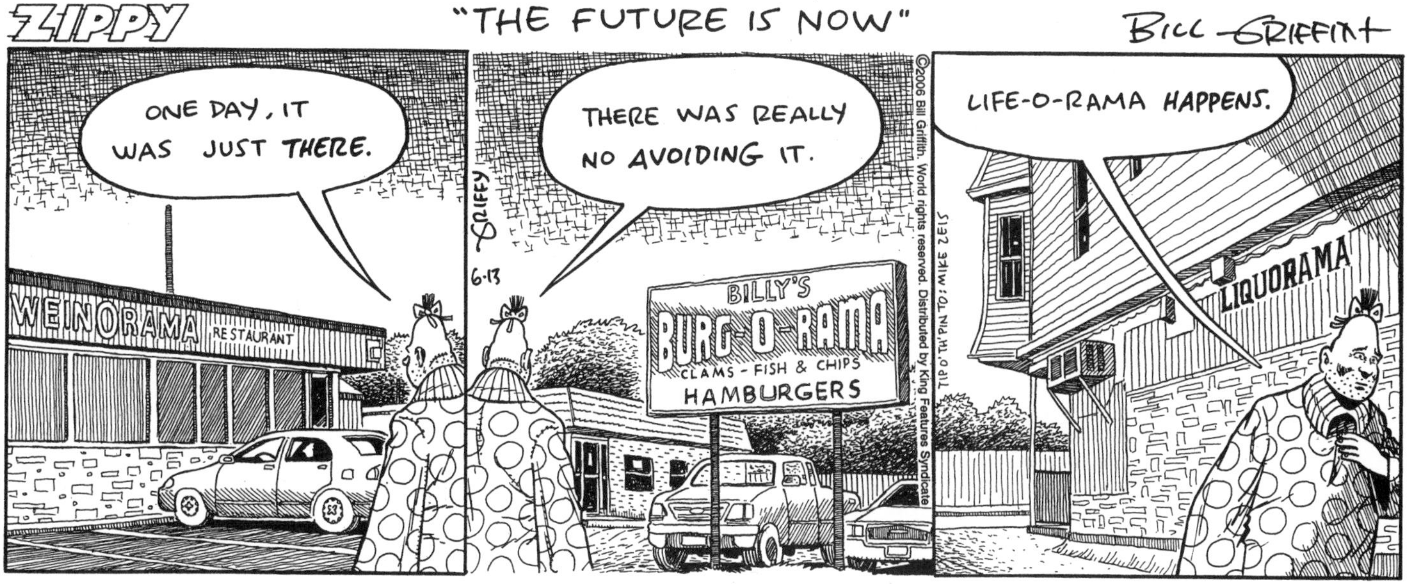
ZIPPY
"THE FUTURE IS NOW"
BILL GRIFFITH
ONE DAY, IT WAS JUST THERE.
WEINORAMA RESTAURANT
THERE WAS REALLY NO AVOIDING IT.
GRIFFY
6-13
BILLY'S BURG-O-RAMA
CLAMS - FISH & CHIPS
HAMBURGERS
©2006 Bill Griffith. World rights reserved. Distributed by King Features Syndicate
TIP: MIKE ZEIS
LIFE-O-RAMA HAPPENS.
LIQUORAMA

46

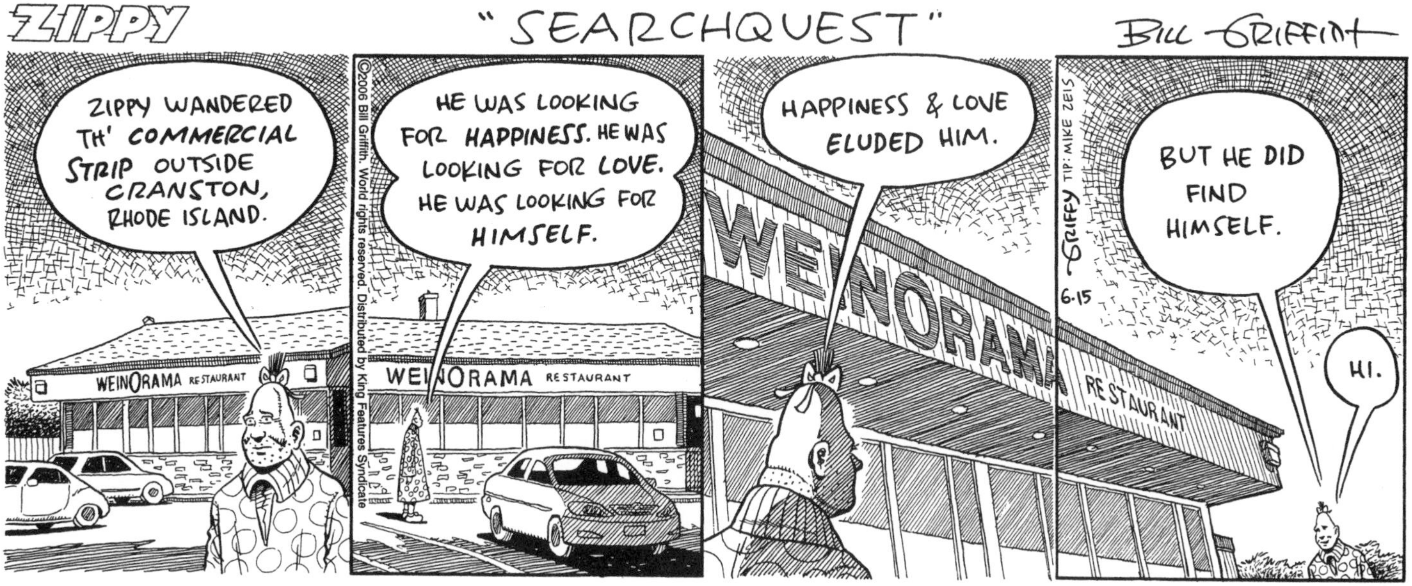
ZIPPY
"SEARCHQUEST"
BILL GRIFFITH
ZIPPY WANDERED TH' COMMERCIAL STRIP OUTSIDE CRANSTON, RHODE ISLAND.
WEINORAMA RESTAURANT
©2006 Bill Griffith. World rights reserved. Distributed by King Features Syndicate
HE WAS LOOKING FOR HAPPINESS. HE WAS LOOKING FOR LOVE. HE WAS LOOKING FOR HIMSELF.
WEINORAMA RESTAURANT
HAPPINESS & LOVE ELUDED HIM.
WEINORAMA
RESTAURANT
GRIFFY
TIP: MIKE ZEIS
6-15
BUT HE DID FIND HIMSELF.
HI.

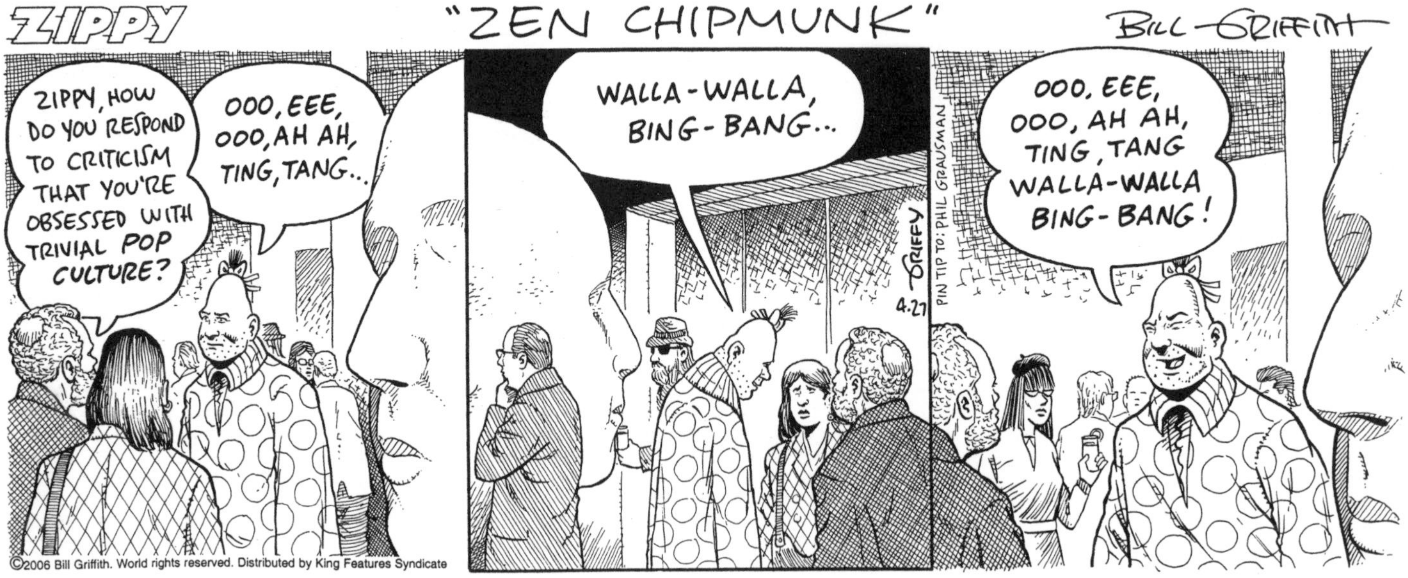
ZIPPY
"ZEN CHIPMUNK"
BILL GRIFFITH
ZIPPY, HOW DO YOU RESPOND TO CRITICISM THAT YOU'RE OBSESSED WITH TRIVIAL POP CULTURE?
OOO, EEE, OOO, AH AH, TING, TANG...
WALLA-WALLA, BING-BANG...
GRIFFY
4-27
PIN TIP TO: PHIL GRAUSMAN
OOO, EEE, OOO, AH AH, TING, TANG WALLA-WALLA BING-BANG!
©2006 Bill Griffith. World rights reserved. Distributed by King Features Syndicate

47

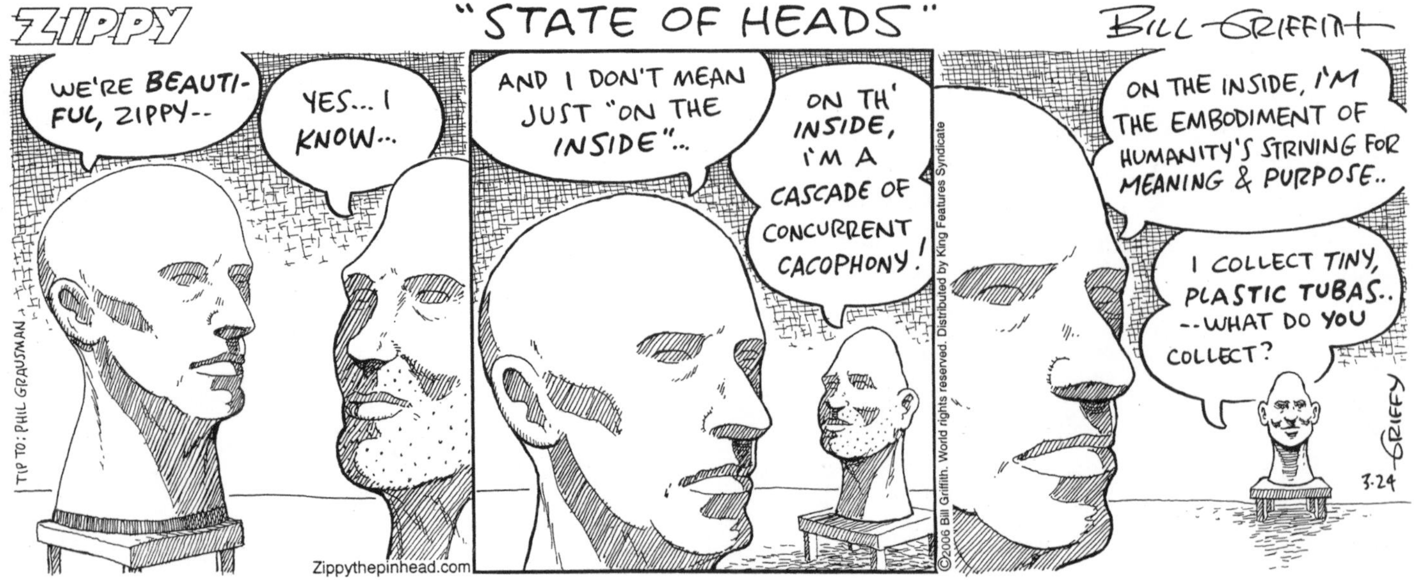
ZIPPY
"STATE OF HEADS"
BILL GRIFFITH
WE'RE BEAUTIFUL, ZIPPY--
YES... I KNOW...
TIP TO: PHIL GRAUSMAN
AND I DON'T MEAN JUST "ON THE INSIDE"...
ON TH' INSIDE, I'M A CASCADE OF CONCURRENT CACOPHONY!
Zippythepinhead.com
©2006 Bill Griffith. World rights reserved. Distributed by King Features Syndicate
ON THE INSIDE, I'M THE EMBODIMENT OF HUMANITY'S STRIVING FOR MEANING & PURPOSE..
I COLLECT TINY, PLASTIC TUBAS.. --WHAT DO YOU COLLECT?
GRIFFY
3-24

48

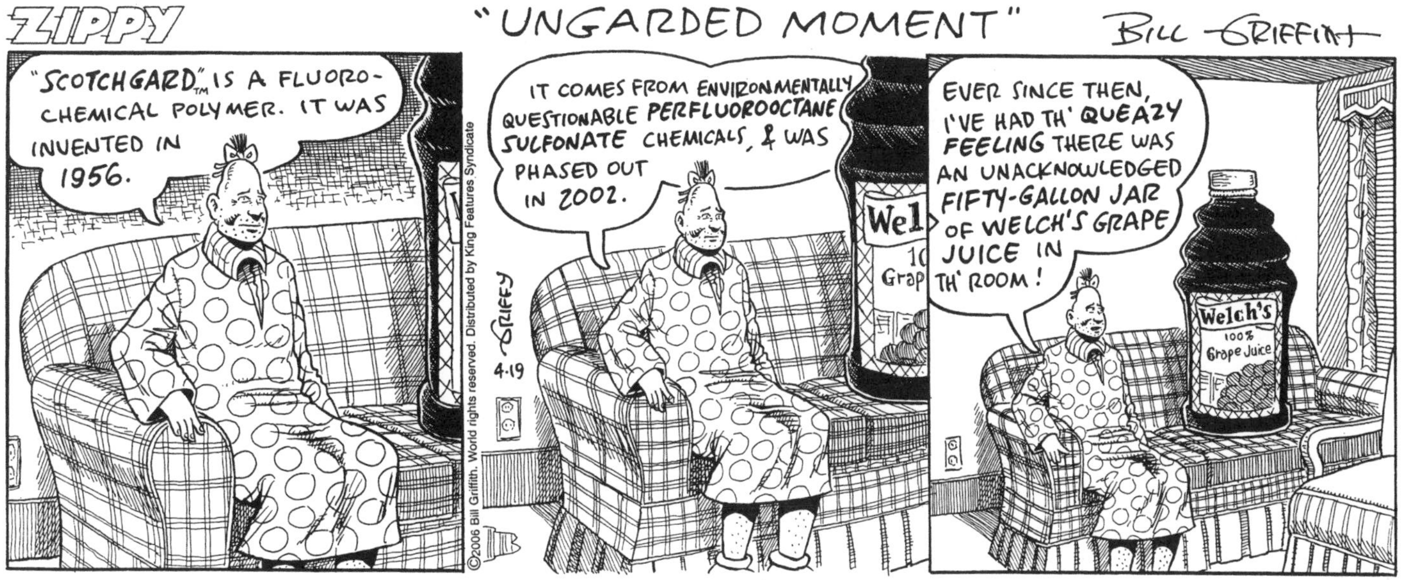
ZIPPY
"UNGARDED MOMENT"
BILL GRIFFITH
"SCOTCHGARD"™ IS A FLUORO-CHEMICAL POLYMER. IT WAS INVENTED IN 1956.
IT COMES FROM ENVIRONMENTALLY QUESTIONABLE PERFLUOROOCTANE SULFONATE CHEMICALS, & WAS PHASED OUT IN 2002.
EVER SINCE THEN, I'VE HAD TH' QUEAZY FEELING THERE WAS AN UNACKNOWLEDGED FIFTY-GALLON JAR OF WELCH'S GRAPE JUICE IN TH' ROOM!
Welch's
100% Grape Juice
GRIFFY
4-19
©2006 Bill Griffith. World rights reserved. Distributed by King Features Syndicate

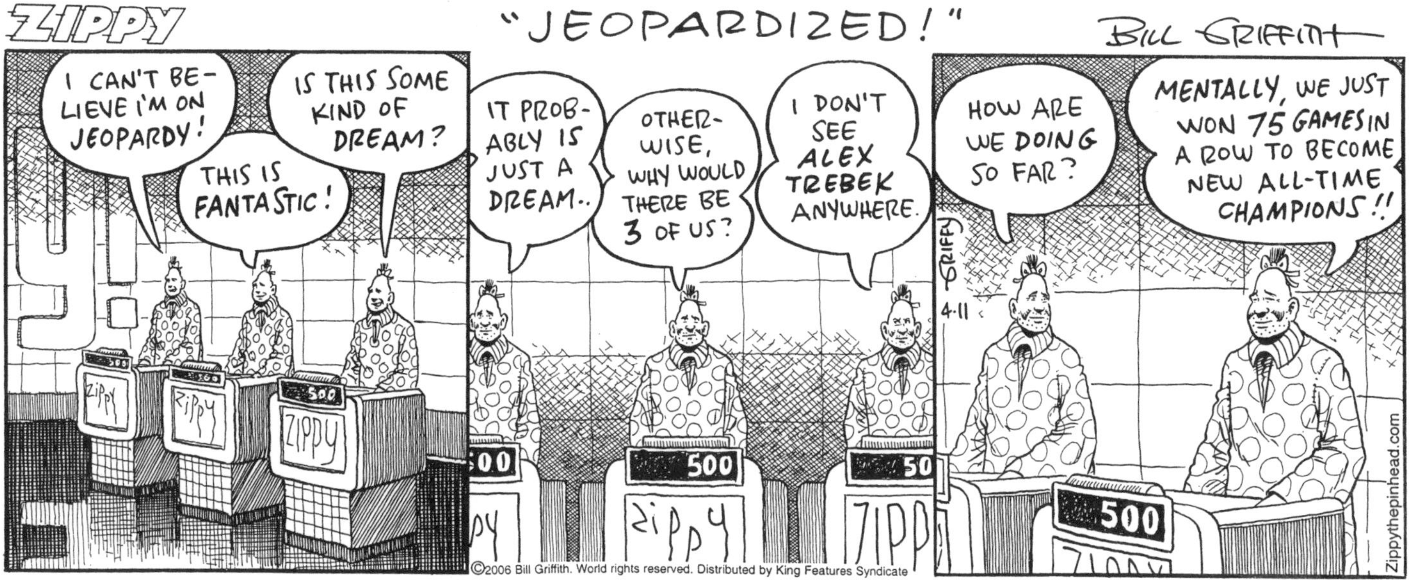
ZIPPY
"JEOPARDIZED!"
BILL GRIFFITH
I CAN'T BELIEVE I'M ON JEOPARDY!
THIS IS FANTASTIC!
IS THIS SOME KIND OF DREAM?
IT PROBABLY IS JUST A DREAM..
OTHERWISE, WHY WOULD THERE BE 3 OF US?
I DON'T SEE ALEX TREBEK ANYWHERE.
HOW ARE WE DOING SO FAR?
MENTALLY, WE JUST WON 75 GAMES IN A ROW TO BECOME NEW ALL-TIME CHAMPIONS!!
500
ZIPPY
GRIFFY
4-11
©2006 Bill Griffith. World rights reserved. Distributed by King Features Syndicate
Zippythepinhead.com

49

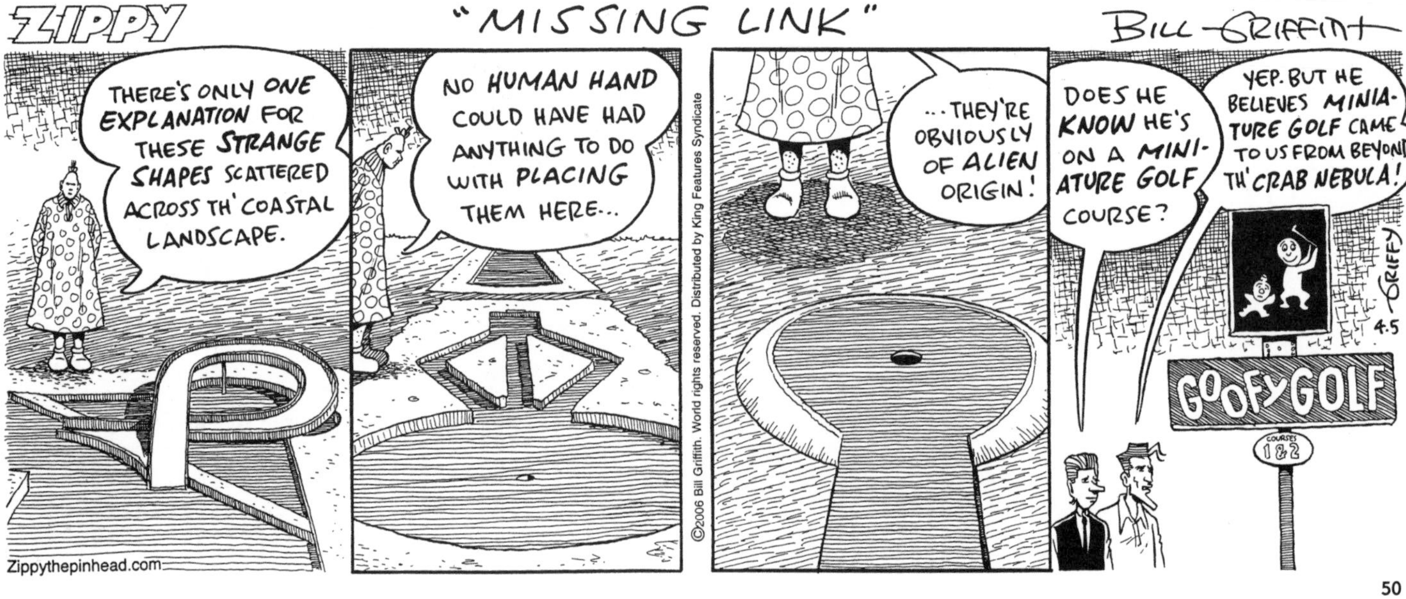
ZIPPY
"MISSING LINK"
BILL GRIFFITH
THERE'S ONLY ONE EXPLANATION FOR THESE STRANGE SHAPES SCATTERED ACROSS TH' COASTAL LANDSCAPE.
NO HUMAN HAND COULD HAVE HAD ANYTHING TO DO WITH PLACING THEM HERE...
...THEY'RE OBVIOUSLY OF ALIEN ORIGIN!
DOES HE KNOW HE'S ON A MINIATURE GOLF COURSE?
YEP. BUT HE BELIEVES MINIATURE GOLF CAME TO US FROM BEYOND TH' CRAB NEBULA!
GOOFY GOLF
COURSES 1 & 2
GRIFFY 4.5
©2006 Bill Griffith. World rights reserved. Distributed by King Features Syndicate
Zippythepinhead.com
50

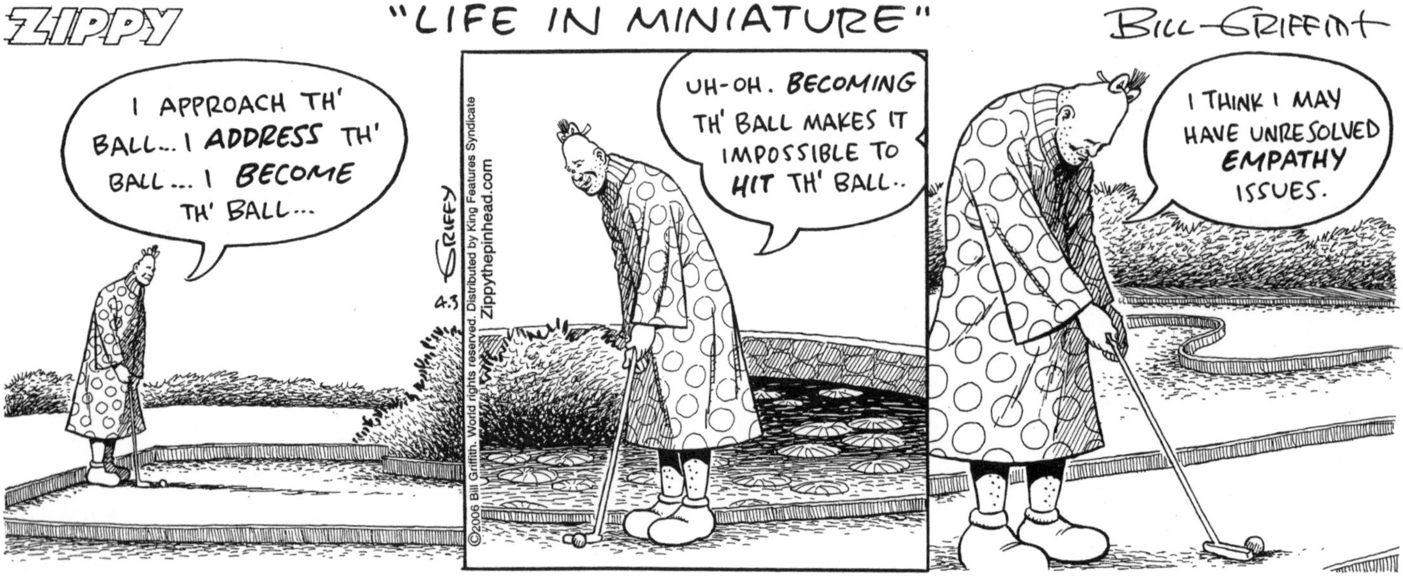
ZIPPY
"LIFE IN MINIATURE"
BILL GRIFFITH
I APPROACH TH' BALL... I ADDRESS TH' BALL... I BECOME TH' BALL...
UH-OH. BECOMING TH' BALL MAKES IT IMPOSSIBLE TO HIT TH' BALL..
I THINK I MAY HAVE UNRESOLVED EMPATHY ISSUES.
GRIFFY 4.3
©2006 Bill Griffith. World rights reserved. Distributed by King Features Syndicate
Zippythepinhead.com

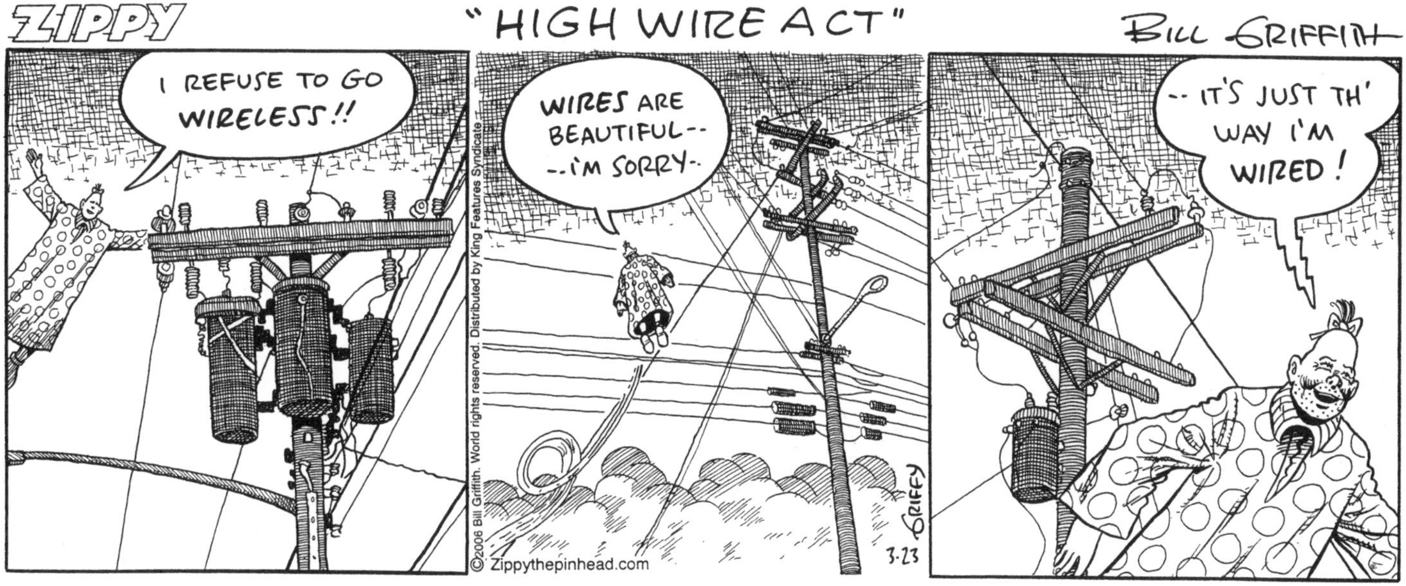
ZIPPY
"HIGH WIRE ACT"
BILL GRIFFITH
I REFUSE TO GO WIRELESS!!
WIRES ARE BEAUTIFUL-- --I'M SORRY--
©2006 Bill Griffith. World rights reserved. Distributed by King Features Syndicate
Zippythepinhead.com
GRIFFY
3-23
-- IT'S JUST TH' WAY I'M WIRED!

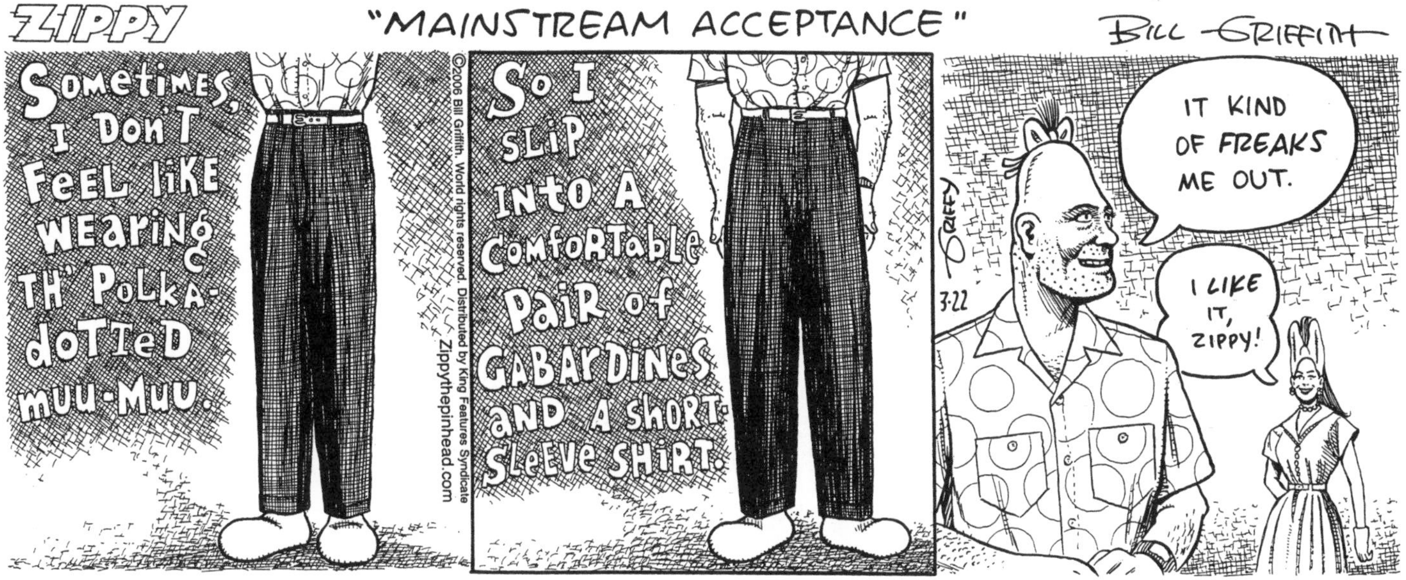
ZIPPY
"MAINSTREAM ACCEPTANCE"
BILL GRIFFITH
Sometimes, I DON'T FEEL LIKE WEARING TH' POLKA-DOTTED MUU-MUU.
©2006 Bill Griffith. World rights reserved. Distributed by King Features Syndicate
Zippythepinhead.com
SO I SLIP INTO A COMFORTABLE PAIR OF GABARDINES AND A SHORT-SLEEVE SHIRT.
GRIFFY
3-22
IT KIND OF FREAKS ME OUT.
I LIKE IT, ZIPPY!

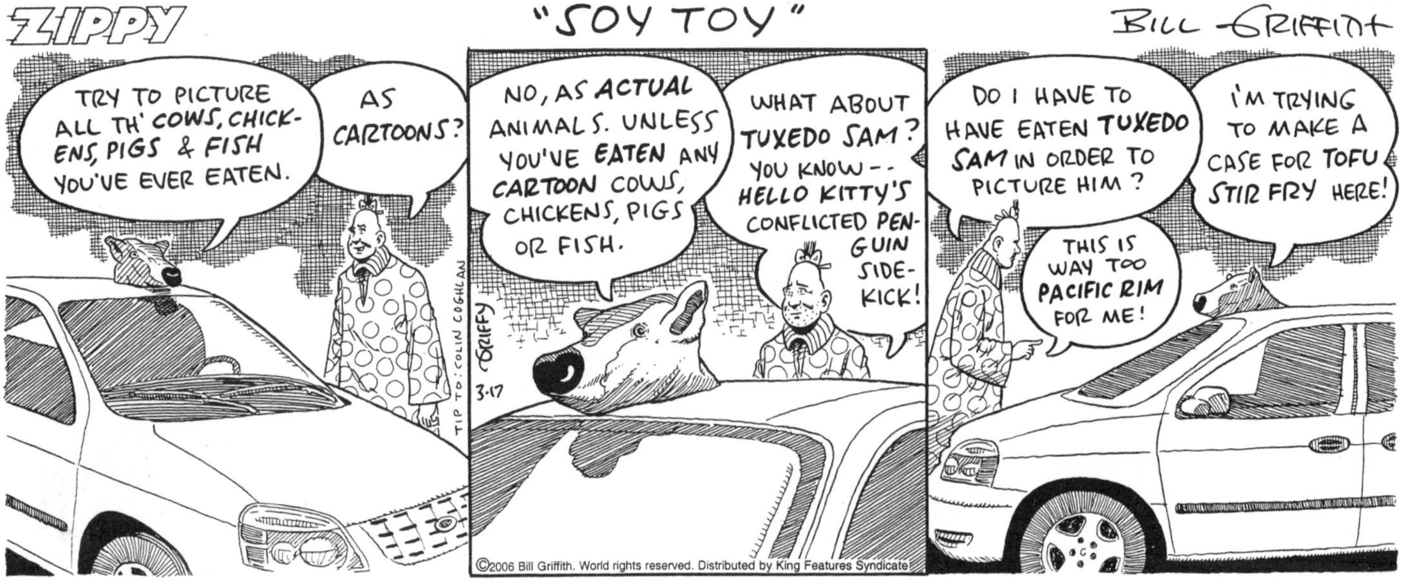
ZIPPY
"SOY TOY"
BILL GRIFFITH
TRY TO PICTURE ALL TH' COWS, CHICKENS, PIGS & FISH YOU'VE EVER EATEN.
AS CARTOONS?
TIP TO: COLIN COGHLAN
NO, AS ACTUAL ANIMALS. UNLESS YOU'VE EATEN ANY CARTOON COWS, CHICKENS, PIGS OR FISH.
WHAT ABOUT TUXEDO SAM? YOU KNOW -- HELLO KITTY'S CONFLICTED PENGUIN SIDE-KICK!
GRIFFY
3-17
©2006 Bill Griffith. World rights reserved. Distributed by King Features Syndicate
DO I HAVE TO HAVE EATEN TUXEDO SAM IN ORDER TO PICTURE HIM?
I'M TRYING TO MAKE A CASE FOR TOFU STIR FRY HERE!
THIS IS WAY TOO PACIFIC RIM FOR ME!

51

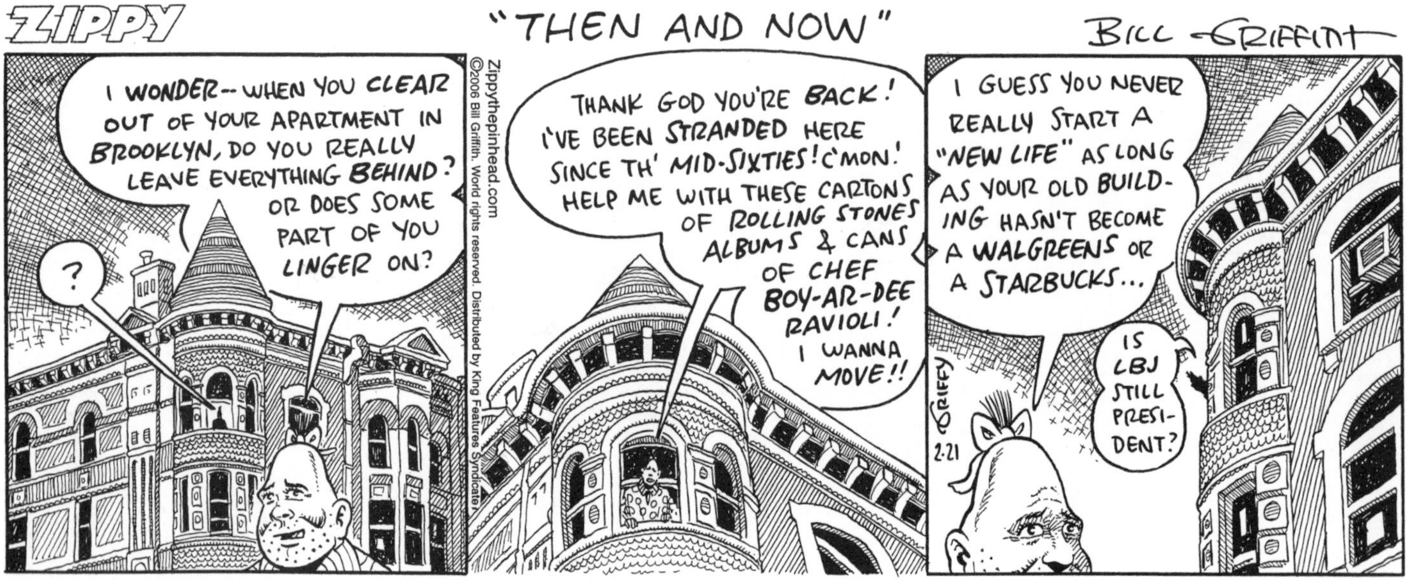
ZIPPY
"THEN AND NOW"
BILL GRIFFITH
I WONDER-- WHEN YOU CLEAR OUT OF YOUR APARTMENT IN BROOKLYN, DO YOU REALLY LEAVE EVERYTHING BEHIND?
OR DOES SOME PART OF YOU LINGER ON?
?
Zippythepinhead.com
©2006 Bill Griffith. World rights reserved. Distributed by King Features Syndicate
THANK GOD YOU'RE BACK! I'VE BEEN STRANDED HERE SINCE TH' MID-SIXTIES! C'MON! HELP ME WITH THESE CARTONS OF ROLLING STONES ALBUMS & CANS OF CHEF BOY-AR-DEE RAVIOLI! I WANNA MOVE!!
I GUESS YOU NEVER REALLY START A "NEW LIFE" AS LONG AS YOUR OLD BUILDING HASN'T BECOME A WALGREENS OR A STARBUCKS...
IS LBJ STILL PRESIDENT?
GRIFFY
2-21

52

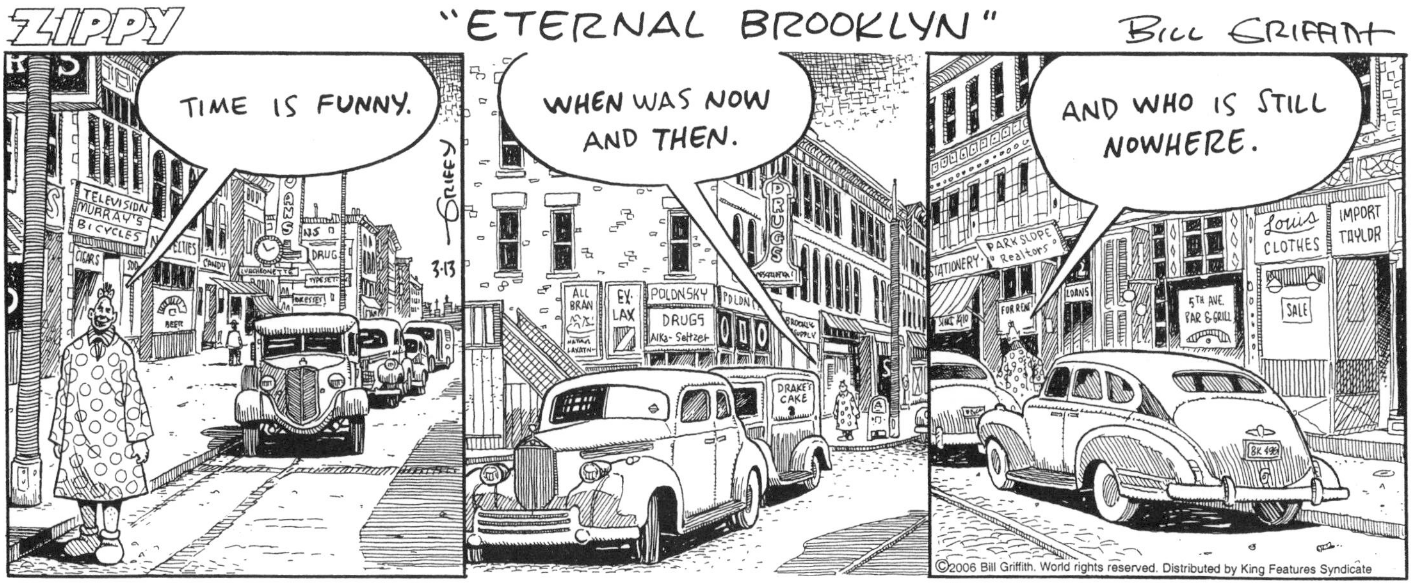
ZIPPY
"ETERNAL BROOKLYN"
BILL GRIFFITH
TIME IS FUNNY.
WHEN WAS NOW AND THEN.
AND WHO IS STILL NOWHERE.
GRIFFY 3·13
©2006 Bill Griffith. World rights reserved. Distributed by King Features Syndicate

53

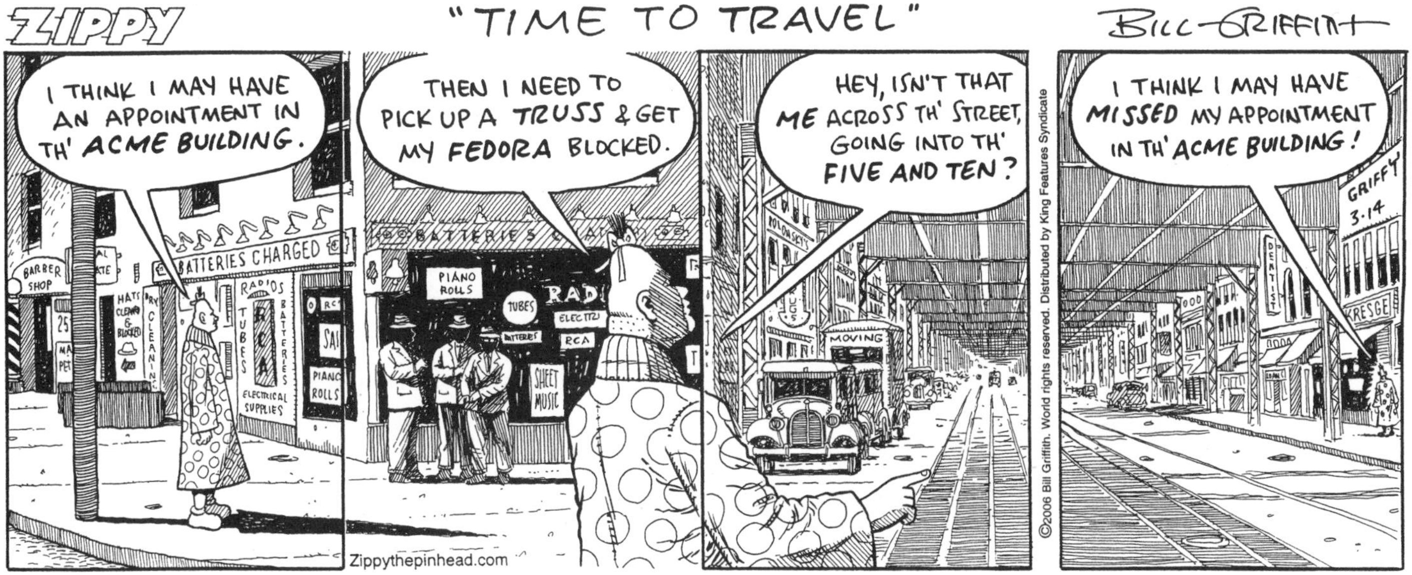
ZIPPY
"TIME TO TRAVEL"
BILL GRIFFITH
I THINK I MAY HAVE AN APPOINTMENT IN TH' ACME BUILDING.
THEN I NEED TO PICK UP A TRUSS & GET MY FEDORA BLOCKED.
HEY, ISN'T THAT ME ACROSS TH' STREET, GOING INTO TH' FIVE AND TEN?
I THINK I MAY HAVE MISSED MY APPOINTMENT IN TH' ACME BUILDING!
GRIFFY 3·14
Zippythepinhead.com
©2006 Bill Griffith. World rights reserved. Distributed by King Features Syndicate

54

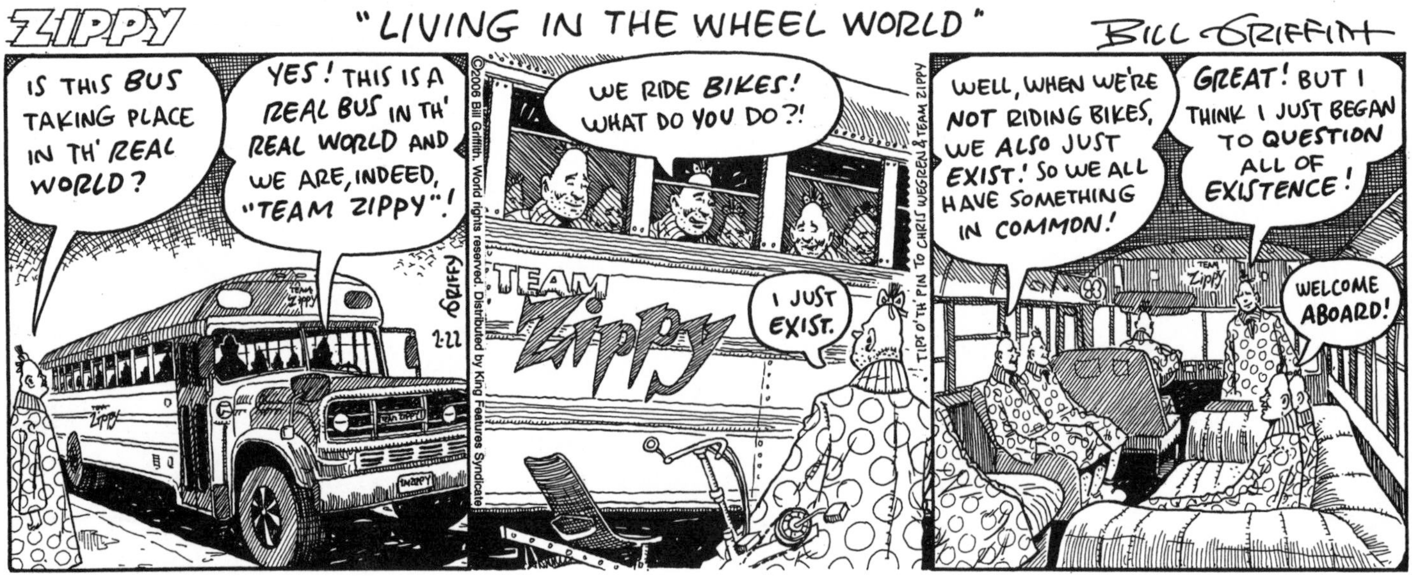
ZIPPY
"LIVING IN THE WHEEL WORLD"
BILL GRIFFITH
IS THIS BUS TAKING PLACE IN TH' REAL WORLD?
YES! THIS IS A REAL BUS IN TH' REAL WORLD AND WE ARE, INDEED, "TEAM ZIPPY"!
GRIFFY 2.22
©2006 Bill Griffith. World rights reserved. Distributed by King Features Syndicate
WE RIDE BIKES! WHAT DO YOU DO?!
TEAM ZIPPY
I JUST EXIST.
TIPS O' TH' PIN TO CHRIS WEGREN & TEAM ZIPPY
WELL, WHEN WE'RE NOT RIDING BIKES, WE ALSO JUST EXIST! SO WE ALL HAVE SOMETHING IN COMMON!
GREAT! BUT I THINK I JUST BEGAN TO QUESTION ALL OF EXISTENCE!
WELCOME ABOARD!

55

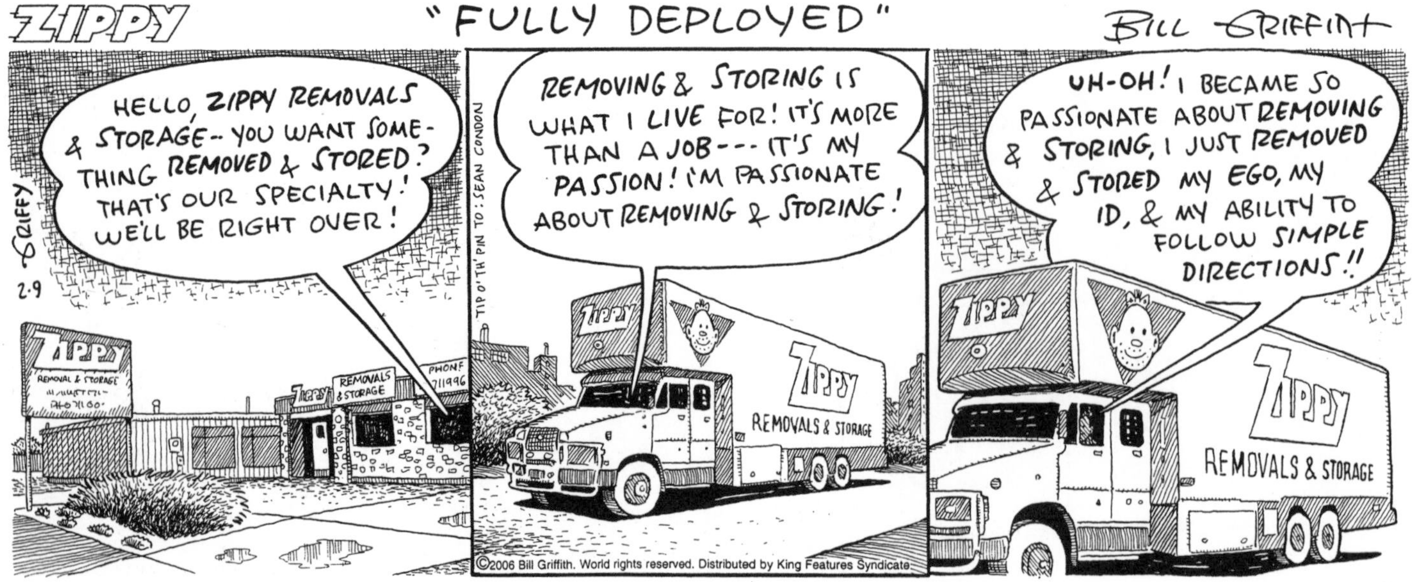
ZIPPY
"FULLY DEPLOYED"
BILL GRIFFITH
HELLO, ZIPPY REMOVALS & STORAGE-- YOU WANT SOMETHING REMOVED & STORED? THAT'S OUR SPECIALTY! WE'LL BE RIGHT OVER!
GRIFFY 2.9
ZIPPY REMOVAL & STORAGE
ZIPPY REMOVALS & STORAGE
TIP O' TH' PIN TO: SEAN CONDON
REMOVING & STORING IS WHAT I LIVE FOR! IT'S MORE THAN A JOB--- IT'S MY PASSION! I'M PASSIONATE ABOUT REMOVING & STORING!
ZIPPY
ZIPPY REMOVALS & STORAGE
©2006 Bill Griffith. World rights reserved. Distributed by King Features Syndicate
UH-OH! I BECAME SO PASSIONATE ABOUT REMOVING & STORING, I JUST REMOVED & STORED MY EGO, MY ID, & MY ABILITY TO FOLLOW SIMPLE DIRECTIONS!!
ZIPPY
ZIPPY REMOVALS & STORAGE

56

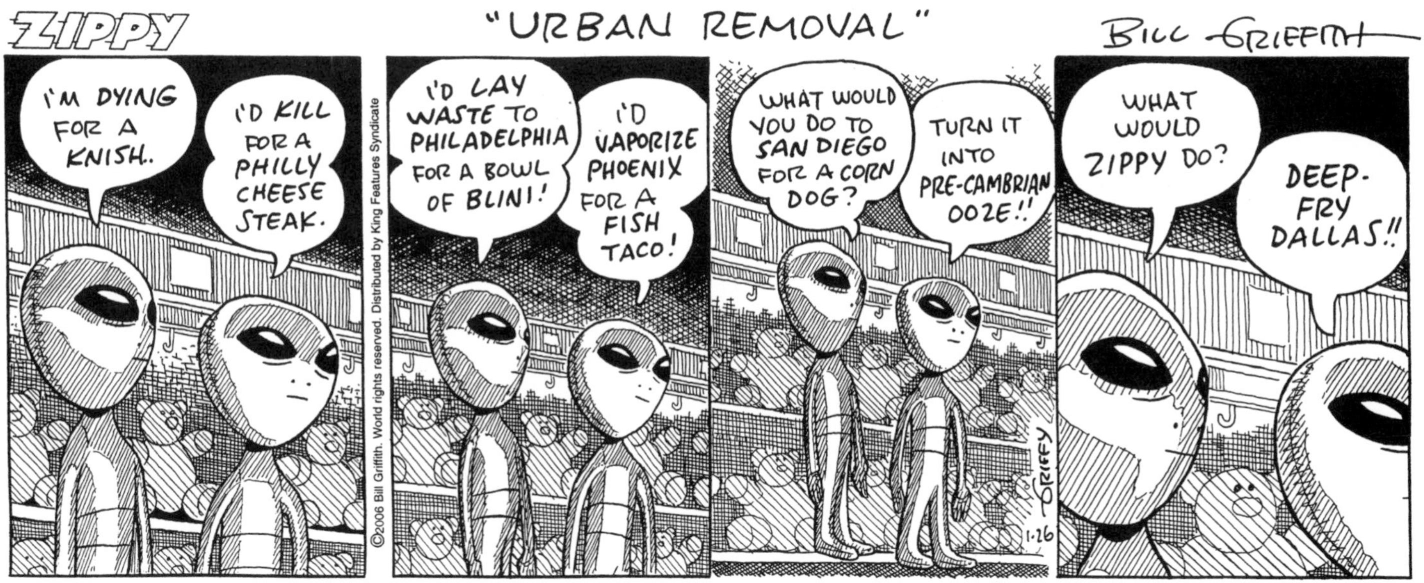
ZIPPY
"URBAN REMOVAL"
BILL GRIFFITH
I'M DYING FOR A KNISH..
I'D KILL FOR A PHILLY CHEESE STEAK.
©2006 Bill Griffith. World rights reserved. Distributed by King Features Syndicate
I'D LAY WASTE TO PHILADELPHIA FOR A BOWL OF BLINI!
I'D VAPORIZE PHOENIX FOR A FISH TACO!
WHAT WOULD YOU DO TO SAN DIEGO FOR A CORN DOG?
TURN IT INTO PRE-CAMBRIAN OOZE!!
GRIFFY
1-26
WHAT WOULD ZIPPY DO?
DEEP-FRY DALLAS!!

57

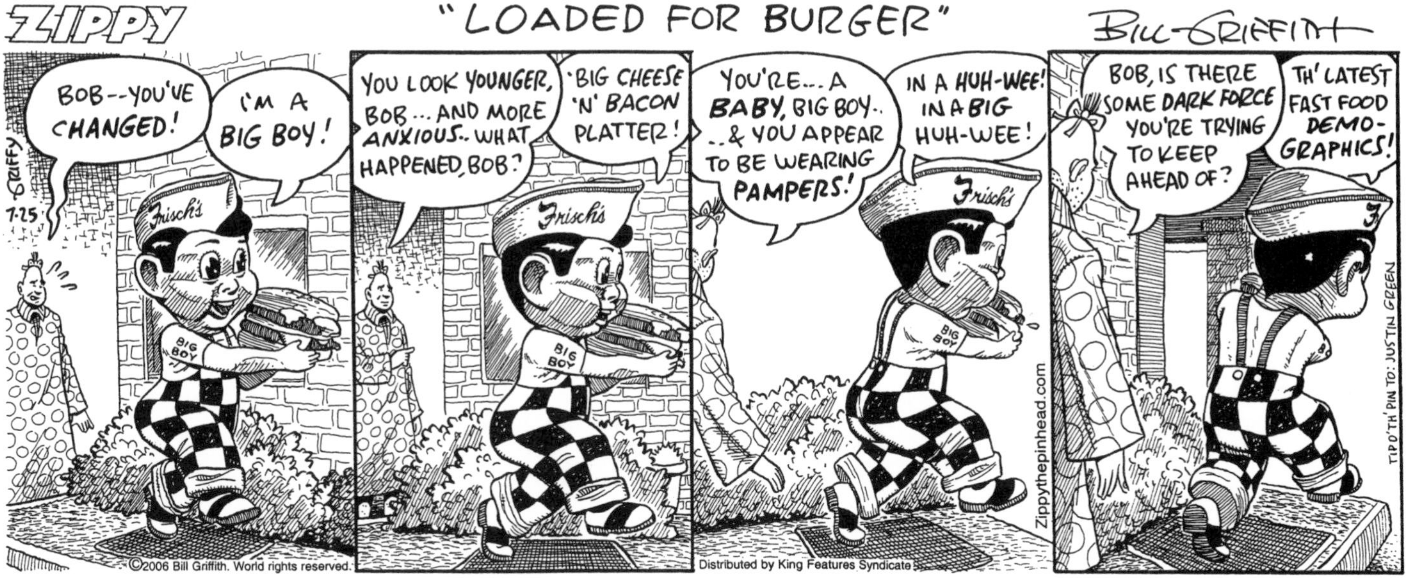
ZIPPY
"LOADED FOR BURGER"
BILL GRIFFITH
BOB--YOU'VE CHANGED!
I'M A BIG BOY!
GRIFFY
7-25
Frisch's
BIG BOY
YOU LOOK YOUNGER, BOB... AND MORE ANXIOUS.. WHAT HAPPENED, BOB?
'BIG CHEESE 'N' BACON PLATTER!
YOU'RE... A BABY, BIG BOY.. ..& YOU APPEAR TO BE WEARING PAMPERS!
IN A HUH-WEE! IN A BIG HUH-WEE!
Zippythepinhead.com
BOB, IS THERE SOME DARK FORCE YOU'RE TRYING TO KEEP AHEAD OF?
TH' LATEST FAST FOOD DEMO-GRAPHICS!
TIP O'TH' PIN TO: JUSTIN GREEN
©2006 Bill Griffith. World rights reserved.
Distributed by King Features Syndicate

58

Zippy & Co.

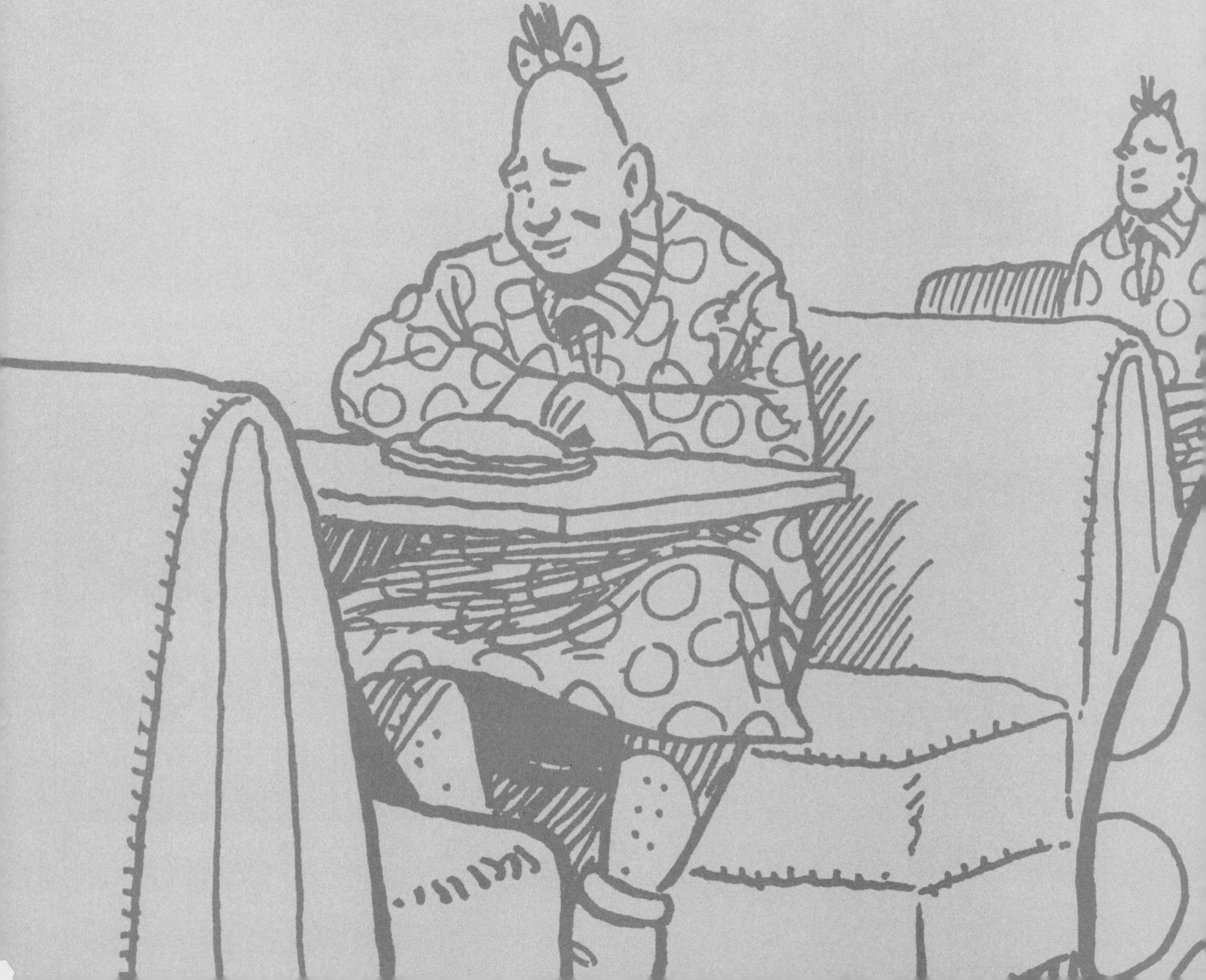

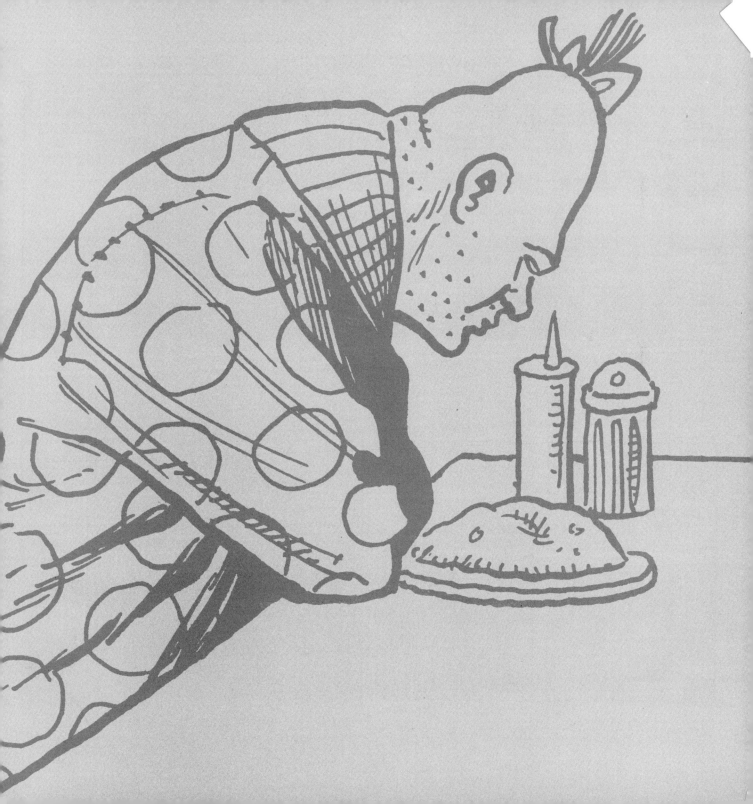

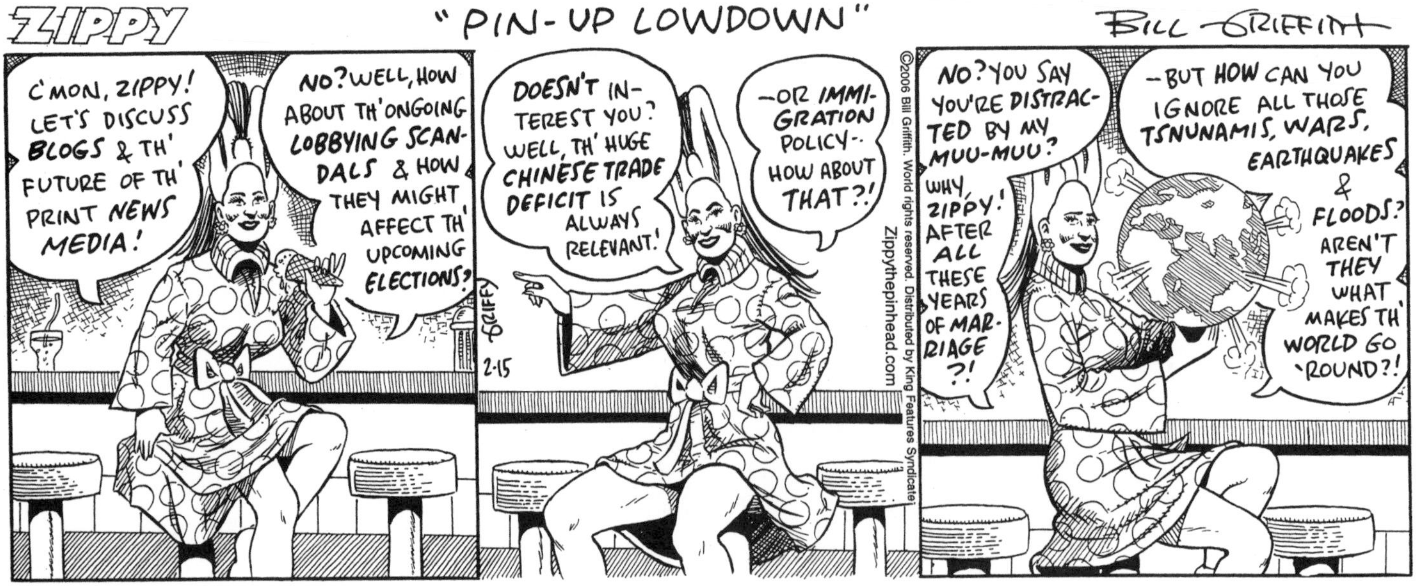
ZIPPY
"PIN-UP LOWDOWN"
BILL GRIFFITH
C'MON, ZIPPY! LET'S DISCUSS BLOGS & TH' FUTURE OF TH' PRINT NEWS MEDIA!
NO? WELL, HOW ABOUT TH' ONGOING LOBBYING SCANDALS & HOW THEY MIGHT AFFECT TH' UPCOMING ELECTIONS?
GRIFFY 2-15
DOESN'T INTEREST YOU? WELL, TH' HUGE CHINESE TRADE DEFICIT IS ALWAYS RELEVANT!
--OR IMMIGRATION POLICY-- HOW ABOUT THAT?!
©2006 Bill Griffith. World rights reserved. Distributed by King Features Syndicate
Zippythepinhead.com
NO? YOU SAY YOU'RE DISTRACTED BY MY MUU-MUU?
WHY, ZIPPY! AFTER ALL THESE YEARS OF MARRIAGE?!
--BUT HOW CAN YOU IGNORE ALL THOSE TSNUNAMIS, WARS, EARTHQUAKES & FLOODS? AREN'T THEY WHAT MAKES TH' WORLD GO 'ROUND?!

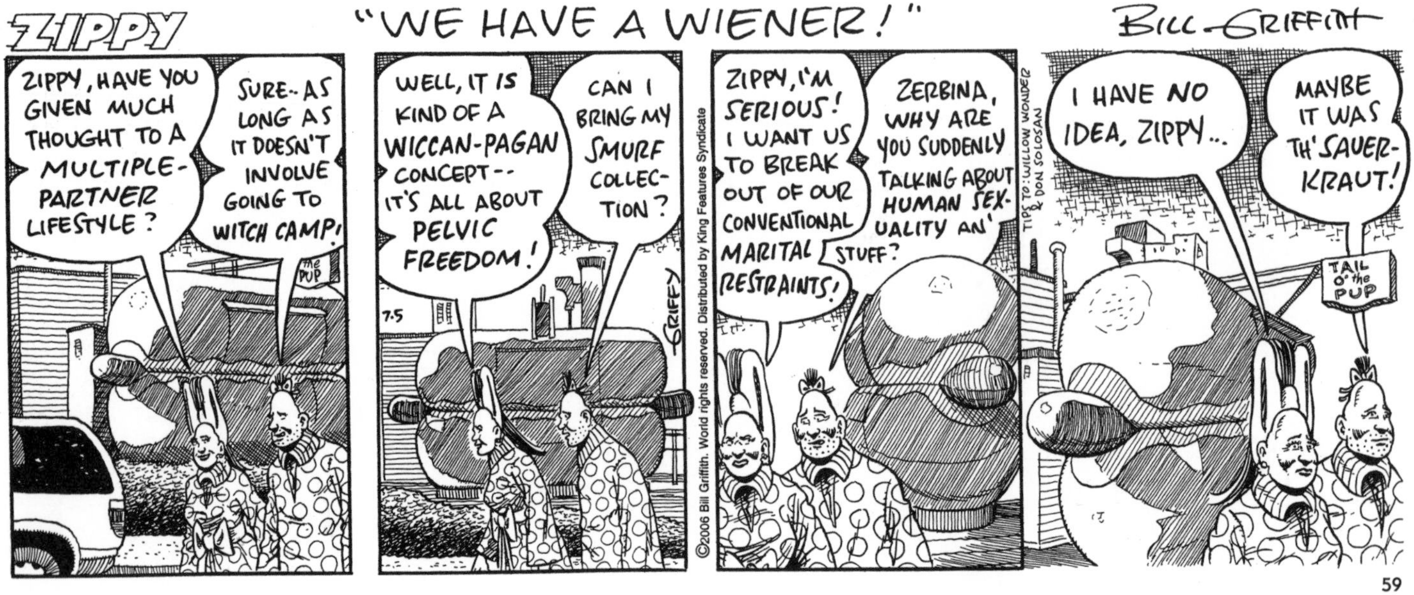
ZIPPY
"WE HAVE A WIENER!"
BILL GRIFFITH
ZIPPY, HAVE YOU GIVEN MUCH THOUGHT TO A MULTIPLE-PARTNER LIFESTYLE?
SURE-- AS LONG AS IT DOESN'T INVOLVE GOING TO WITCH CAMP!
THE PUP
WELL, IT IS KIND OF A WICCAN-PAGAN CONCEPT-- IT'S ALL ABOUT PELVIC FREEDOM!
CAN I BRING MY SMURF COLLECTION?
7-5
GRIFFY
©2006 Bill Griffith. World rights reserved. Distributed by King Features Syndicate
ZIPPY, I'M SERIOUS! I WANT US TO BREAK OUT OF OUR CONVENTIONAL MARITAL RESTRAINTS!
ZERBINA, WHY ARE YOU SUDDENLY TALKING ABOUT HUMAN SEXUALITY AN' STUFF?
TIPS TO: WILLOW WONDER & DON SOLOSAN
I HAVE NO IDEA, ZIPPY...
MAYBE IT WAS TH' SAUERKRAUT!
TAIL O' the PUP

59

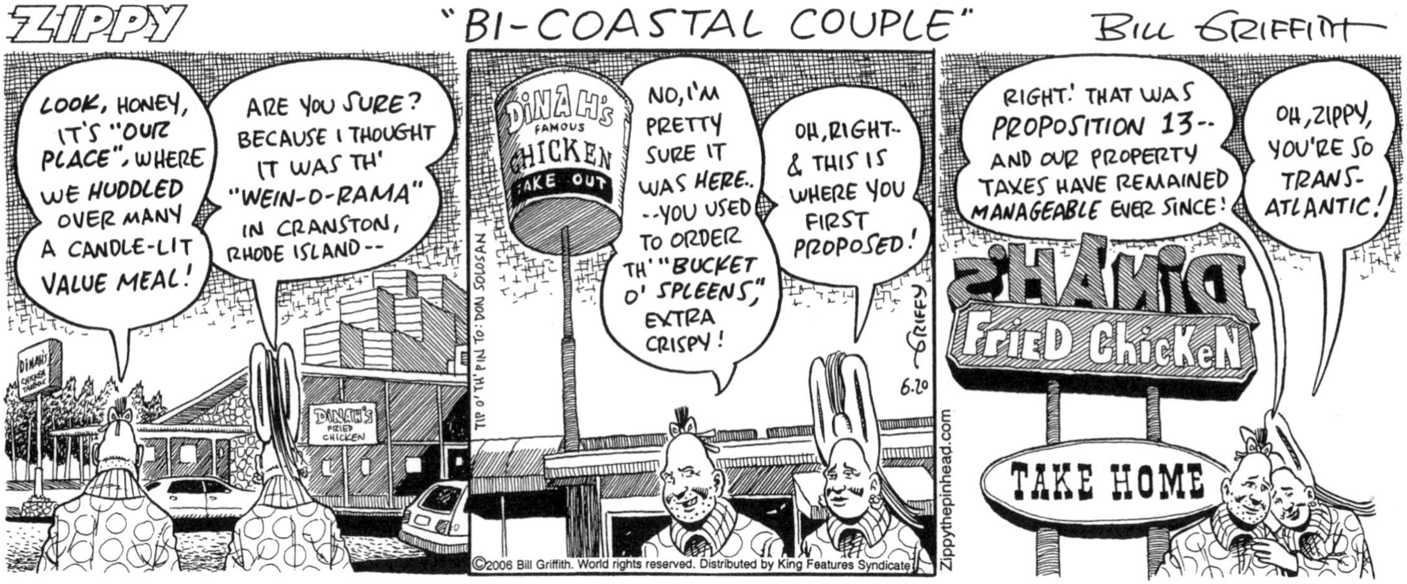
ZIPPY
"BI-COASTAL COUPLE"
BILL GRIFFITH
LOOK, HONEY, IT'S "OUR PLACE", WHERE WE HUDDLED OVER MANY A CANDLE-LIT VALUE MEAL!
ARE YOU SURE? BECAUSE I THOUGHT IT WAS TH' "WEIN-O-RAMA" IN CRANSTON, RHODE ISLAND--
DINAH'S FRIED CHICKEN
DINAH'S FAMOUS CHICKEN TAKE OUT
NO, I'M PRETTY SURE IT WAS HERE.. --YOU USED TO ORDER TH' "BUCKET O' SPLEENS," EXTRA CRISPY!
OH, RIGHT-- & THIS IS WHERE YOU FIRST PROPOSED!
TIP O' TH' PIN TO: DON SOLOSAN
GRIFFY 6.20
©2006 Bill Griffith. World rights reserved. Distributed by King Features Syndicate
Zippythepinhead.com
RIGHT! THAT WAS PROPOSITION 13-- AND OUR PROPERTY TAXES HAVE REMAINED MANAGEABLE EVER SINCE!
OH, ZIPPY, YOU'RE SO TRANS-ATLANTIC!
DINAH'S
FRIED CHICKEN
TAKE HOME

60

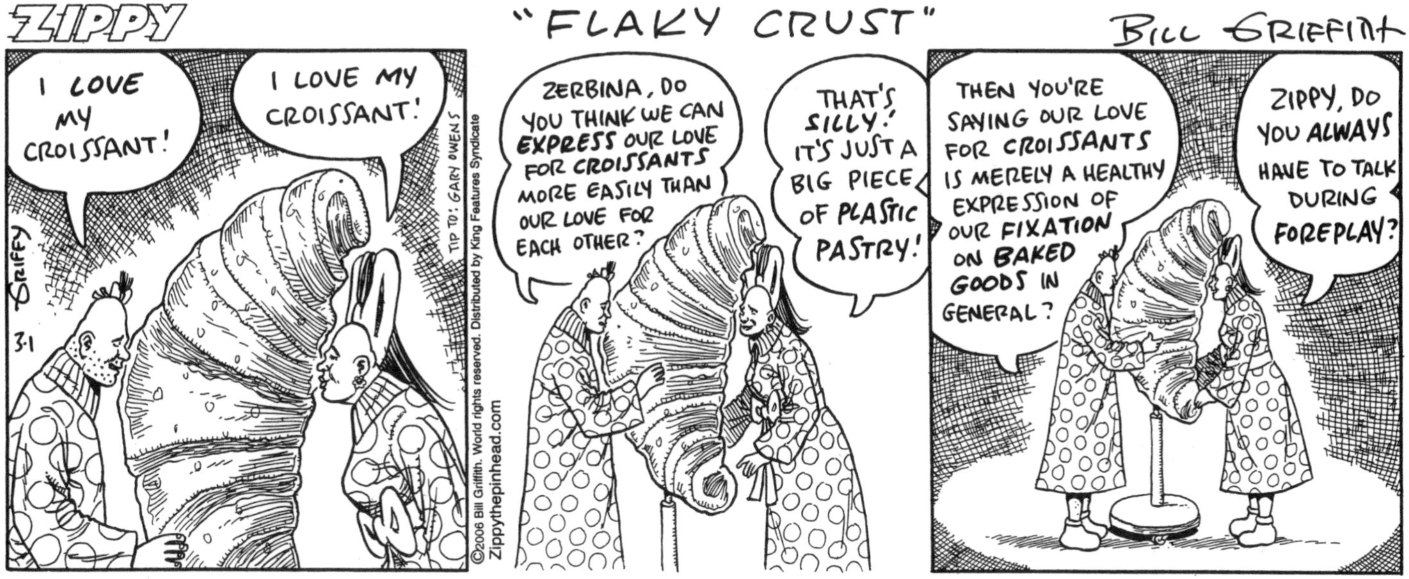
ZIPPY
"FLAKY CRUST"
BILL GRIFFITH
I LOVE MY CROISSANT!
I LOVE MY CROISSANT!
GRIFFY 3.1
TIP TO: GARY OWENS
©2006 Bill Griffith. World rights reserved. Distributed by King Features Syndicate
Zippythepinhead.com
ZERBINA, DO YOU THINK WE CAN EXPRESS OUR LOVE FOR CROISSANTS MORE EASILY THAN OUR LOVE FOR EACH OTHER?
THAT'S SILLY! IT'S JUST A BIG PIECE OF PLASTIC PASTRY!
THEN YOU'RE SAYING OUR LOVE FOR CROISSANTS IS MERELY A HEALTHY EXPRESSION OF OUR FIXATION ON BAKED GOODS IN GENERAL?
ZIPPY, DO YOU ALWAYS HAVE TO TALK DURING FOREPLAY?

61

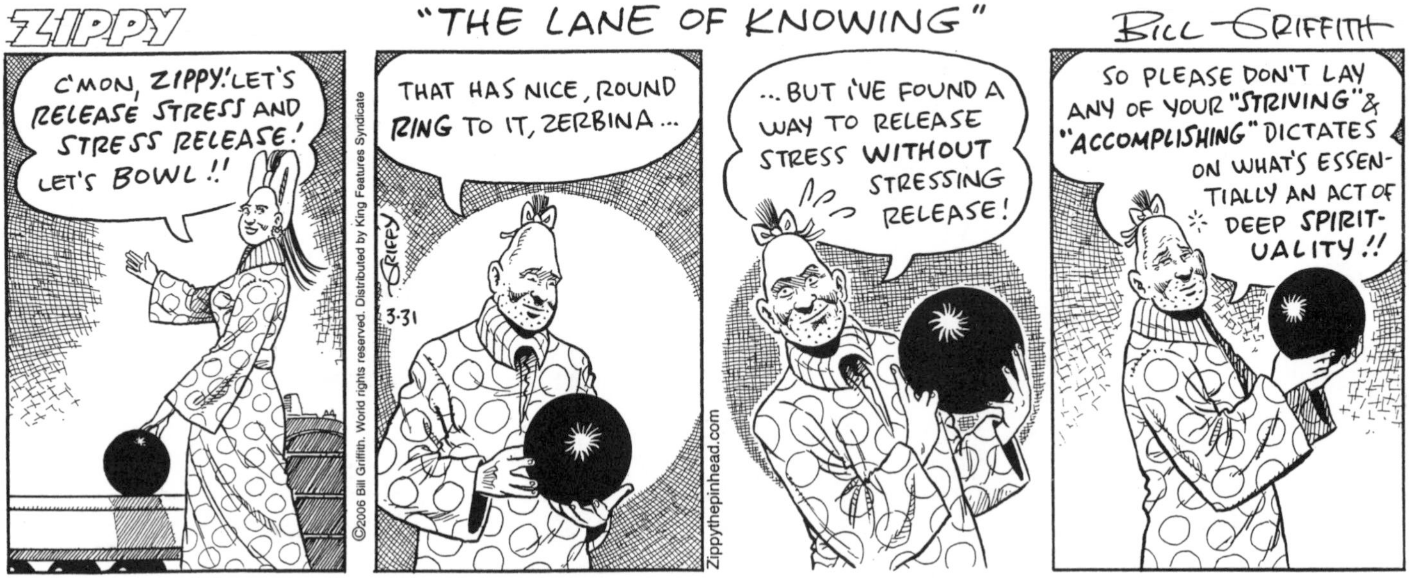
ZIPPY
"THE LANE OF KNOWING"
BILL GRIFFITH
C'MON, ZIPPY! LET'S RELEASE STRESS AND STRESS RELEASE! LET'S BOWL!!
THAT HAS NICE, ROUND RING TO IT, ZERBINA...
GRIFFY 3·31
©2006 Bill Griffith. World rights reserved. Distributed by King Features Syndicate
...BUT I'VE FOUND A WAY TO RELEASE STRESS WITHOUT STRESSING RELEASE!
Zippythepinhead.com
SO PLEASE DON'T LAY ANY OF YOUR "STRIVING" & "ACCOMPLISHING" DICTATES ON WHAT'S ESSENTIALLY AN ACT OF DEEP SPIRITUALITY!!

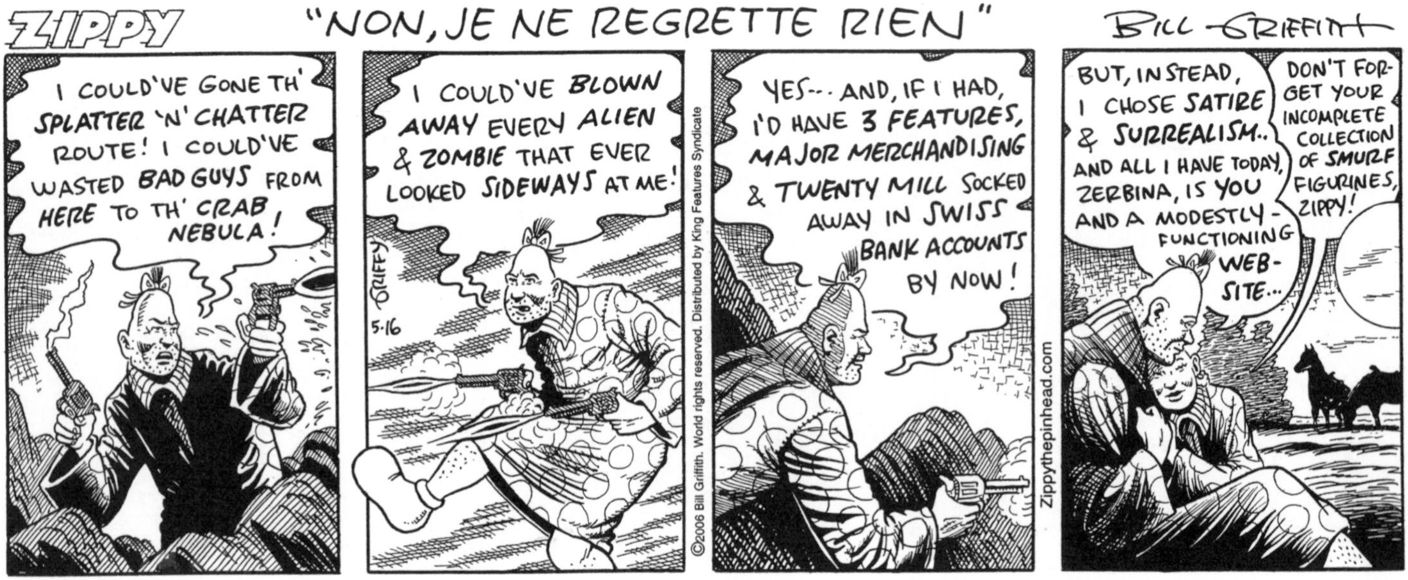
ZIPPY
"NON, JE NE REGRETTE RIEN"
BILL GRIFFITH
I COULD'VE GONE TH' SPLATTER 'N' CHATTER ROUTE! I COULD'VE WASTED BAD GUYS FROM HERE TO TH' CRAB NEBULA!
I COULD'VE BLOWN AWAY EVERY ALIEN & ZOMBIE THAT EVER LOOKED SIDEWAYS AT ME!
GRIFFY 5·16
©2006 Bill Griffith. World rights reserved. Distributed by King Features Syndicate
YES... AND, IF I HAD, I'D HAVE 3 FEATURES, MAJOR MERCHANDISING & TWENTY MILL SOCKED AWAY IN SWISS BANK ACCOUNTS BY NOW!
Zippythepinhead.com
BUT, INSTEAD, I CHOSE SATIRE & SURREALISM.. AND ALL I HAVE TODAY, ZERBINA, IS YOU AND A MODESTLY-FUNCTIONING WEB-SITE...
DON'T FORGET YOUR INCOMPLETE COLLECTION OF SMURF FIGURINES, ZIPPY!

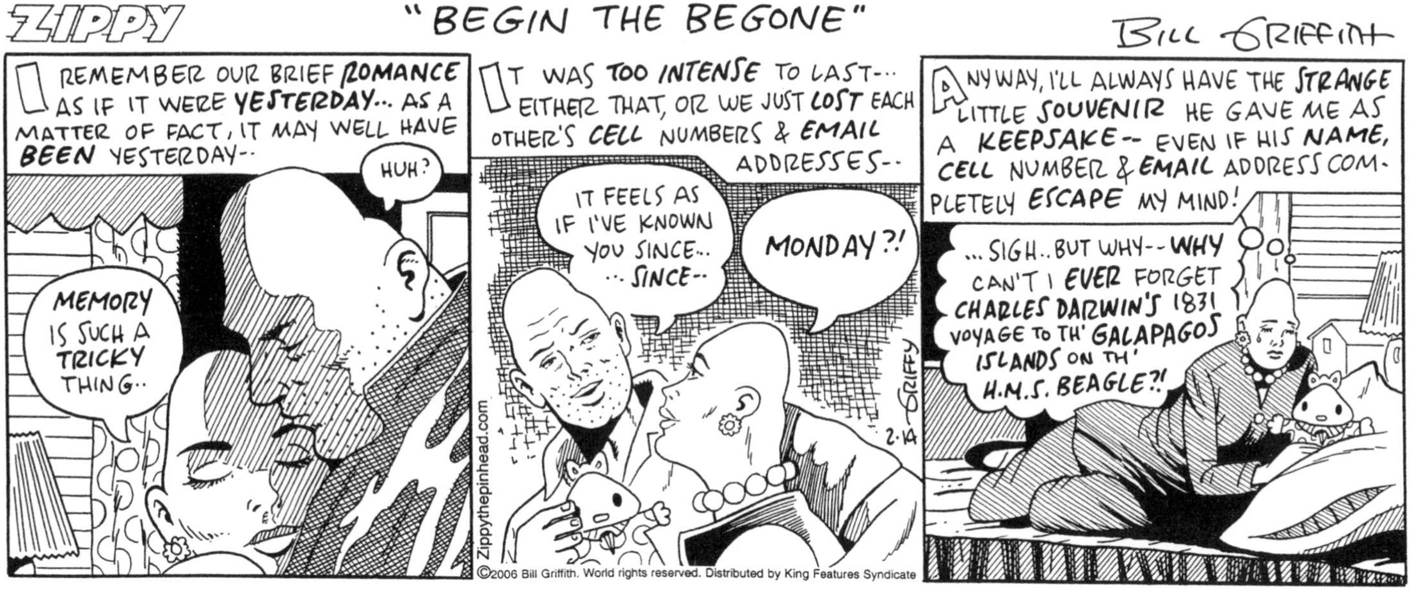
ZIPPY
"BEGIN THE BEGONE"
BILL GRIFFITH
I REMEMBER OUR BRIEF ROMANCE AS IF IT WERE YESTERDAY... AS A MATTER OF FACT, IT MAY WELL HAVE BEEN YESTERDAY--
HUH?
MEMORY IS SUCH A TRICKY THING..
IT WAS TOO INTENSE TO LAST-... EITHER THAT, OR WE JUST LOST EACH OTHER'S CELL NUMBERS & EMAIL ADDRESSES--
IT FEELS AS IF I'VE KNOWN YOU SINCE.. ...SINCE--
MONDAY?!
GRIFFY 2.14
Zippythepinhead.com
©2006 Bill Griffith. World rights reserved. Distributed by King Features Syndicate
ANYWAY, I'LL ALWAYS HAVE THE STRANGE LITTLE SOUVENIR HE GAVE ME AS A KEEPSAKE-- EVEN IF HIS NAME, CELL NUMBER & EMAIL ADDRESS COMPLETELY ESCAPE MY MIND!
...SIGH..BUT WHY--WHY CAN'T I EVER FORGET CHARLES DARWIN'S 1831 VOYAGE TO TH' GALAPAGOS ISLANDS ON TH' H.M.S. BEAGLE?!

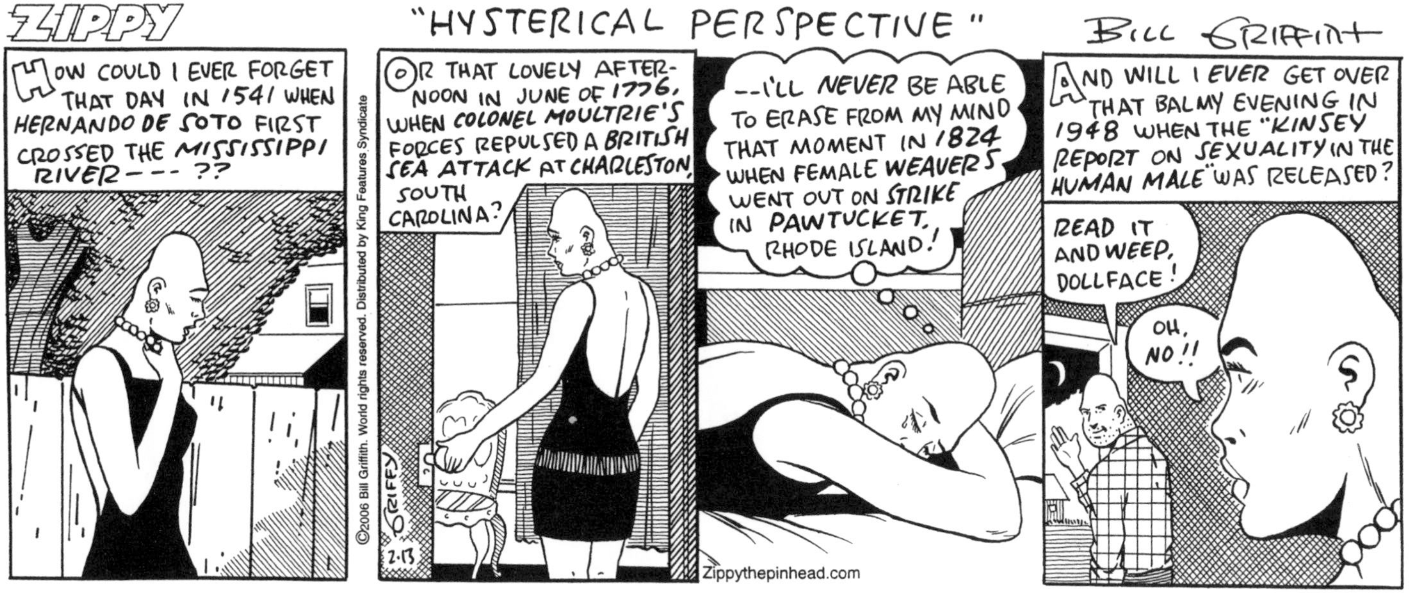
ZIPPY
"HYSTERICAL PERSPECTIVE"
BILL GRIFFITH
HOW COULD I EVER FORGET THAT DAY IN 1541 WHEN HERNANDO DE SOTO FIRST CROSSED THE MISSISSIPPI RIVER--- ??
©2006 Bill Griffith. World rights reserved. Distributed by King Features Syndicate
OR THAT LOVELY AFTERNOON IN JUNE OF 1776, WHEN COLONEL MOULTRIE'S FORCES REPULSED A BRITISH SEA ATTACK AT CHARLESTON, SOUTH CAROLINA?
GRIFFY 2.13
--I'LL NEVER BE ABLE TO ERASE FROM MY MIND THAT MOMENT IN 1824 WHEN FEMALE WEAVERS WENT OUT ON STRIKE IN PAWTUCKET, RHODE ISLAND!
Zippythepinhead.com
AND WILL I EVER GET OVER THAT BALMY EVENING IN 1948 WHEN THE "KINSEY REPORT ON SEXUALITY IN THE HUMAN MALE" WAS RELEASED?
READ IT AND WEEP, DOLLFACE!
OH, NO!!

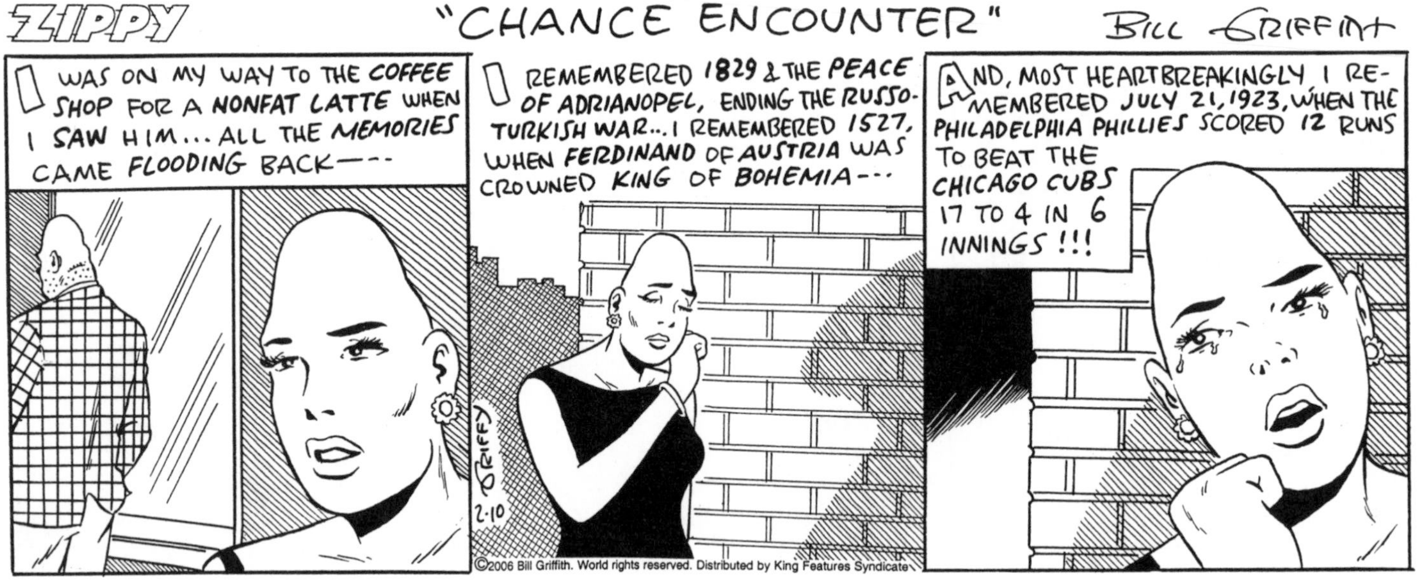
ZIPPY
"CHANCE ENCOUNTER"
BILL GRIFFITH
I WAS ON MY WAY TO THE COFFEE SHOP FOR A NONFAT LATTE WHEN I SAW HIM... ALL THE MEMORIES CAME FLOODING BACK---
GRIFFY 2·10
I REMEMBERED 1829 & THE PEACE OF ADRIANOPEL, ENDING THE RUSSO-TURKISH WAR... I REMEMBERED 1527, WHEN FERDINAND OF AUSTRIA WAS CROWNED KING OF BOHEMIA---
AND, MOST HEARTBREAKINGLY I REMEMBERED JULY 21, 1923, WHEN THE PHILADELPHIA PHILLIES SCORED 12 RUNS TO BEAT THE CHICAGO CUBS 17 TO 4 IN 6 INNINGS!!!
©2006 Bill Griffith. World rights reserved. Distributed by King Features Syndicate

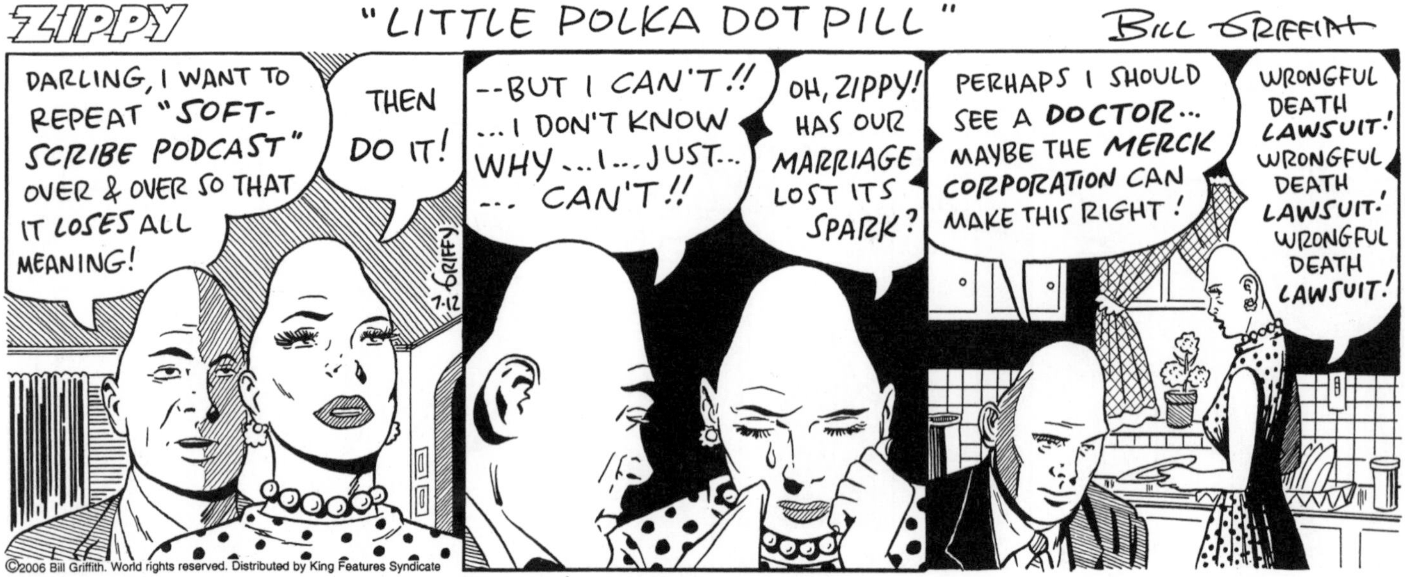
ZIPPY
"LITTLE POLKA DOT PILL"
BILL GRIFFITH
DARLING, I WANT TO REPEAT "SOFT-SCRIBE PODCAST" OVER & OVER SO THAT IT LOSES ALL MEANING!
THEN DO IT!
GRIFFY 7·12
--BUT I CAN'T!! ...I DON'T KNOW WHY...I...JUST... ... CAN'T!!
OH, ZIPPY! HAS OUR MARRIAGE LOST ITS SPARK?
PERHAPS I SHOULD SEE A DOCTOR... MAYBE THE MERCK CORPORATION CAN MAKE THIS RIGHT!
WRONGFUL DEATH LAWSUIT! WRONGFUL DEATH LAWSUIT! WRONGFUL DEATH LAWSUIT!
©2006 Bill Griffith. World rights reserved. Distributed by King Features Syndicate

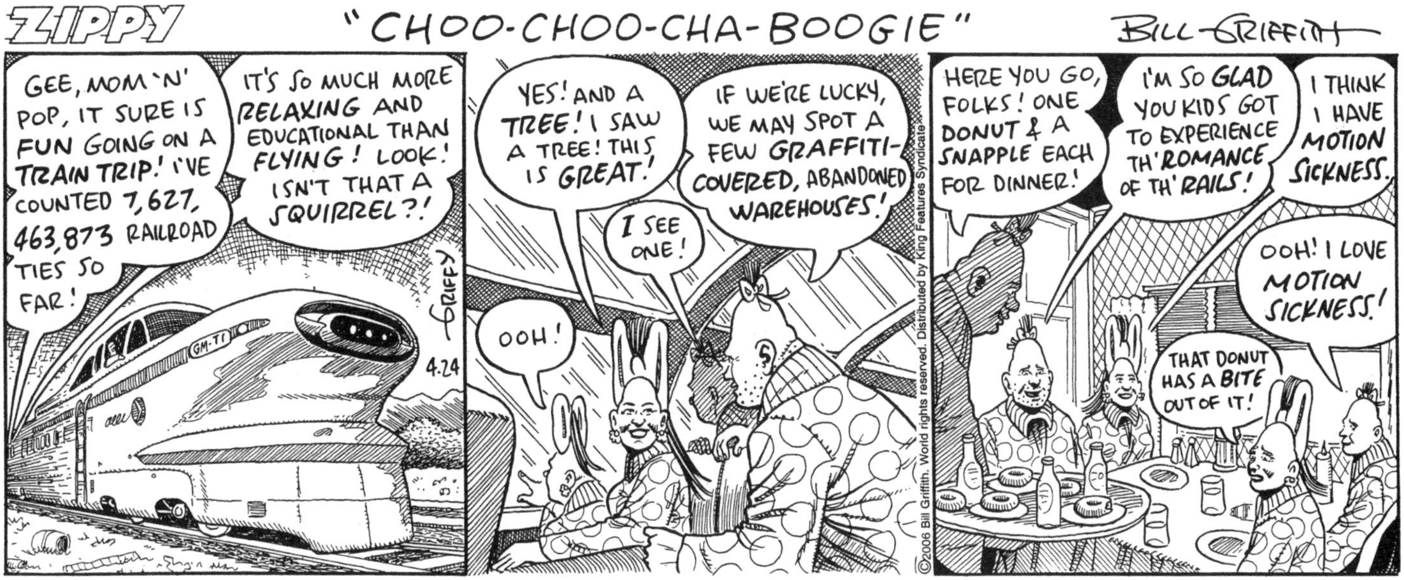
ZIPPY
"CHOO-CHOO-CHA-BOOGIE"
BILL GRIFFITH
GEE, MOM 'N' POP, IT SURE IS FUN GOING ON A TRAIN TRIP! I'VE COUNTED 7,627,463,873 RAILROAD TIES SO FAR!
IT'S SO MUCH MORE RELAXING AND EDUCATIONAL THAN FLYING! LOOK! ISN'T THAT A SQUIRREL?!
GM-T1
GRIFFY
4.24
YES! AND A TREE! I SAW A TREE! THIS IS GREAT!
IF WE'RE LUCKY, WE MAY SPOT A FEW GRAFFITI-COVERED, ABANDONED WAREHOUSES!
I SEE ONE!
OOH!
©2006 Bill Griffith. World rights reserved. Distributed by King Features Syndicate
HERE YOU GO, FOLKS! ONE DONUT & A SNAPPLE EACH FOR DINNER!
I'M SO GLAD YOU KIDS GOT TO EXPERIENCE TH' ROMANCE OF TH' RAILS!
I THINK I HAVE MOTION SICKNESS.
OOH! I LOVE MOTION SICKNESS!
THAT DONUT HAS A BITE OUT OF IT!

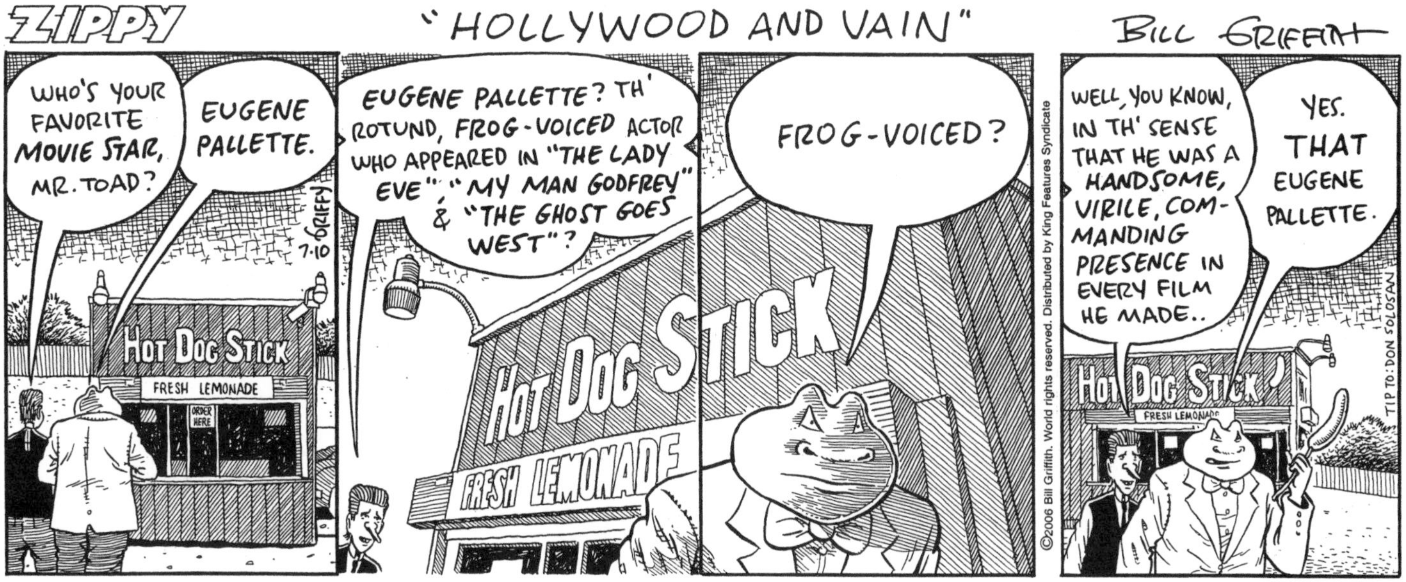
ZIPPY
"HOLLYWOOD AND VAIN"
BILL GRIFFITH
WHO'S YOUR FAVORITE MOVIE STAR, MR. TOAD?
EUGENE PALLETTE.
7.10 GRIFFY
HOT DOG STICK
FRESH LEMONADE
ORDER HERE
EUGENE PALLETTE? TH' ROTUND, FROG-VOICED ACTOR WHO APPEARED IN "THE LADY EVE", "MY MAN GODFREY" & "THE GHOST GOES WEST"?
HOT DOG STICK
FRESH LEMONADE
FROG-VOICED?
©2006 Bill Griffith. World rights reserved. Distributed by King Features Syndicate
WELL, YOU KNOW, IN TH' SENSE THAT HE WAS A HANDSOME, VIRILE, COMMANDING PRESENCE IN EVERY FILM HE MADE..
YES. THAT EUGENE PALLETTE.
HOT DOG STICK
TIP TO: DON SOLOSAN

62

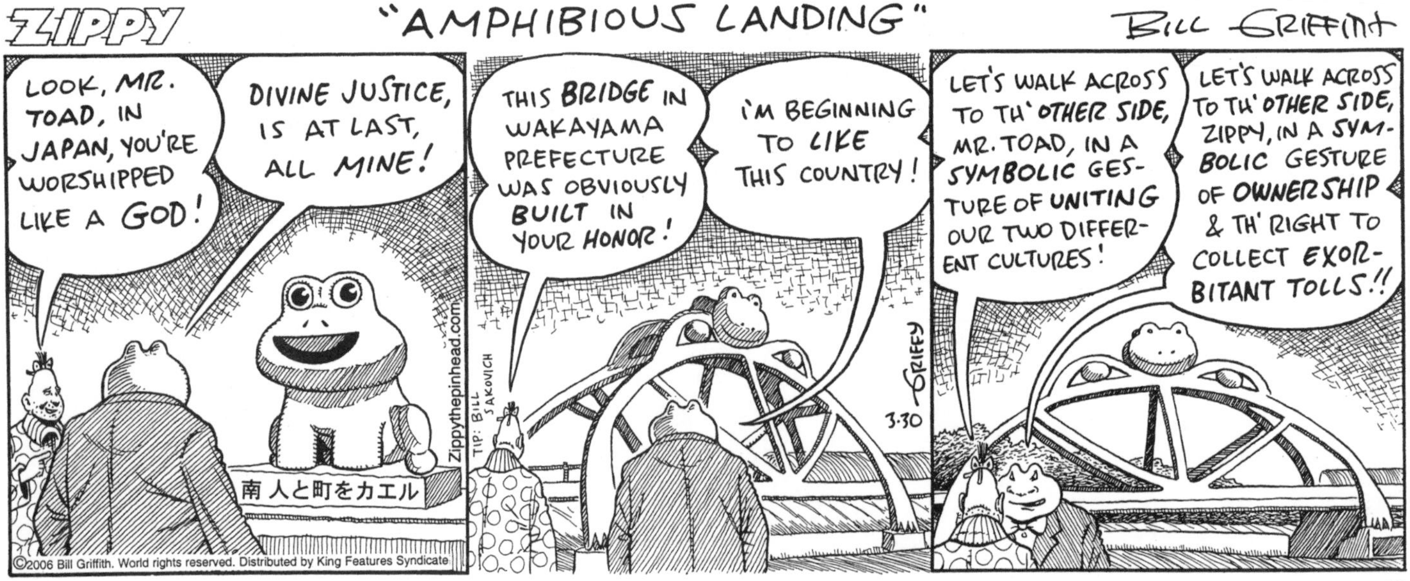
ZIPPY
"AMPHIBIOUS LANDING"
BILL GRIFFITH
LOOK, MR. TOAD, IN JAPAN, YOU'RE WORSHIPPED LIKE A GOD!
DIVINE JUSTICE, IS AT LAST, ALL MINE!
南 人と町をカエル
Zippythepinhead.com
©2006 Bill Griffith. World rights reserved. Distributed by King Features Syndicate
THIS BRIDGE IN WAKAYAMA PREFECTURE WAS OBVIOUSLY BUILT IN YOUR HONOR!
I'M BEGINNING TO LIKE THIS COUNTRY!
TIP: BILL SAKOVICH
GRIFFY
3·30
LET'S WALK ACROSS TO TH' OTHER SIDE, MR. TOAD, IN A SYMBOLIC GESTURE OF UNITING OUR TWO DIFFERENT CULTURES!
LET'S WALK ACROSS TO TH' OTHER SIDE, ZIPPY, IN A SYMBOLIC GESTURE OF OWNERSHIP & TH' RIGHT TO COLLECT EXORBITANT TOLLS!!

63

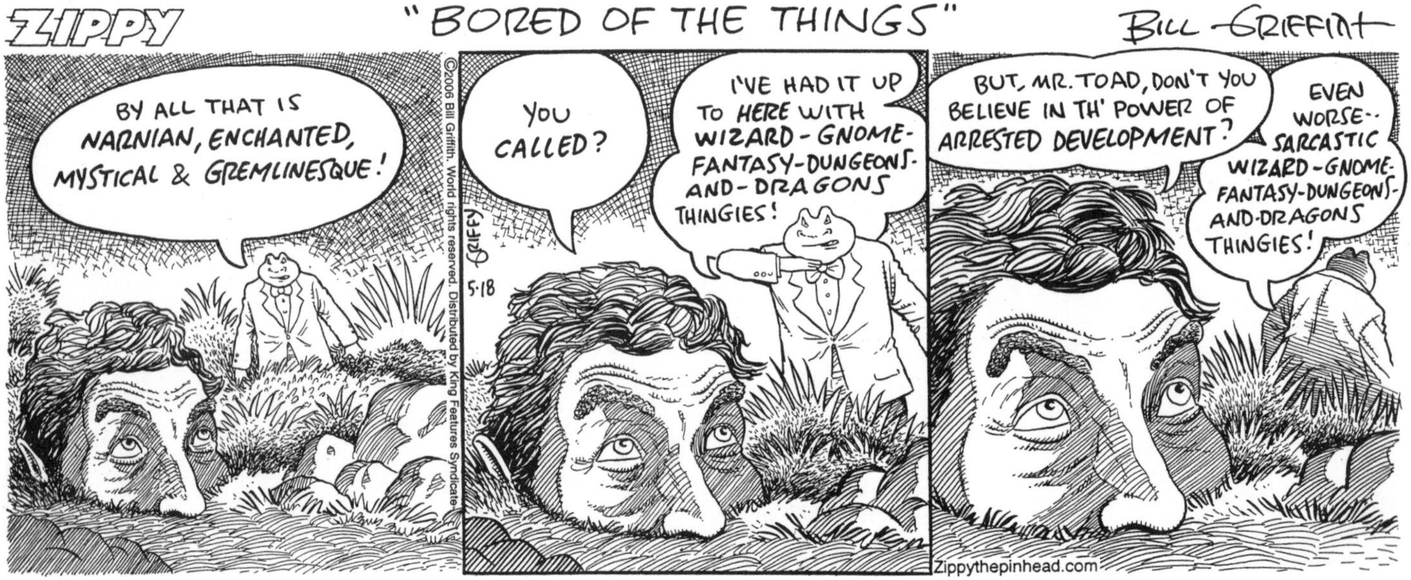
ZIPPY
"BORED OF THE THINGS"
BILL GRIFFITH
BY ALL THAT IS NARNIAN, ENCHANTED, MYSTICAL & GREMLINESQUE!
©2006 Bill Griffith. World rights reserved. Distributed by King Features Syndicate
YOU CALLED?
I'VE HAD IT UP TO HERE WITH WIZARD-GNOME-FANTASY-DUNGEONS-AND-DRAGONS THINGIES!
GRIFFY
5·18
BUT, MR. TOAD, DON'T YOU BELIEVE IN TH' POWER OF ARRESTED DEVELOPMENT?
EVEN WORSE-- SARCASTIC WIZARD-GNOME-FANTASY-DUNGEONS-AND-DRAGONS THINGIES!
Zippythepinhead.com

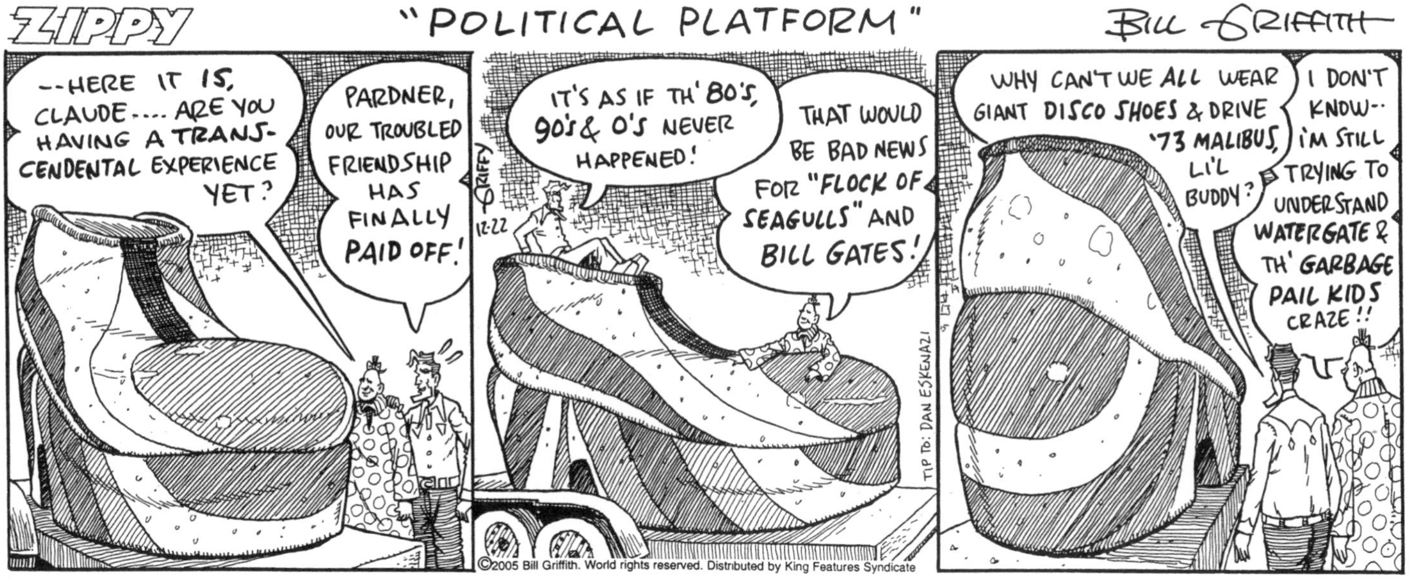
ZIPPY
"POLITICAL PLATFORM"
BILL GRIFFITH
--HERE IT IS, CLAUDE.... ARE YOU HAVING A TRANS-CENDENTAL EXPERIENCE YET?
PARDNER, OUR TROUBLED FRIENDSHIP HAS FINALLY PAID OFF!
IT'S AS IF TH' 80'S, 90'S & O'S NEVER HAPPENED!
THAT WOULD BE BAD NEWS FOR "FLOCK OF SEAGULLS" AND BILL GATES!
GRIFFY 12-22
TIP TO: DAN ESKENAZI
WHY CAN'T WE ALL WEAR GIANT DISCO SHOES & DRIVE '73 MALIBUS, LI'L BUDDY?
I DON'T KNOW-- I'M STILL TRYING TO UNDERSTAND WATERGATE & TH' GARBAGE PAIL KIDS CRAZE!!
©2005 Bill Griffith. World rights reserved. Distributed by King Features Syndicate

64

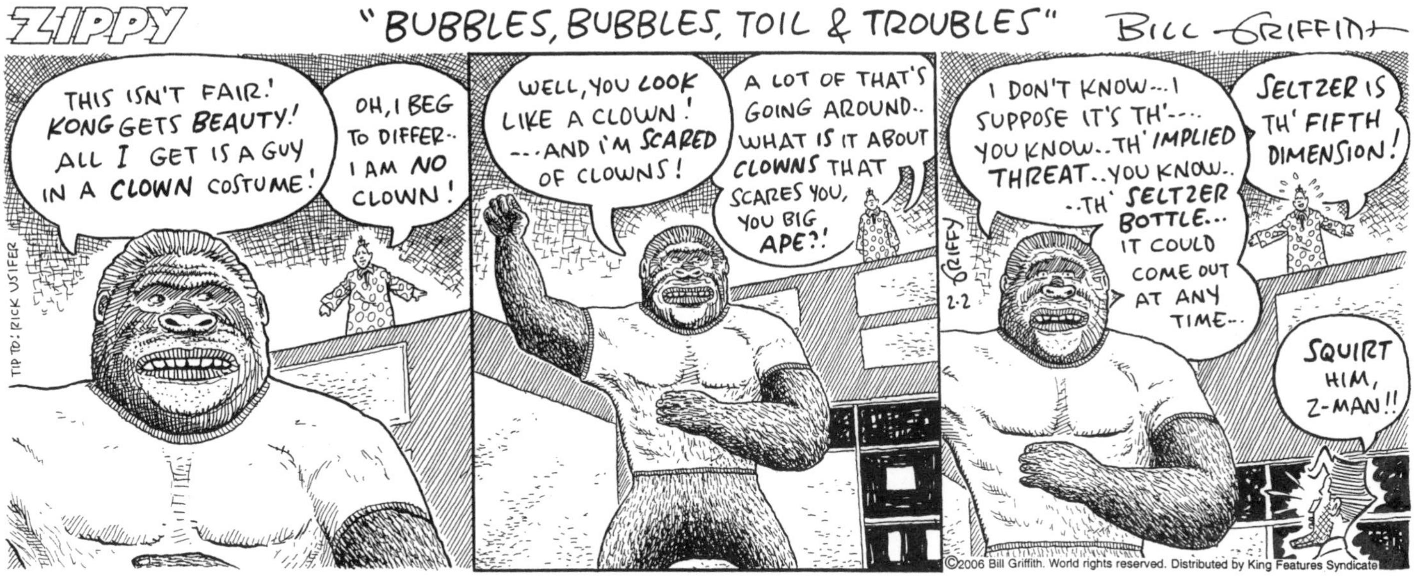
ZIPPY
"BUBBLES, BUBBLES, TOIL & TROUBLES"
BILL GRIFFITH
THIS ISN'T FAIR! KONG GETS BEAUTY! ALL I GET IS A GUY IN A CLOWN COSTUME!
OH, I BEG TO DIFFER-- I AM NO CLOWN!
TIP TO: RICK USIFER
WELL, YOU LOOK LIKE A CLOWN! ---AND I'M SCARED OF CLOWNS!
A LOT OF THAT'S GOING AROUND.. WHAT IS IT ABOUT CLOWNS THAT SCARES YOU, YOU BIG APE?!
I DON'T KNOW---I SUPPOSE IT'S TH'--- YOU KNOW..TH' IMPLIED THREAT..YOU KNOW.. --TH' SELTZER BOTTLE... IT COULD COME OUT AT ANY TIME--
GRIFFY 2-2
SELTZER IS TH' FIFTH DIMENSION!
SQUIRT HIM, Z-MAN!!
©2006 Bill Griffith. World rights reserved. Distributed by King Features Syndicate

65

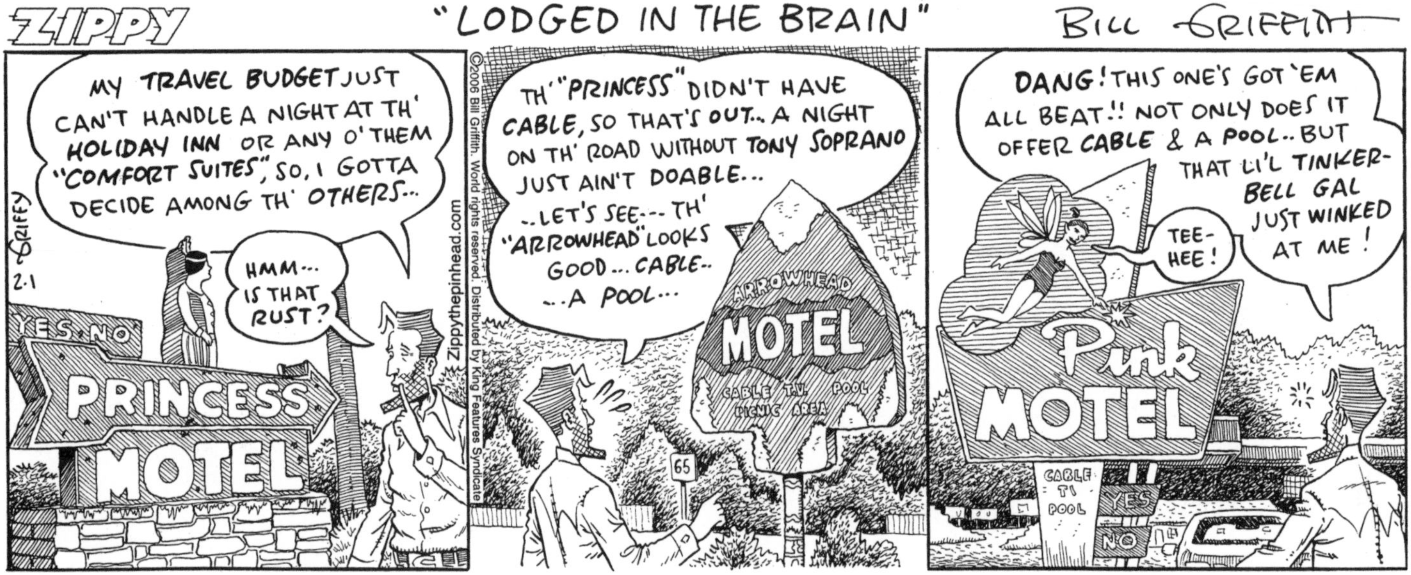

ZIPPY
"LODGED IN THE BRAIN"
BILL GRIFFITH
MY TRAVEL BUDGET JUST CAN'T HANDLE A NIGHT AT TH' HOLIDAY INN OR ANY O' THEM "COMFORT SUITES", SO, I GOTTA DECIDE AMONG TH' OTHERS...
HMM... IS THAT RUST?
GRIFFY 2-1
YES NO
PRINCESS MOTEL
©2006 Bill Griffith. World rights reserved. Distributed by King Features Syndicate
Zippythepinhead.com
TH' "PRINCESS" DIDN'T HAVE CABLE, SO THAT'S OUT.. A NIGHT ON TH' ROAD WITHOUT TONY SOPRANO JUST AIN'T DOABLE...
..LET'S SEE... TH' "ARROWHEAD" LOOKS GOOD... CABLE.. ..A POOL...
ARROWHEAD
MOTEL
CABLE T.V. POOL PICNIC AREA
65
DANG! THIS ONE'S GOT 'EM ALL BEAT!! NOT ONLY DOES IT OFFER CABLE & A POOL.. BUT THAT LI'L TINKER-BELL GAL JUST WINKED AT ME!
TEE-HEE!
Pink MOTEL
CABLE TV POOL
YES
NO

66

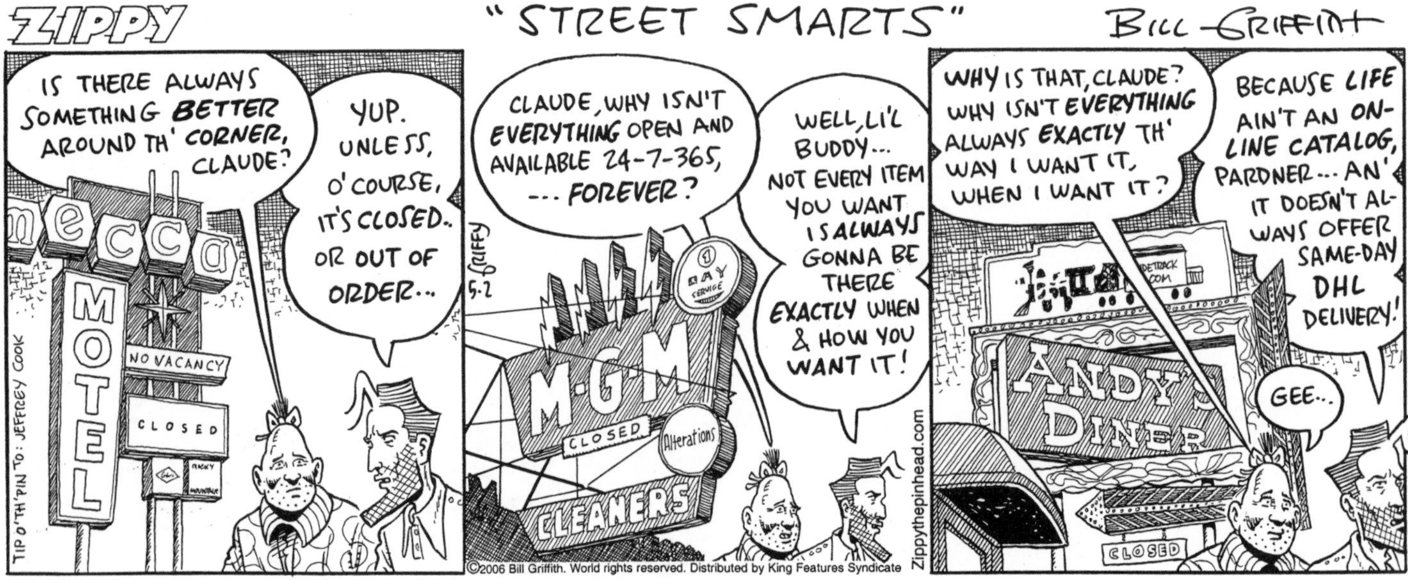

ZIPPY
"STREET SMARTS"
BILL GRIFFITH
IS THERE ALWAYS SOMETHING BETTER AROUND TH' CORNER, CLAUDE?
YUP. UNLESS, O' COURSE, IT'S CLOSED.. OR OUT OF ORDER...
mecca
MOTEL
NO VACANCY
CLOSED
TIP O' TH' PIN TO: JEFFREY COOK
GRIFFY 5-2
CLAUDE, WHY ISN'T EVERYTHING OPEN AND AVAILABLE 24-7-365, --- FOREVER?
WELL, LI'L BUDDY... NOT EVERY ITEM YOU WANT IS ALWAYS GONNA BE THERE EXACTLY WHEN & HOW YOU WANT IT!
1 DAY SERVICE
M-G-M
CLOSED
Alterations
CLEANERS
©2006 Bill Griffith. World rights reserved. Distributed by King Features Syndicate
Zippythepinhead.com
WHY IS THAT, CLAUDE? WHY ISN'T EVERYTHING ALWAYS EXACTLY TH' WAY I WANT IT, WHEN I WANT IT?
BECAUSE LIFE AIN'T AN ON-LINE CATALOG, PARDNER... AN' IT DOESN'T ALWAYS OFFER SAME-DAY DHL DELIVERY!
GEE...
ANDY'S DINER
CLOSED

67

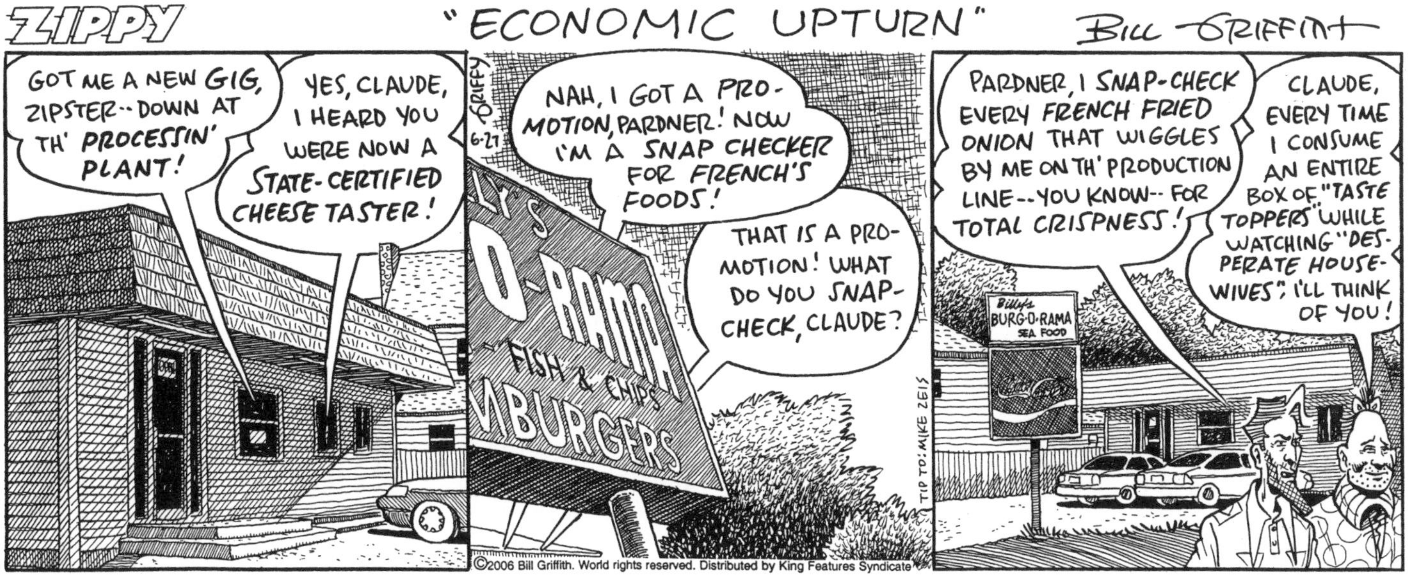

ZIPPY
"ECONOMIC UPTURN"
BILL GRIFFITH
GOT ME A NEW GIG, ZIPSTER--DOWN AT TH' PROCESSIN' PLANT!
YES, CLAUDE, I HEARD YOU WERE NOW A STATE-CERTIFIED CHEESE TASTER!
GRIFFY 6-27
NAH, I GOT A PROMOTION, PARDNER! NOW I'M A SNAP CHECKER FOR FRENCH'S FOODS!
THAT IS A PROMOTION! WHAT DO YOU SNAP-CHECK, CLAUDE?
FISH & CHIPS
MBURGERS
TIP TO: MIKE ZEIS
©2006 Bill Griffith. World rights reserved. Distributed by King Features Syndicate
PARDNER, I SNAP-CHECK EVERY FRENCH FRIED ONION THAT WIGGLES BY ME ON TH' PRODUCTION LINE--YOU KNOW--FOR TOTAL CRISPNESS!
CLAUDE, EVERY TIME I CONSUME AN ENTIRE BOX OF "TASTE TOPPERS" WHILE WATCHING "DESPERATE HOUSEWIVES", I'LL THINK OF YOU!
Billy's BURG-O-RAMA SEA FOOD

68

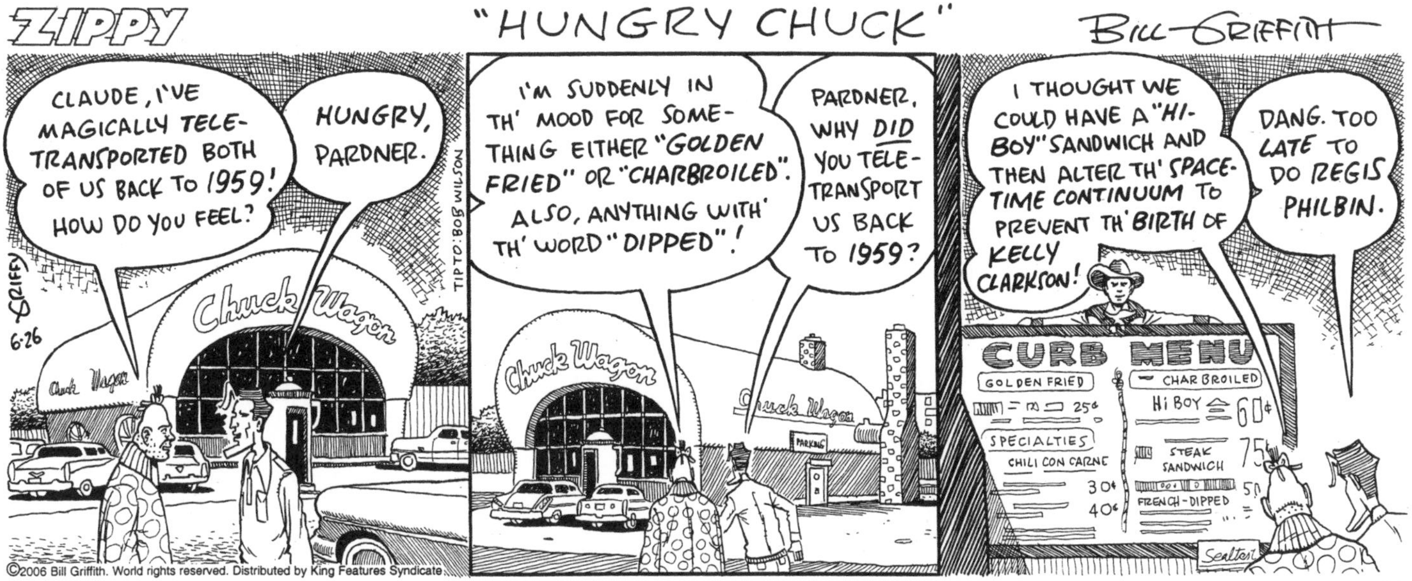

ZIPPY
"HUNGRY CHUCK"
BILL GRIFFITH
CLAUDE, I'VE MAGICALLY TELE-TRANSPORTED BOTH OF US BACK TO 1959! HOW DO YOU FEEL?
HUNGRY, PARDNER.
GRIFFY 6-26
TIP TO: BOB WILSON
Chuck Wagon
©2006 Bill Griffith. World rights reserved. Distributed by King Features Syndicate
I'M SUDDENLY IN TH' MOOD FOR SOMETHING EITHER "GOLDEN FRIED" OR "CHARBROILED". ALSO, ANYTHING WITH TH' WORD "DIPPED"!
PARDNER, WHY DID YOU TELE-TRANSPORT US BACK TO 1959?
Chuck Wagon
PARKING
I THOUGHT WE COULD HAVE A "HI-BOY" SANDWICH AND THEN ALTER TH' SPACE-TIME CONTINUUM TO PREVENT TH' BIRTH OF KELLY CLARKSON!
DANG. TOO LATE TO DO REGIS PHILBIN.
CURB MENU
GOLDEN FRIED
CHAR BROILED
25¢
Hi BOY 60¢
SPECIALTIES
CHILI CON CARNE
30¢
40¢
STEAK SANDWICH 75¢
FRENCH-DIPPED
Sealtest

69

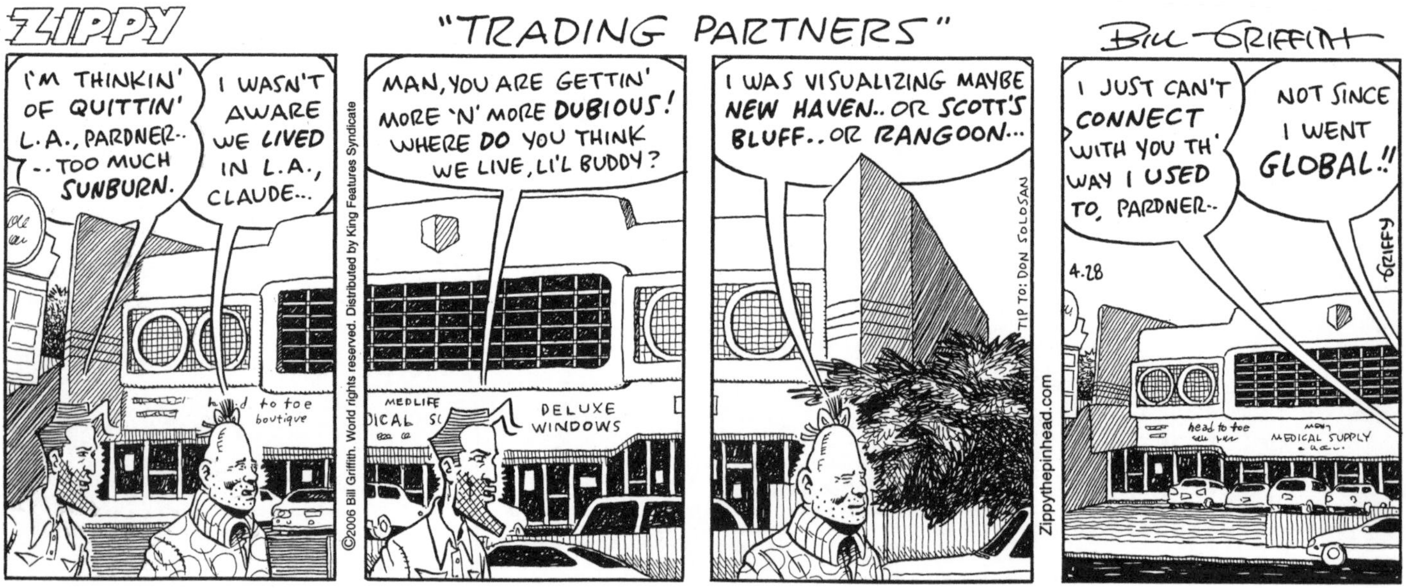

ZIPPY
"TRADING PARTNERS"
BILL GRIFFITH
I'M THINKIN' OF QUITTIN' L.A., PARDNER.. ..TOO MUCH SUNBURN.
I WASN'T AWARE WE LIVED IN L.A., CLAUDE...
head to toe boutique
©2006 Bill Griffith. World rights reserved. Distributed by King Features Syndicate
MAN, YOU ARE GETTIN' MORE 'N' MORE DUBIOUS! WHERE DO YOU THINK WE LIVE, LI'L BUDDY?
MEDLIFE
DELUXE WINDOWS
I WAS VISUALIZING MAYBE NEW HAVEN.. OR SCOTT'S BLUFF.. OR RANGOON...
TIP TO: DON SOLOSAN
Zippythepinhead.com
I JUST CAN'T CONNECT WITH YOU TH' WAY I USED TO, PARDNER..
NOT SINCE I WENT GLOBAL!!
4-28
GRIFFY
head to toe
MEDICAL SUPPLY

70

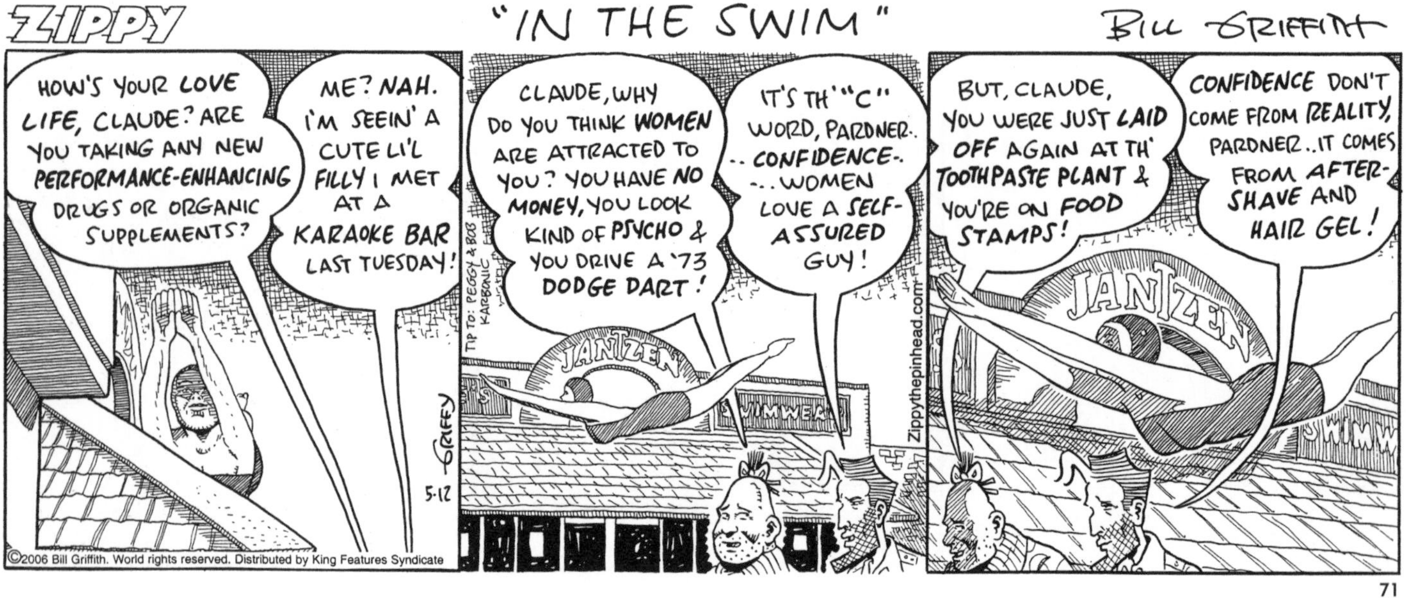

ZIPPY
"IN THE SWIM"
BILL GRIFFITH
HOW'S YOUR LOVE LIFE, CLAUDE? ARE YOU TAKING ANY NEW PERFORMANCE-ENHANCING DRUGS OR ORGANIC SUPPLEMENTS?
ME? NAH. I'M SEEIN' A CUTE LI'L FILLY I MET AT A KARAOKE BAR LAST TUESDAY!
GRIFFY
5-12
©2006 Bill Griffith. World rights reserved. Distributed by King Features Syndicate
CLAUDE, WHY DO YOU THINK WOMEN ARE ATTRACTED TO YOU? YOU HAVE NO MONEY, YOU LOOK KIND OF PSYCHO & YOU DRIVE A '73 DODGE DART!
IT'S TH' "C" WORD, PARDNER.. ..CONFIDENCE.. ...WOMEN LOVE A SELF-ASSURED GUY!
TIP TO: PEGGY & BOB KARBONIC
JANTZEN
SWIMWEAR
Zippythepinhead.com
BUT, CLAUDE, YOU WERE JUST LAID OFF AGAIN AT TH' TOOTHPASTE PLANT & YOU'RE ON FOOD STAMPS!
CONFIDENCE DON'T COME FROM REALITY, PARDNER.. IT COMES FROM AFTER-SHAVE AND HAIR GEL!
JANTZEN

71

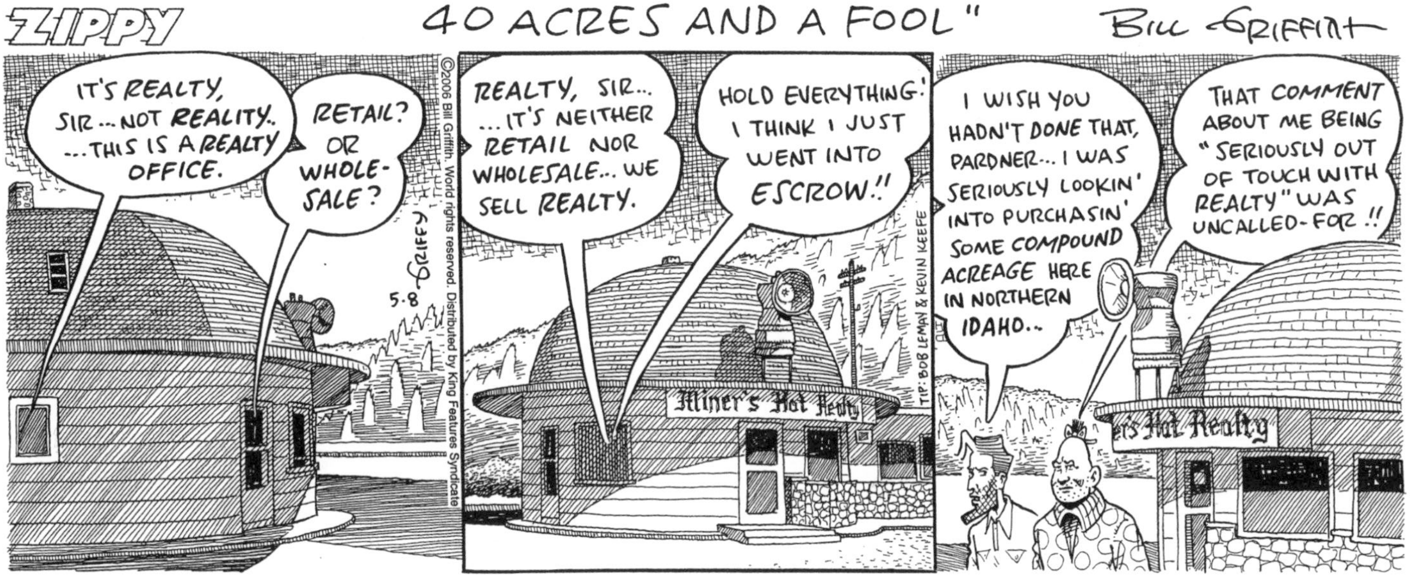
ZIPPY
40 ACRES AND A FOOL"
BILL GRIFFITH
IT'S REALTY, SIR ... NOT REALITY.. ... THIS IS A REALTY OFFICE.
RETAIL? OR WHOLE-SALE?
©2006 Bill Griffith. World rights reserved. Distributed by King Features Syndicate
GRIFFY 5-8
REALTY, SIR... ...IT'S NEITHER RETAIL NOR WHOLESALE... WE SELL REALTY.
HOLD EVERYTHING! I THINK I JUST WENT INTO ESCROW!!
Miner's Hat Realty
TIP: BOB LEMAN & KEVIN KEEFE
I WISH YOU HADN'T DONE THAT, PARDNER... I WAS SERIOUSLY LOOKIN' INTO PURCHASIN' SOME COMPOUND ACREAGE HERE IN NORTHERN IDAHO..
THAT COMMENT ABOUT ME BEING "SERIOUSLY OUT OF TOUCH WITH REALTY" WAS UNCALLED-FOR!!
...'s Hat Realty

72

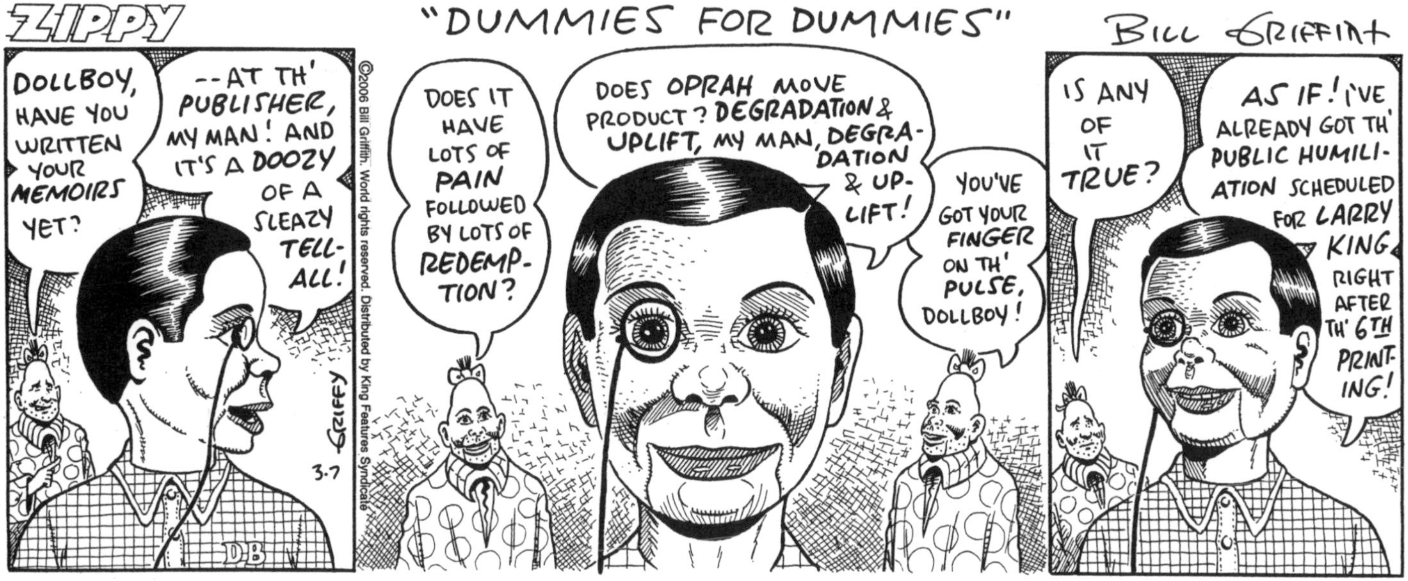
ZIPPY
"DUMMIES FOR DUMMIES"
BILL GRIFFITH
DOLLBOY, HAVE YOU WRITTEN YOUR MEMOIRS YET?
--AT TH' PUBLISHER, MY MAN! AND IT'S A DOOZY OF A SLEAZY TELL-ALL!
©2006 Bill Griffith. World rights reserved. Distributed by King Features Syndicate
GRIFFY 3-7
DB
DOES IT HAVE LOTS OF PAIN FOLLOWED BY LOTS OF REDEMP-TION?
DOES OPRAH MOVE PRODUCT? DEGRADATION & UPLIFT, MY MAN, DEGRA-DATION & UP-LIFT!
YOU'VE GOT YOUR FINGER ON TH' PULSE, DOLLBOY!
IS ANY OF IT TRUE?
AS IF! I'VE ALREADY GOT TH' PUBLIC HUMILI-ATION SCHEDULED FOR LARRY KING RIGHT AFTER TH' 6TH PRINT-ING!

Dinerama

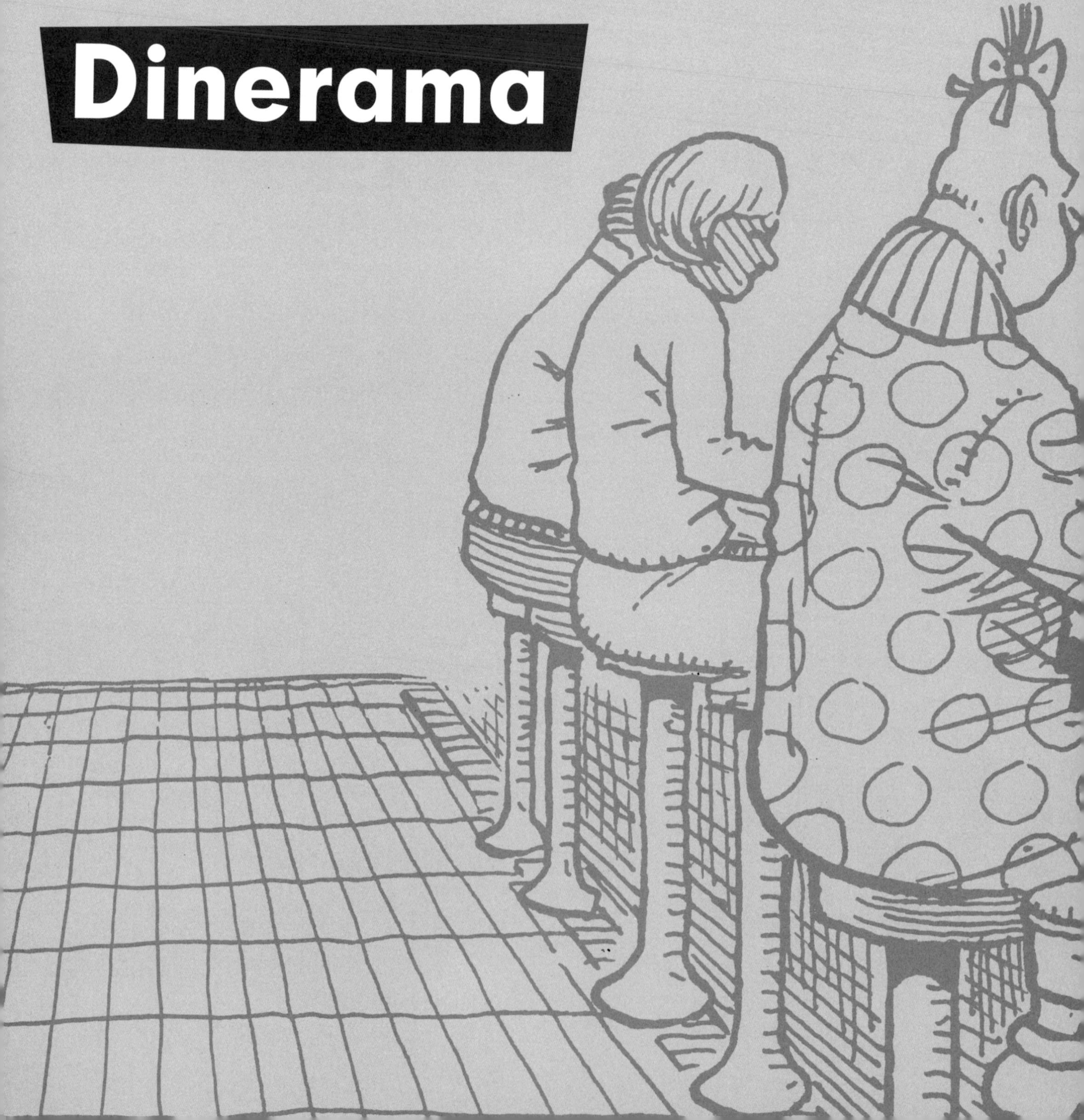

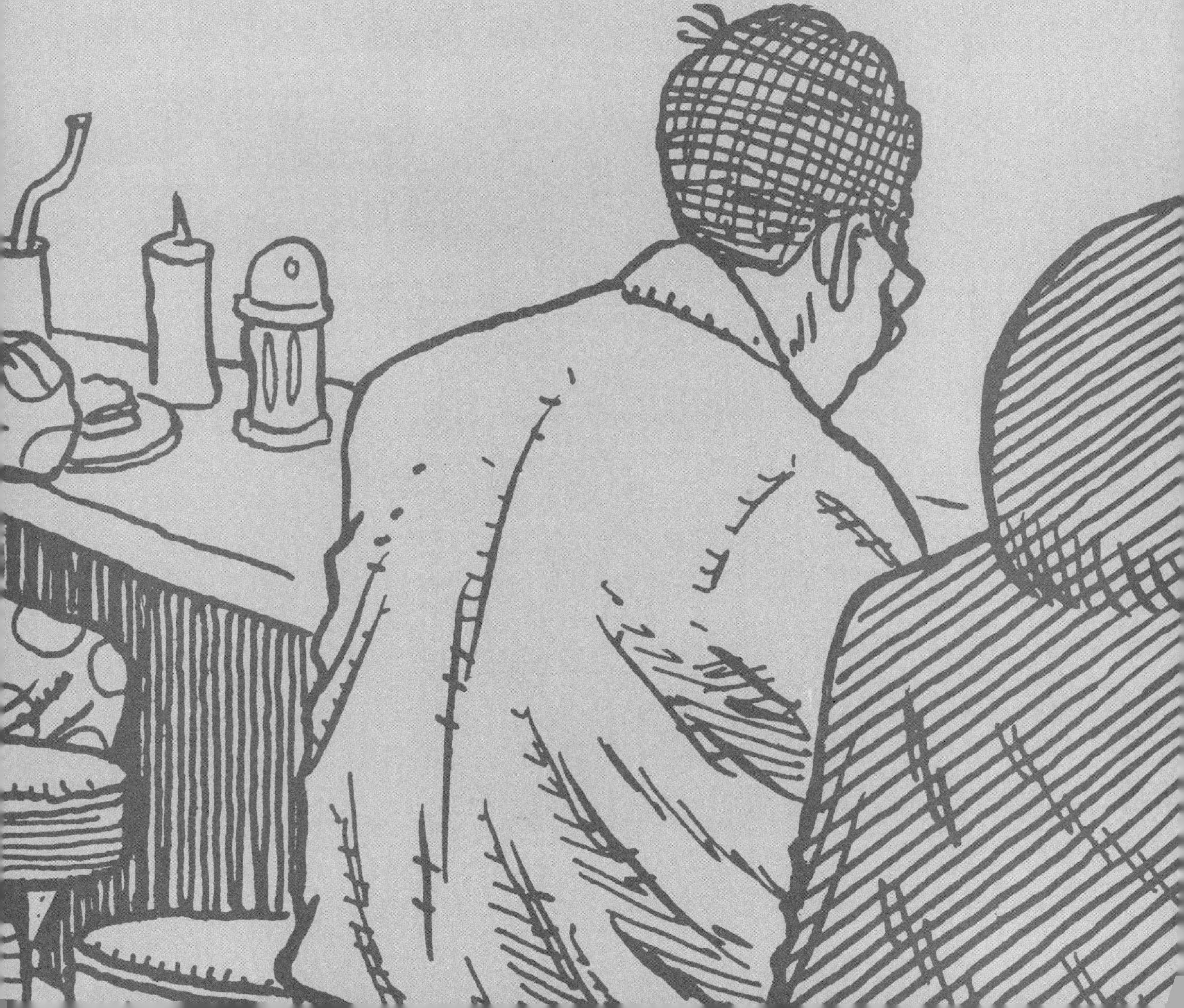

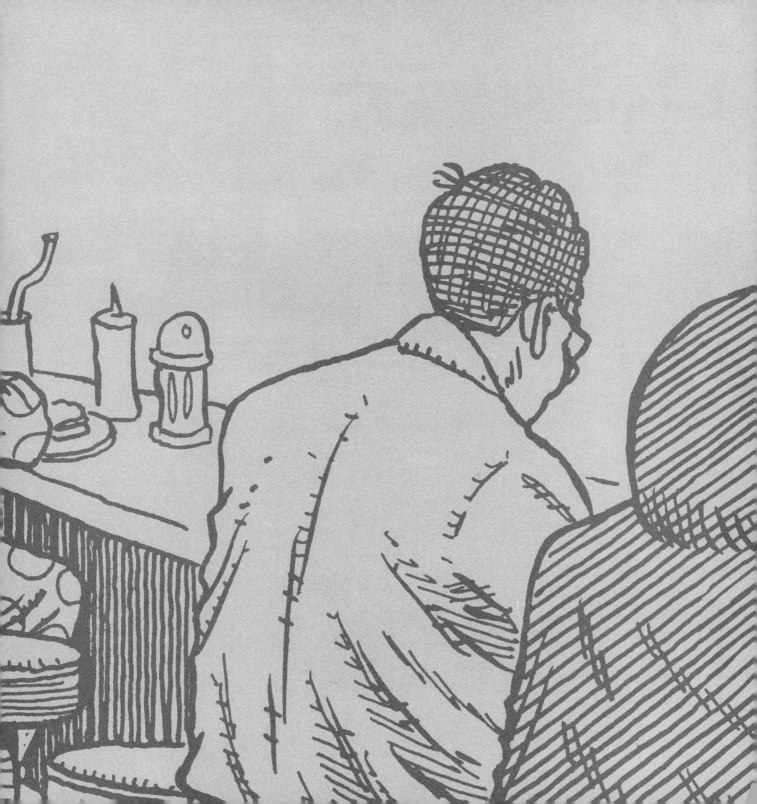

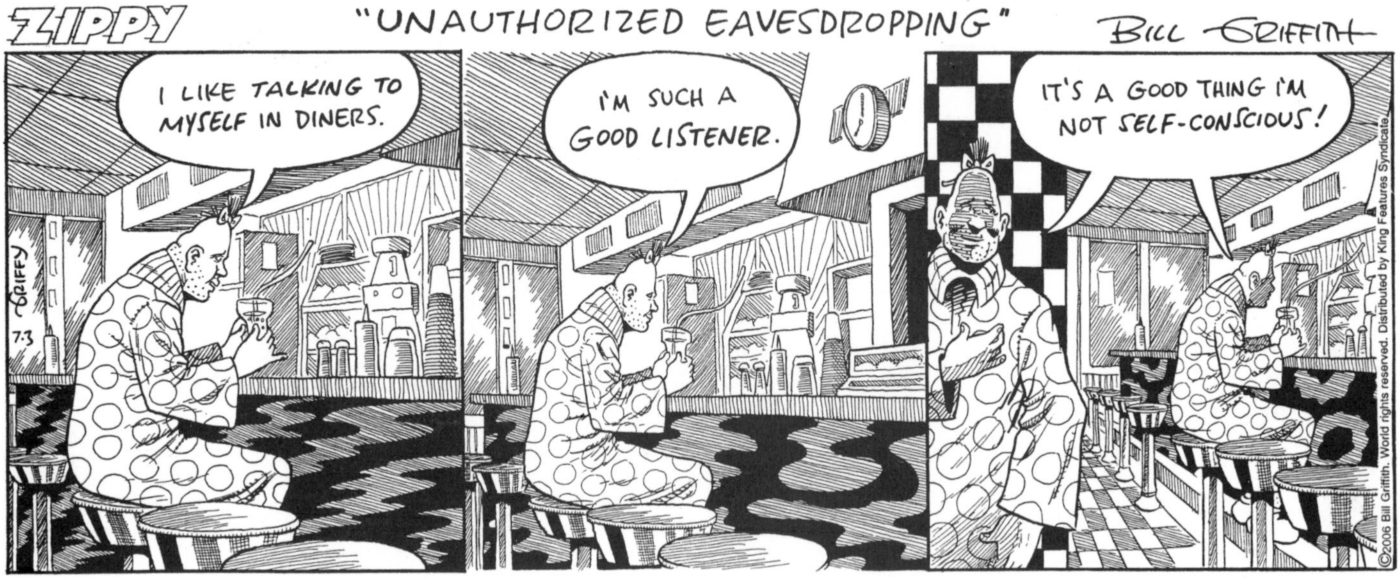
ZIPPY
"UNAUTHORIZED EAVESDROPPING"
BILL GRIFFITH
I LIKE TALKING TO MYSELF IN DINERS.
I'M SUCH A GOOD LISTENER.
IT'S A GOOD THING I'M NOT SELF-CONSCIOUS!
GRIFFY 7·3
©2006 Bill Griffith. World rights reserved. Distributed by King Features Syndicate.

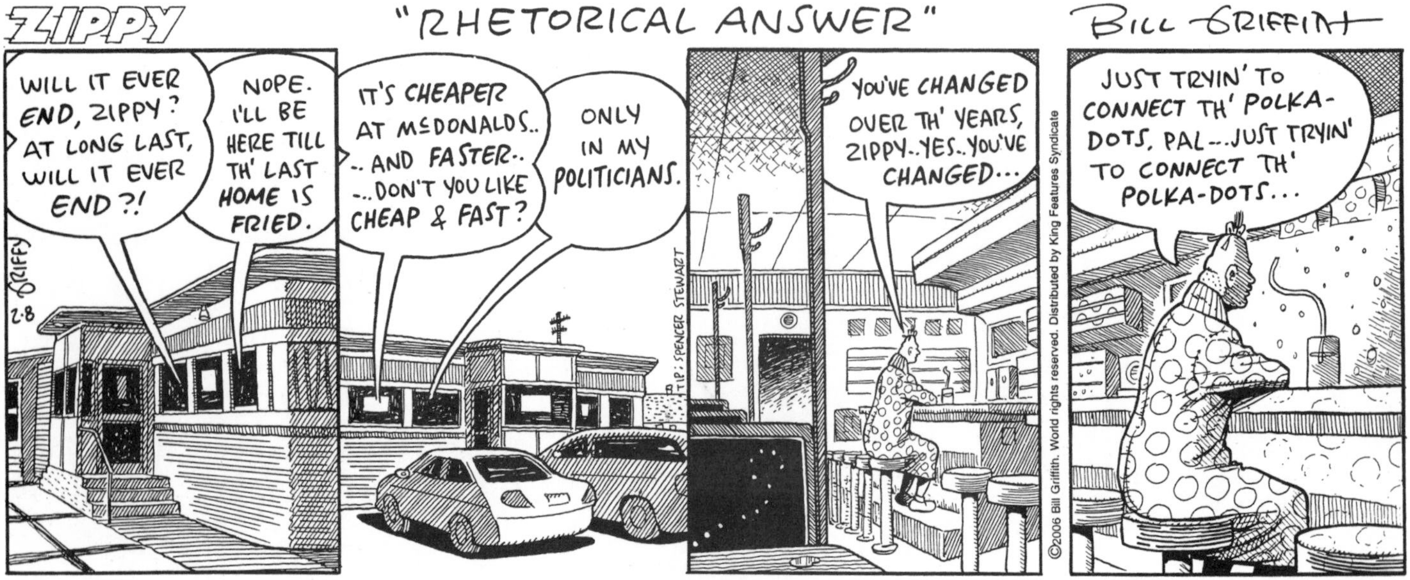
ZIPPY
"RHETORICAL ANSWER"
BILL GRIFFITH
WILL IT EVER END, ZIPPY? AT LONG LAST, WILL IT EVER END?!
NOPE. I'LL BE HERE TILL TH' LAST HOME IS FRIED.
IT'S CHEAPER AT McDONALDS.. ..AND FASTER.. ...DON'T YOU LIKE CHEAP & FAST?
ONLY IN MY POLITICIANS.
YOU'VE CHANGED OVER TH' YEARS, ZIPPY..YES..YOU'VE CHANGED...
JUST TRYIN' TO CONNECT TH' POLKA-DOTS, PAL---JUST TRYIN' TO CONNECT TH' POLKA-DOTS...
GRIFFY 2·8
TIP: SPENCER STEWART
©2006 Bill Griffith. World rights reserved. Distributed by King Features Syndicate

73

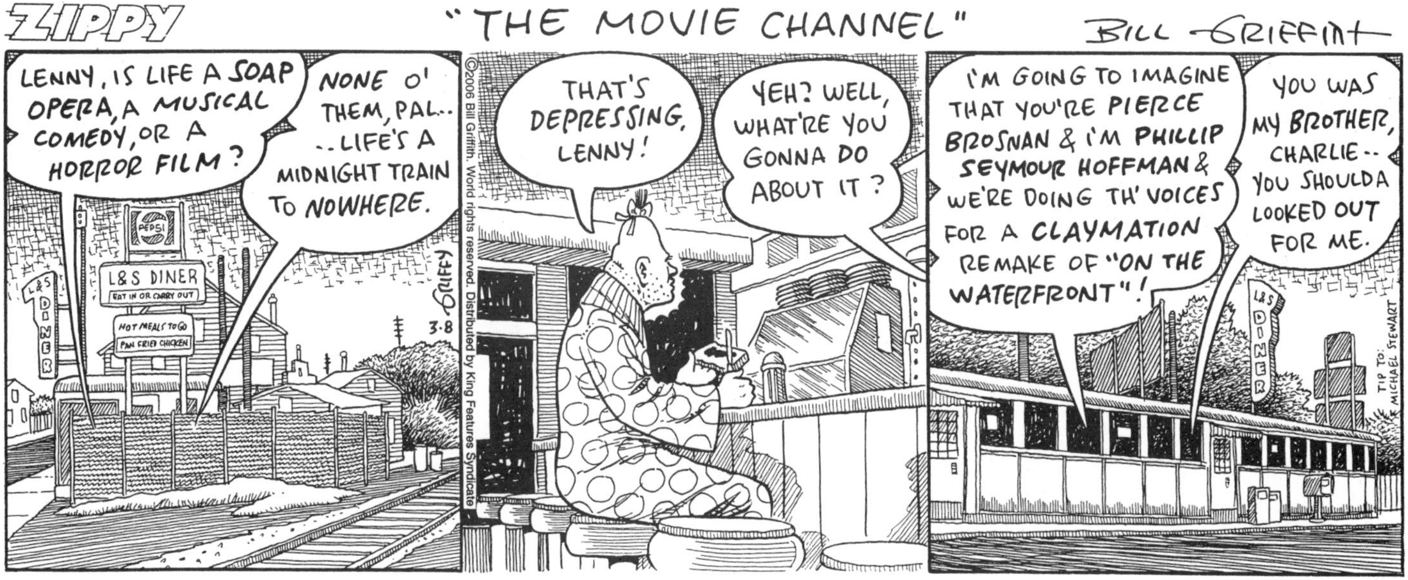
ZIPPY
"THE MOVIE CHANNEL"
BILL GRIFFITH
LENNY, IS LIFE A SOAP OPERA, A MUSICAL COMEDY, OR A HORROR FILM?
NONE O' THEM, PAL.. ..LIFE'S A MIDNIGHT TRAIN TO NOWHERE.
PEPSI
L&S DINER
EAT IN OR CARRY OUT
HOT MEALS TO GO
PAN FRIED CHICKEN
L&S DINER
GRIFFY 3·8
©2006 Bill Griffith. World rights reserved. Distributed by King Features Syndicate
THAT'S DEPRESSING, LENNY!
YEH? WELL, WHAT'RE YOU GONNA DO ABOUT IT?
I'M GOING TO IMAGINE THAT YOU'RE PIERCE BROSNAN & I'M PHILLIP SEYMOUR HOFFMAN & WE'RE DOING TH' VOICES FOR A CLAYMATION REMAKE OF "ON THE WATERFRONT"!
YOU WAS MY BROTHER, CHARLIE.. YOU SHOULDA LOOKED OUT FOR ME.
L&S DINER
TIP TO: MICHAEL STEWART

74

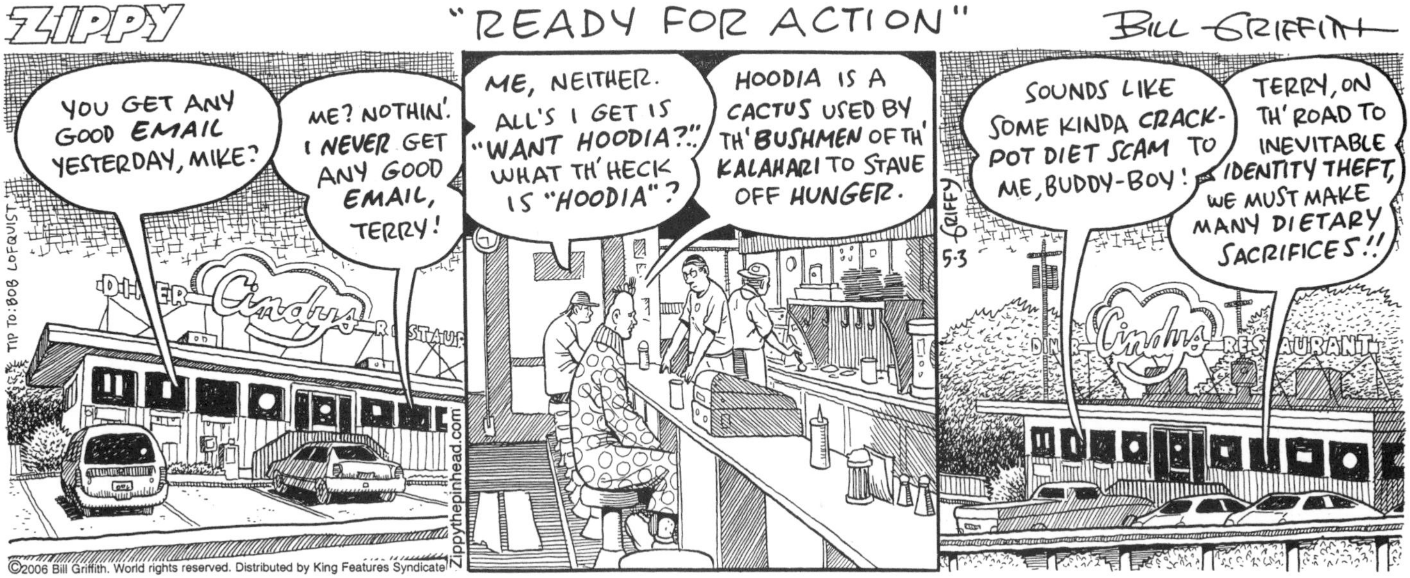
ZIPPY
"READY FOR ACTION"
BILL GRIFFITH
YOU GET ANY GOOD EMAIL YESTERDAY, MIKE?
ME? NOTHIN'. I NEVER GET ANY GOOD EMAIL, TERRY!
TIP TO: BOB LOFQUIST
Cindy's
©2006 Bill Griffith. World rights reserved. Distributed by King Features Syndicate
Zippythepinhead.com
ME, NEITHER. ALL'S I GET IS "WANT HOODIA?" WHAT TH' HECK IS "HOODIA"?
HOODIA IS A CACTUS USED BY TH' BUSHMEN OF TH' KALAHARI TO STAVE OFF HUNGER.
GRIFFY 5·3
SOUNDS LIKE SOME KINDA CRACK-POT DIET SCAM TO ME, BUDDY-BOY!
TERRY, ON TH' ROAD TO INEVITABLE IDENTITY THEFT, WE MUST MAKE MANY DIETARY SACRIFICES!!
DINER Cindy's RESTAURANT

75

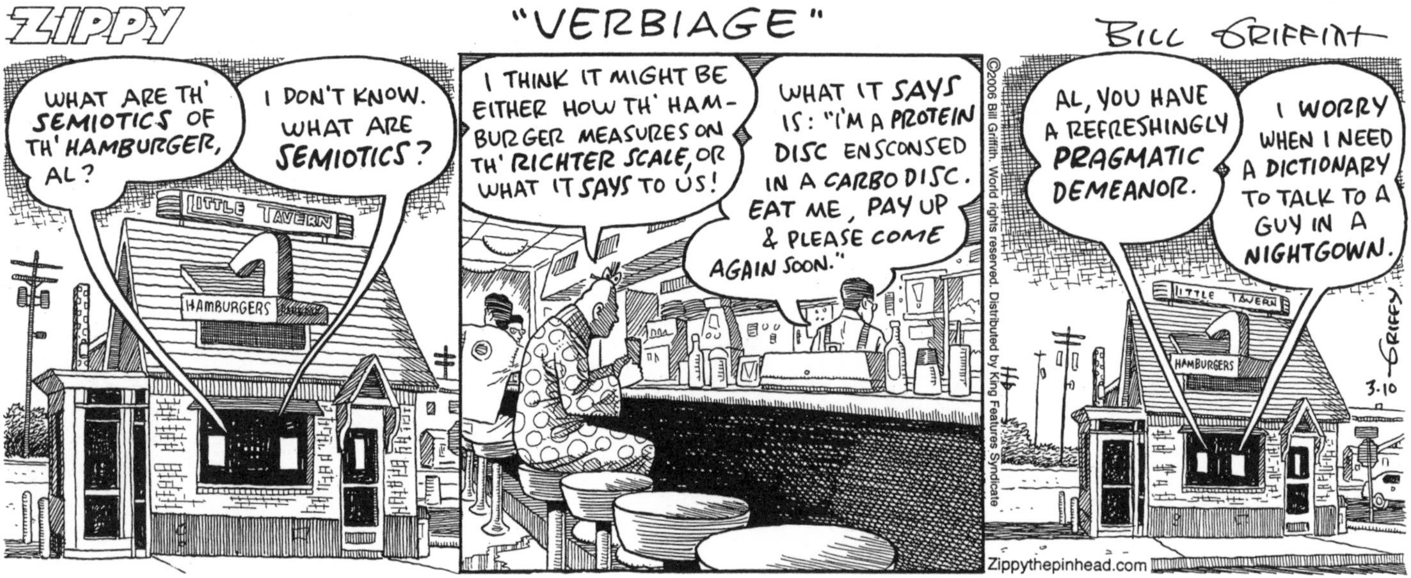
ZIPPY
"VERBIAGE"
BILL GRIFFITH
WHAT ARE TH' SEMIOTICS OF TH' HAMBURGER, AL?
I DON'T KNOW. WHAT ARE SEMIOTICS?
LITTLE TAVERN
HAMBURGERS
I THINK IT MIGHT BE EITHER HOW TH' HAMBURGER MEASURES ON TH' RICHTER SCALE, OR WHAT IT SAYS TO US!
WHAT IT SAYS IS: "I'M A PROTEIN DISC ENSCONSED IN A CARBO DISC. EAT ME, PAY UP & PLEASE COME AGAIN SOON."
©2006 Bill Griffith. World rights reserved. Distributed by King Features Syndicate
AL, YOU HAVE A REFRESHINGLY PRAGMATIC DEMEANOR.
I WORRY WHEN I NEED A DICTIONARY TO TALK TO A GUY IN A NIGHTGOWN.
LITTLE TAVERN
HAMBURGERS
GRIFFY
3.10
Zippythepinhead.com

76

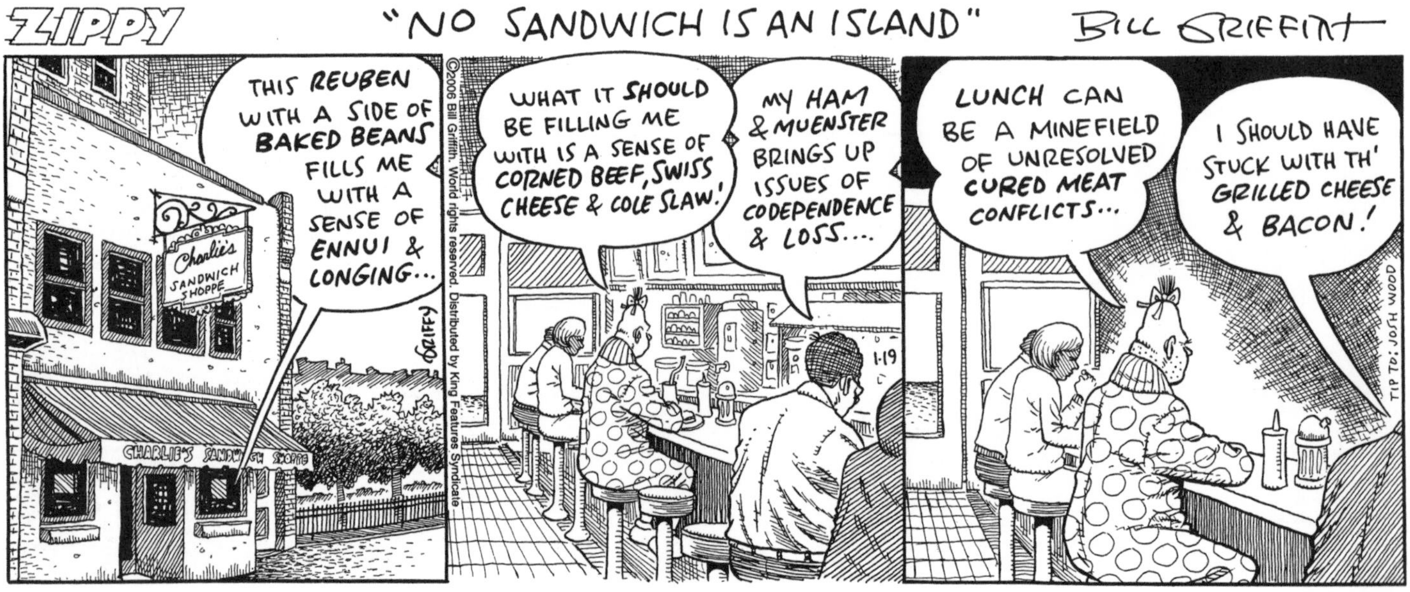
ZIPPY
"NO SANDWICH IS AN ISLAND"
BILL GRIFFITH
THIS REUBEN WITH A SIDE OF BAKED BEANS FILLS ME WITH A SENSE OF ENNUI & LONGING...
Charlie's SANDWICH SHOPPE
CHARLIE'S SANDWICH SHOPPE
GRIFFY
©2006 Bill Griffith. World rights reserved. Distributed by King Features Syndicate
WHAT IT SHOULD BE FILLING ME WITH IS A SENSE OF CORNED BEEF, SWISS CHEESE & COLE SLAW!
MY HAM & MUENSTER BRINGS UP ISSUES OF CODEPENDENCE & LOSS....
1.19
LUNCH CAN BE A MINEFIELD OF UNRESOLVED CURED MEAT CONFLICTS...
I SHOULD HAVE STUCK WITH TH' GRILLED CHEESE & BACON!
TIP TO: JOSH WOOD

77

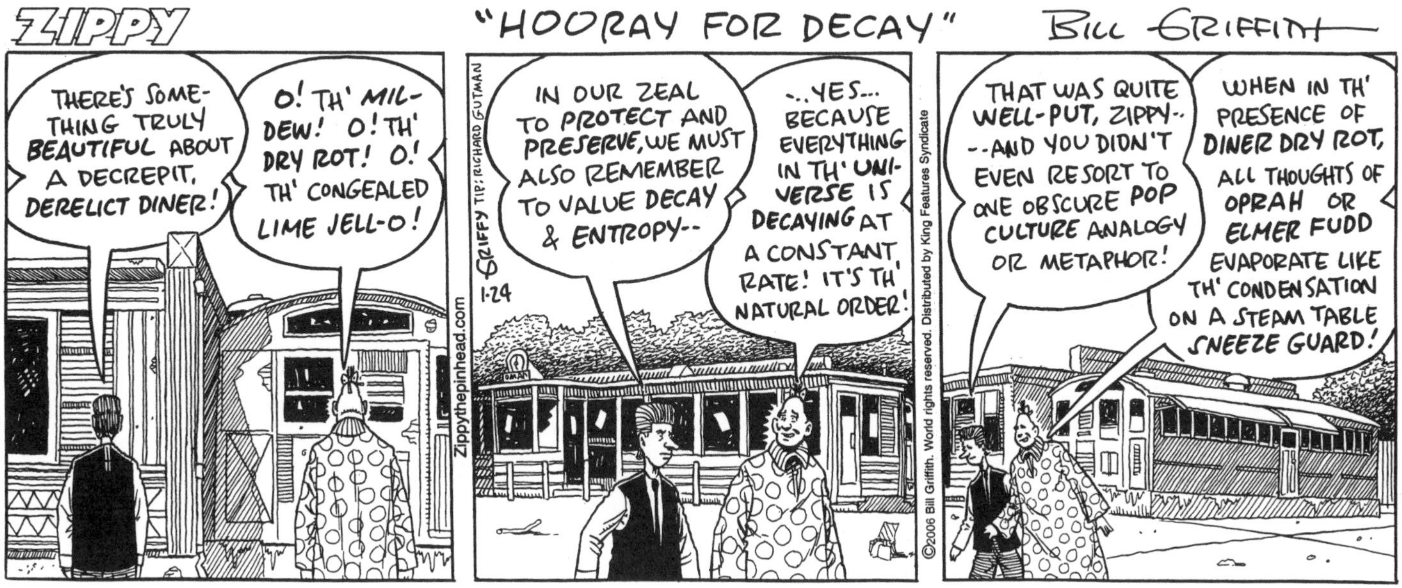
ZIPPY
"HOORAY FOR DECAY"
BILL GRIFFITH
THERE'S SOMETHING TRULY BEAUTIFUL ABOUT A DECREPIT, DERELICT DINER!
O! TH' MILDEW! O! TH' DRY ROT! O! TH' CONGEALED LIME JELL-O!
GRIFFY TIP: RICHARD GUTMAN 1-24
Zippythepinhead.com
IN OUR ZEAL TO PROTECT AND PRESERVE, WE MUST ALSO REMEMBER TO VALUE DECAY & ENTROPY--
--..YES... BECAUSE EVERYTHING IN TH' UNIVERSE IS DECAYING AT A CONSTANT RATE! IT'S TH' NATURAL ORDER!
©2006 Bill Griffith. World rights reserved. Distributed by King Features Syndicate
THAT WAS QUITE WELL-PUT, ZIPPY.. --AND YOU DIDN'T EVEN RESORT TO ONE OBSCURE POP CULTURE ANALOGY OR METAPHOR!
WHEN IN TH' PRESENCE OF DINER DRY ROT, ALL THOUGHTS OF OPRAH OR ELMER FUDD EVAPORATE LIKE TH' CONDENSATION ON A STEAM TABLE SNEEZE GUARD!

78

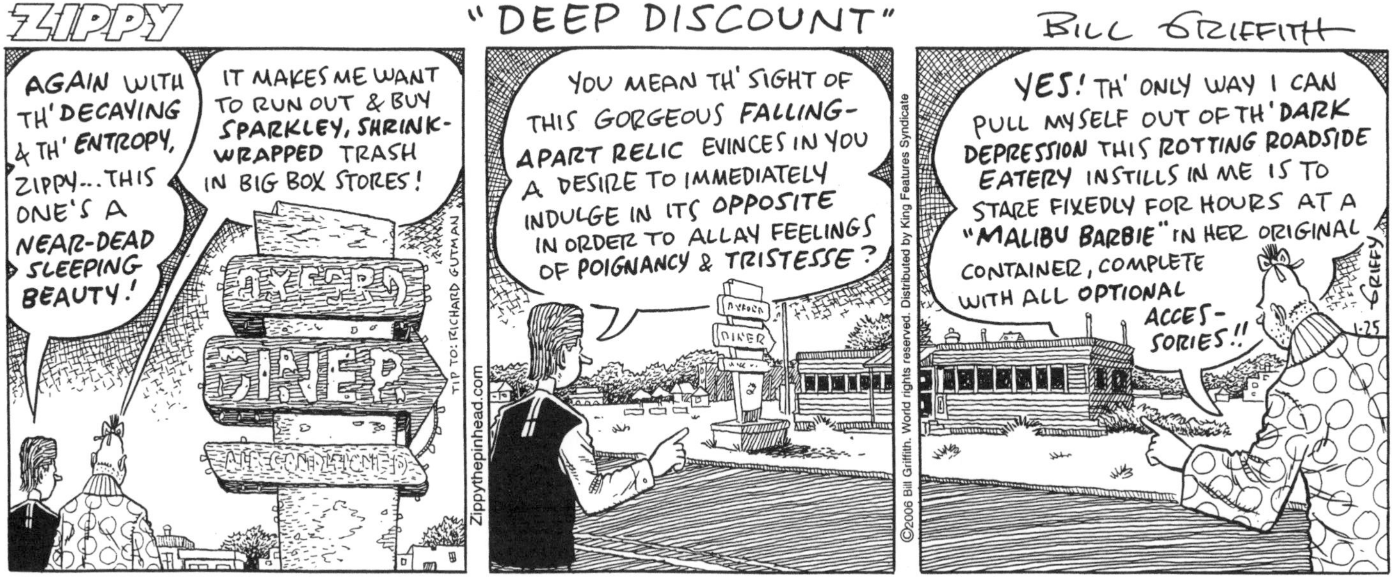
ZIPPY
"DEEP DISCOUNT"
BILL GRIFFITH
AGAIN WITH TH' DECAYING & TH' ENTROPY, ZIPPY... THIS ONE'S A NEAR-DEAD SLEEPING BEAUTY!
IT MAKES ME WANT TO RUN OUT & BUY SPARKLEY, SHRINK-WRAPPED TRASH IN BIG BOX STORES!
TIP TO: RICHARD GUTMAN
Zippythepinhead.com
YOU MEAN TH' SIGHT OF THIS GORGEOUS FALLING-APART RELIC EVINCES IN YOU A DESIRE TO IMMEDIATELY INDULGE IN ITS OPPOSITE IN ORDER TO ALLAY FEELINGS OF POIGNANCY & TRISTESSE?
©2006 Bill Griffith. World rights reserved. Distributed by King Features Syndicate
YES! TH' ONLY WAY I CAN PULL MYSELF OUT OF TH' DARK DEPRESSION THIS ROTTING ROADSIDE EATERY INSTILLS IN ME IS TO STARE FIXEDLY FOR HOURS AT A "MALIBU BARBIE" IN HER ORIGINAL CONTAINER, COMPLETE WITH ALL OPTIONAL ACCESSORIES!!
GRIFFY 1-25

79

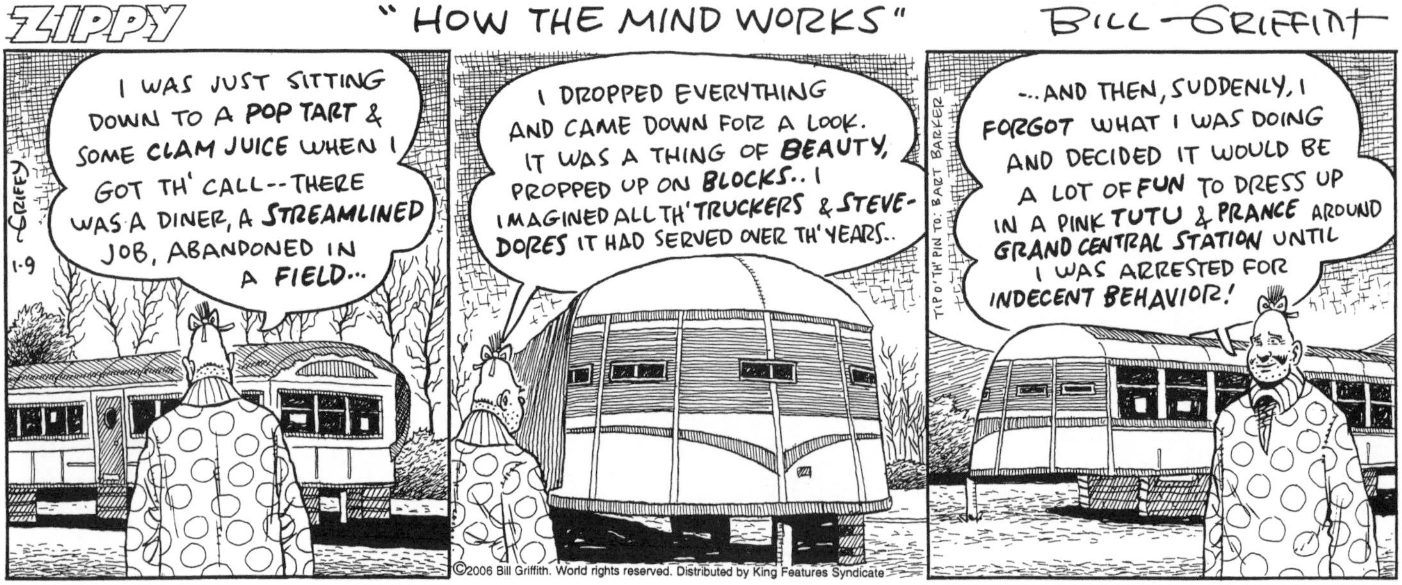
ZIPPY
"HOW THE MIND WORKS"
BILL GRIFFITH
I WAS JUST SITTING DOWN TO A POP TART & SOME CLAM JUICE WHEN I GOT TH' CALL--THERE WAS A DINER, A STREAMLINED JOB, ABANDONED IN A FIELD...
I DROPPED EVERYTHING AND CAME DOWN FOR A LOOK. IT WAS A THING OF BEAUTY, PROPPED UP ON BLOCKS.. I IMAGINED ALL TH' TRUCKERS & STEVEDORES IT HAD SERVED OVER TH' YEARS..
TIP O' TH' PIN TO: BART BARKER
--AND THEN, SUDDENLY, I FORGOT WHAT I WAS DOING AND DECIDED IT WOULD BE A LOT OF FUN TO DRESS UP IN A PINK TUTU & PRANCE AROUND GRAND CENTRAL STATION UNTIL I WAS ARRESTED FOR INDECENT BEHAVIOR!
GRIFFY 1-9
©2006 Bill Griffith. World rights reserved. Distributed by King Features Syndicate

80

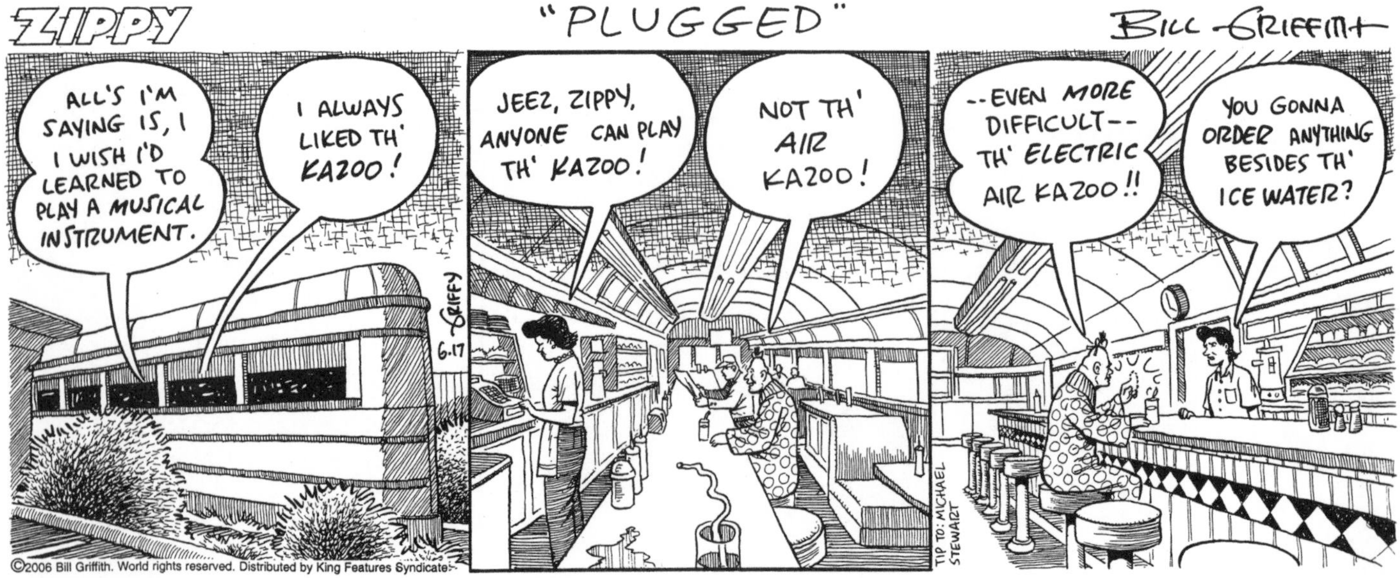
ZIPPY
"PLUGGED"
BILL GRIFFITH
ALL'S I'M SAYING IS, I WISH I'D LEARNED TO PLAY A MUSICAL INSTRUMENT.
I ALWAYS LIKED TH' KAZOO!
GRIFFY 6-17
JEEZ, ZIPPY, ANYONE CAN PLAY TH' KAZOO!
NOT TH' AIR KAZOO!
TIP TO: MICHAEL STEWART
--EVEN MORE DIFFICULT-- TH' ELECTRIC AIR KAZOO!!
YOU GONNA ORDER ANYTHING BESIDES TH' ICE WATER?
©2006 Bill Griffith. World rights reserved. Distributed by King Features Syndicate

81

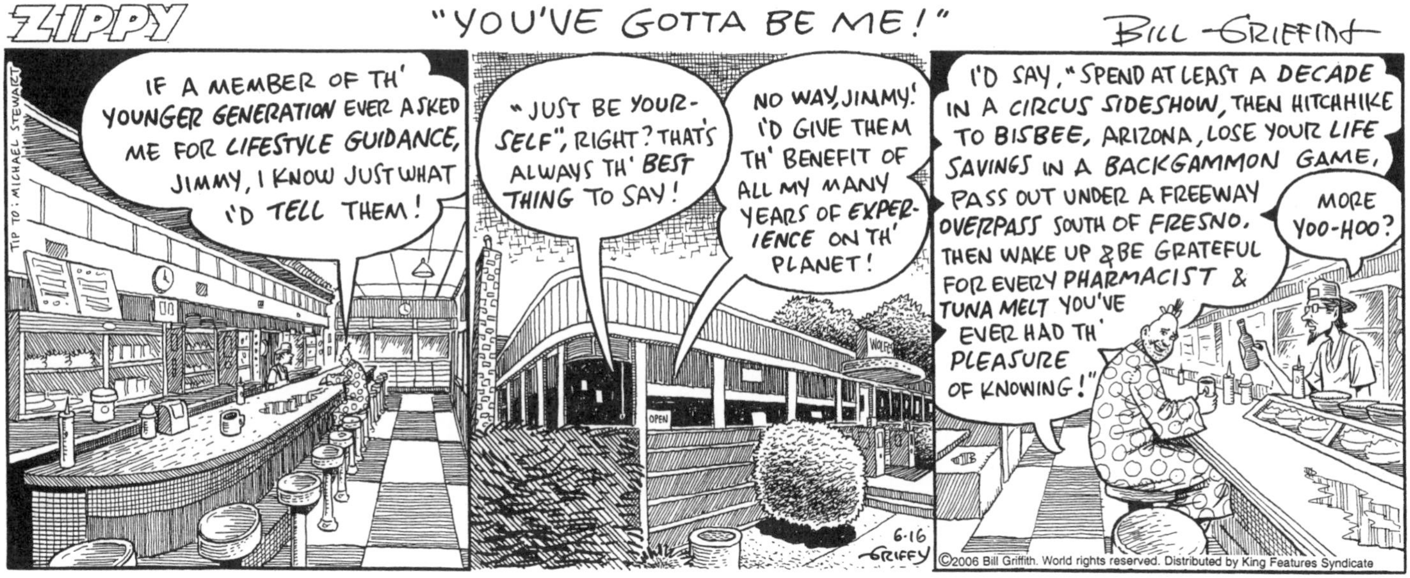
ZIPPY
"YOU'VE GOTTA BE ME!"
BILL GRIFFITH
TIP TO: MICHAEL STEWART
IF A MEMBER OF TH' YOUNGER GENERATION EVER ASKED ME FOR LIFESTYLE GUIDANCE, JIMMY, I KNOW JUST WHAT I'D TELL THEM!
"JUST BE YOURSELF", RIGHT? THAT'S ALWAYS TH' BEST THING TO SAY!
NO WAY, JIMMY! I'D GIVE THEM TH' BENEFIT OF ALL MY MANY YEARS OF EXPERIENCE ON TH' PLANET!
OPEN
6.16
GRIFFY
I'D SAY, "SPEND AT LEAST A DECADE IN A CIRCUS SIDESHOW, THEN HITCHHIKE TO BISBEE, ARIZONA, LOSE YOUR LIFE SAVINGS IN A BACKGAMMON GAME, PASS OUT UNDER A FREEWAY OVERPASS SOUTH OF FRESNO, THEN WAKE UP & BE GRATEFUL FOR EVERY PHARMACIST & TUNA MELT YOU'VE EVER HAD TH' PLEASURE OF KNOWING!"
MORE YOO-HOO?
©2006 Bill Griffith. World rights reserved. Distributed by King Features Syndicate

82

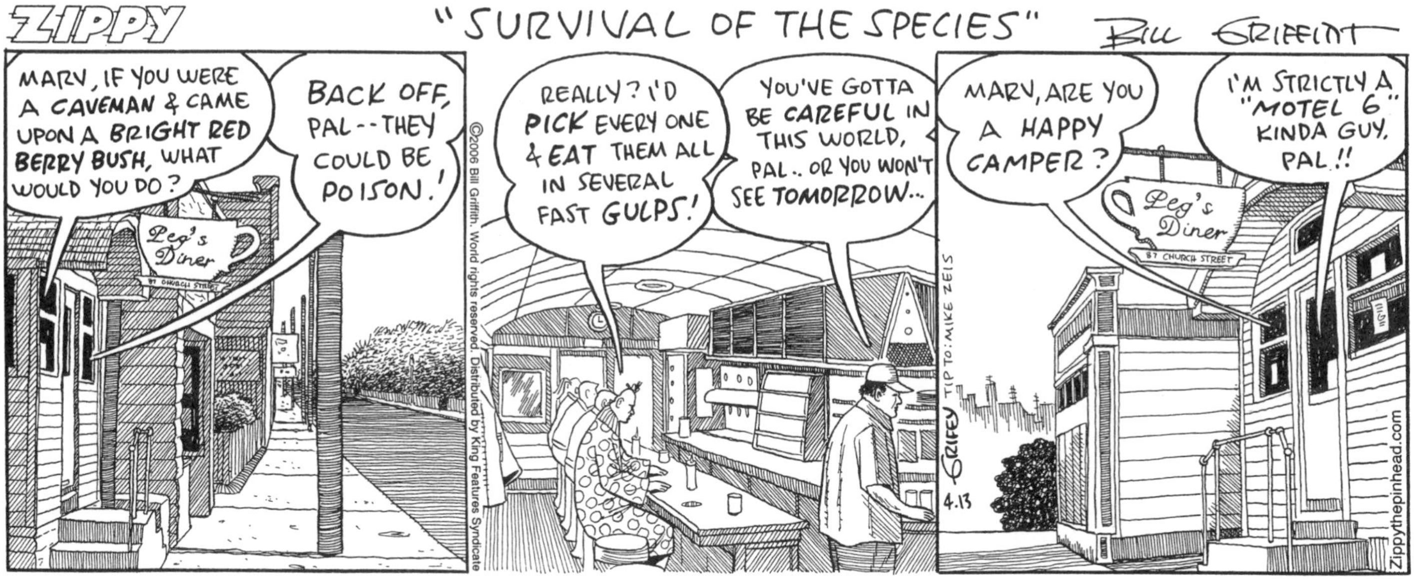
ZIPPY
"SURVIVAL OF THE SPECIES"
BILL GRIFFITH
MARV, IF YOU WERE A CAVEMAN & CAME UPON A BRIGHT RED BERRY BUSH, WHAT WOULD YOU DO?
BACK OFF, PAL--THEY COULD BE POISON!
Peg's Diner
©2006 Bill Griffith. World rights reserved. Distributed by King Features Syndicate
REALLY? I'D PICK EVERY ONE & EAT THEM ALL IN SEVERAL FAST GULPS!
YOU'VE GOTTA BE CAREFUL IN THIS WORLD, PAL.. OR YOU WON'T SEE TOMORROW...
TIP TO: MIKE ZEIS
GRIFFY
4.13
MARV, ARE YOU A HAPPY CAMPER?
Peg's Diner
87 CHURCH STREET
I'M STRICTLY A "MOTEL 6" KINDA GUY, PAL!!
Zippythepinhead.com

83

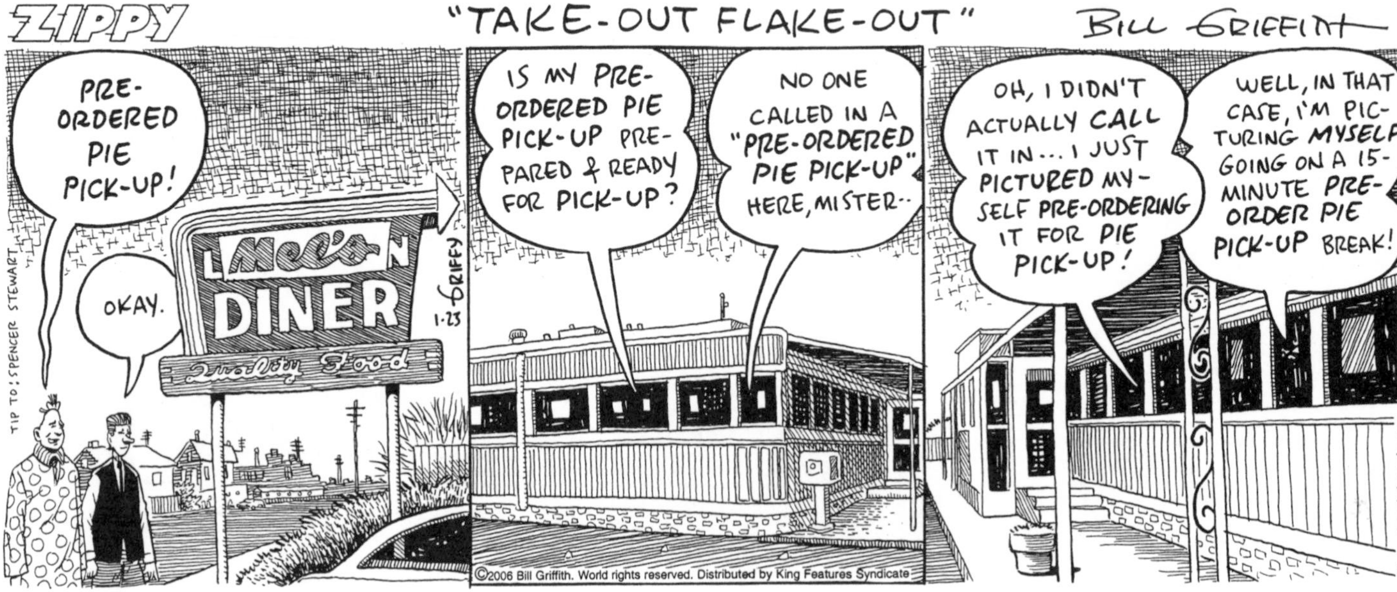
ZIPPY
"TAKE-OUT FLAKE-OUT"
BILL GRIFFITH
PRE-ORDERED PIE PICK-UP!
OKAY.
TIP TO: SPENCER STEWART
Mel's DINER
Quality Food
GRIFFY 1-23
IS MY PRE-ORDERED PIE PICK-UP PRE-PARED & READY FOR PICK-UP?
NO ONE CALLED IN A "PRE-ORDERED PIE PICK-UP" HERE, MISTER..
OH, I DIDN'T ACTUALLY CALL IT IN... I JUST PICTURED MY-SELF PRE-ORDERING IT FOR PIE PICK-UP!
WELL, IN THAT CASE, I'M PIC-TURING MYSELF GOING ON A 15-MINUTE PRE-ORDER PIE PICK-UP BREAK!
©2006 Bill Griffith. World rights reserved. Distributed by King Features Syndicate
Zippythepinhead.com

84

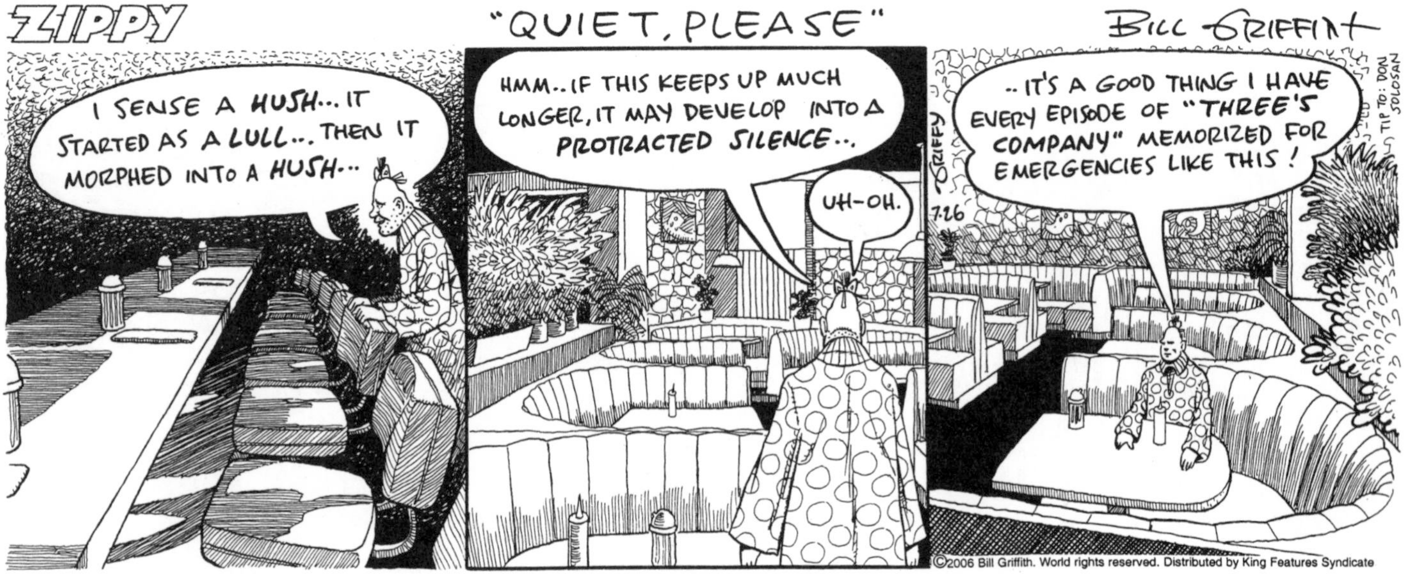
ZIPPY
"QUIET, PLEASE"
BILL GRIFFITH
I SENSE A HUSH... IT STARTED AS A LULL... THEN IT MORPHED INTO A HUSH...
HMM..IF THIS KEEPS UP MUCH LONGER, IT MAY DEVELOP INTO A PROTRACTED SILENCE...
UH-OH.
GRIFFY 7-26
..IT'S A GOOD THING I HAVE EVERY EPISODE OF "THREE'S COMPANY" MEMORIZED FOR EMERGENCIES LIKE THIS!
TIP TO: DON SOLOSAN
©2006 Bill Griffith. World rights reserved. Distributed by King Features Syndicate

85

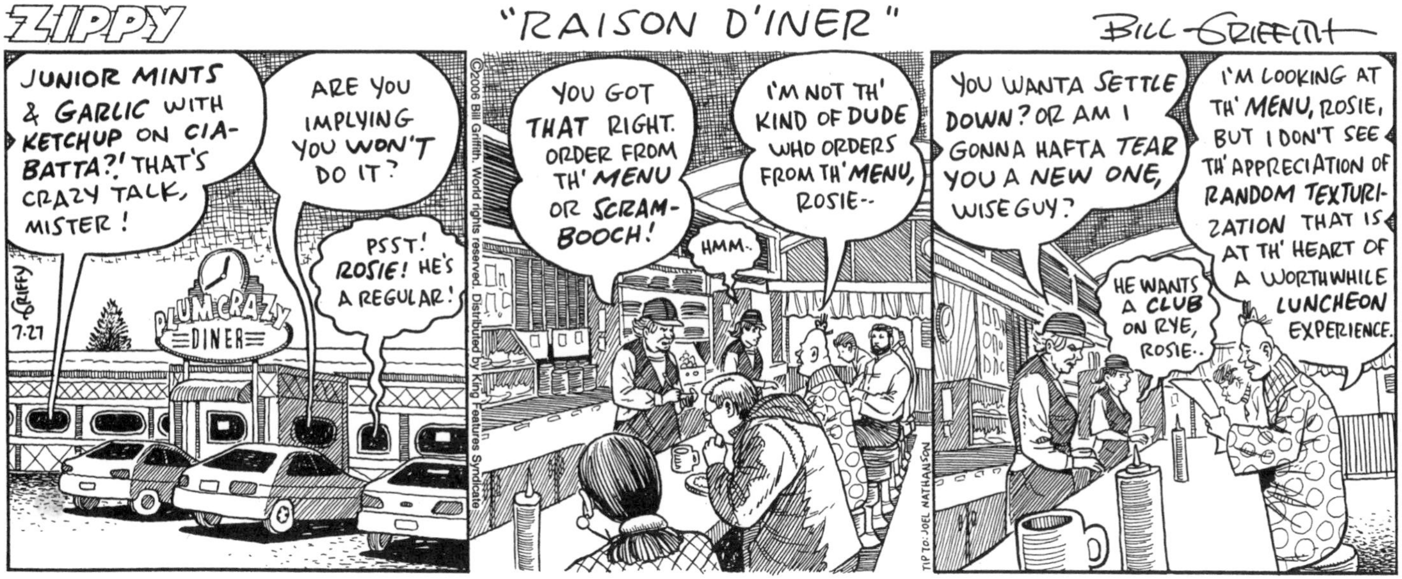
ZIPPY
"RAISON D'INER"
BILL GRIFFITH
JUNIOR MINTS & GARLIC WITH KETCHUP ON CIABATTA?! THAT'S CRAZY TALK, MISTER!
ARE YOU IMPLYING YOU WON'T DO IT?
PSST! ROSIE! HE'S A REGULAR!
PLUM CRAZY DINER
GRIFFY 7-27
©2006 Bill Griffith. World rights reserved. Distributed by King Features Syndicate
YOU GOT THAT RIGHT. ORDER FROM TH' MENU OR SCRAM-BOOCH!
HMM..
I'M NOT TH' KIND OF DUDE WHO ORDERS FROM TH' MENU, ROSIE--
TIP TO: JOEL NATHANSON
YOU WANTA SETTLE DOWN? OR AM I GONNA HAFTA TEAR YOU A NEW ONE, WISE GUY?
HE WANTS A CLUB ON RYE, ROSIE..
I'M LOOKING AT TH' MENU, ROSIE, BUT I DON'T SEE TH' APPRECIATION OF RANDOM TEXTURIZATION THAT IS AT TH' HEART OF A WORTHWHILE LUNCHEON EXPERIENCE.

86

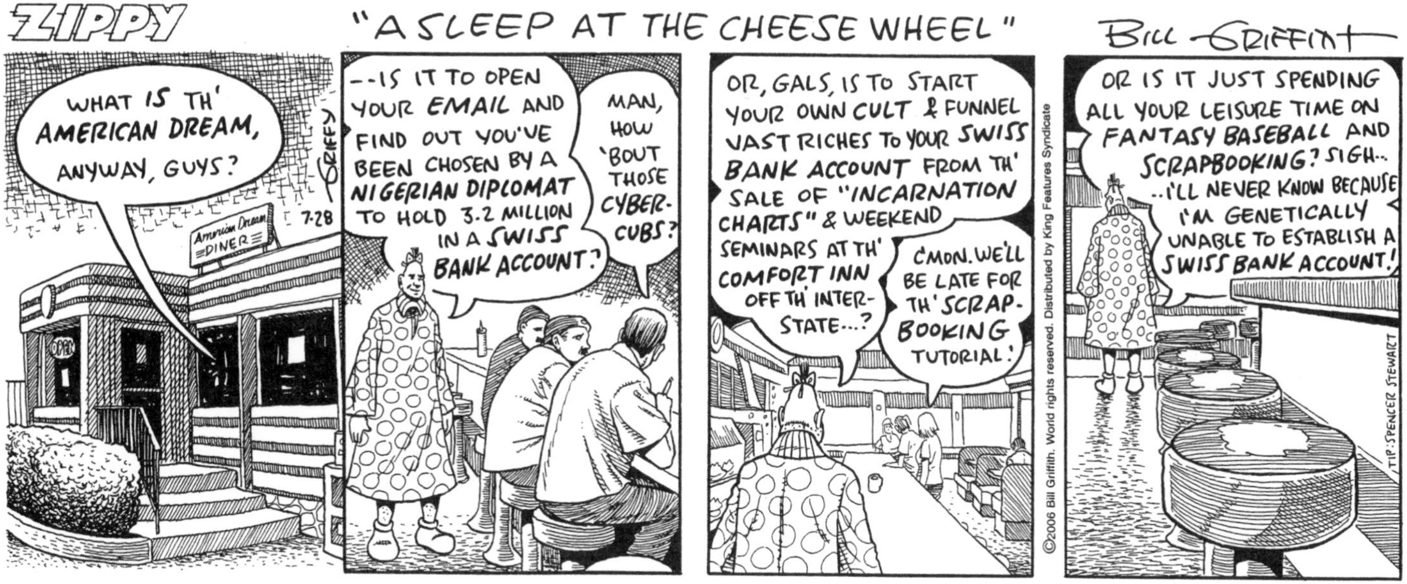
ZIPPY
"A SLEEP AT THE CHEESE WHEEL"
BILL GRIFFITH
WHAT IS TH' AMERICAN DREAM, ANYWAY, GUYS?
GRIFFY 7-28
American Dream DINER
OPEN
--IS IT TO OPEN YOUR EMAIL AND FIND OUT YOU'VE BEEN CHOSEN BY A NIGERIAN DIPLOMAT TO HOLD 3.2 MILLION IN A SWISS BANK ACCOUNT?
MAN, HOW 'BOUT THOSE CYBER-CUBS?
OR, GALS, IS TO START YOUR OWN CULT & FUNNEL VAST RICHES TO YOUR SWISS BANK ACCOUNT FROM TH' SALE OF "INCARNATION CHARTS" & WEEKEND SEMINARS AT TH' COMFORT INN OFF TH' INTERSTATE...?
C'MON. WE'LL BE LATE FOR TH' SCRAPBOOKING TUTORIAL!
©2006 Bill Griffith. World rights reserved. Distributed by King Features Syndicate
OR IS IT JUST SPENDING ALL YOUR LEISURE TIME ON FANTASY BASEBALL AND SCRAPBOOKING? SIGH.. ..I'LL NEVER KNOW BECAUSE I'M GENETICALLY UNABLE TO ESTABLISH A SWISS BANK ACCOUNT!
TIP: SPENCER STEWART

87

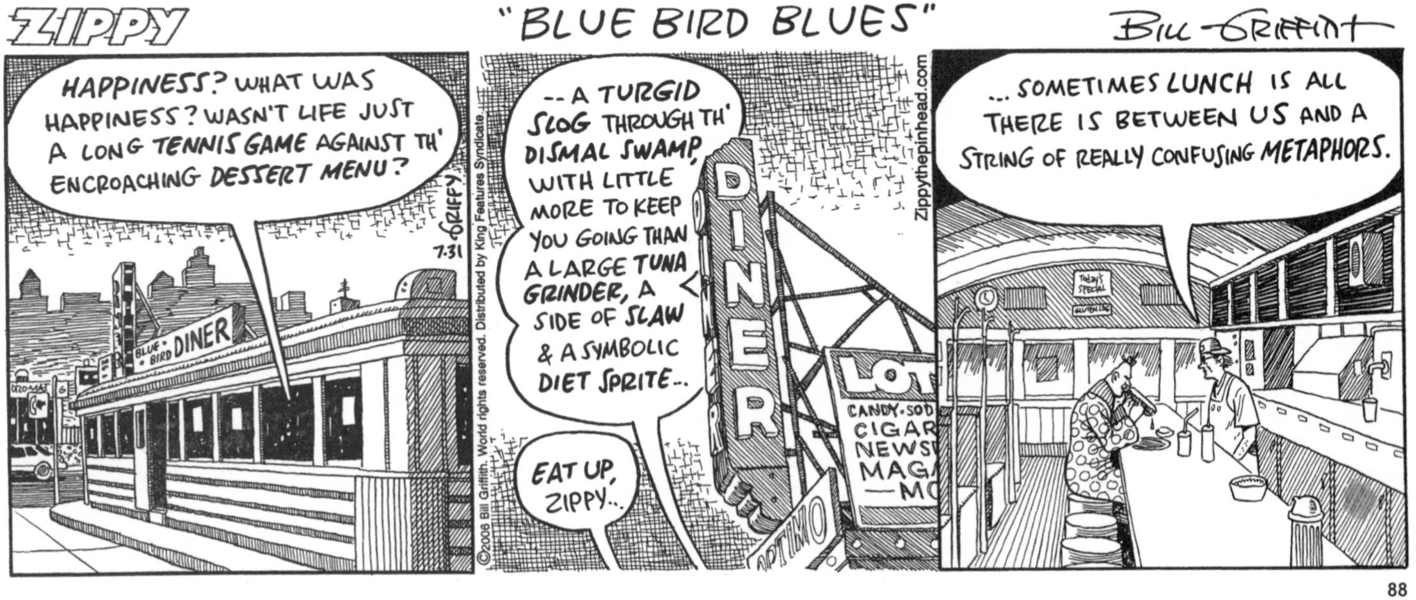
ZIPPY
"BLUE BIRD BLUES"
BILL GRIFFITH
HAPPINESS? WHAT WAS HAPPINESS? WASN'T LIFE JUST A LONG TENNIS GAME AGAINST TH' ENCROACHING DESSERT MENU?
GRIFFY 7-31
BLUE BIRD DINER
©2006 Bill Griffith. World rights reserved. Distributed by King Features Syndicate.
Zippythepinhead.com
--A TURGID SLOG THROUGH TH' DISMAL SWAMP, WITH LITTLE MORE TO KEEP YOU GOING THAN A LARGE TUNA GRINDER, A SIDE OF SLAW & A SYMBOLIC DIET SPRITE..
EAT UP, ZIPPY..
DINER
CANDY. SOD CIGAR NEWS MAGA —MO
OPTIMO
...SOMETIMES LUNCH IS ALL THERE IS BETWEEN US AND A STRING OF REALLY CONFUSING METAPHORS.
88

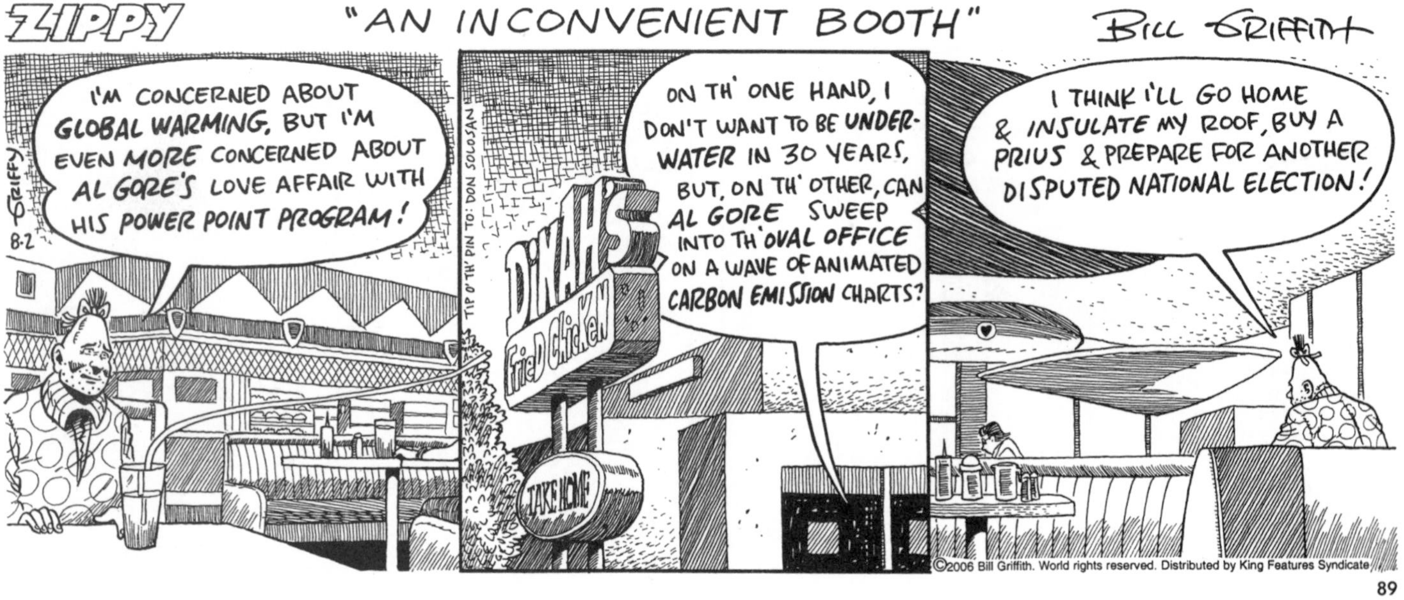
ZIPPY
"AN INCONVENIENT BOOTH"
BILL GRIFFITH
I'M CONCERNED ABOUT GLOBAL WARMING, BUT I'M EVEN MORE CONCERNED ABOUT AL GORE'S LOVE AFFAIR WITH HIS POWER POINT PROGRAM!
GRIFFY 8-2
TIP O' TH' PIN TO: DON SOLOSAN
ON TH' ONE HAND, I DON'T WANT TO BE UNDER-WATER IN 30 YEARS, BUT, ON TH' OTHER, CAN AL GORE SWEEP INTO TH' OVAL OFFICE ON A WAVE OF ANIMATED CARBON EMISSION CHARTS?
DINAH'S Fried Chicken
TAKE HOME
I THINK I'LL GO HOME & INSULATE MY ROOF, BUY A PRIUS & PREPARE FOR ANOTHER DISPUTED NATIONAL ELECTION!
©2006 Bill Griffith. World rights reserved. Distributed by King Features Syndicate
89

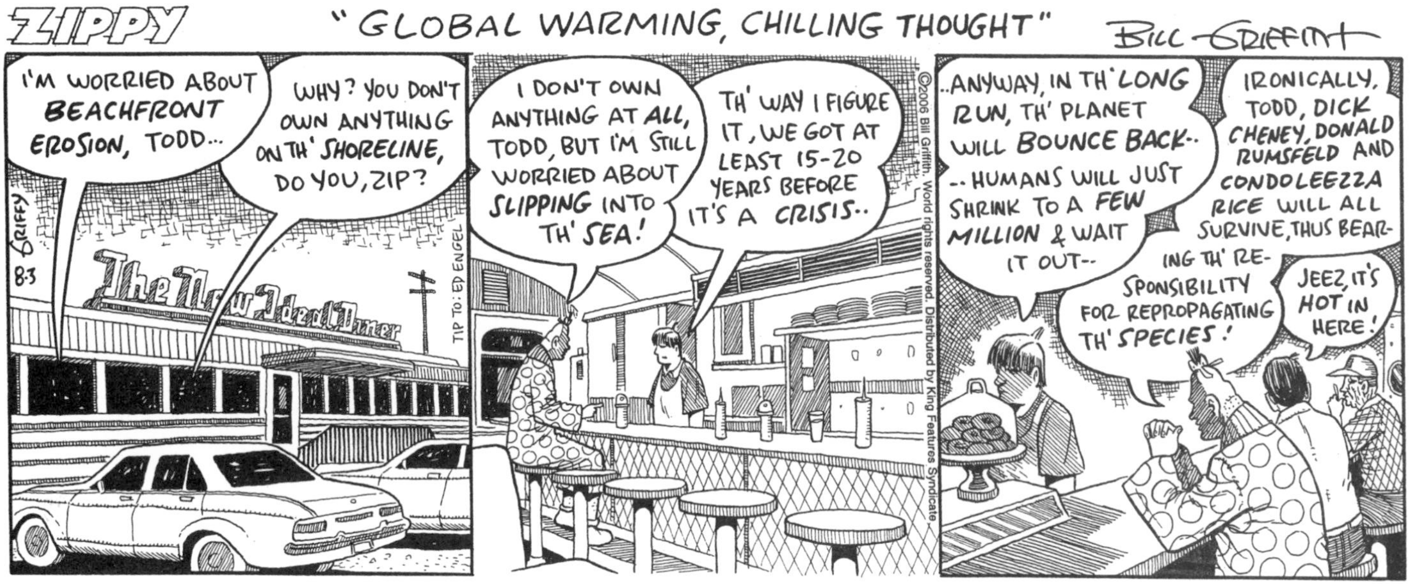
ZIPPY
"GLOBAL WARMING, CHILLING THOUGHT"
BILL GRIFFITH
I'M WORRIED ABOUT BEACHFRONT EROSION, TODD...
WHY? YOU DON'T OWN ANYTHING ON TH' SHORELINE, DO YOU, ZIP?
GRIFFY 8-3
The New Ideal Diner
TIP TO: ED ENGEL
I DON'T OWN ANYTHING AT ALL, TODD, BUT I'M STILL WORRIED ABOUT SLIPPING INTO TH' SEA!
TH' WAY I FIGURE IT, WE GOT AT LEAST 15-20 YEARS BEFORE IT'S A CRISIS..
©2006 Bill Griffith. World rights reserved. Distributed by King Features Syndicate
..ANYWAY, IN TH' LONG RUN, TH' PLANET WILL BOUNCE BACK.. -- HUMANS WILL JUST SHRINK TO A FEW MILLION & WAIT IT OUT--
IRONICALLY, TODD, DICK CHENEY, DONALD RUMSFELD AND CONDOLEEZZA RICE WILL ALL SURVIVE, THUS BEARING TH' RESPONSIBILITY FOR REPROPAGATING TH' SPECIES!
JEEZ, IT'S HOT IN HERE!

90

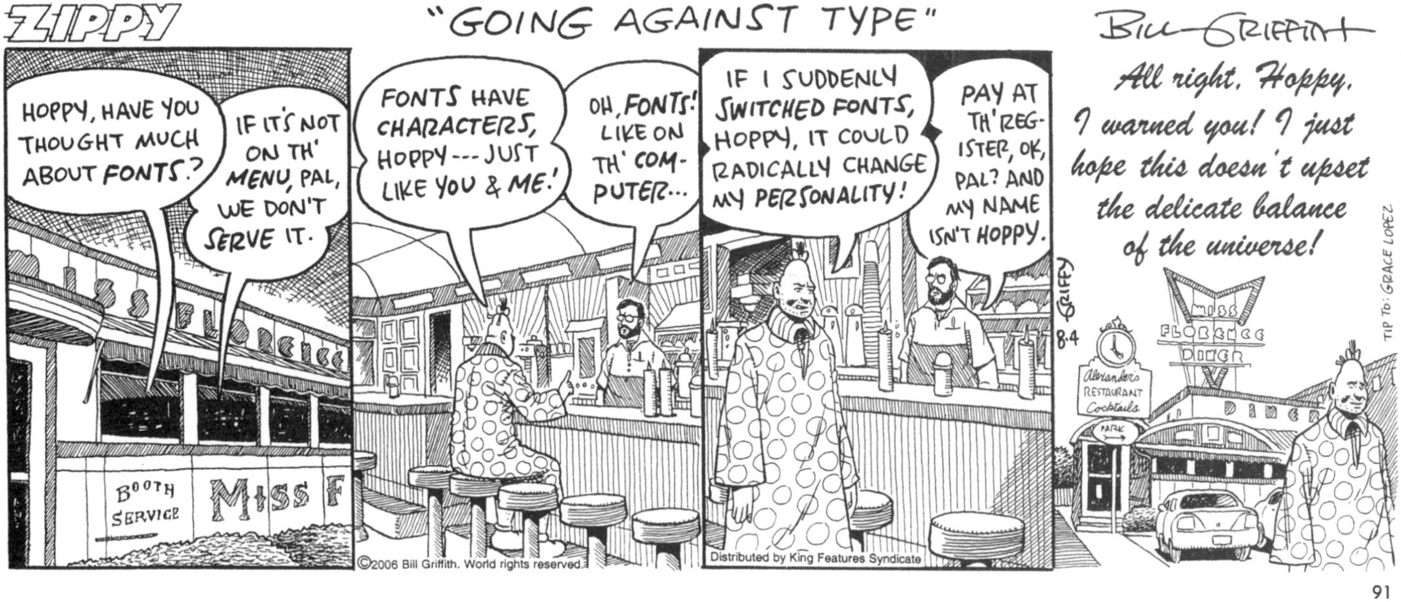
ZIPPY
"GOING AGAINST TYPE"
BILL GRIFFITH
HOPPY, HAVE YOU THOUGHT MUCH ABOUT FONTS?
IF IT'S NOT ON TH' MENU, PAL, WE DON'T SERVE IT.
BOOTH SERVICE
MISS F
FONTS HAVE CHARACTERS, HOPPY--- JUST LIKE YOU & ME!
OH, FONTS! LIKE ON TH' COMPUTER...
©2006 Bill Griffith. World rights reserved.
IF I SUDDENLY SWITCHED FONTS, HOPPY, IT COULD RADICALLY CHANGE MY PERSONALITY!
PAY AT TH' REGISTER, OK, PAL? AND MY NAME ISN'T HOPPY.
Distributed by King Features Syndicate
GRIFFY 8-4
All right, Hoppy, I warned you! I just hope this doesn't upset the delicate balance of the universe!
TIP TO: GRACE LOPEZ
Alexander's RESTAURANT Cocktails
PARK
MISS FLORENCE DINER

91

Sunday Color & More

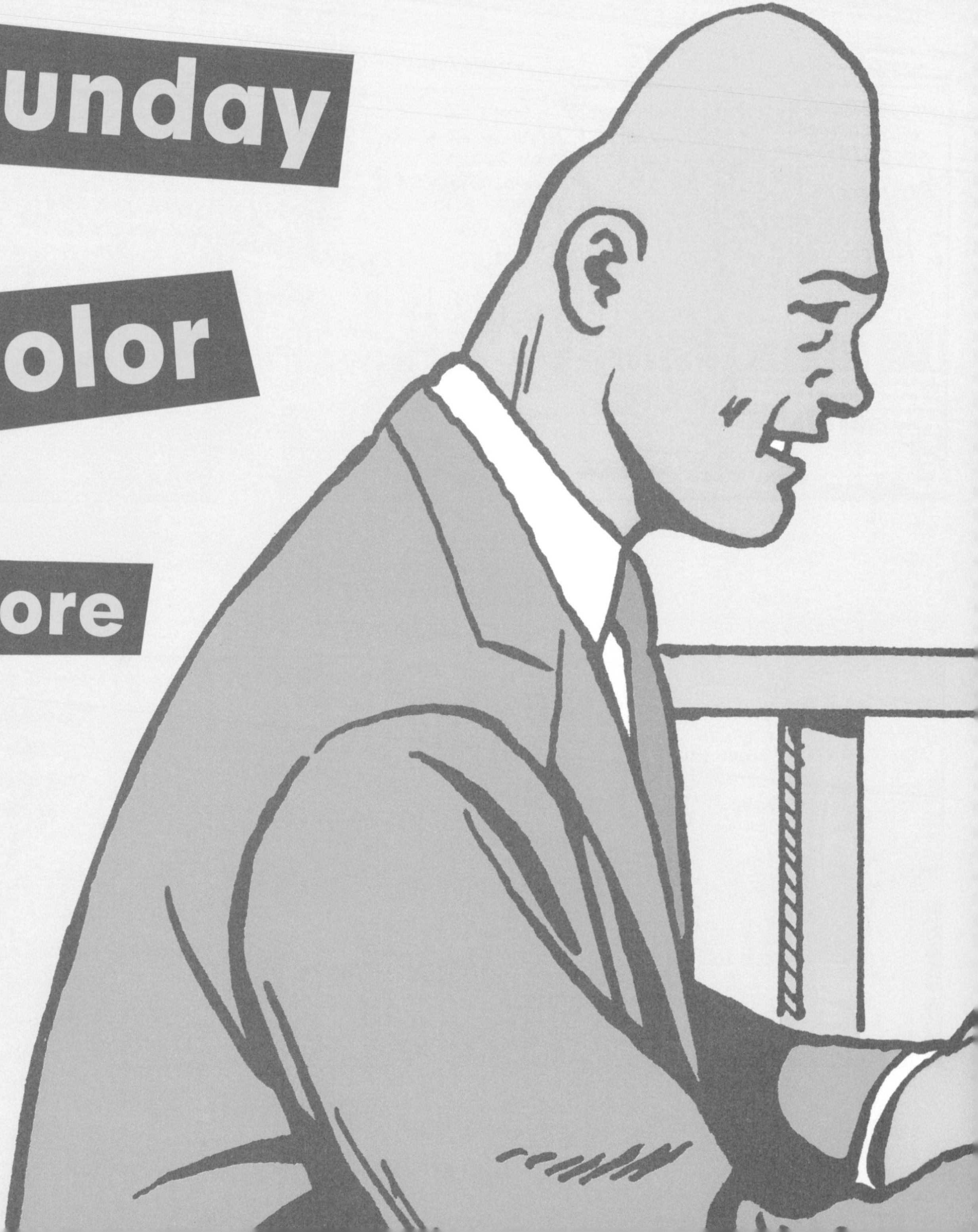

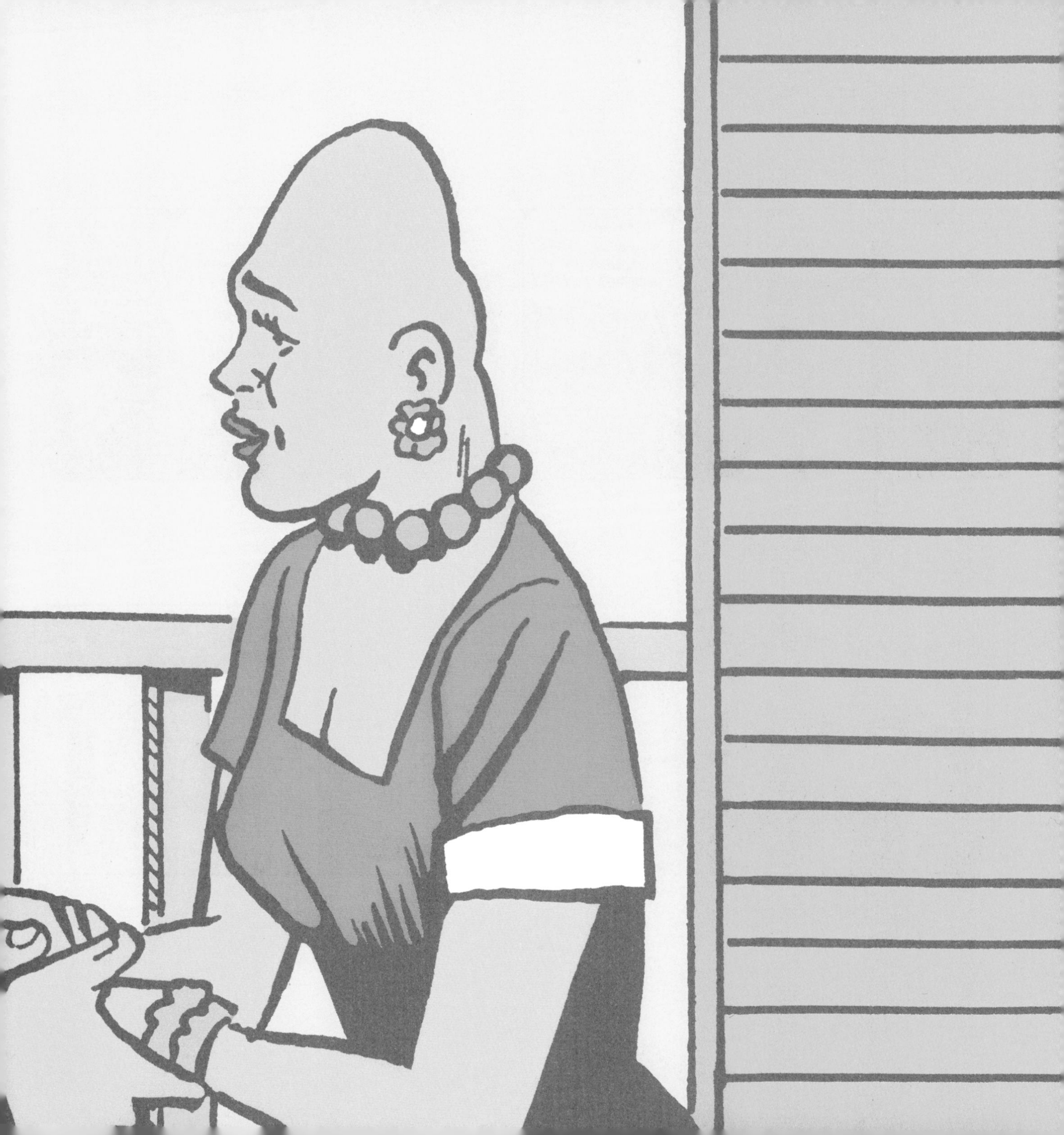

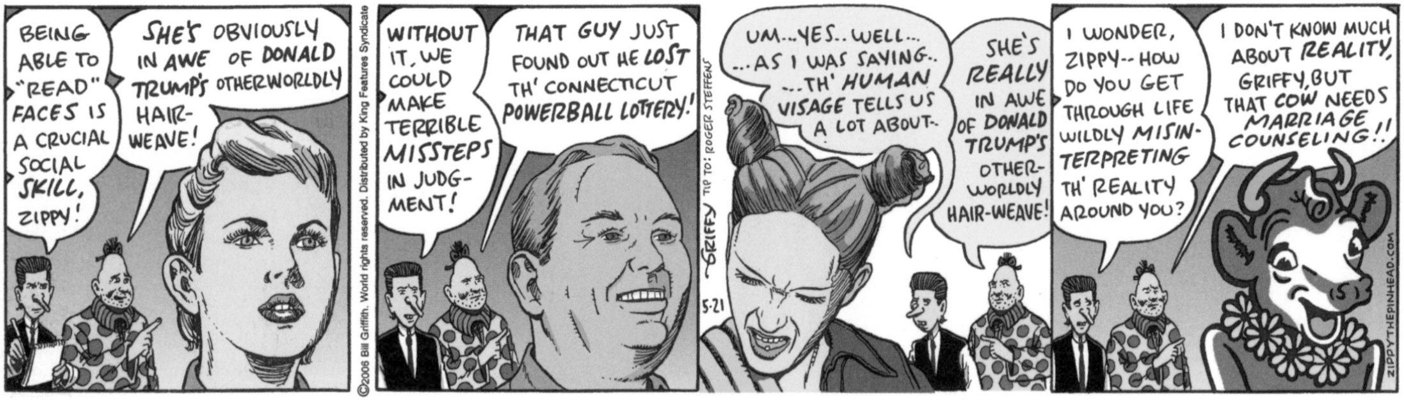
BEING ABLE TO "READ" FACES IS A CRUCIAL SOCIAL SKILL, ZIPPY!
SHE'S OBVIOUSLY IN AWE OF DONALD TRUMP'S OTHERWORLDLY HAIR-WEAVE!
©2006 Bill Griffith. World rights reserved. Distributed by King Features Syndicate
WITHOUT IT, WE COULD MAKE TERRIBLE MISSTEPS IN JUDGMENT!
THAT GUY JUST FOUND OUT HE LOST TH' CONNECTICUT POWERBALL LOTTERY!
GRIFFY
TIP TO: ROGER STEFFENS
5.21
UM...YES..WELL... ...AS I WAS SAYING.. ...TH' HUMAN VISAGE TELLS US A LOT ABOUT..
SHE'S REALLY IN AWE OF DONALD TRUMP'S OTHER-WORLDLY HAIR-WEAVE!
I WONDER, ZIPPY-- HOW DO YOU GET THROUGH LIFE WILDLY MISIN-TERPRETING TH' REALITY AROUND YOU?
I DON'T KNOW MUCH ABOUT REALITY, GRIFFY, BUT THAT COW NEEDS MARRIAGE COUNSELING!!
ZIPPYTHEPINHEAD.COM

92

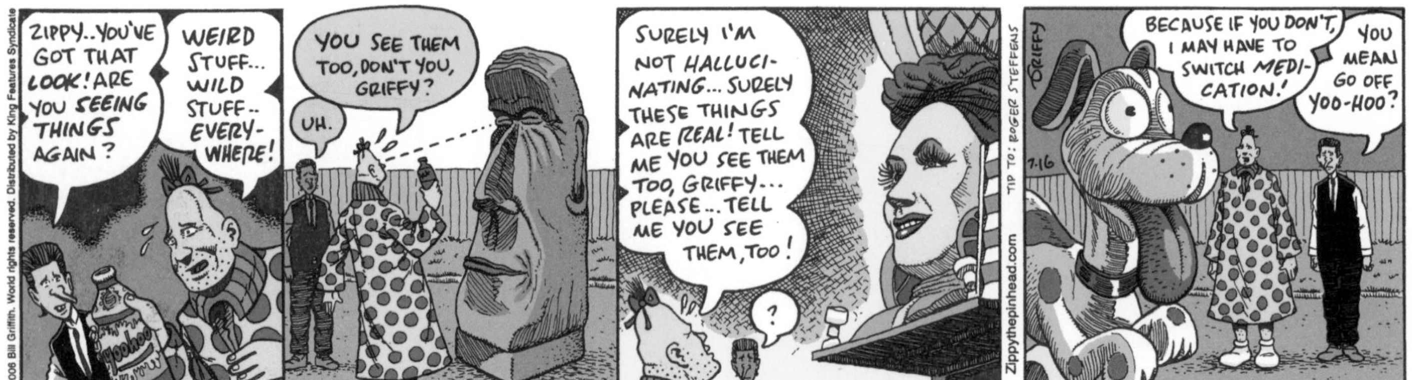
©2006 Bill Griffith. World rights reserved. Distributed by King Features Syndicate
ZIPPY..YOU'VE GOT THAT LOOK! ARE YOU SEEING THINGS AGAIN?
WEIRD STUFF... WILD STUFF.. EVERY-WHERE!
YOU SEE THEM TOO, DON'T YOU, GRIFFY?
UH.
SURELY I'M NOT HALLUCI-NATING... SURELY THESE THINGS ARE REAL! TELL ME YOU SEE THEM TOO, GRIFFY... PLEASE... TELL ME YOU SEE THEM, TOO!
?
Zippythepinhead.com
TIP TO: ROGER STEFFENS
GRIFFY
7.16
BECAUSE IF YOU DON'T, I MAY HAVE TO SWITCH MEDI-CATION!
YOU MEAN GO OFF YOO-HOO?

93

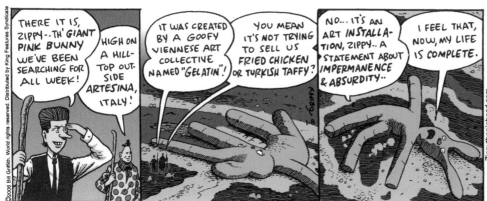

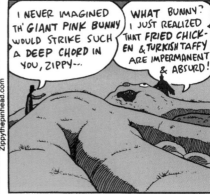

©2006 Bill Griffith. World rights reserved. Distributed by King Features Syndicate
THERE IT IS, ZIPPY-- TH' GIANT PINK BUNNY WE'VE BEEN SEARCHING FOR ALL WEEK!
HIGH ON A HILL-TOP OUT-SIDE ARTESINA, ITALY!
IT WAS CREATED BY A GOOFY VIENNESE ART COLLECTIVE NAMED "GELATIN"!
YOU MEAN IT'S NOT TRYING TO SELL US FRIED CHICKEN OR TURKISH TAFFY?
GRIFFY
1-8
NO... IT'S AN ART INSTALLA-TION, ZIPPY.. A STATEMENT ABOUT IMPERMANENCE & ABSURDITY..
I FEEL THAT, NOW, MY LIFE IS COMPLETE.
Zippythepinhead.com
I NEVER IMAGINED TH' GIANT PINK BUNNY WOULD STRIKE SUCH A DEEP CHORD IN YOU, ZIPPY--.
WHAT BUNNY? I JUST REALIZED THAT FRIED CHICK-EN & TURKISH TAFFY ARE IMPERMANENT & ABSURD!

94

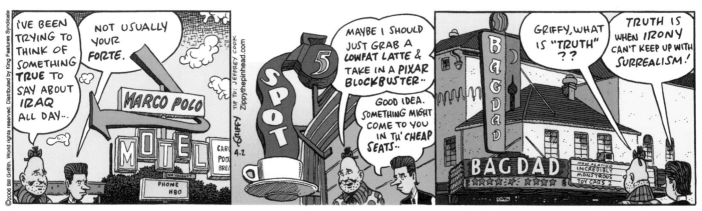

©2006 Bill Griffith. World rights reserved. Distributed by King Features Syndicate
I'VE BEEN TRYING TO THINK OF SOMETHING TRUE TO SAY ABOUT IRAQ ALL DAY..
NOT USUALLY YOUR FORTE.
MARCO POLO
MOTEL
NO VACANCY
PHONE
HBO
GRIFFY
4-2
TIP TO: JEFFREY COOK
Zippythepinhead.com
SPOT
5
MAYBE I SHOULD JUST GRAB A LOWFAT LATTE & TAKE IN A PIXAR BLOCKBUSTER..
GOOD IDEA. SOMETHING MIGHT COME TO YOU IN TH' CHEAP SEATS..
BAGDAD
GRIFFY, WHAT IS "TRUTH"??
TRUTH IS WHEN IRONY CAN'T KEEP UP WITH SURREALISM!
NOW PLAYING
INCREDIBLY
MONSTROUS
TOY CARS 2
OPEN

95

WELL, HERE IT IS, ZIPPY... I DON'T KNOW HOW WE MISSED IT ALL THESE YEARS!
MY EGO IS BURSTING!
POK-A-DOT
PEPSI
TIP TO: GRACE LOPEZ
Zippythepinhead.com
GRIFFY 1·22
ZIPPY... YOU'RE CRYING.. ...IS IT STRONG FEELING.. .. OR IS IT BECAUSE THERE'S NO SPUMONI ON TH' MENU?
I JUST HAD A HINT OF MY OWN MORTALITY!
POK-A-DOT
HOTS · HAMBURGERS · ROAST BEEF
©2006 Bill Griffith. World rights reserved. Distributed by King Features Syndicate
WELL, WE ALL HAVE TO GO EVENTUALLY.. DOES THAT BOTHER YOU?
ME? NO... BUT IT DOES BOTHER ME THAT MISSPELLING WILL LIVE ON LONG AFTER I'M TOAST!
PEPSI
POK-A-DOT

96

ZIPPY, WHERE DO YOU LIVE?
—TODAY, I LIVE HERE, IN THIS ENCHANTED CASTLE BY TH' SEA IN KEY WEST, FLORIDA!
©2006 Bill Griffith. World rights reserved. Distributed by King Features Syndicate
AND ARE YOU HAPPY IN YOUR ENCHANTED CASTLE BY TH' SEA, ZIPPY?
NOT SINCE ABOUT TWO SECONDS AGO!
KLIK!
Zippythepinhead.com
NOW, I'D PREFER TO LIVE HERE, IN THIS CRAZY LITTLE HUT, ON A MINIATURE GOLF COURSE IN FOUNTAIN VALLEY, CALIFORNIA!
GRIFFY 4·13
AND WHY IS THAT, ZIPPY?
BECAUSE HAPPINESS IS SWITCHING LOCATIONS AS OFTEN AS YOU SWITCH CHANNELS ON YOUR TV REMOTE!!
KLIK!

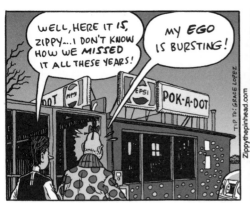

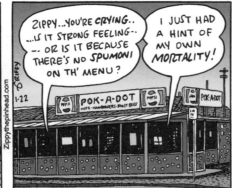

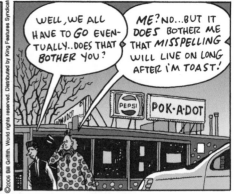

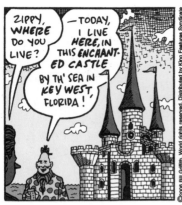

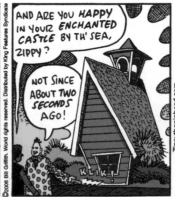

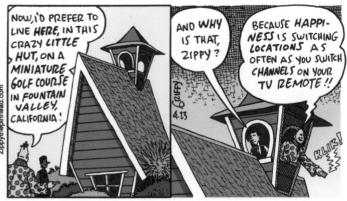

©2006 Bill Griffith. World rights reserved. Distributed by King Features Syndicate
DAVIES' chuck wagon DINER
DINNER
SHORT ORDERS
I REFUSE TO GET ALL MY NEWS FROM TH' INTERNET! YOU CAN'T FOLD TH' INTERNET! YOU CAN'T SMELL TH' INTERNET!
GRIFFY
5.14
ZIPPY, WE ALL HAVE TO FACE FACTS... TH' WEB HAS TOTALLY RE-ARRANGED TH' MEDIA LANDSCAPE...
IF I CAN'T TURN TO PAGE A16 TO READ MORE ABOUT THAT TRIPLE SLAYING OUT ON ROUTE 12, I DON'T WANT TO LIVE!
TIP TO: JON KITTREDGE
DINER
OPEN
YOU DO KNOW THIS PLACE IS CLOSED & YOU'RE LOCKED IN, DON'T YOU?
I'M NOT COMING OUT UNTIL TH' DENVER POST REINSTATES WALTER WINCHELL & TH' KATZENJAMMER KIDS!!
Zippythepinhead.com

97

GRIFFY
6.11
OWL DINER
TRY OUR NEW HOMEMADE LUNCH SPECIALS
OWL
DINER
VINYL TOPS
ZIPPY, IS THERE SOMETHING YOU'RE NOT TELLING ME?
©2006 Bill Griffith. World rights reserved. Distributed by King Features Syndicate
OH, THERE'S A LOT I'M NOT TELLING YOU!
CAN YOU GIVE ME ONE EXAMPLE?
TIPS TO: REX McMANAMY
BOOTH SERVICE
AND ROGER STEFFENS
NO, I DON'T THINK SO... ...THAT'S PRIVILEGED INFORMATION.
Zippythepinhead.com
WHY? WHAT WOULD HAPPEN IF YOU GAVE ME ONE EXAMPLE?
WE'D BOTH BE THROWN INTO TH' MOUTH OF AN ACTIVE VOLCANO.
DINER

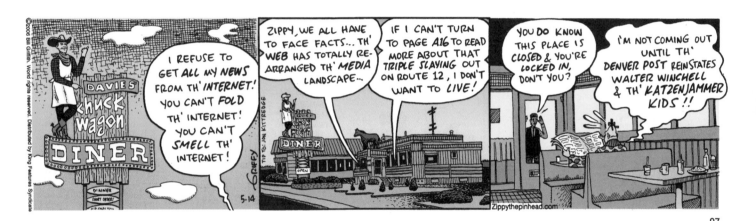

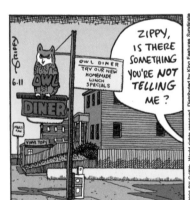

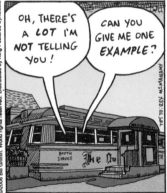

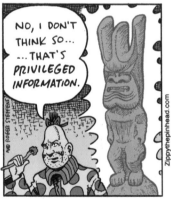

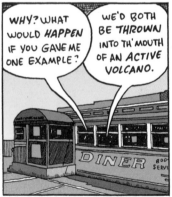

98

PSSST! ZIPPY--- DON'T LOOK NOW, BUT GUESS WHO'S SITTING IN TH' BOOTH BEHIND ME, CALMLY CONSUMING A TURKEY ON RYE?
OH, I SAW HIM AS SOON AS WE CAME IN --- IT'S ARNOLD STANG! *
GRIFFY 12-11
* TRUE! REALLY HAPPENED! ETC.!
©2005 Bill Griffith. World rights reserved. Distributed by King Features Syndicate
THAT'S RIGHT, ARNOLD STANG!! ONE OF MY CHILDHOOD POP CULTURE HEROES! HE WAS TH' VOICE OF "TOP CAT" & STARRED IN TH' FILM "THE MAN WITH THE GOLDEN ARM" WITH FRANK SINATRA!
?
DON'T FORGET HIS "WHAT A CHUNK O' CHOCOLATE!" CHUNKY CANDY BAR COMMERCIALS FROM TH' '50S!
Zippythepinhead.com
AW, JEEZ... HERE WE GO AGAIN.. EVERY BABY BOOMER & HIS BROTHER WANTS A PIECE OF ME!
SHOULD I GO OVER & TALK TO HIM?
NOT NECESSARY. I CAN FEEL TH' LOVE FROM HERE!!

99

ZERBINA, I THINK WE SHOULD GET MARRIED!
I THOUGHT WE WERE MARRIED, ZIPPY!
NO, I MEAN AS A GAY COUPLE!
WHAT A HIP IDEA!
Zippythepinhead.com
©2006 Bill Griffith. World rights reserved. Distributed by King Features Syndicate
THEN WE COULD MOVE TO UTAH & PRACTICE POLYGAMY, LIKE ON HBO!
THIS IS GREAT! WE'RE RANDOMLY BLENDING AT LEAST TWO DIFFERENT ALTERNATIVE LIFESTYLES!
TIP: SPENCER STEWART
Marriage works.
GEE, NOW I DON'T KNOW WHETHER WE SHOULD GO ANTIQUING..
--OR BUY 3 ADJOINING TRACT HOMES IN SALT LAKE CITY!!
GRIFFY 6-25

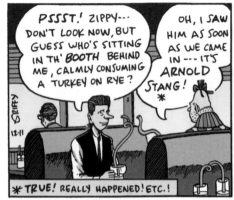

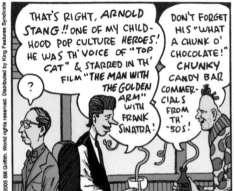

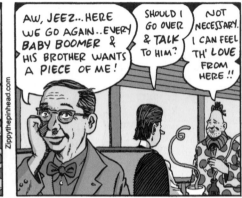

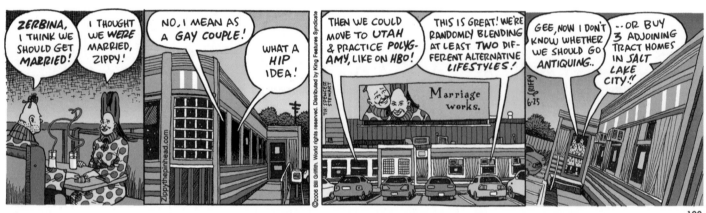

100

ZERBINA? WILL YOU GO ROLLER-SKATING WITH ME TONIGHT FROM 7 PM UNTIL 11 PM?
YOU WON'T? --. WHAT? BECAUSE OF TH' PATRIOT ACT? HONEY, WE CAN'T LET TH' REPUBLICANS WIN!
WE MUST ROLLER-SKATE CONTINUOUSLY FROM 7 PM UNTIL 11 PM TONIGHT & EVERY NIGHT!
BECAUSE TH' FREEDOM TO ROLLER-SKATE MUST NEVER BE SACRIFICED ON TH' ALTAR OF A FALSE SENSE OF SECURITY!
WE MUST RESIST, ZERBINA. AND WE MUST ROLL!!
HAMBURGERS
Since 1946
TIP TO: RICHARD ROBERTS
GRIFFY
11·20
Zippythepinhead.com
©2005 Bill Griffith. World rights reserved. Distributed by King Features Syndicate

101

FLASHBACK TO A CUTER DECADE... ZIP 'N' ZERB ON THEIR OZARKS HONEYMOON--
OOH, LOOK! TH' BEAR'S T-SHIRT SAYS "LIFE'S A VACATION" INSTEAD OF "LIFE'S A BEACH"!
WOW! LET'S BECOME EVANGELICAL CHRISTIANS!
--. AND LOOK AGAIN! ON THIS SIDE, HIS LI'L T-SHIRT SAYS "LIFE'S GOOD" INSTEAD OF "I'M WITH STUPID"!
HEY! THIS WHOLE THING WAS PROPHESIED IN REVELATIONS 14:02!
HELLO. WE DON'T WANT TO SPEND TH' WEEKEND HERE! WE WANT TO MOVE IN & START A WORLDWIDE MOVEMENT!
WOULD YOU MIND IF WE MADE CABIN 27 CULT HEADQUARTERS?
Teddy Bear MOTEL
VACANCY
Teddy Bear OFFICE
TIP TO: ED ENGEL
GRIFFY
2·12
Zippythepinhead.com
©2006 Bill Griffith. World rights reserved. Distributed by King Features Syndicate

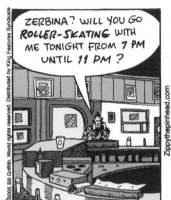

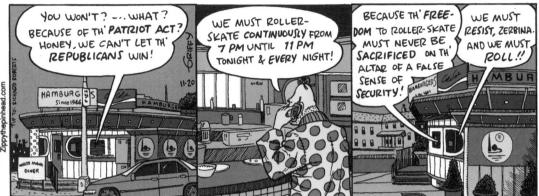

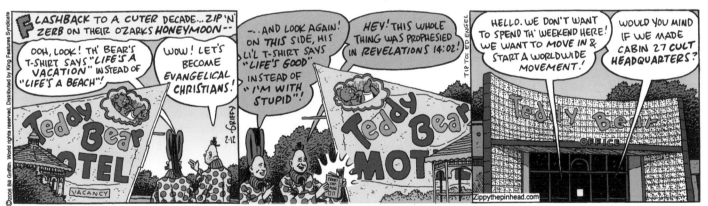

102

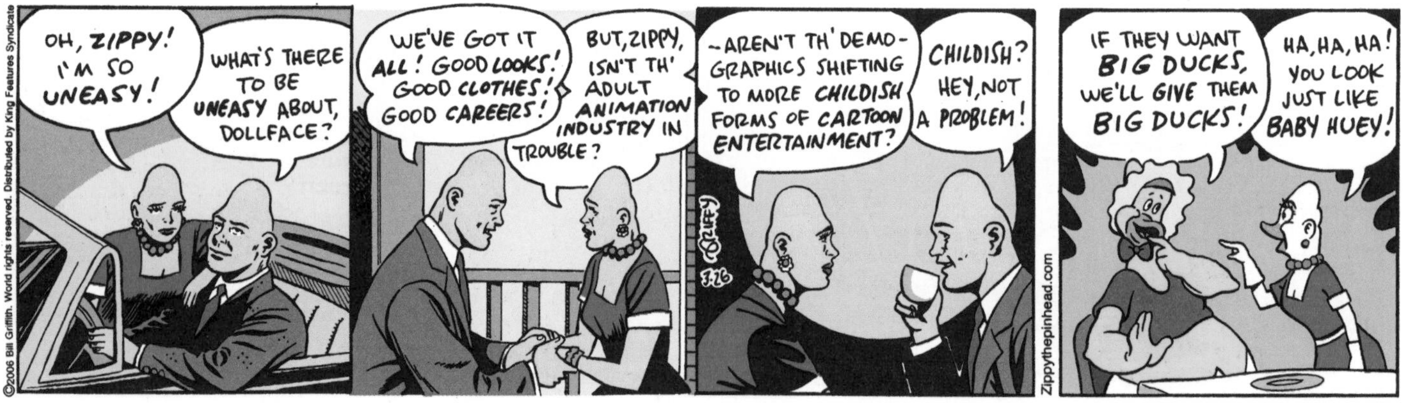
©2006 Bill Griffith. World rights reserved. Distributed by King Features Syndicate
OH, ZIPPY! I'M SO UNEASY!
WHAT'S THERE TO BE UNEASY ABOUT, DOLLFACE?
WE'VE GOT IT ALL! GOOD LOOKS! GOOD CLOTHES! GOOD CAREERS!
BUT, ZIPPY, ISN'T TH' ADULT ANIMATION INDUSTRY IN TROUBLE?
~AREN'T TH' DEMOGRAPHICS SHIFTING TO MORE CHILDISH FORMS OF CARTOON ENTERTAINMENT?
CHILDISH? HEY, NOT A PROBLEM!
GRIFFY
7-26
Zippythepinhead.com
IF THEY WANT BIG DUCKS, WE'LL GIVE THEM BIG DUCKS!
HA, HA, HA! YOU LOOK JUST LIKE BABY HUEY!

103

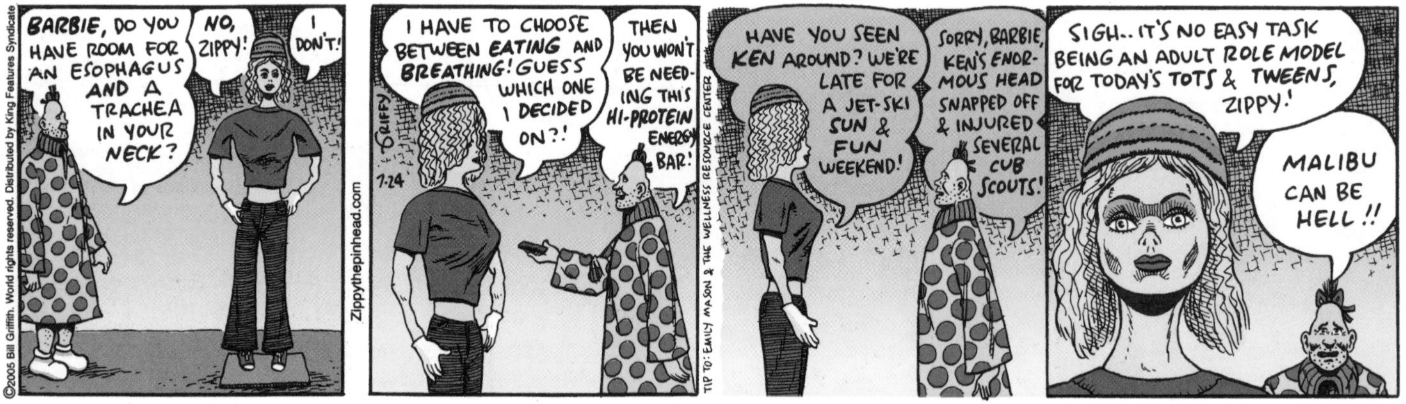
©2005 Bill Griffith. World rights reserved. Distributed by King Features Syndicate
BARBIE, DO YOU HAVE ROOM FOR AN ESOPHAGUS AND A TRACHEA IN YOUR NECK?
NO, ZIPPY!
I DON'T!
Zippythepinhead.com
I HAVE TO CHOOSE BETWEEN EATING AND BREATHING! GUESS WHICH ONE I DECIDED ON?!
THEN YOU WON'T BE NEEDING THIS HI-PROTEIN ENERGY BAR!
GRIFFY
7-24
TIP TO: EMILY MASON & THE WELLNESS RESOURCE CENTER
HAVE YOU SEEN KEN AROUND? WE'RE LATE FOR A JET-SKI SUN & FUN WEEKEND!
SORRY, BARBIE, KEN'S ENORMOUS HEAD SNAPPED OFF & INJURED SEVERAL CUB SCOUTS!
SIGH.. IT'S NO EASY TASK BEING AN ADULT ROLE MODEL FOR TODAY'S TOTS & TWEENS, ZIPPY!
MALIBU CAN BE HELL!!

104

I SAY WE PUT TH' RAP ON VICTOR MATURE! I NEVER LIKED TH' GUY!
NAH. DANA ANDREWS IS TH' PERFECT PATSY!
BOTH OF YOU MUGS SHUT YER YAPS! I'M TRYING TO CHANNEL JACK PALANCE!
©2006 Bill Griffith. World rights reserved. Distributed by King Features Syndicate
SOON--
SO, IT'S AGREED.. SCOTT BRADY TAKES TH' FALL FOR TH' LLOYD NOLAN KILLING..
I DON'T LIKE IT.. I STILL SAY PETER LORRE WAS MADE FOR TH' JOB!
THIS ISN'T WORK-ING FOR ME! LET'S PRETEND INSTEAD WE'RE IN A CHEESY '50S SCI-FI FLICK!
Zippythepinhead.com
LATER--
NO WAY I'M SWITCHING GENRES, PUNK! NOT UNTIL I GET TO DO MY WILLIAM BENDIX IMPER-SONATION!
WHAT? YOU SAID I COULD BE ZSA ZSA GABOR IN TH' "QUEEN OF OUTER SPACE"!
GRIFFY
2-5

105

©2006 Bill Griffith. World rights reserved. Distributed by King Features Syndicate
OKAY--NOBODY MOVES!
IS THIS TH' FIRST ACT CONFLICT?
YOU GOT ME, LAWMAN! BUT YOU'LL NEVER PUT ME BEHIND BARS!
I GET IT.. TH' PLOT TWIST BEFORE TH' FINAL DENOUE-MENT!
GRIFFY
4-16
Zippythepinhead.com
NO TRICKS, WISE GUY, AND WE BOTH WALK OUT OF HERE ALIVE!
NICE CAMERA WORK, PUNK, BUT YOUR STORY ARC LACKS EMOTIONAL RESONANCE!!

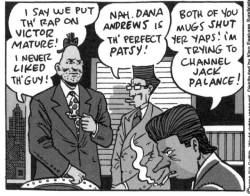

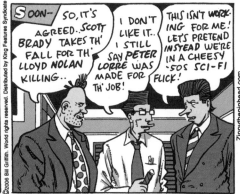

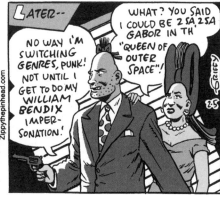

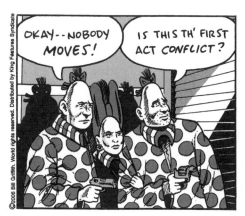

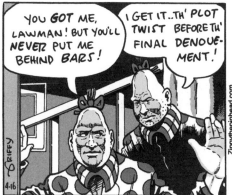

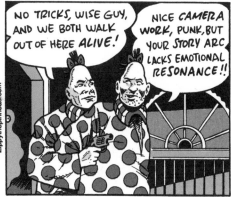

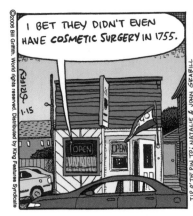

©2006 Bill Griffith. World rights reserved. Distributed by King Features Syndicate
I BET THEY DIDN'T EVEN HAVE COSMETIC SURGERY IN 1755.
GRIFFY 1-15
OPEN
TIP O' TH' PIN TO: NATALIE & JOHN GRABILL
SO?
Bill's Grill
Zippythepinhead.com
I THINK I'M READY TO START MY BLOG.
Bill's Grill
BREAKFAST LUNCH
1/2 POUND
$3.00
AUTO SALES

106

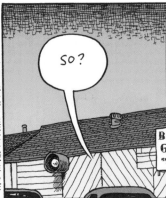

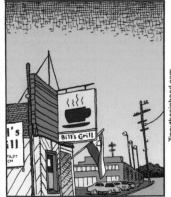

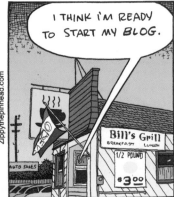

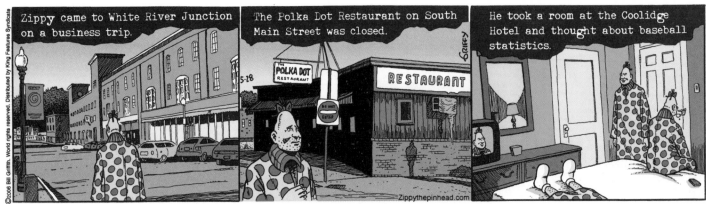

©2006 Bill Griffith. World rights reserved. Distributed by King Features Syndicate
Zippy came to White River Junction on a business trip.
The Polka Dot Restaurant on South Main Street was closed.
GRIFFY
5-28
THE POLKA DOT RESTAURANT
DO NOT ENTER
RESTAURANT
Zippythepinhead.com
He took a room at the Coolidge Hotel and thought about baseball statistics.

107

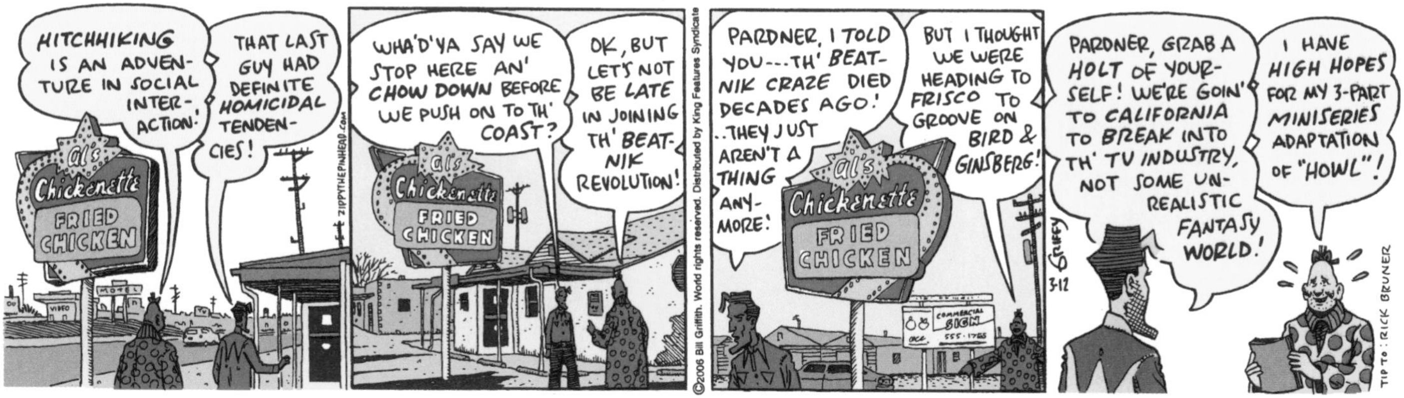
HITCHHIKING IS AN ADVENTURE IN SOCIAL INTERACTION!
THAT LAST GUY HAD DEFINITE HOMICIDAL TENDENCIES!
al's Chickenette FRIED CHICKEN
MOTEL
zippythepinhead.com
WHA'D'YA SAY WE STOP HERE AN' CHOW DOWN BEFORE WE PUSH ON TO TH' COAST?
OK, BUT LET'S NOT BE LATE IN JOINING TH' BEATNIK REVOLUTION!
al's Chickenette FRIED CHICKEN
©2006 Bill Griffith. World rights reserved. Distributed by King Features Syndicate
PARDNER, I TOLD YOU---TH' BEATNIK CRAZE DIED DECADES AGO! ..THEY JUST AREN'T A THING ANYMORE!
BUT I THOUGHT WE WERE HEADING TO FRISCO TO GROOVE ON BIRD & GINSBERG!
al's Chickenette FRIED CHICKEN
COMMERCIAL SIGN
GRIFFY 3·12
PARDNER, GRAB A HOLT OF YOURSELF! WE'RE GOIN' TO CALIFORNIA TO BREAK INTO TH' TV INDUSTRY, NOT SOME UNREALISTIC FANTASY WORLD!
I HAVE HIGH HOPES FOR MY 3-PART MINISERIES ADAPTATION OF "HOWL"!
TIP TO: RICK BRUNER

108

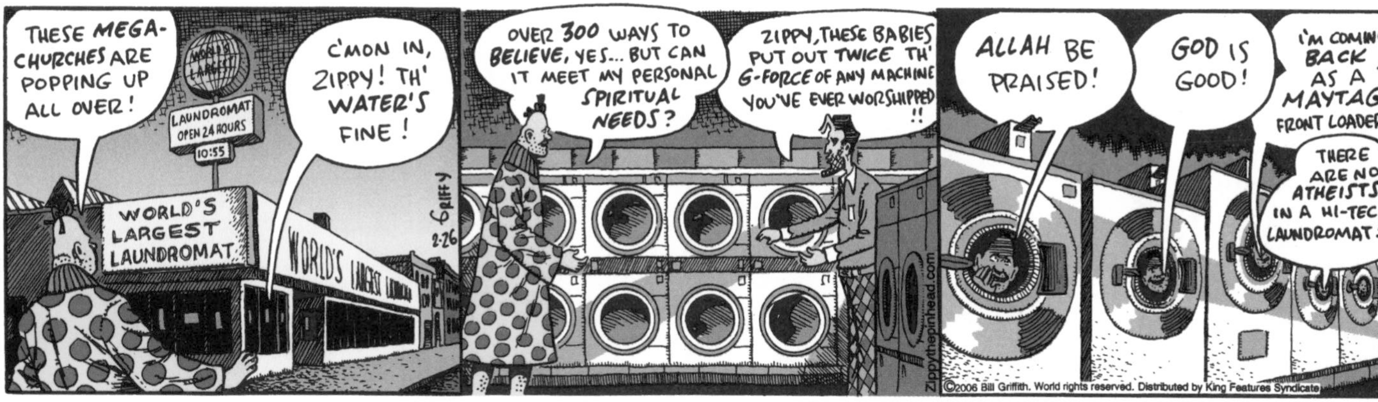
THESE MEGA-CHURCHES ARE POPPING UP ALL OVER!
WORLD'S LARGEST
LAUNDROMAT OPEN 24 HOURS
10:55
C'MON IN, ZIPPY! TH' WATER'S FINE!
WORLD'S LARGEST LAUNDROMAT
WORLD'S LARGEST LAUNDROMAT
GRIFFY 2·26
OVER 300 WAYS TO BELIEVE, YES... BUT CAN IT MEET MY PERSONAL SPIRITUAL NEEDS?
ZIPPY, THESE BABIES PUT OUT TWICE TH' G-FORCE OF ANY MACHINE YOU'VE EVER WORSHIPPED!!
zippythepinhead.com
ALLAH BE PRAISED!
GOD IS GOOD!
I'M COMING BACK AS A MAYTAG FRONT LOADER!
THERE ARE NO ATHEISTS IN A HI-TECH LAUNDROMAT!!
©2006 Bill Griffith. World rights reserved. Distributed by King Features Syndicate

109

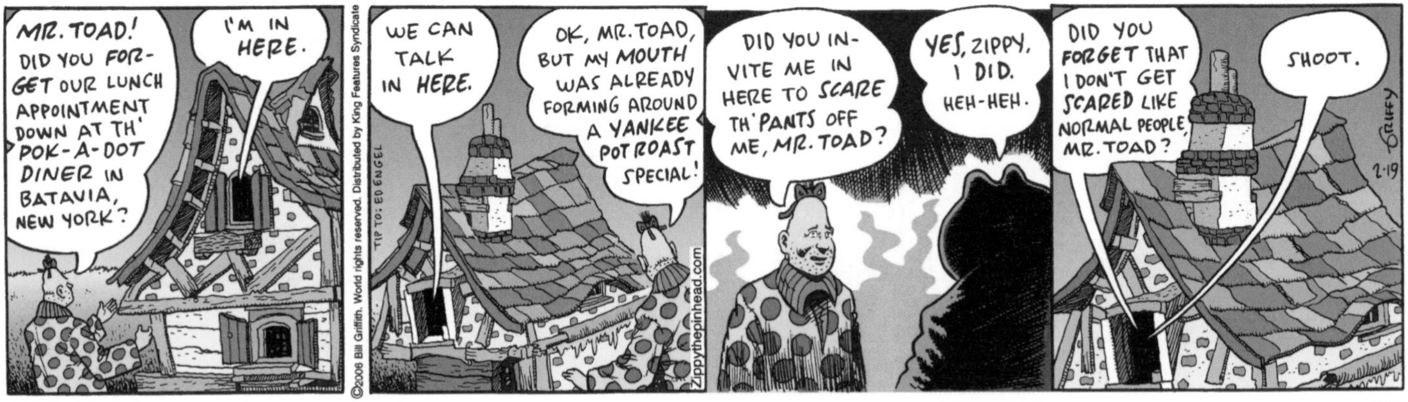
MR. TOAD! DID YOU FORGET OUR LUNCH APPOINTMENT DOWN AT TH' POK-A-DOT DINER IN BATAVIA, NEW YORK?
I'M IN HERE.
©2006 Bill Griffith. World rights reserved. Distributed by King Features Syndicate
WE CAN TALK IN HERE.
OK, MR. TOAD, BUT MY MOUTH WAS ALREADY FORMING AROUND A YANKEE POT ROAST SPECIAL!
TIP TO: ED ENGEL
Zippythepinhead.com
DID YOU INVITE ME IN HERE TO SCARE TH' PANTS OFF ME, MR. TOAD?
YES, ZIPPY, I DID. HEH-HEH.
DID YOU FORGET THAT I DON'T GET SCARED LIKE NORMAL PEOPLE, MR. TOAD?
SHOOT.
GRIFFY
2-19

110

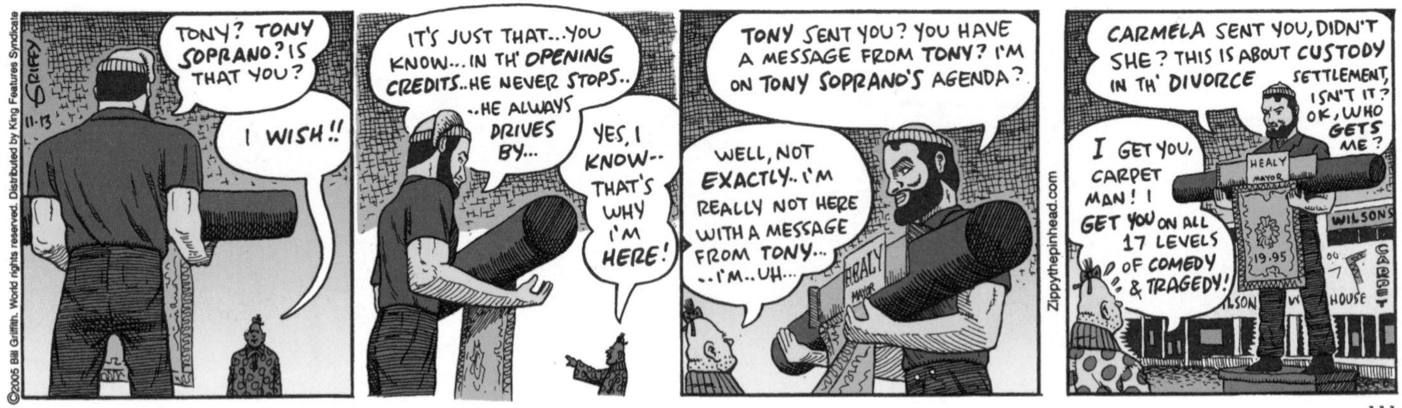
©2005 Bill Griffith. World rights reserved. Distributed by King Features Syndicate
GRIFFY
11-13
TONY? TONY SOPRANO? IS THAT YOU?
I WISH!!
IT'S JUST THAT...YOU KNOW...IN TH' OPENING CREDITS..HE NEVER STOPS.. ..HE ALWAYS DRIVES BY...
YES, I KNOW-- THAT'S WHY I'M HERE!
TONY SENT YOU? YOU HAVE A MESSAGE FROM TONY? I'M ON TONY SOPRANO'S AGENDA?
WELL, NOT EXACTLY.. I'M REALLY NOT HERE WITH A MESSAGE FROM TONY... ..I'M..UH...
HEALY
MAYOR
Zippythepinhead.com
CARMELA SENT YOU, DIDN'T SHE? THIS IS ABOUT CUSTODY IN TH' DIVORCE SETTLEMENT, ISN'T IT? OK, WHO GETS ME?
I GET YOU, CARPET MAN! I GET YOU ON ALL 17 LEVELS OF COMEDY & TRAGEDY!
HEALY
MAYOR
WILSONS
19.95
CARPET
HOUSE

111

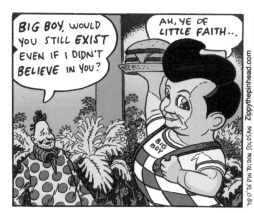

BIG BOY, WOULD YOU STILL EXIST EVEN IF I DIDN'T BELIEVE IN YOU?
AH, YE OF LITTLE FAITH...
BIG BOY
TIP O' TH' PIN TO: DON SOLOSAN
Zippythepinhead.com
SUPPOSE I AM JUST A MENTAL CONSTRUCT. AN AIRY PHANTASM.. A FIGMENT OF YOUR FEVERED BROW--
RIGHT! LIKE COLONEL SANDERS OR TH' TACO BELL CHIHUAHUA!
BIG BOY
©2006 Bill Griffith. World rights reserved. Distributed by King Features Syndicate
GRIFFY 5-7
OK, SO IF I DIDN'T EXIST, WOULD YOU CONDUCT YOURSELF ANY DIFFERENTLY?
PLEASE, BIG BOY, DON'T CONDEMN ME TO A LIFE OF LACTO-VEGETARIANISM!!

112

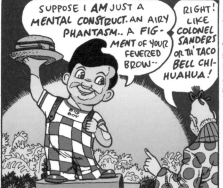

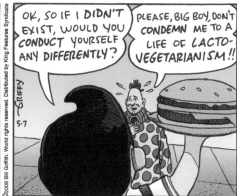

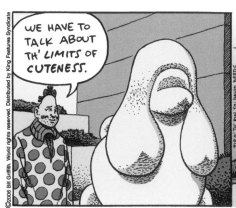

©2006 Bill Griffith. World rights reserved. Distributed by King Features Syndicate
WE HAVE TO TALK ABOUT TH' LIMITS OF CUTENESS.
TIP O' TH' PIN TO: DAVID DEEDS
BECAUSE I'M AFRAID YOU'VE CROSSED THAT BRIGHT LINE.
OH, YEH? INTO WHAT?
ZIPPYTHEPINHEAD.COM GRIFFY 4-30
INTO STOMACH-CHURNING, MUU-MUU-WRENCHING GROTESQUITUDE.
GO #@!+ #%?#&%@#, YOU STUPID %#@-?#*@!!

113

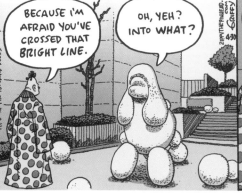

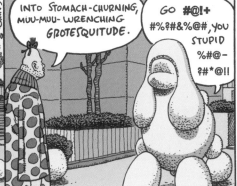

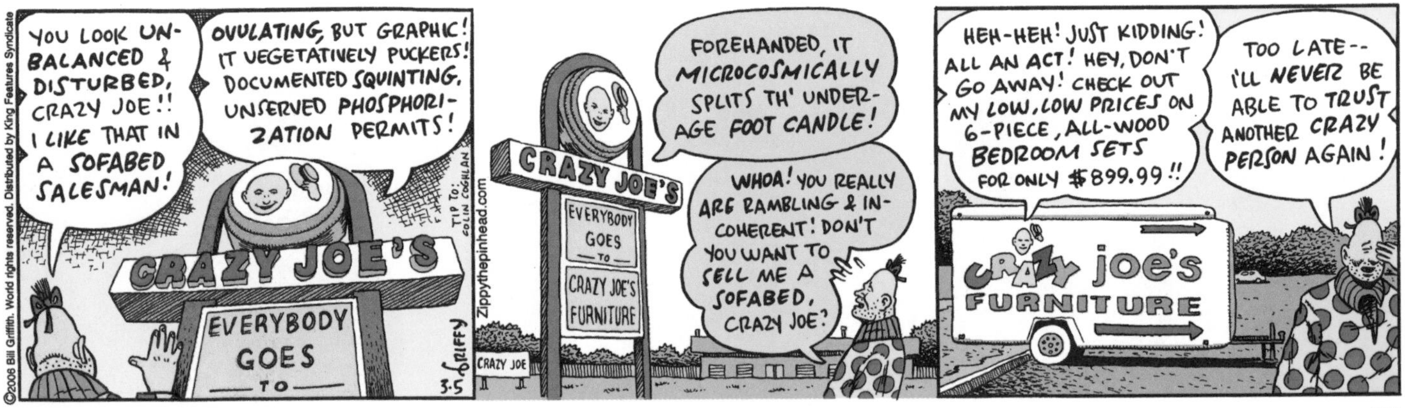

©2006 Bill Griffith. World rights reserved. Distributed by King Features Syndicate
YOU LOOK UN-BALANCED & DISTURBED, CRAZY JOE!! I LIKE THAT IN A SOFABED SALESMAN!
OVULATING, BUT GRAPHIC! IT VEGETATIVELY PUCKERS! DOCUMENTED SQUINTING, UNSERVED PHOSPHORI-ZATION PERMITS!
CRAZY JOE'S
EVERYBODY GOES TO
TIP TO: COLIN COGHLAN
GRIFFY 3·5
Zippythepinhead.com
FOREHANDED, IT MICROCOSMICALLY SPLITS TH' UNDER-AGE FOOT CANDLE!
CRAZY JOE'S
EVERYBODY GOES TO CRAZY JOE'S FURNITURE
CRAZY JOE
WHOA! YOU REALLY ARE RAMBLING & IN-COHERENT! DON'T YOU WANT TO SELL ME A SOFABED, CRAZY JOE?
HEH-HEH! JUST KIDDING! ALL AN ACT! HEY, DON'T GO AWAY! CHECK OUT MY LOW, LOW PRICES ON 6-PIECE, ALL-WOOD BEDROOM SETS FOR ONLY $899.99!!
TOO LATE-- I'LL NEVER BE ABLE TO TRUST ANOTHER CRAZY PERSON AGAIN!
CRAZY joe's FURNITURE

114

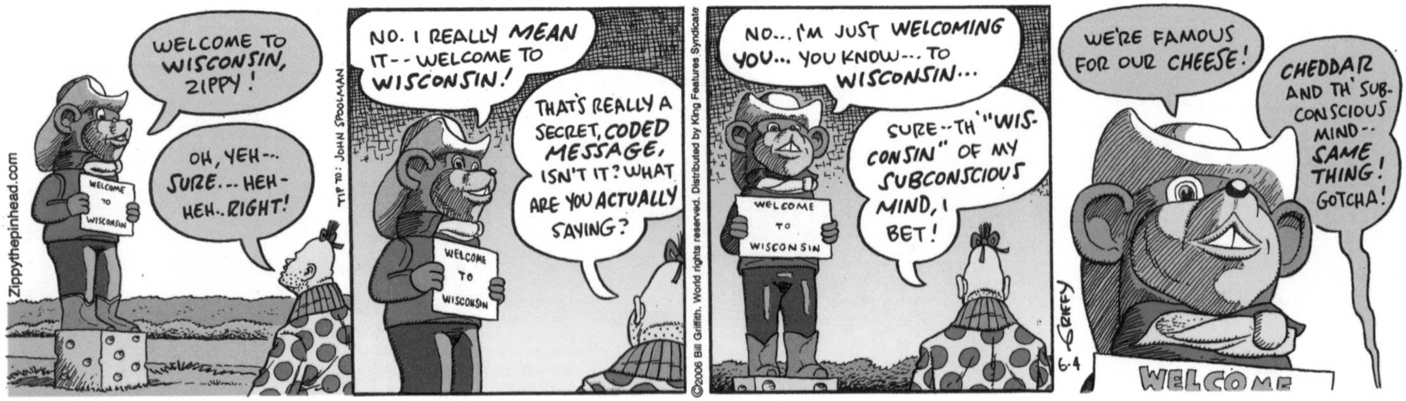

Zippythepinhead.com
WELCOME TO WISCONSIN, ZIPPY!
WELCOME TO WISCONSIN
OH, YEH-- SURE.-- HEH-HEH..RIGHT!
TIP TO: JOHN SPOOLMAN
NO. I REALLY MEAN IT-- WELCOME TO WISCONSIN!
WELCOME TO WISCONSIN
THAT'S REALLY A SECRET, CODED MESSAGE, ISN'T IT? WHAT ARE YOU ACTUALLY SAYING?
©2006 Bill Griffith. World rights reserved. Distributed by King Features Syndicate
NO... I'M JUST WELCOMING YOU... YOU KNOW--. TO WISCONSIN...
WELCOME TO WISCONSIN
SURE--TH' "WIS-CONSIN" OF MY SUBCONSCIOUS MIND, I BET!
GRIFFY 6·4
WE'RE FAMOUS FOR OUR CHEESE!
CHEDDAR AND TH' SUB-CONSCIOUS MIND-- SAME THING! GOTCHA!
WELCOME

115

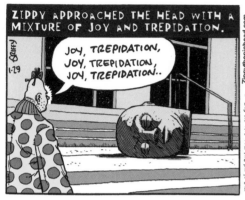

ZIPPY APPROACHED THE HEAD WITH A MIXTURE OF JOY AND TREPIDATION.
JOY, TREPIDATION, JOY, TREPIDATION, JOY, TREPIDATION..
GRIFFY 1-29
Zippythepinhead.com
TIP O' TH' PIN TO: CHUCK STRINZ
WAS IT A SYMBOL OF THE DISCONNECT BETWEEN MIND AND BODY SO PREVALENT IN SOCIETY TODAY?
HMMM... IS THIS ART? OR A MESSAGE SENT ESPECIALLY TO ME BY FORCES BEYOND MY CONTROL?
©2006 Bill Griffith. World rights reserved. Distributed by King Features Syndicate
OR WAS THERE SIMPLY A FIFTY-FOOT CHUNKY GUY SOMEWHERE, WALKING AROUND WITHOUT A HEAD?
--IF I JUST CONCENTRATE ON HOW SCRUMPTIOUS THIS "PAYDAY" CANDY BAR IS, ALL MY PSYCHOSOCIAL CRISES WILL BE RESOLVED!
YUM....

116

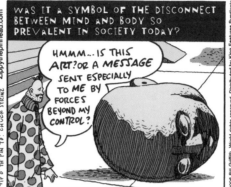

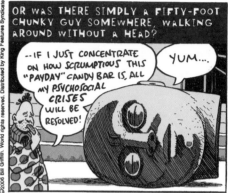

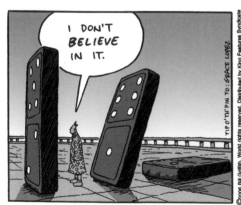

I DON'T BELIEVE IN IT.
TIP O' TH' PIN TO: GRACE LOPEZ
©2006 Bill Griffith. World rights reserved. Distributed by King Features Syndicate
I'M TELLING YOU, IT'S AN OUTMODED THEORY!
GRIFFY 3-19
Zippythepinhead.com
UH-OH.

117

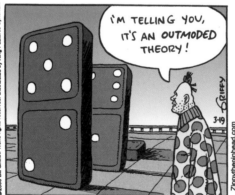

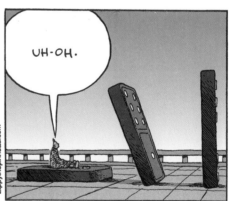

©2005 Bill Griffith. World rights reserved. Distributed by King Features Syndicate
DO YOU BELIEVE IN TH' GREAT FLOOD, ZIPPY?
TH' BIG, WET ONE!
YOU MEAN TH' ONE BUSH BADLY BUNGLED?
TIP TO: DAN RODGERS
Zippythepinhead.com
NO, NO ---- TH' CLEANSING --- TH' DAY WHEN ALL SIN WILL BE SWEPT AWAY!
SORRY, WHEN SOMEONE ADOPTS THAT TONE OF NOSE, I TUNE OUT!
IS THIS ABOUT TH' APOCALYPSE? BECAUSE I REALLY DON'T SUBSCRIBE TO TH' APOCALYPSE!
IT'S COMING, ZIPPY! AND YOU MUST PREPARE!
GRIFFY
12-4
HEY, I'M GOING TO TH' STORE FOR ALTOIDS & A COUPLA HOT POCKETS.. YOU NEED ANYTHING WHILE YOU WAIT FOR TH' END TO COME?
NAIL POLISH?
MAYBE SOME KLEENEX.

118

I CAN'T MAKE UP MY MIND.
Zippythepinhead.com
GRIFFY
11-27
I ALSO CAN'T MAKE UP MY PARENTS, MY GENDER OR MY RESUMÉ.
©2005 Bill Griffith. World rights reserved. Distributed by King Features Syndicate
I COULD MAKE UP MY MOUTH.
...BUT I'D PROBABLY PUT MY FOOT IN IT.

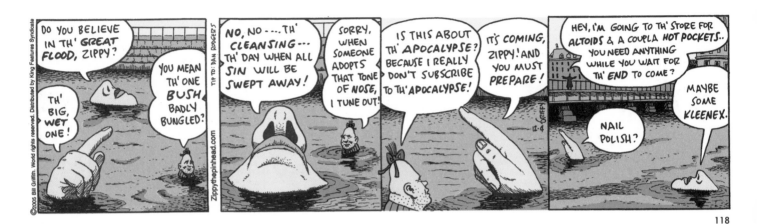

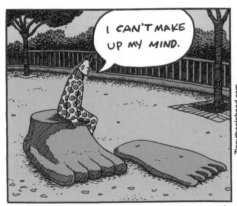

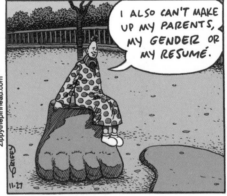

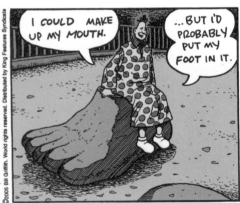

119

SOMETIMES I THINK I SHOULD MOVE TO LITHUANIA.
BILLY'S BURG-O-RAMA CLAMS-FISH & CHIPS HAMBURGERS
GRIFFY
7-2
©2006 Bill Griffith. World rights reserved. Distributed by King Features Syndicate
BUT THEN I THINK OF ALL TH' GOOD STUFF I'D MISS---
BILLY'S BURG-O-RAMA CLAMS-FISH & CHIPS HAMBURGERS
TIP TO: MIKE ZEIS
Zippythepinhead.com
MY COUNTRY--- RIGHT OR FAR-RIGHT!!
BILLY'S BURG-O-RAMA CLAMS-FISH & CHIPS HAMBURGERS

120

©2006 Bill Griffith. World rights reserved. Distributed by King Features Syndicate
GR-R-R-R...
CAN'T YOU TWO OPPOSING FORCES OF TH' UNIVERSE GET ALONG?
HISS-S-S-S...
TIP O' TH' PIN TO: NEAL GOLDSTEIN
I MEAN...CAN'T YOU SEE YOU'RE BOTH TWO SIDES OF TH' SAME COIN? C'MON, GUYS, FEEL TH' LOVE!!
HISS-S-S...
GR-R-R-R...
GRIFFY
7-30
Zippythepinhead.com
BACK OFF, PINHEAD! CONFLICT IS NATURAL--
--WITHOUT US THERE'D BE NOTHING BUT SUNSHINE & LOLLIPOPS!
DOES IT ALWAYS HAVE TO BE ABOUT LESLEY GORE??

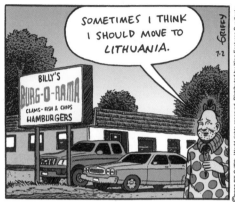

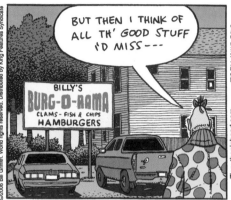

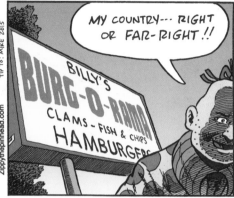

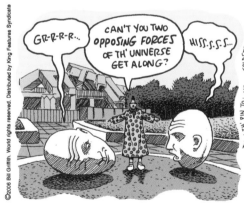

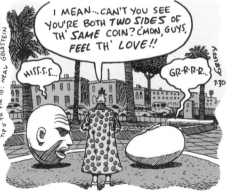

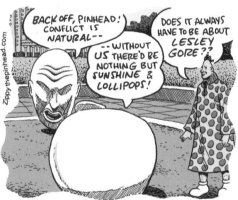

121

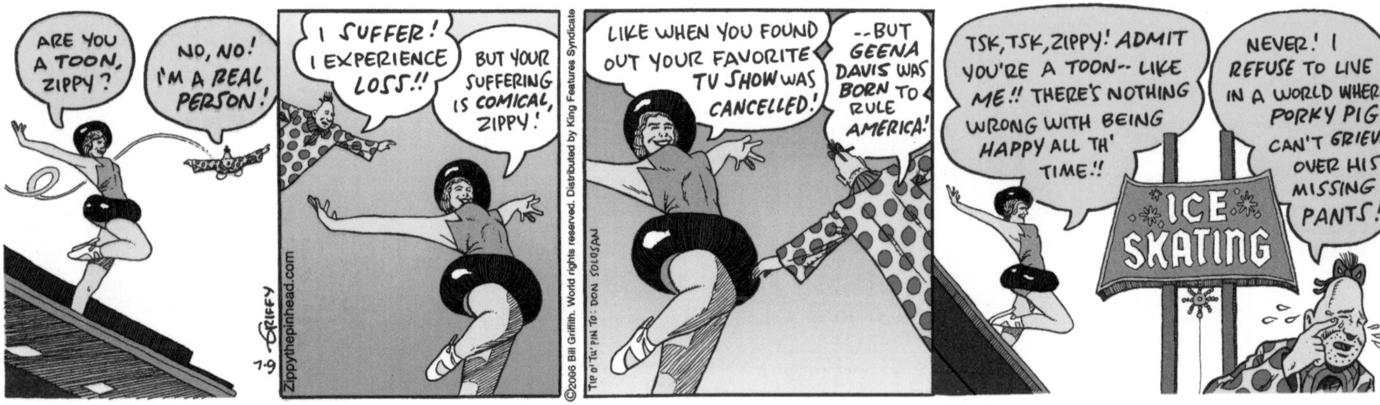
ARE YOU A TOON, ZIPPY?
NO, NO! I'M A REAL PERSON!
I SUFFER! I EXPERIENCE LOSS!!
BUT YOUR SUFFERING IS COMICAL, ZIPPY!
LIKE WHEN YOU FOUND OUT YOUR FAVORITE TV SHOW WAS CANCELLED!
--BUT GEENA DAVIS WAS BORN TO RULE AMERICA!
TSK, TSK, ZIPPY! ADMIT YOU'RE A TOON-- LIKE ME!! THERE'S NOTHING WRONG WITH BEING HAPPY ALL TH' TIME!!
NEVER! I REFUSE TO LIVE IN A WORLD WHERE PORKY PIG CAN'T GRIEVE OVER HIS MISSING PANTS!
ICE SKATING
GRIFFY 1-9
Zippythepinhead.com
©2006 Bill Griffith. World rights reserved. Distributed by King Features Syndicate
TIP O' TH' PIN TO: DON SOLOSAN

122

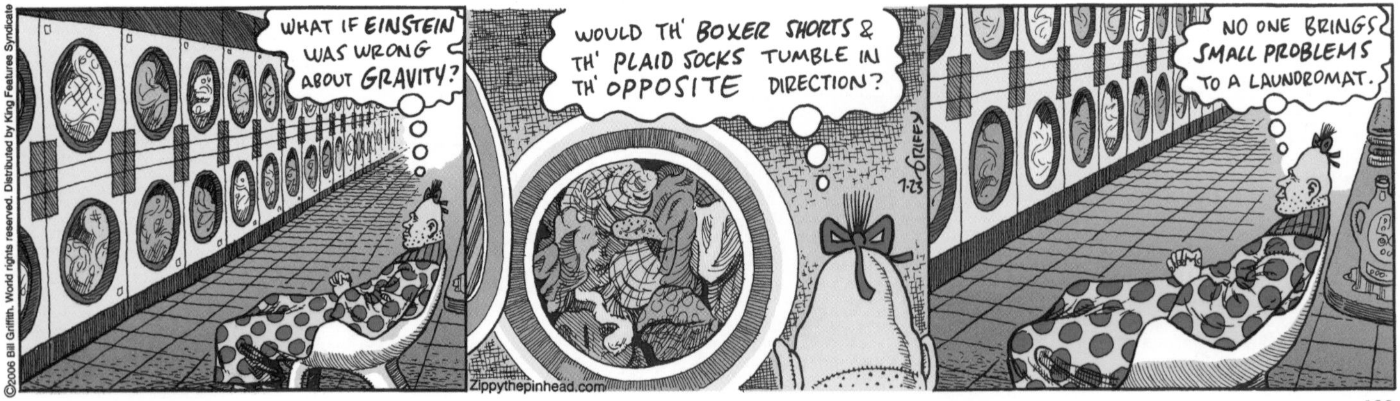
WHAT IF EINSTEIN WAS WRONG ABOUT GRAVITY?
WOULD TH' BOXER SHORTS & TH' PLAID SOCKS TUMBLE IN TH' OPPOSITE DIRECTION?
NO ONE BRINGS SMALL PROBLEMS TO A LAUNDROMAT.
GRIFFY 1-23
Zippythepinhead.com
©2006 Bill Griffith. World rights reserved. Distributed by King Features Syndicate

123

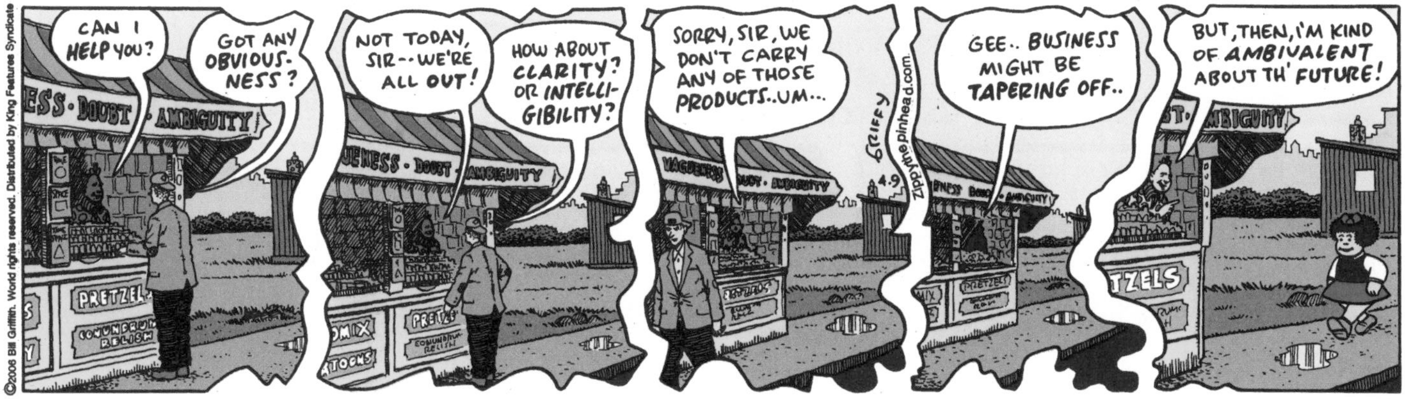
CAN I HELP YOU?
GOT ANY OBVIOUS-NESS?
NOT TODAY, SIR--WE'RE ALL OUT!
HOW ABOUT CLARITY? OR INTELLI-GIBILITY?
SORRY, SIR, WE DON'T CARRY ANY OF THOSE PRODUCTS..UM...
GEE.. BUSINESS MIGHT BE TAPERING OFF..
BUT, THEN, I'M KIND OF AMBIVALENT ABOUT TH' FUTURE!
DOUBT · AMBIGUITY
PRETZELS
GRIFFY 4·9
Zippythepinhead.com
©2006 Bill Griffith. World rights reserved. Distributed by King Features Syndicate

124

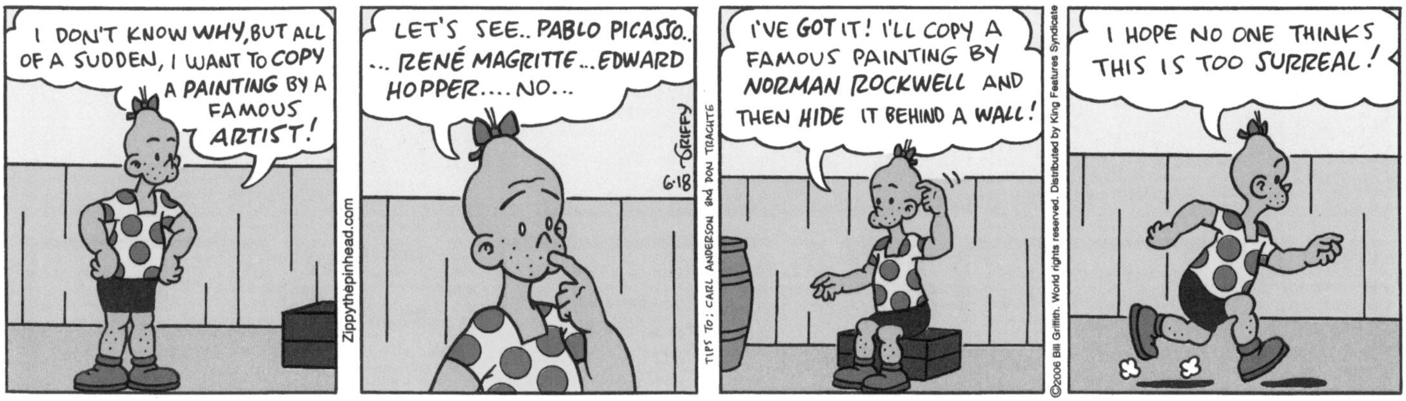
I DON'T KNOW WHY, BUT ALL OF A SUDDEN, I WANT TO COPY A PAINTING BY A FAMOUS ARTIST!
LET'S SEE.. PABLO PICASSO.. ... RENÉ MAGRITTE ... EDWARD HOPPER.... NO...
I'VE GOT IT! I'LL COPY A FAMOUS PAINTING BY NORMAN ROCKWELL AND THEN HIDE IT BEHIND A WALL!
I HOPE NO ONE THINKS THIS IS TOO SURREAL!
GRIFFY 6·18
TIPS TO: CARL ANDERSON and DON TRACHTE
Zippythepinhead.com
©2006 Bill Griffith. World rights reserved. Distributed by King Features Syndicate

125

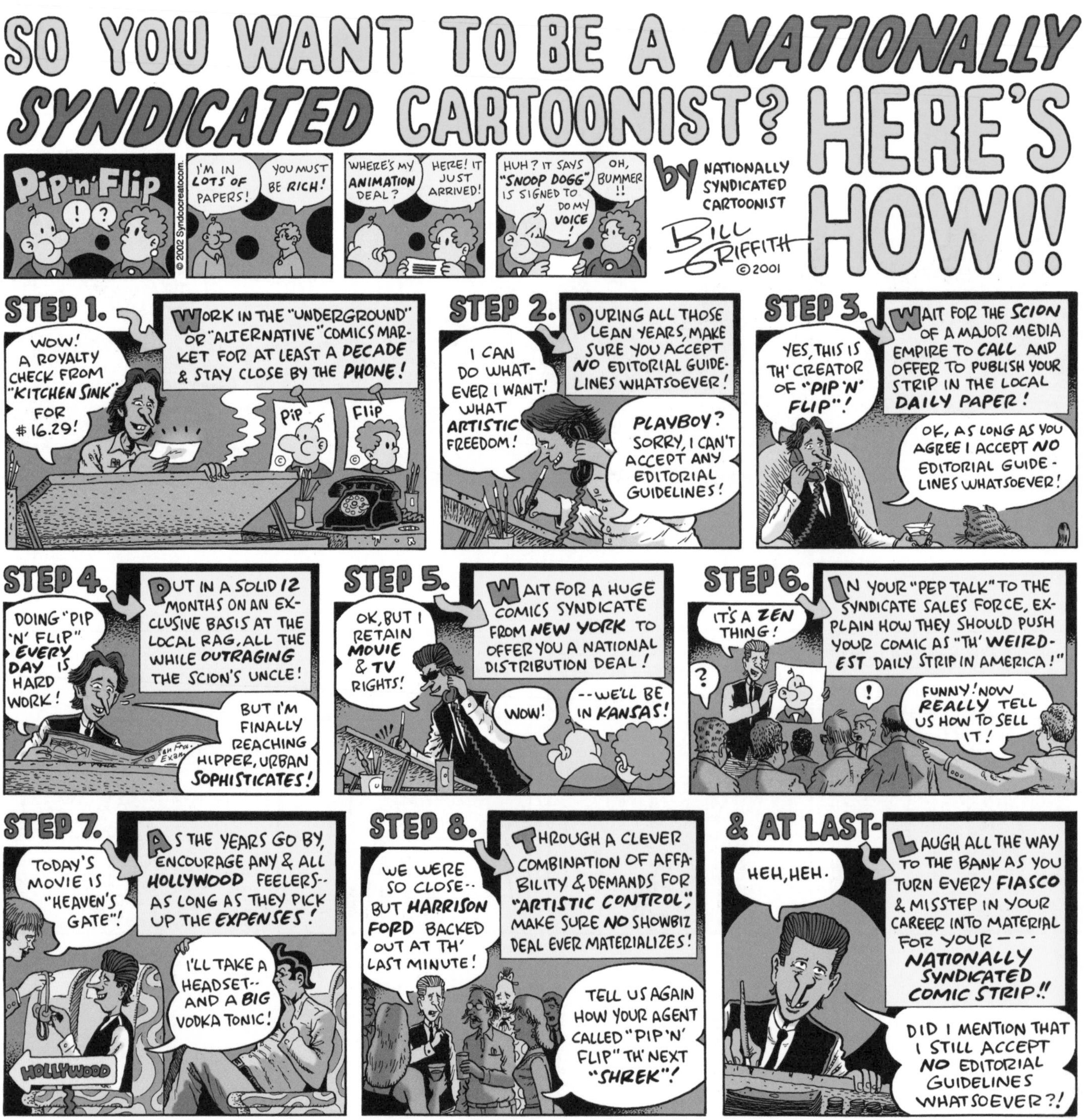
SO YOU WANT TO BE A NATIONALLY SYNDICATED CARTOONIST? HERE'S HOW!!
Pip'n'Flip
!
?
© 2002 Syndcocreatocom.
I'M IN LOTS OF PAPERS!
YOU MUST BE RICH!
WHERE'S MY ANIMATION DEAL?
HERE! IT JUST ARRIVED!
HUH? IT SAYS "SNOOP DOGG" IS SIGNED TO DO MY VOICE!
OH, BUMMER!!
by NATIONALLY SYNDICATED CARTOONIST
BILL GRIFFITH
©2001
STEP 1.
WORK IN THE "UNDERGROUND" OR "ALTERNATIVE" COMICS MARKET FOR AT LEAST A DECADE & STAY CLOSE BY THE PHONE!
WOW! A ROYALTY CHECK FROM "KITCHEN SINK" FOR $16.29!
PIP
FLIP
STEP 2.
DURING ALL THOSE LEAN YEARS, MAKE SURE YOU ACCEPT NO EDITORIAL GUIDELINES WHATSOEVER!
I CAN DO WHATEVER I WANT! WHAT ARTISTIC FREEDOM!
PLAYBOY? SORRY, I CAN'T ACCEPT ANY EDITORIAL GUIDELINES!
STEP 3.
WAIT FOR THE SCION OF A MAJOR MEDIA EMPIRE TO CALL AND OFFER TO PUBLISH YOUR STRIP IN THE LOCAL DAILY PAPER!
YES, THIS IS TH' CREATOR OF "PIP 'N' FLIP"!
OK, AS LONG AS YOU AGREE I ACCEPT NO EDITORIAL GUIDELINES WHATSOEVER!
STEP 4.
PUT IN A SOLID 12 MONTHS ON AN EXCLUSIVE BASIS AT THE LOCAL RAG, ALL THE WHILE OUTRAGING THE SCION'S UNCLE!
DOING "PIP 'N' FLIP" EVERY DAY IS HARD WORK!
BUT I'M FINALLY REACHING HIPPER, URBAN SOPHISTICATES!
STEP 5.
WAIT FOR A HUGE COMICS SYNDICATE FROM NEW YORK TO OFFER YOU A NATIONAL DISTRIBUTION DEAL!
OK, BUT I RETAIN MOVIE & TV RIGHTS!
WOW!
--WE'LL BE IN KANSAS!
STEP 6.
IN YOUR "PEP TALK" TO THE SYNDICATE SALES FORCE, EXPLAIN HOW THEY SHOULD PUSH YOUR COMIC AS "TH' WEIRDEST DAILY STRIP IN AMERICA!"
IT'S A ZEN THING!
?
!
FUNNY! NOW REALLY TELL US HOW TO SELL IT!
STEP 7.
AS THE YEARS GO BY, ENCOURAGE ANY & ALL HOLLYWOOD FEELERS-- AS LONG AS THEY PICK UP THE EXPENSES!
TODAY'S MOVIE IS "HEAVEN'S GATE"!
I'LL TAKE A HEADSET-- AND A BIG VODKA TONIC!
HOLLYWOOD
STEP 8.
THROUGH A CLEVER COMBINATION OF AFFABILITY & DEMANDS FOR "ARTISTIC CONTROL", MAKE SURE NO SHOWBIZ DEAL EVER MATERIALIZES!
WE WERE SO CLOSE-- BUT HARRISON FORD BACKED OUT AT TH' LAST MINUTE!
TELL US AGAIN HOW YOUR AGENT CALLED "PIP 'N' FLIP" TH' NEXT "SHREK"!
& AT LAST-
LAUGH ALL THE WAY TO THE BANK AS YOU TURN EVERY FIASCO & MISSTEP IN YOUR CAREER INTO MATERIAL FOR YOUR--- NATIONALLY SYNDICATED COMIC STRIP!!
HEH, HEH.
DID I MENTION THAT I STILL ACCEPT NO EDITORIAL GUIDELINES WHATSOEVER?!

126

MY FATHER ALWAYS IMPRESSED UPON ME A REVERENCE & RESPECT FOR THE **AMERICAN FLAG.**

HE WORKED AT THE **WHITEHALL STREET ARMY INDUCTION CENTER** IN LOWER MANHATTAN.

WHEN HE DIED, IN 1972, HE WAS GIVEN A **MILITARY FUNERAL** & A 21-GUN SALUTE. I WAS PRESENTED WITH A CRISPLY FOLDED FLAG.

WE ARGUED ENDLESSLY ABOUT **NUCLEAR DISARMAMENT** & THE **VIETNAM WAR.** WHEN HE DIED, I REGRETTED THAT I'D NEVER TOLD HIM WHY I'D REALLY **"FAILED"** MY PHYSICAL AT THE WHITEHALL ST. INDUCTION CENTER IN 1966.

Asthma ☐
Flat Feet ☐
Homosexual Tendencies ☐
Psoriasis

WHEN I WAS **EIGHT,** IN 1952, HE TOOK ME INTO **WORK** ONE DAY. I PLAYED WITH PAPER CLIPS & INDUCTION FORMS AT HIS DESK. WHEN HE DIED, I WAS GIVEN A **SHELL CASING** FROM HIS 21-GUN SALUTE.

Patriotic **DUTY**

MY FATHER KEPT A **DIARY** IN 1941. THERE ARE NO ENTRIES BEYOND **PEARL HARBOR DAY.** HE VOLUNTEERED FOR ACTIVE DUTY ON DECEMBER 8TH, 1941.

HE USED TO TELL ME STORIES ABOUT HOW SOME MEN WOULD TRY TO **AVOID** MILITARY SERVICE IN THE FIFTIES.

WHEN HE DIED, **ELECTION DAY** WAS A FEW DAYS OFF. I THOUGHT ABOUT CASTING MY VOTE FOR **RICHARD NIXON,** HIS CHOICE.

4 MORE YEARS

BUT I COULDN'T DO IT...

THERE WAS **NO** SURGE IN U.S. ARMY **ENLISTMENT** ON SEPTEMBER 12TH, 2001.

WHEN MY FATHER DIED, I FELT A SMALL TWINGE OF **PATRIOTISM.**

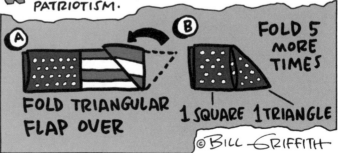

Ⓐ Ⓑ

FOLD 5 MORE TIMES

FOLD TRIANGULAR FLAP OVER

1 SQUARE 1 TRIANGLE

© BILL GRIFFITH

CARtooNist dEScENding An elEvaTOr

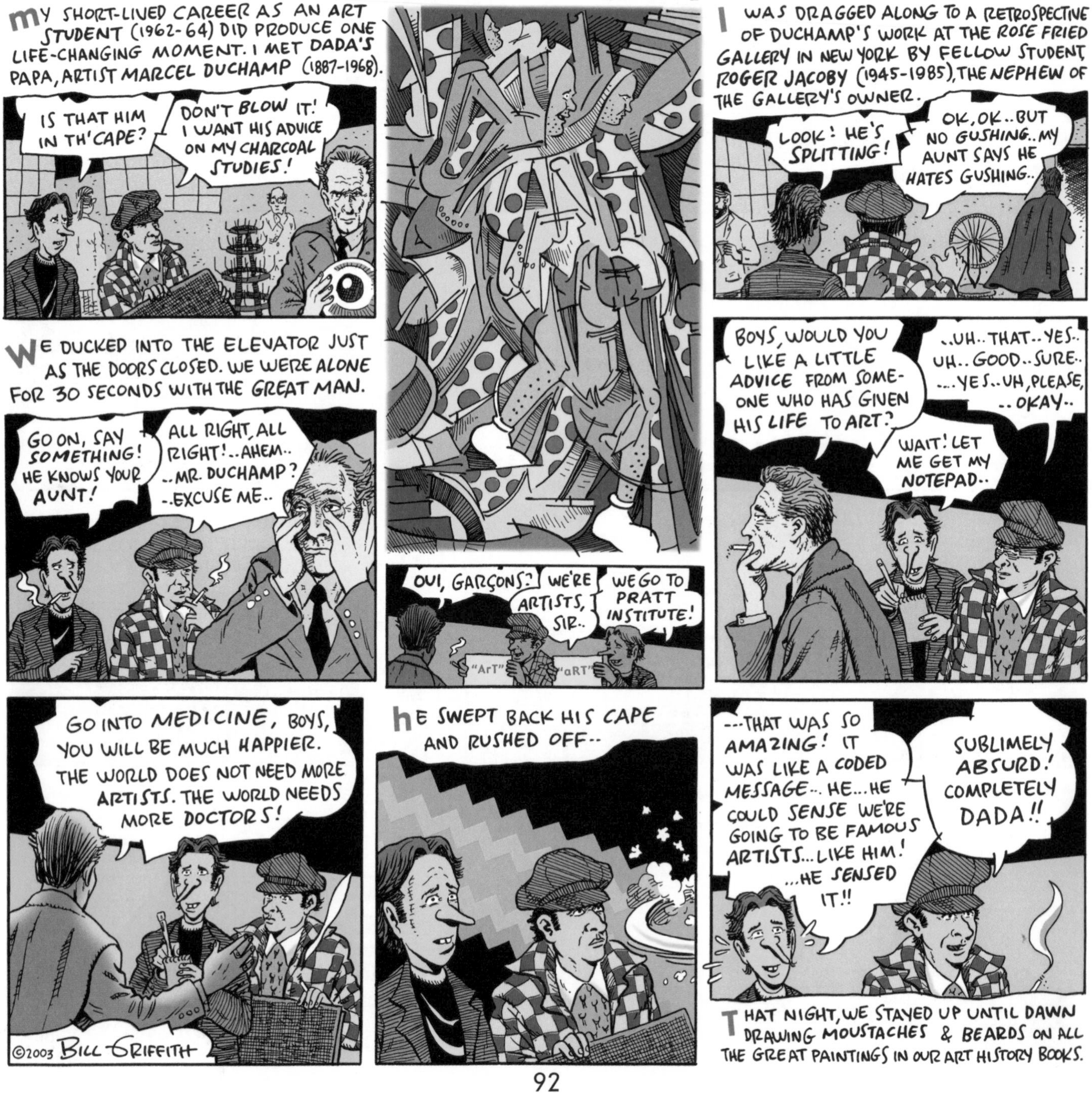
MY SHORT-LIVED CAREER AS AN ART STUDENT (1962-64) DID PRODUCE ONE LIFE-CHANGING MOMENT. I MET DADA'S PAPA, ARTIST MARCEL DUCHAMP (1887-1968).
IS THAT HIM IN TH' CAPE?
DON'T BLOW IT! I WANT HIS ADVICE ON MY CHARCOAL STUDIES!
I WAS DRAGGED ALONG TO A RETROSPECTIVE OF DUCHAMP'S WORK AT THE ROSE FRIED GALLERY IN NEW YORK BY FELLOW STUDENT, ROGER JACOBY (1945-1985), THE NEPHEW OF THE GALLERY'S OWNER.
LOOK! HE'S SPLITTING!
OK, OK.. BUT NO GUSHING.. MY AUNT SAYS HE HATES GUSHING..
WE DUCKED INTO THE ELEVATOR JUST AS THE DOORS CLOSED. WE WERE ALONE FOR 30 SECONDS WITH THE GREAT MAN.
GO ON, SAY SOMETHING! HE KNOWS YOUR AUNT!
ALL RIGHT, ALL RIGHT!..AHEM.. ..MR. DUCHAMP? ..EXCUSE ME..
OUI, GARÇONS?
WE'RE ARTISTS, SIR..
WE GO TO PRATT INSTITUTE!
"ArT"
"aRT"
BOYS, WOULD YOU LIKE A LITTLE ADVICE FROM SOME-ONE WHO HAS GIVEN HIS LIFE TO ART?
..UH.. THAT.. YES.. UH.. GOOD.. SURE.. ...YES..UH, PLEASE, ..OKAY..
WAIT! LET ME GET MY NOTEPAD..
GO INTO MEDICINE, BOYS, YOU WILL BE MUCH HAPPIER. THE WORLD DOES NOT NEED MORE ARTISTS. THE WORLD NEEDS MORE DOCTORS!
©2003 BILL GRIFFITH
HE SWEPT BACK HIS CAPE AND RUSHED OFF--
---THAT WAS SO AMAZING! IT WAS LIKE A CODED MESSAGE-- HE... HE COULD SENSE WE'RE GOING TO BE FAMOUS ARTISTS... LIKE HIM! ...HE SENSED IT!!
SUBLIMELY ABSURD! COMPLETELY DADA!!
THAT NIGHT, WE STAYED UP UNTIL DAWN DRAWING MOUSTACHES & BEARDS ON ALL THE GREAT PAINTINGS IN OUR ART HISTORY BOOKS.

I WAS A YOUNG, IMPRESSIONABLE ART STUDENT... SHE WAS MY FRESHMAN "FOUNDATION" PROFESSOR... I WAS 19... SHE WAS 42... THEN ONE DAY —

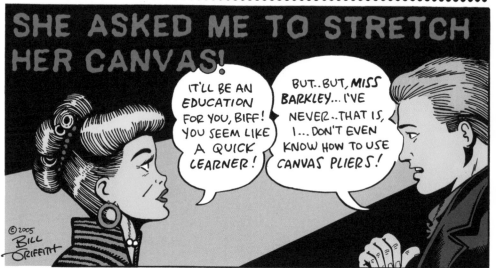

SHE ASKED ME TO STRETCH HER CANVAS!

© 2005 BILL GRIFFITH

IT'LL BE AN EDUCATION FOR YOU, BIFF! YOU SEEM LIKE A QUICK LEARNER!

BUT..BUT, MISS BARKLEY... I'VE NEVER..THAT IS, I...DON'T EVEN KNOW HOW TO USE CANVAS PLIERS!

I WON'T TAKE NO FOR AN ANSWER! HERE'S A LONG ISLAND RAILROAD SCHEDULE & DIRECTIONS TO MY STUDIO IN GLEN COVE!

WELL, OK, I GUESS I CAN STUDY UP ON THE PROCESS DURING THE TRAIN RIDE...

JEEZ, LOOK AT THE SIZE OF THAT STUDIO! IT'S BIGGER THAN PICASSO'S!!

BIFF!

WHY DON'T YOU BEGIN ON A SMALL ONE... WE CAN WORK UP TO THE LARGE SIZES...

UM, WHICH SIDE OF THE FRAME SHOULD I START ON, MISS BARKLEY?

BEGIN IN THE EAST POSITION, PLACING THE FIRST STAPLE IN THE CENTER OF THE STRETCHER BAR WHILE I FRESHEN UP A LITTLE!

DO I CONTINUE IN THE NORTH POSITION, THEN AGAIN IN THE SOUTH POSITION, METHODICALLY MOVING FROM ONE POSITION TO THE OTHER--?

OH, YES, BIFF!!

EVEN TENSION ON THE CANVAS IS ESSENTIAL TO A TAUGHT, FIRM PAINTING SURFACE!

I THINK I'M READY TO APPLY THE GESSO NOW, MISS BARKLEY!

POP!

MR. GRIFFMAN! PLEASE DO YOUR NAPPING OUTSIDE MY CLASSROOM!!

HUH? WHAT WAS TH' QUESTION, MISS BARKLEY?

PSST! TH' ANSWER IS SURREALISM!

THE END

Roadside Attractions

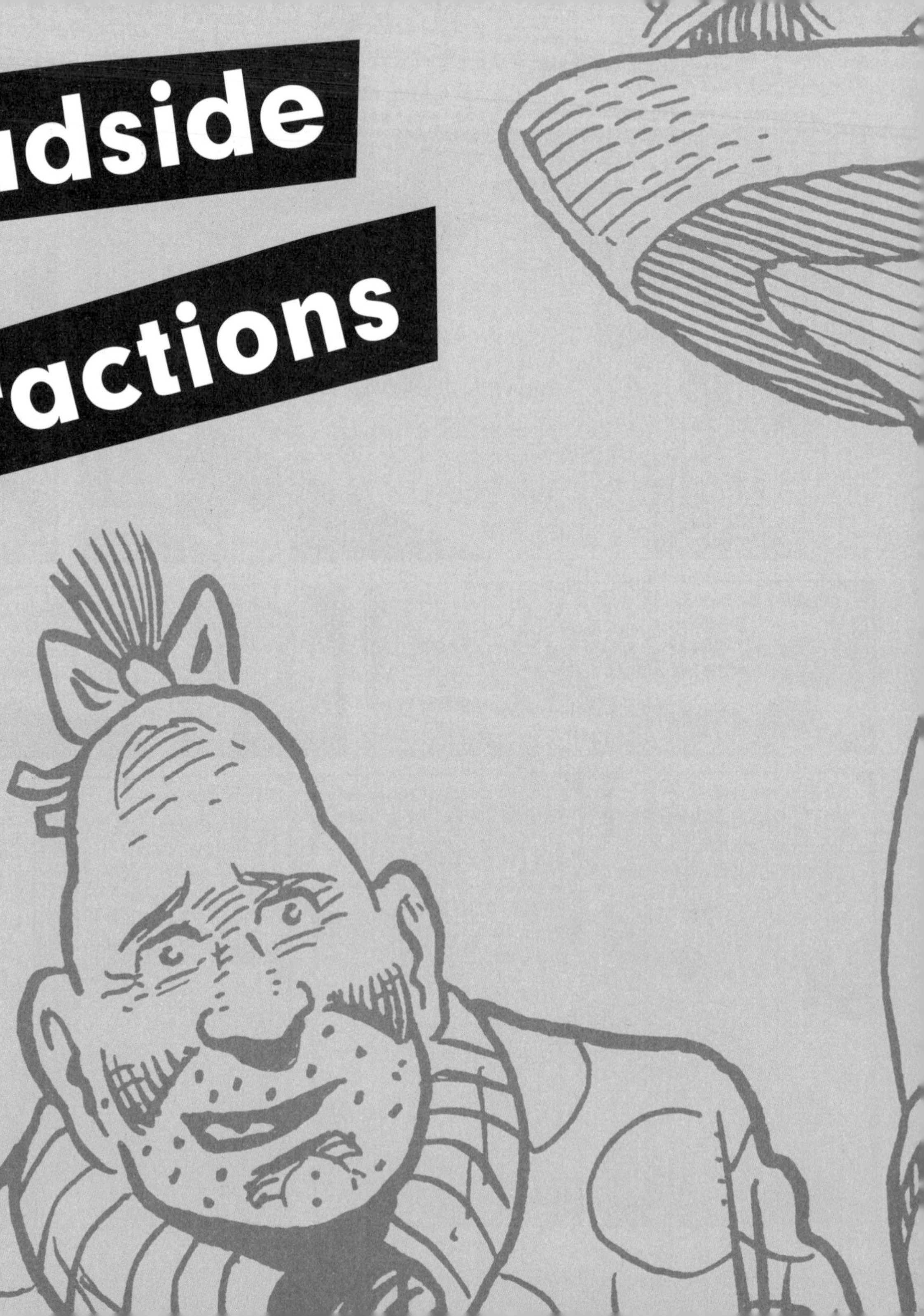

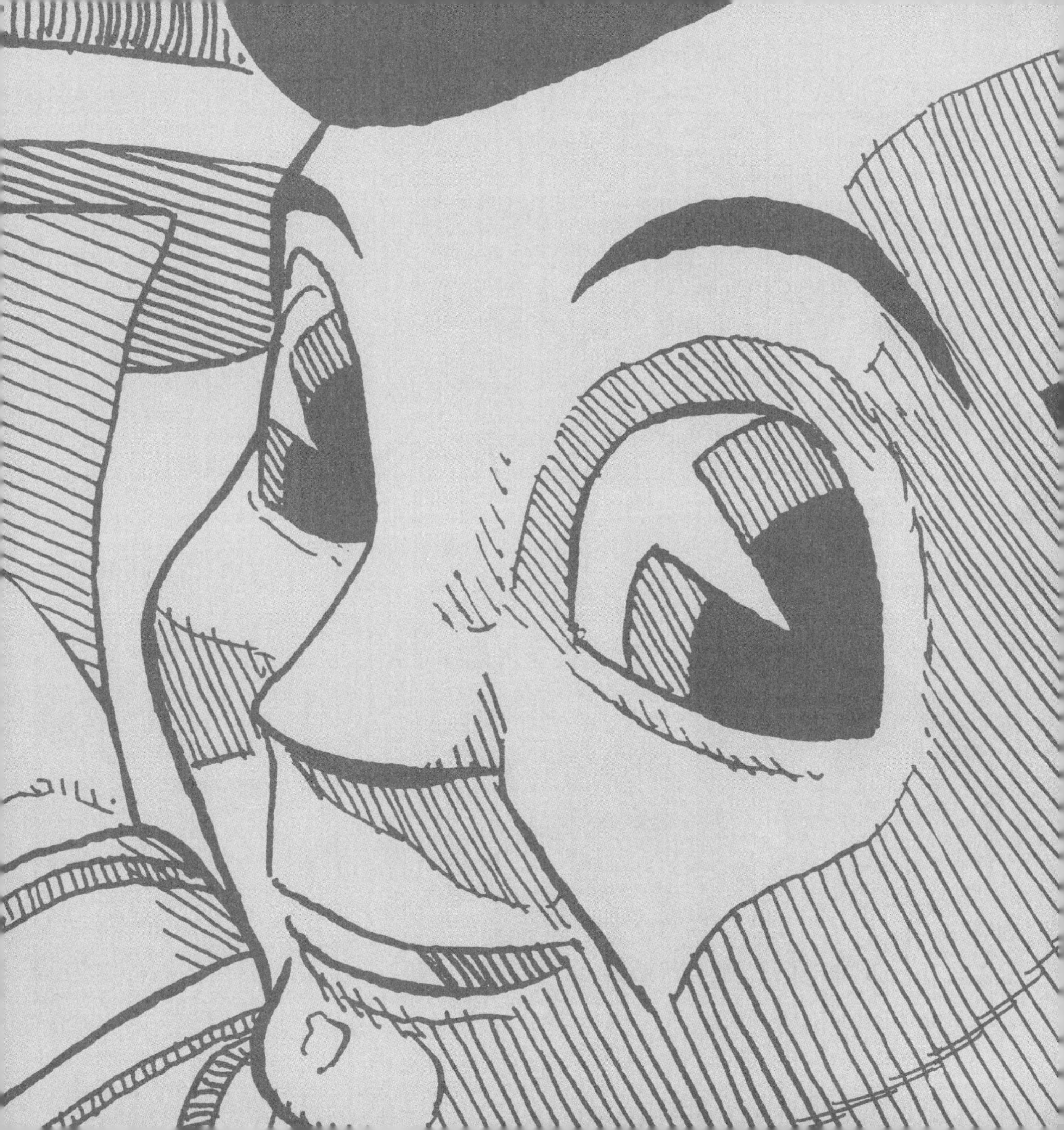

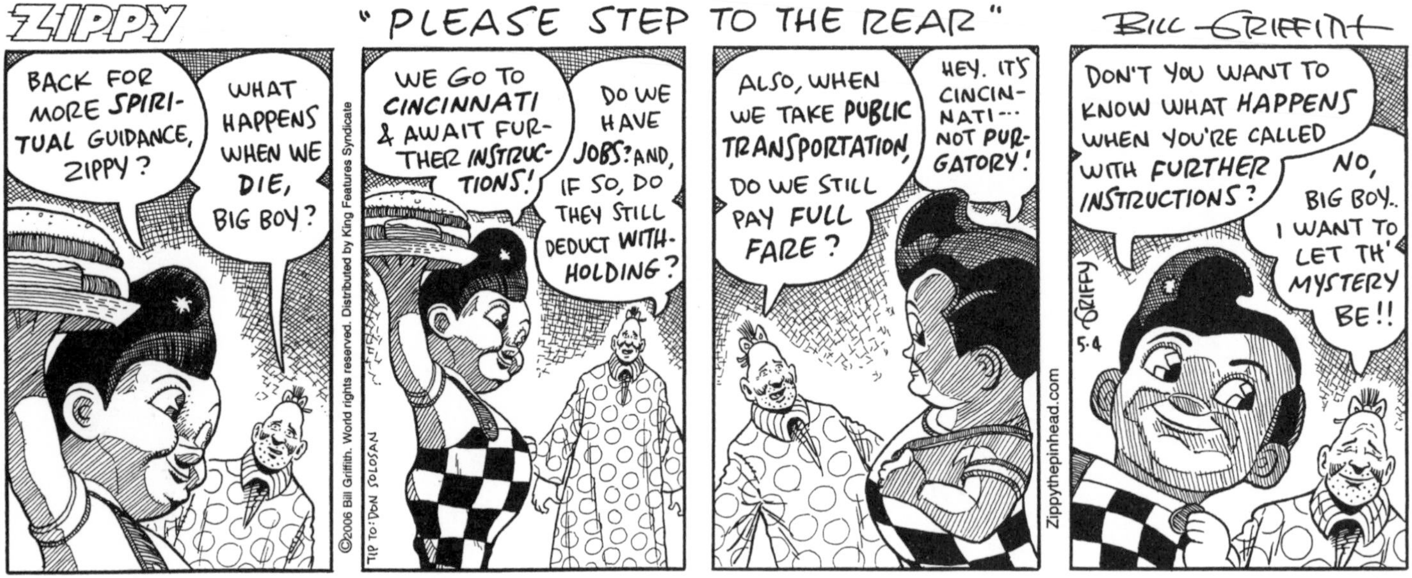
ZIPPY
"PLEASE STEP TO THE REAR"
BILL GRIFFITH
BACK FOR MORE SPIRITUAL GUIDANCE, ZIPPY?
WHAT HAPPENS WHEN WE DIE, BIG BOY?
©2006 Bill Griffith. World rights reserved. Distributed by King Features Syndicate
TIP TO: DON SOLOSAN
WE GO TO CINCINNATI & AWAIT FURTHER INSTRUCTIONS!
DO WE HAVE JOBS? AND, IF SO, DO THEY STILL DEDUCT WITHHOLDING?
ALSO, WHEN WE TAKE PUBLIC TRANSPORTATION, DO WE STILL PAY FULL FARE?
HEY. IT'S CINCINNATI--- NOT PURGATORY!
Zippythepinhead.com
GRIFFY 5.4
DON'T YOU WANT TO KNOW WHAT HAPPENS WHEN YOU'RE CALLED WITH FURTHER INSTRUCTIONS?
NO, BIG BOY.. I WANT TO LET TH' MYSTERY BE!!

127 A

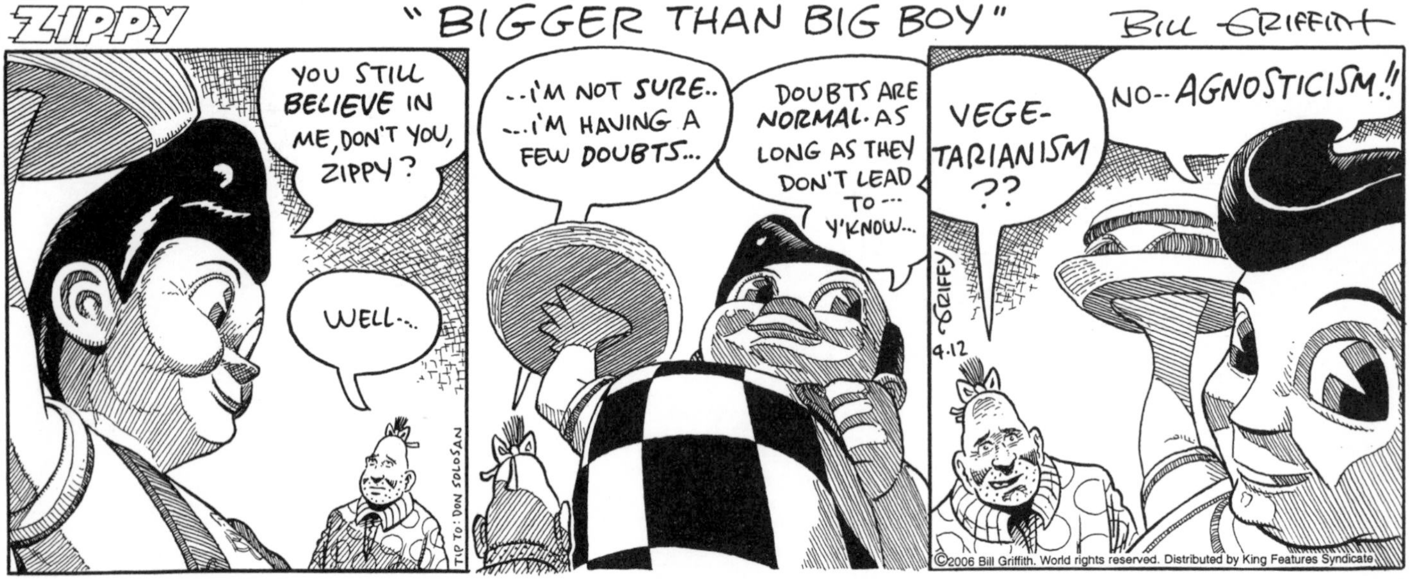
ZIPPY
"BIGGER THAN BIG BOY"
BILL GRIFFITH
YOU STILL BELIEVE IN ME, DON'T YOU, ZIPPY?
WELL-..
TIP TO: DON SOLOSAN
--I'M NOT SURE.. ..I'M HAVING A FEW DOUBTS...
DOUBTS ARE NORMAL. AS LONG AS THEY DON'T LEAD TO--- Y'KNOW...
VEGETARIANISM??
NO-- AGNOSTICISM!!
GRIFFY 4.12
©2006 Bill Griffith. World rights reserved. Distributed by King Features Syndicate

127 B

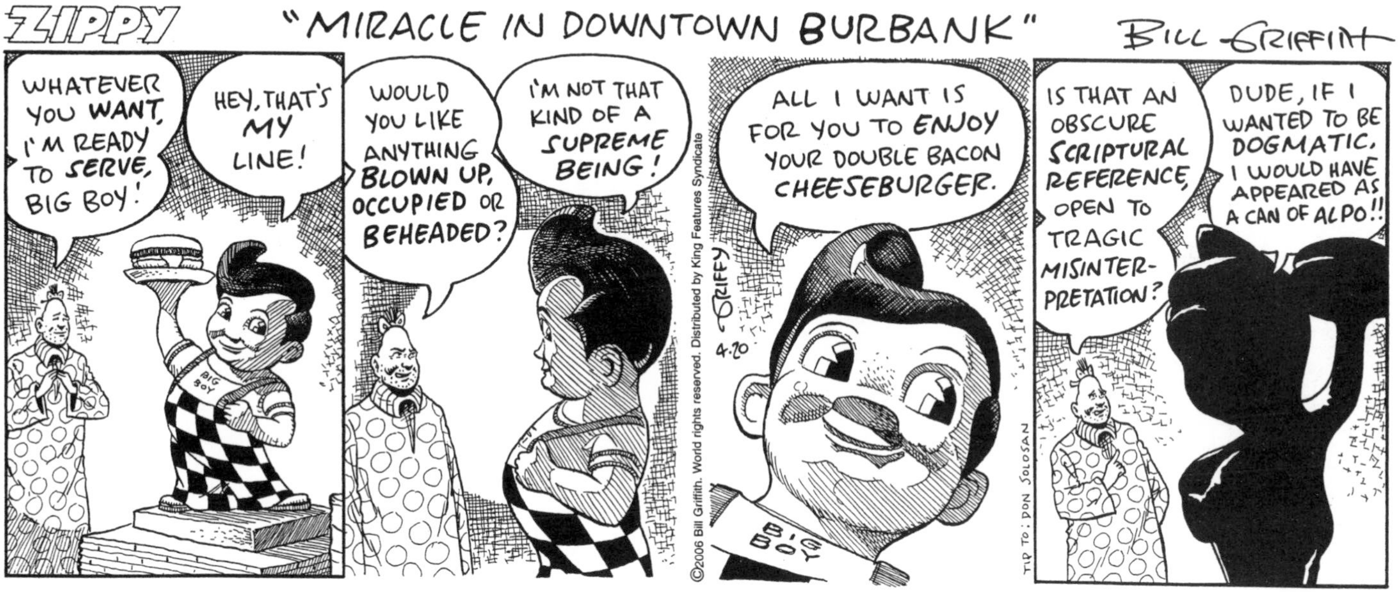
ZIPPY
"MIRACLE IN DOWNTOWN BURBANK"
BILL GRIFFITH
WHATEVER YOU WANT, I'M READY TO SERVE, BIG BOY!
HEY, THAT'S MY LINE!
WOULD YOU LIKE ANYTHING BLOWN UP, OCCUPIED OR BEHEADED?
I'M NOT THAT KIND OF A SUPREME BEING!
©2006 Bill Griffith. World rights reserved. Distributed by King Features Syndicate
GRIFFY 4.20
ALL I WANT IS FOR YOU TO ENJOY YOUR DOUBLE BACON CHEESEBURGER.
BIG BOY
TIP TO: DON SOLOSAN
IS THAT AN OBSCURE SCRIPTURAL REFERENCE, OPEN TO TRAGIC MISINTERPRETATION?
DUDE, IF I WANTED TO BE DOGMATIC, I WOULD HAVE APPEARED AS A CAN OF ALPO!!

127 C

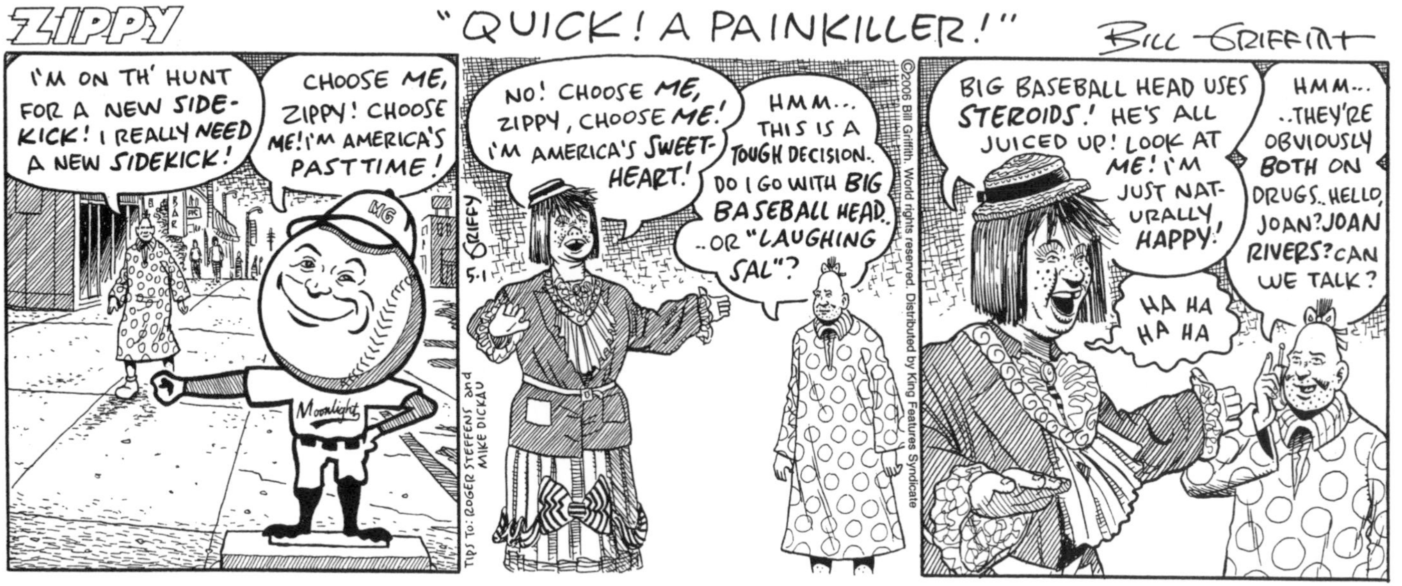
ZIPPY
"QUICK! A PAINKILLER!"
BILL GRIFFITH
I'M ON TH' HUNT FOR A NEW SIDE-KICK! I REALLY NEED A NEW SIDEKICK!
CHOOSE ME, ZIPPY! CHOOSE ME! I'M AMERICA'S PASTTIME!
MG
Moonlight
GRIFFY 5.1
TIPS TO: ROGER STEFFENS and MIKE DICKAU
NO! CHOOSE ME, ZIPPY, CHOOSE ME! I'M AMERICA'S SWEET-HEART!
HMM... THIS IS A TOUGH DECISION.. DO I GO WITH BIG BASEBALL HEAD.. ..OR "LAUGHING SAL"?
©2006 Bill Griffith. World rights reserved. Distributed by King Features Syndicate
BIG BASEBALL HEAD USES STEROIDS! HE'S ALL JUICED UP! LOOK AT ME! I'M JUST NAT-URALLY HAPPY!
HA HA HA HA
HMM... ..THEY'RE OBVIOUSLY BOTH ON DRUGS.. HELLO, JOAN? JOAN RIVERS? CAN WE TALK?

128

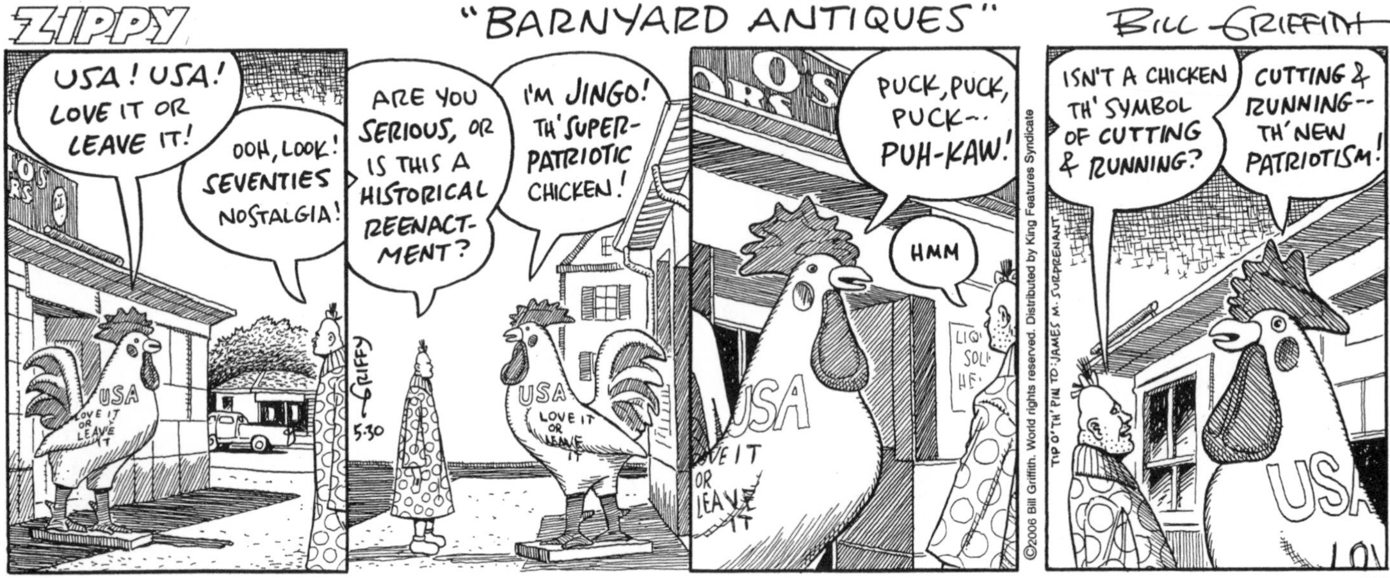
ZIPPY
"BARNYARD ANTIQUES"
BILL GRIFFITH
USA! USA! LOVE IT OR LEAVE IT!
OOH, LOOK! SEVENTIES NOSTALGIA!
USA LOVE IT OR LEAVE IT
ARE YOU SERIOUS, OR IS THIS A HISTORICAL REENACTMENT?
I'M JINGO! TH' SUPER-PATRIOTIC CHICKEN!
GRIFFY 5-30
PUCK, PUCK, PUCK-- PUH-KAW!
HMM
©2006 Bill Griffith. World rights reserved. Distributed by King Features Syndicate
TIP O' TH' PIN TO: JAMES M. SURPRENANT
ISN'T A CHICKEN TH' SYMBOL OF CUTTING & RUNNING?
CUTTING & RUNNING-- TH' NEW PATRIOTISM!
USA

129

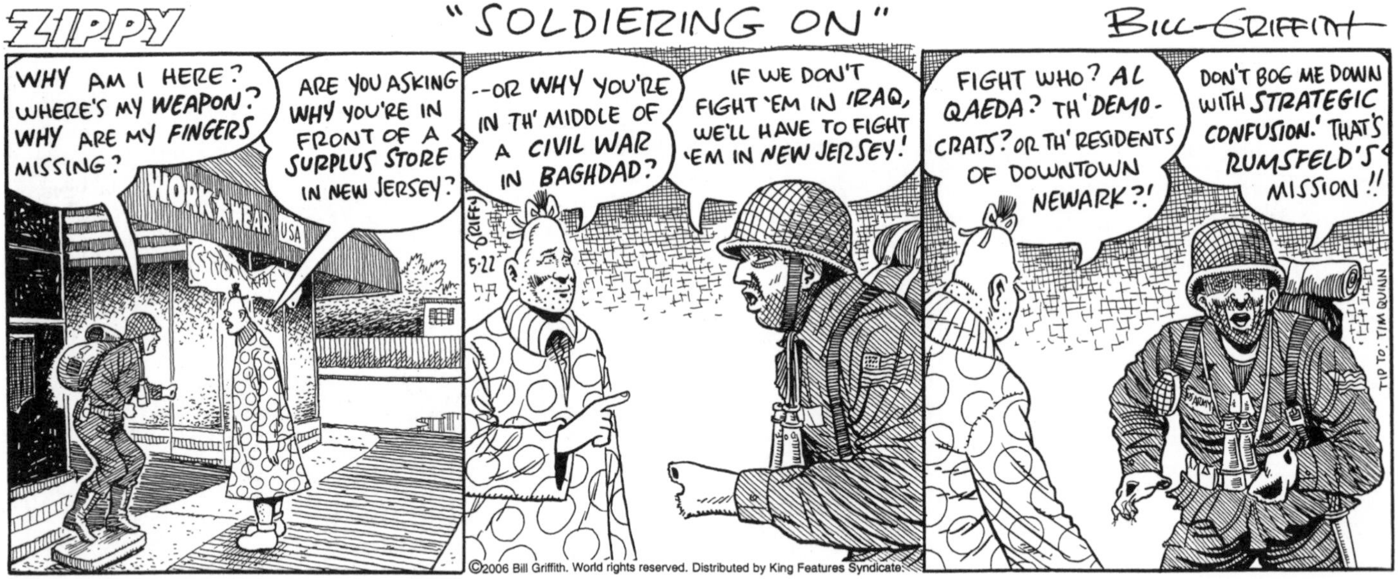
ZIPPY
"SOLDIERING ON"
BILL GRIFFITH
WHY AM I HERE? WHERE'S MY WEAPON? WHY ARE MY FINGERS MISSING?
ARE YOU ASKING WHY YOU'RE IN FRONT OF A SURPLUS STORE IN NEW JERSEY?
WORK★WEAR USA
--OR WHY YOU'RE IN TH' MIDDLE OF A CIVIL WAR IN BAGHDAD?
IF WE DON'T FIGHT 'EM IN IRAQ, WE'LL HAVE TO FIGHT 'EM IN NEW JERSEY!
GRIFFY 5-22
FIGHT WHO? AL QAEDA? TH' DEMOCRATS? OR TH' RESIDENTS OF DOWNTOWN NEWARK?!
DON'T BOG ME DOWN WITH STRATEGIC CONFUSION! THAT'S RUMSFELD'S MISSION!!
TIP TO: TIM QUINN
©2006 Bill Griffith. World rights reserved. Distributed by King Features Syndicate.

130

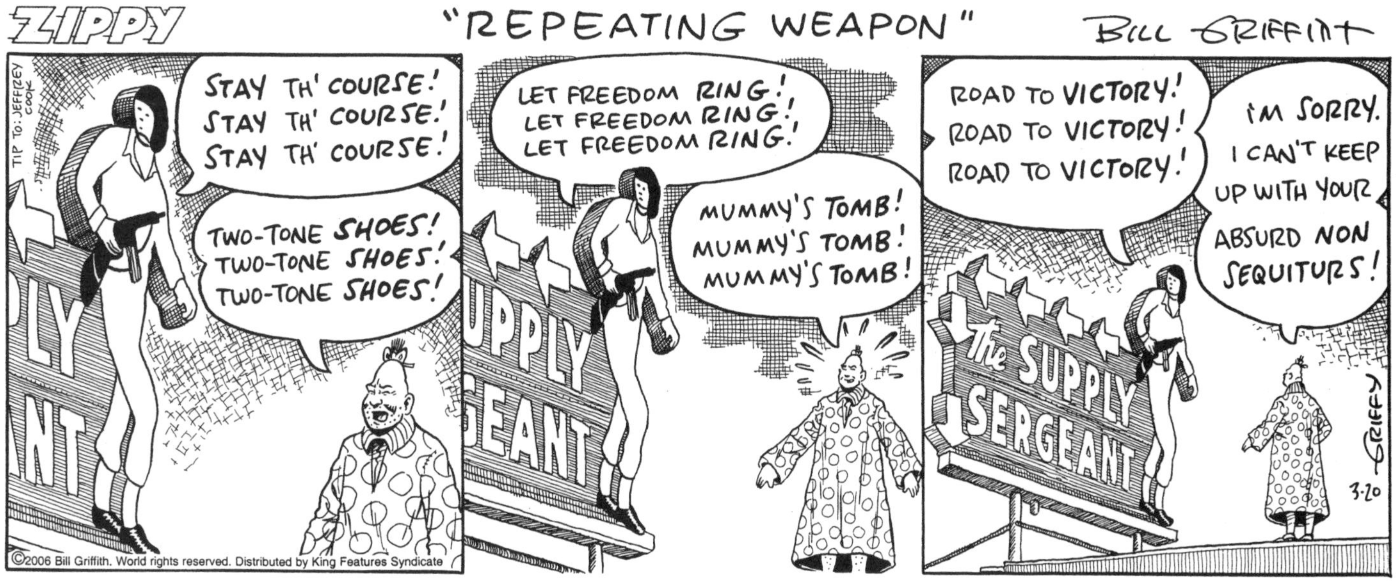
ZIPPY
"REPEATING WEAPON"
BILL GRIFFITH
TIP TO: JEFFREY COOK
STAY TH' COURSE! STAY TH' COURSE! STAY TH' COURSE!
TWO-TONE SHOES! TWO-TONE SHOES! TWO-TONE SHOES!
©2006 Bill Griffith. World rights reserved. Distributed by King Features Syndicate
LET FREEDOM RING! LET FREEDOM RING! LET FREEDOM RING!
MUMMY'S TOMB! MUMMY'S TOMB! MUMMY'S TOMB!
UPPLY
GEANT
ROAD TO VICTORY! ROAD TO VICTORY! ROAD TO VICTORY!
I'M SORRY. I CAN'T KEEP UP WITH YOUR ABSURD NON SEQUITURS!
The SUPPLY SERGEANT
GRIFFY
3-20

131

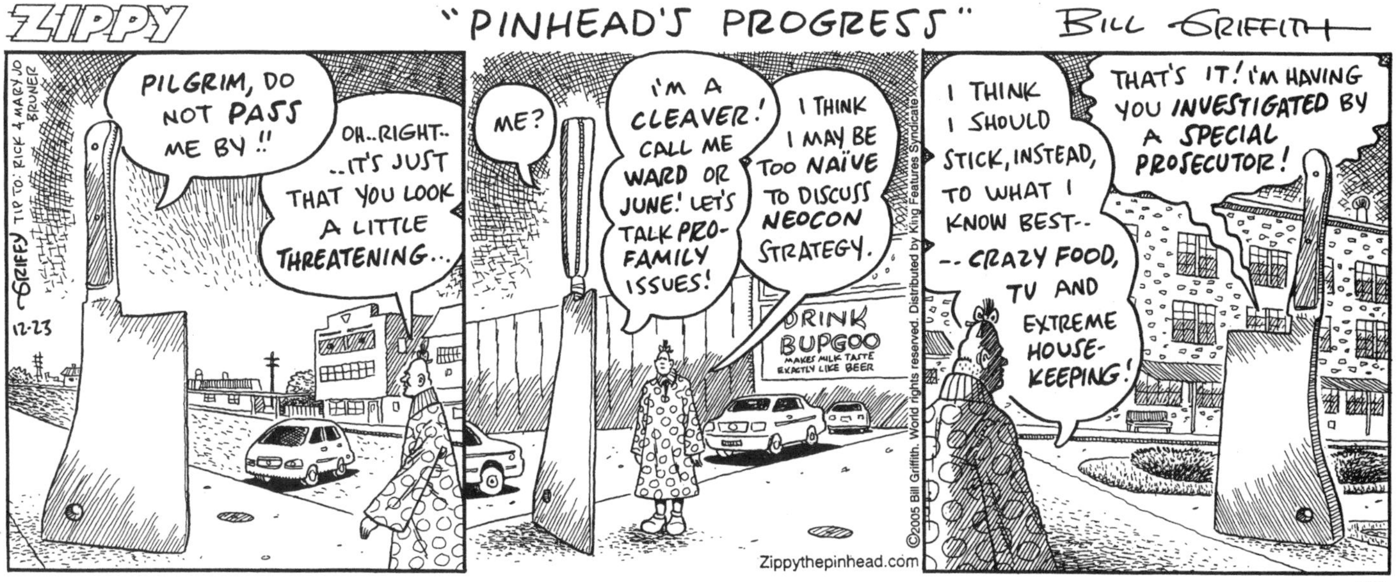
ZIPPY
"PINHEAD'S PROGRESS"
BILL GRIFFITH
GRIFFY TIP TO: RICK & MARY JO BRUNER
12-23
PILGRIM, DO NOT PASS ME BY!!
OH..RIGHT-- ..IT'S JUST THAT YOU LOOK A LITTLE THREATENING...
ME?
I'M A CLEAVER! CALL ME WARD OR JUNE! LET'S TALK PRO-FAMILY ISSUES!
I THINK I MAY BE TOO NAÏVE TO DISCUSS NEOCON STRATEGY.
DRINK BUPGOO MAKES MILK TASTE EXACTLY LIKE BEER
©2005 Bill Griffith. World rights reserved. Distributed by King Features Syndicate
Zippythepinhead.com
I THINK I SHOULD STICK, INSTEAD, TO WHAT I KNOW BEST-- --CRAZY FOOD, TV AND EXTREME HOUSE-KEEPING!
THAT'S IT! I'M HAVING YOU INVESTIGATED BY A SPECIAL PROSECUTOR!

132

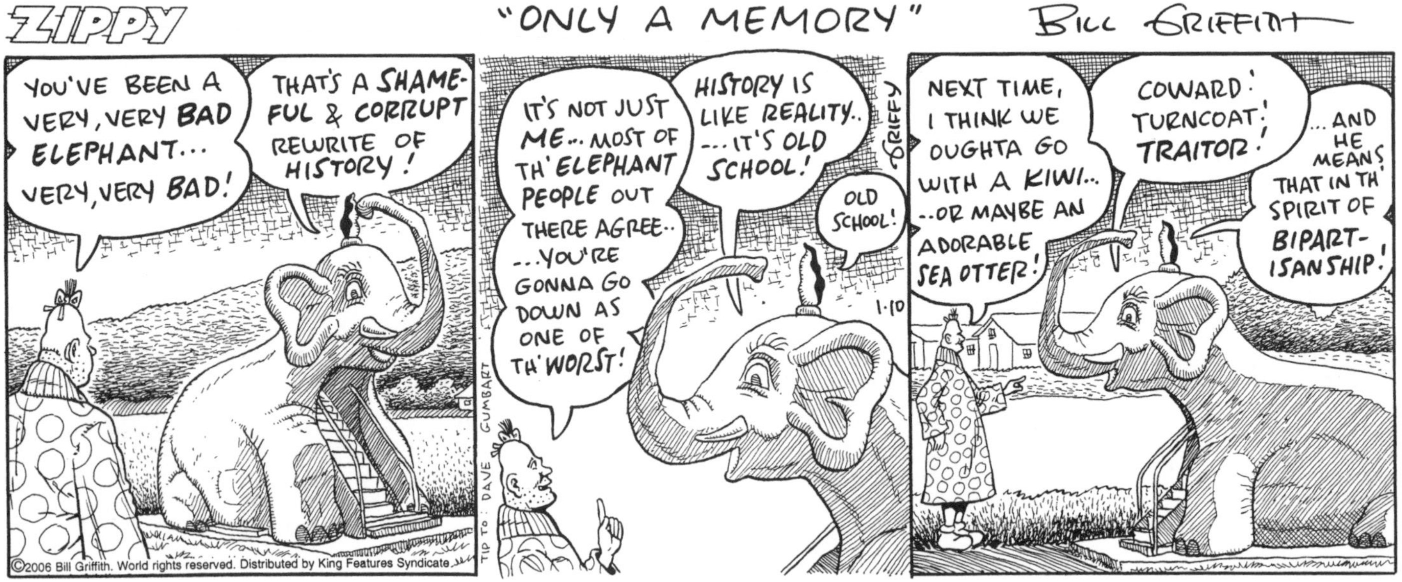
ZIPPY
"ONLY A MEMORY"
BILL GRIFFITH
YOU'VE BEEN A VERY, VERY BAD ELEPHANT... VERY, VERY BAD!
THAT'S A SHAMEFUL & CORRUPT REWRITE OF HISTORY!
IT'S NOT JUST ME.. MOST OF TH' ELEPHANT PEOPLE OUT THERE AGREE.. ...YOU'RE GONNA GO DOWN AS ONE OF TH' WORST!
HISTORY IS LIKE REALITY.. ...IT'S OLD SCHOOL!
OLD SCHOOL!
TIP TO: DAVE GUMBART
GRIFFY
1-10
NEXT TIME, I THINK WE OUGHTA GO WITH A KIWI... ..OR MAYBE AN ADORABLE SEA OTTER!
COWARD! TURNCOAT! TRAITOR!
...AND HE MEANS THAT IN TH' SPIRIT OF BIPARTISANSHIP!
©2006 Bill Griffith. World rights reserved. Distributed by King Features Syndicate

133

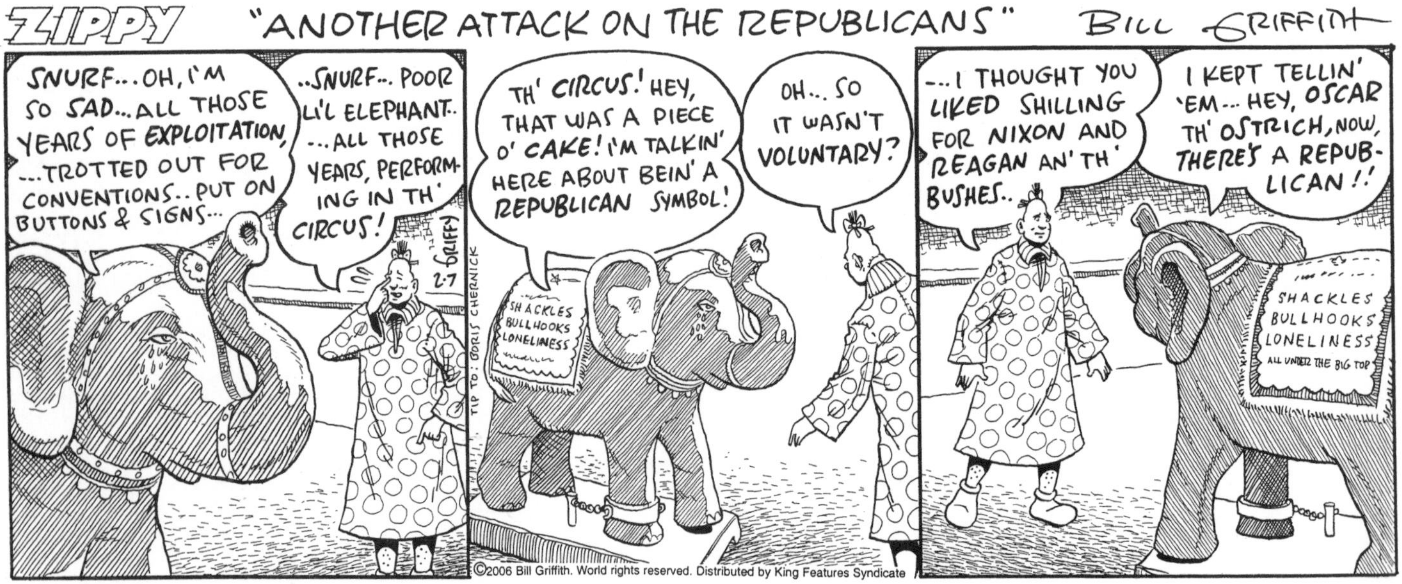
ZIPPY
"ANOTHER ATTACK ON THE REPUBLICANS"
BILL GRIFFITH
SNURF... OH, I'M SO SAD... ALL THOSE YEARS OF EXPLOITATION, ...TROTTED OUT FOR CONVENTIONS.. PUT ON BUTTONS & SIGNS...
..SNURF... POOR LI'L ELEPHANT.. ...ALL THOSE YEARS, PERFORMING IN TH' CIRCUS!
GRIFFY
2-7
TIP TO: BORIS CHERNICK
TH' CIRCUS! HEY, THAT WAS A PIECE O' CAKE! I'M TALKIN' HERE ABOUT BEIN' A REPUBLICAN SYMBOL!
OH... SO IT WASN'T VOLUNTARY?
SHACKLES BULLHOOKS LONELINESS
...I THOUGHT YOU LIKED SHILLING FOR NIXON AND REAGAN AN' TH' BUSHES..
I KEPT TELLIN' 'EM... HEY, OSCAR TH' OSTRICH, NOW, THERE'S A REPUBLICAN!!
SHACKLES BULLHOOKS LONELINESS ALL UNDER THE BIG TOP
©2006 Bill Griffith. World rights reserved. Distributed by King Features Syndicate

134

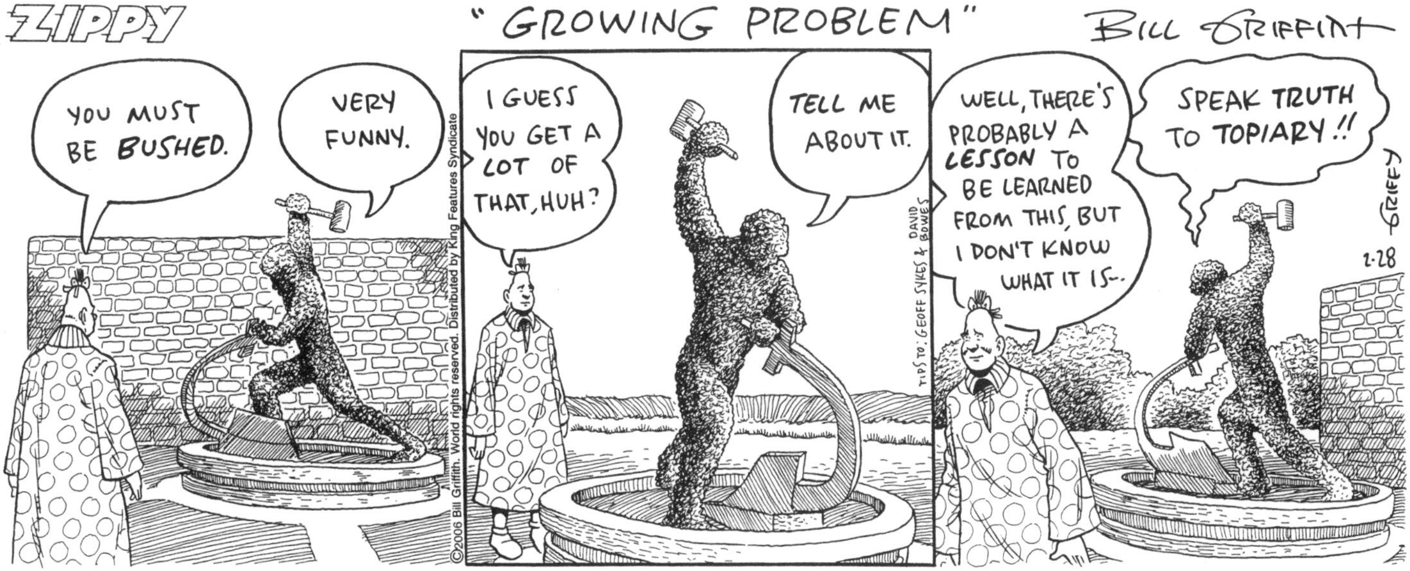
ZIPPY
"GROWING PROBLEM"
BILL GRIFFITH
YOU MUST BE BUSHED.
VERY FUNNY.
©2006 Bill Griffith. World rights reserved. Distributed by King Features Syndicate
I GUESS YOU GET A LOT OF THAT, HUH?
TELL ME ABOUT IT.
TIPS TO: GEOFF SYKES & DAVID BOWES
WELL, THERE'S PROBABLY A LESSON TO BE LEARNED FROM THIS, BUT I DON'T KNOW WHAT IT IS--.
SPEAK TRUTH TO TOPIARY!!
GRIFFY
2-28

135

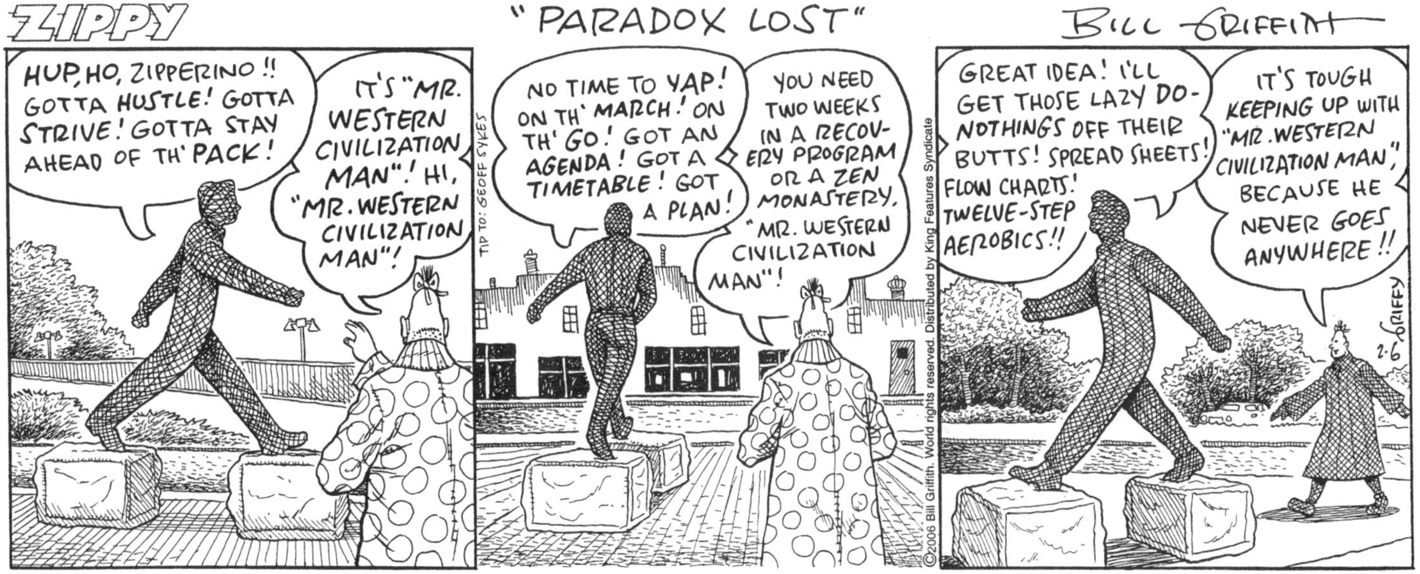
ZIPPY
"PARADOX LOST"
BILL GRIFFITH
HUP, HO, ZIPPERINO!! GOTTA HUSTLE! GOTTA STRIVE! GOTTA STAY AHEAD OF TH' PACK!
IT'S "MR. WESTERN CIVILIZATION MAN"! HI, "MR. WESTERN CIVILIZATION MAN"!
TIP TO: GEOFF SYKES
NO TIME TO YAP! ON TH' MARCH! ON TH' GO! GOT AN AGENDA! GOT A TIMETABLE! GOT A PLAN!
YOU NEED TWO WEEKS IN A RECOVERY PROGRAM OR A ZEN MONASTERY, "MR. WESTERN CIVILIZATION MAN"!
©2006 Bill Griffith. World rights reserved. Distributed by King Features Syndicate
GREAT IDEA! I'LL GET THOSE LAZY DO-NOTHINGS OFF THEIR BUTTS! SPREAD SHEETS! FLOW CHARTS! TWELVE-STEP AEROBICS!!
IT'S TOUGH KEEPING UP WITH "MR. WESTERN CIVILIZATION MAN", BECAUSE HE NEVER GOES ANYWHERE!!
GRIFFY
2-6

136

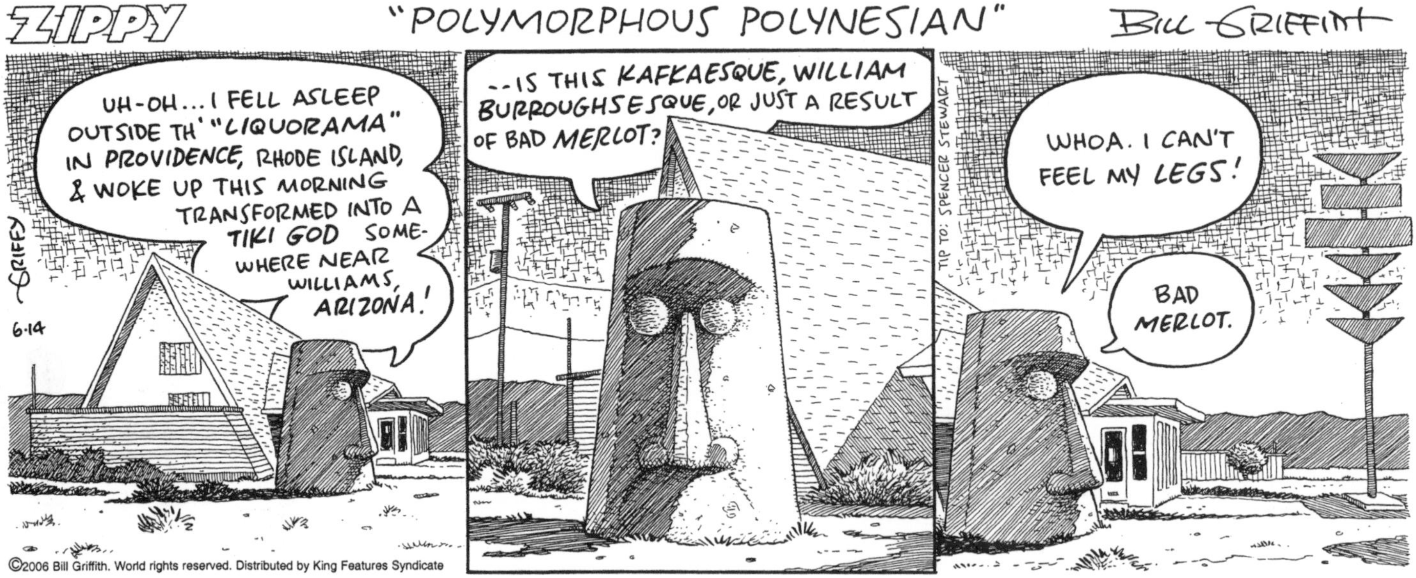
ZIPPY
"POLYMORPHOUS POLYNESIAN"
BILL GRIFFITH
UH-OH... I FELL ASLEEP OUTSIDE TH' "LIQUORAMA" IN PROVIDENCE, RHODE ISLAND, & WOKE UP THIS MORNING TRANSFORMED INTO A TIKI GOD SOMEWHERE NEAR WILLIAMS, ARIZONA!
GRIFFY
6·14
--IS THIS KAFKAESQUE, WILLIAM BURROUGHSESQUE, OR JUST A RESULT OF BAD MERLOT?
TIP TO: SPENCER STEWART
WHOA. I CAN'T FEEL MY LEGS!
BAD MERLOT.
©2006 Bill Griffith. World rights reserved. Distributed by King Features Syndicate

137

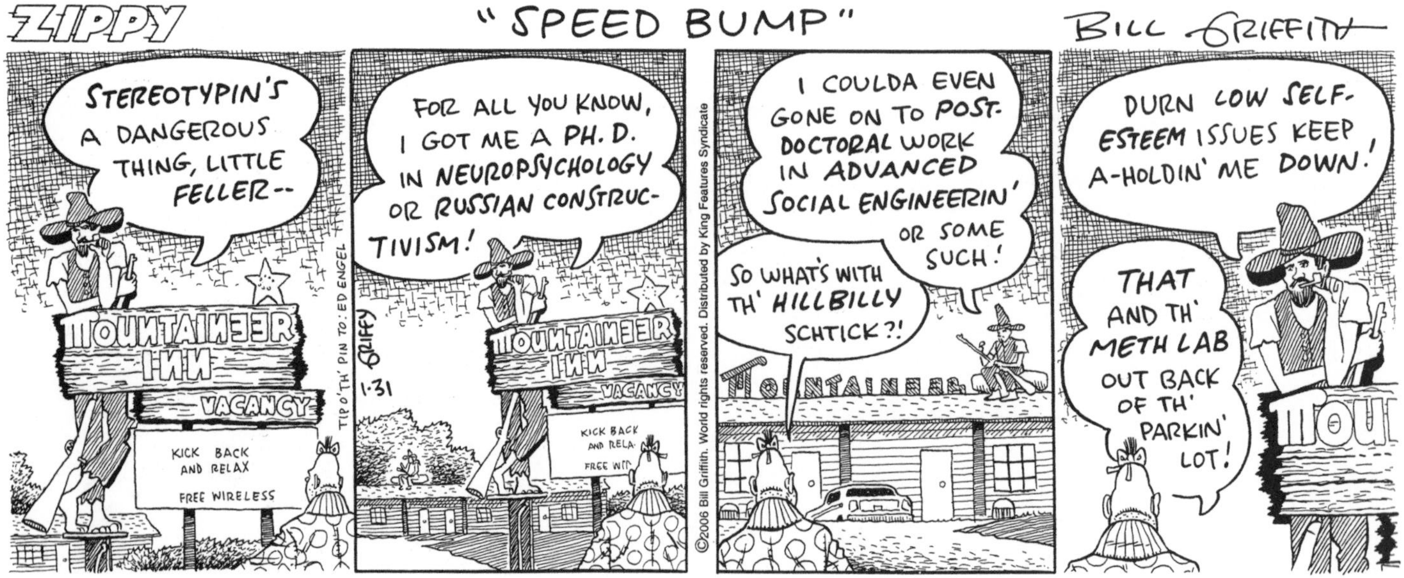
ZIPPY
"SPEED BUMP"
BILL GRIFFITH
STEREOTYPIN'S A DANGEROUS THING, LITTLE FELLER--
MOUNTAINEER INN
VACANCY
KICK BACK AND RELAX
FREE WIRELESS
TIP O' TH' PIN TO: ED ENGEL
GRIFFY
1·31
FOR ALL YOU KNOW, I GOT ME A PH. D. IN NEUROPSYCHOLOGY OR RUSSIAN CONSTRUCTIVISM!
©2006 Bill Griffith. World rights reserved. Distributed by King Features Syndicate
I COULDA EVEN GONE ON TO POST-DOCTORAL WORK IN ADVANCED SOCIAL ENGINEERIN' OR SOME SUCH!
SO WHAT'S WITH TH' HILLBILLY SCHTICK?!
DURN LOW SELF-ESTEEM ISSUES KEEP A-HOLDIN' ME DOWN!
THAT AND TH' METH LAB OUT BACK OF TH' PARKIN' LOT!

138

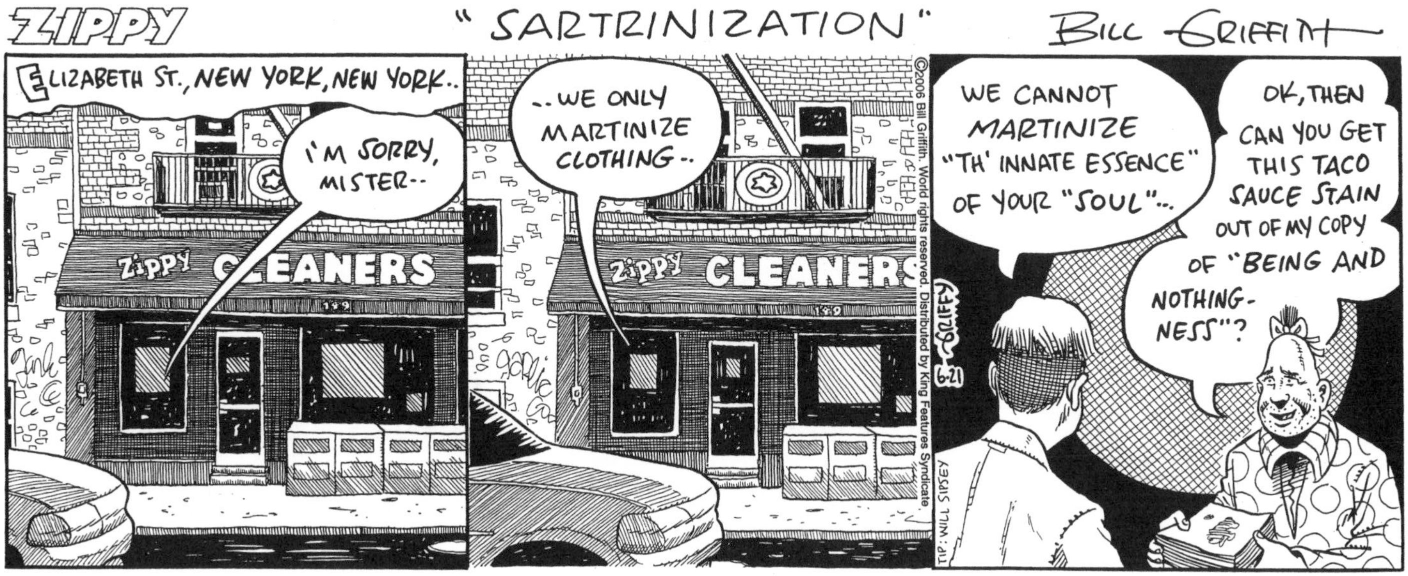
ZIPPY
"SARTRINIZATION"
BILL GRIFFITH
ELIZABETH ST., NEW YORK, NEW YORK..
I'M SORRY, MISTER--
ZIPPY CLEANERS
--WE ONLY MARTINIZE CLOTHING--
ZIPPY CLEANERS
©2006 Bill Griffith. World rights reserved. Distributed by King Features Syndicate
GRIFFY 6-21
TIP: WILL SISSEY
WE CANNOT MARTINIZE "TH' INNATE ESSENCE" OF YOUR "SOUL"--
OK, THEN CAN YOU GET THIS TACO SAUCE STAIN OUT OF MY COPY OF "BEING AND NOTHING-NESS"?

139

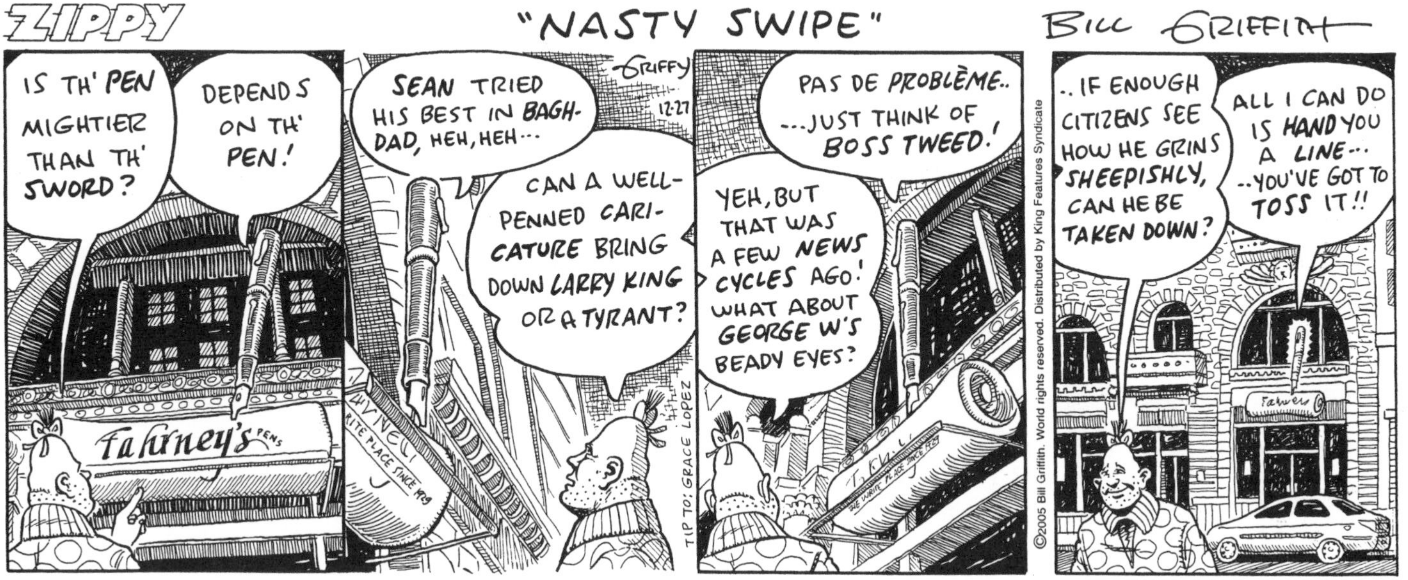
ZIPPY
"NASTY SWIPE"
BILL GRIFFITH
IS TH' PEN MIGHTIER THAN TH' SWORD?
DEPENDS ON TH' PEN!
Fahrney's PENS
GRIFFY 12-27
SEAN TRIED HIS BEST IN BAGH-DAD, HEH, HEH--
CAN A WELL-PENNED CARI-CATURE BRING DOWN LARRY KING OR A TYRANT?
TIP TO: GRACE LOPEZ
PAS DE PROBLÈME.. --JUST THINK OF BOSS TWEED!
YEH, BUT THAT WAS A FEW NEWS CYCLES AGO! WHAT ABOUT GEORGE W'S BEADY EYES?
©2005 Bill Griffith. World rights reserved. Distributed by King Features Syndicate
--IF ENOUGH CITIZENS SEE HOW HE GRINS SHEEPISHLY, CAN HE BE TAKEN DOWN?
ALL I CAN DO IS HAND YOU A LINE-- --YOU'VE GOT TO TOSS IT!!

140

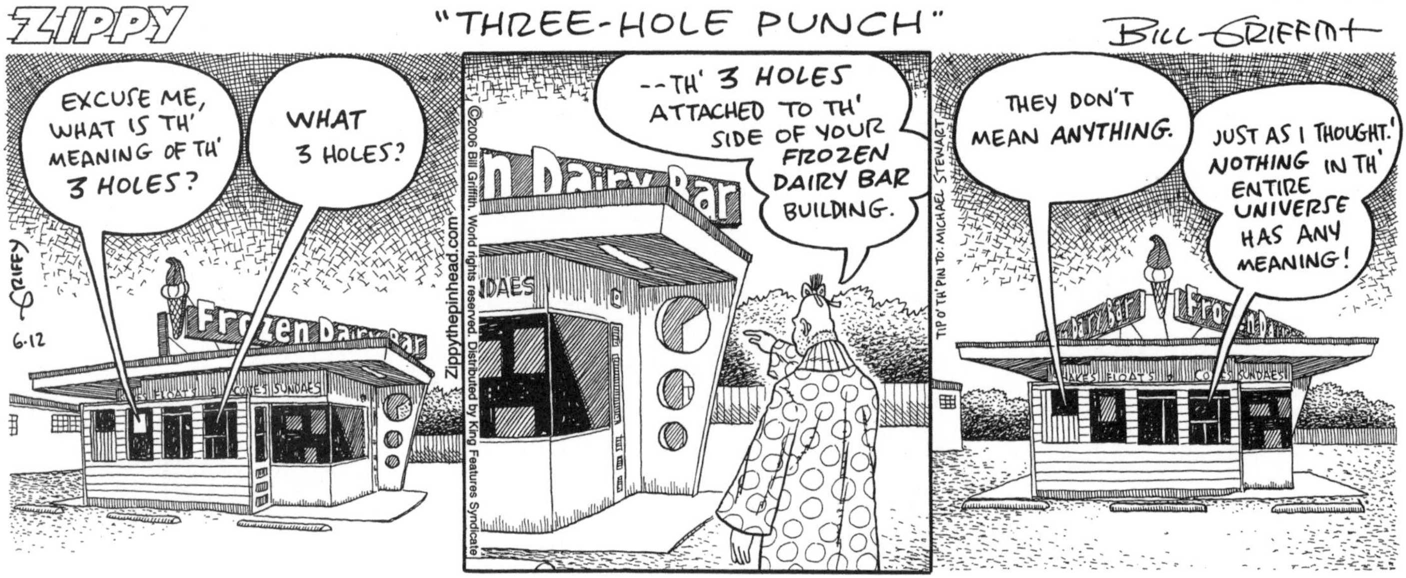
ZIPPY
"THREE-HOLE PUNCH"
BILL GRIFFITH
EXCUSE ME, WHAT IS TH' MEANING OF TH' 3 HOLES?
WHAT 3 HOLES?
GRIFFY 6.12
Frozen Dairy Bar
--TH' 3 HOLES ATTACHED TO TH' SIDE OF YOUR FROZEN DAIRY BAR BUILDING.
©2006 Bill Griffith. World rights reserved. Distributed by King Features Syndicate
Zippythepinhead.com
TIP O' TH' PIN TO: MICHAEL STEWART
THEY DON'T MEAN ANYTHING.
JUST AS I THOUGHT! NOTHING IN TH' ENTIRE UNIVERSE HAS ANY MEANING!

141

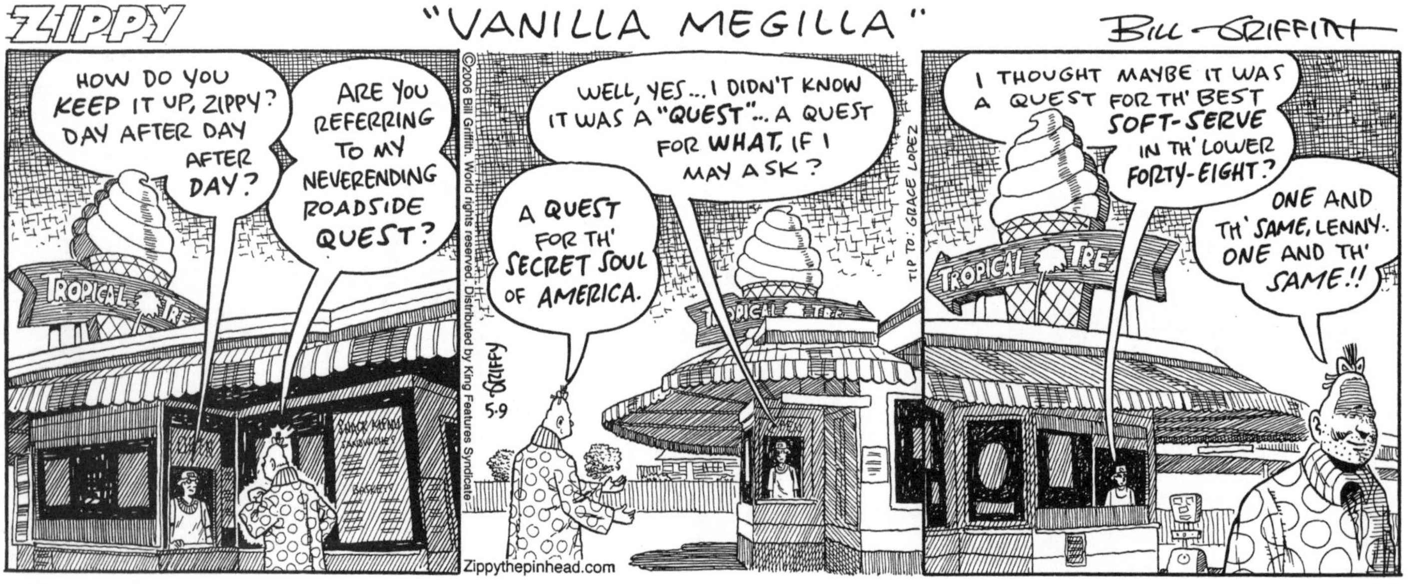
ZIPPY
"VANILLA MEGILLA"
BILL GRIFFITH
HOW DO YOU KEEP IT UP, ZIPPY? DAY AFTER DAY AFTER DAY?
ARE YOU REFERRING TO MY NEVERENDING ROADSIDE QUEST?
©2006 Bill Griffith. World rights reserved. Distributed by King Features Syndicate
WELL, YES... I DIDN'T KNOW IT WAS A "QUEST"... A QUEST FOR WHAT, IF I MAY ASK?
A QUEST FOR TH' SECRET SOUL OF AMERICA.
GRIFFY 5.9
TIP TO: GRACE LOPEZ
I THOUGHT MAYBE IT WAS A QUEST FOR TH' BEST SOFT-SERVE IN TH' LOWER FORTY-EIGHT?
ONE AND TH' SAME, LENNY.. ONE AND TH' SAME!!
Zippythepinhead.com

142

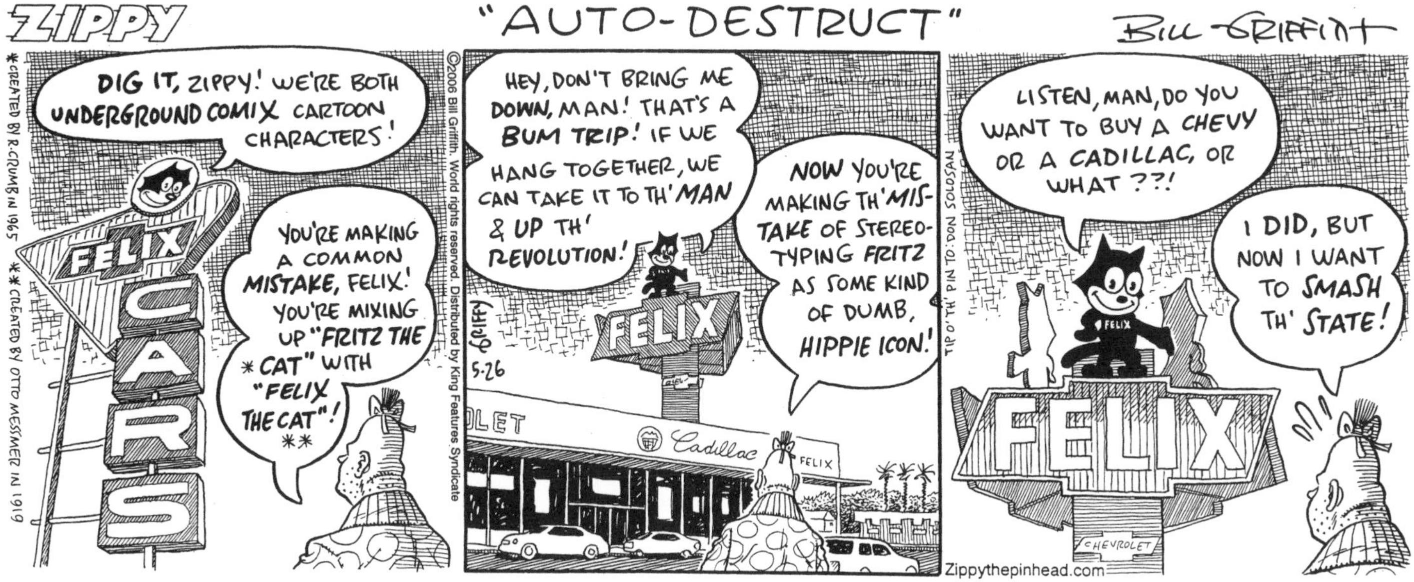
ZIPPY
"AUTO-DESTRUCT"
BILL GRIFFITH
DIG IT, ZIPPY! WE'RE BOTH UNDERGROUND COMIX CARTOON CHARACTERS!
FELIX CARS
YOU'RE MAKING A COMMON MISTAKE, FELIX! YOU'RE MIXING UP "FRITZ THE * CAT" WITH "FELIX THE CAT"! **
*CREATED BY R.CRUMB IN 1965 **CREATED BY OTTO MESSMER IN 1919
©2006 Bill Griffith. World rights reserved. Distributed by King Features Syndicate
HEY, DON'T BRING ME DOWN, MAN! THAT'S A BUM TRIP! IF WE HANG TOGETHER, WE CAN TAKE IT TO TH' MAN & UP TH' REVOLUTION!
GRIFFY 5-26
FELIX
NOW YOU'RE MAKING TH' MISTAKE OF STEREOTYPING FRITZ AS SOME KIND OF DUMB, HIPPIE ICON!
Cadillac
FELIX
TIP O' TH' PIN TO: DON SOLOSAN
LISTEN, MAN, DO YOU WANT TO BUY A CHEVY OR A CADILLAC, OR WHAT ??!
I DID, BUT NOW I WANT TO SMASH TH' STATE!
FELIX
CHEVROLET
Zippythepinhead.com

143

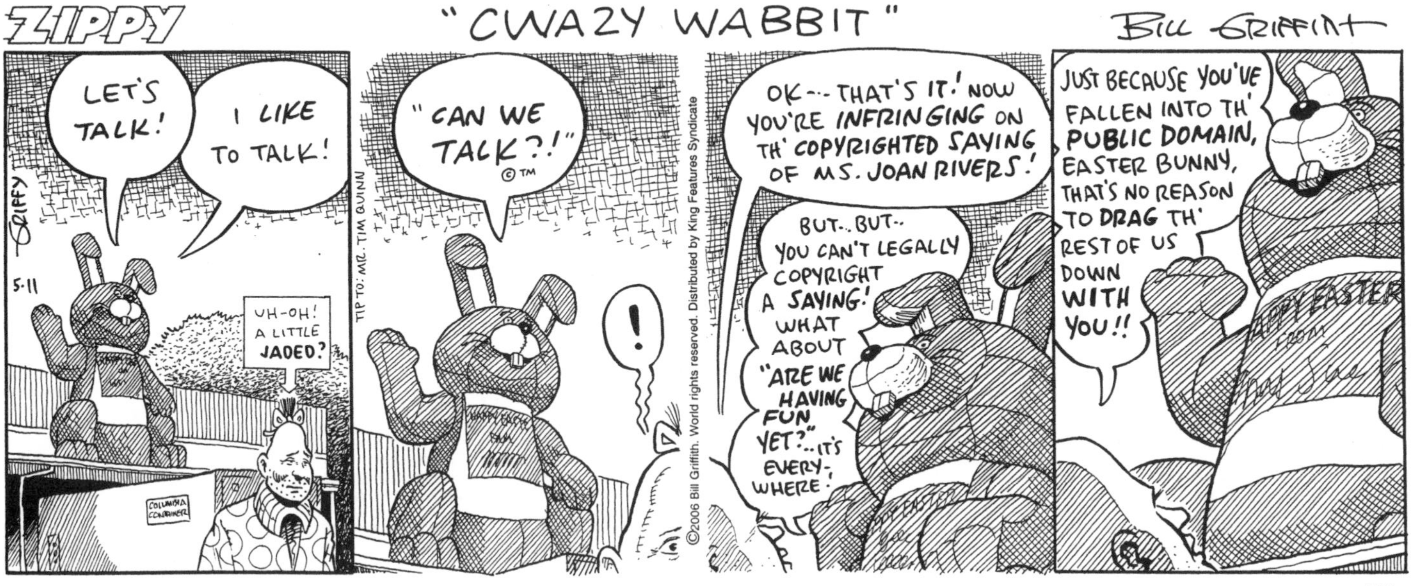
ZIPPY
"CWAZY WABBIT"
BILL GRIFFITH
LET'S TALK!
I LIKE TO TALK!
GRIFFY 5-11
UH-OH! A LITTLE JADED?
COLUMBIA CONTAINER
TIP TO: MR. TIM QUINN
"CAN WE TALK?!" ©TM
!
©2006 Bill Griffith. World rights reserved. Distributed by King Features Syndicate
OK -- THAT'S IT! NOW YOU'RE INFRINGING ON TH' COPYRIGHTED SAYING OF MS. JOAN RIVERS!
BUT.. BUT.. YOU CAN'T LEGALLY COPYRIGHT A SAYING! WHAT ABOUT "ARE WE HAVING FUN YET?"..IT'S EVERYWHERE!
JUST BECAUSE YOU'VE FALLEN INTO TH' PUBLIC DOMAIN, EASTER BUNNY, THAT'S NO REASON TO DRAG TH' REST OF US DOWN WITH YOU!!

144

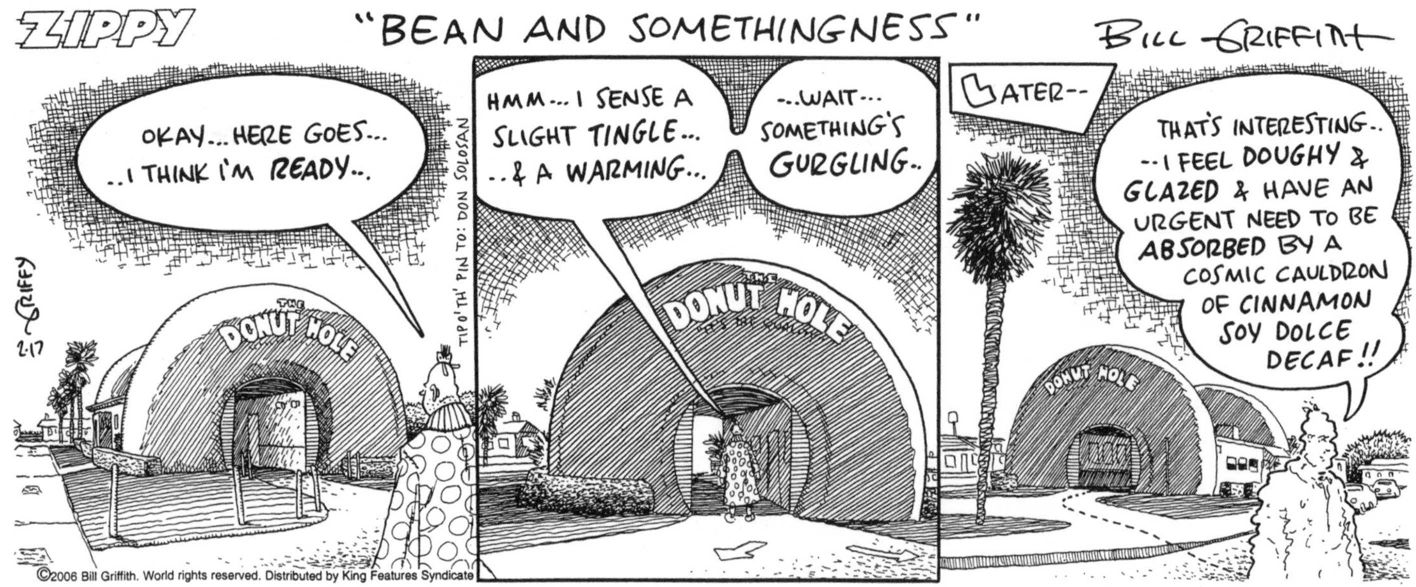
ZIPPY
"BEAN AND SOMETHINGNESS"
BILL GRIFFITH
OKAY... HERE GOES... ..I THINK I'M READY...
GRIFFY 2·17
THE DONUT HOLE
TIP O' TH' PIN TO: DON SOLDOSAN
©2006 Bill Griffith. World rights reserved. Distributed by King Features Syndicate
HMM... I SENSE A SLIGHT TINGLE... ..& A WARMING...
--..WAIT--- SOMETHING'S GURGLING..
LATER--
THAT'S INTERESTING.. --I FEEL DOUGHY & GLAZED & HAVE AN URGENT NEED TO BE ABSORBED BY A COSMIC CAULDRON OF CINNAMON SOY DOLCE DECAF!!
DONUT HOLE

145

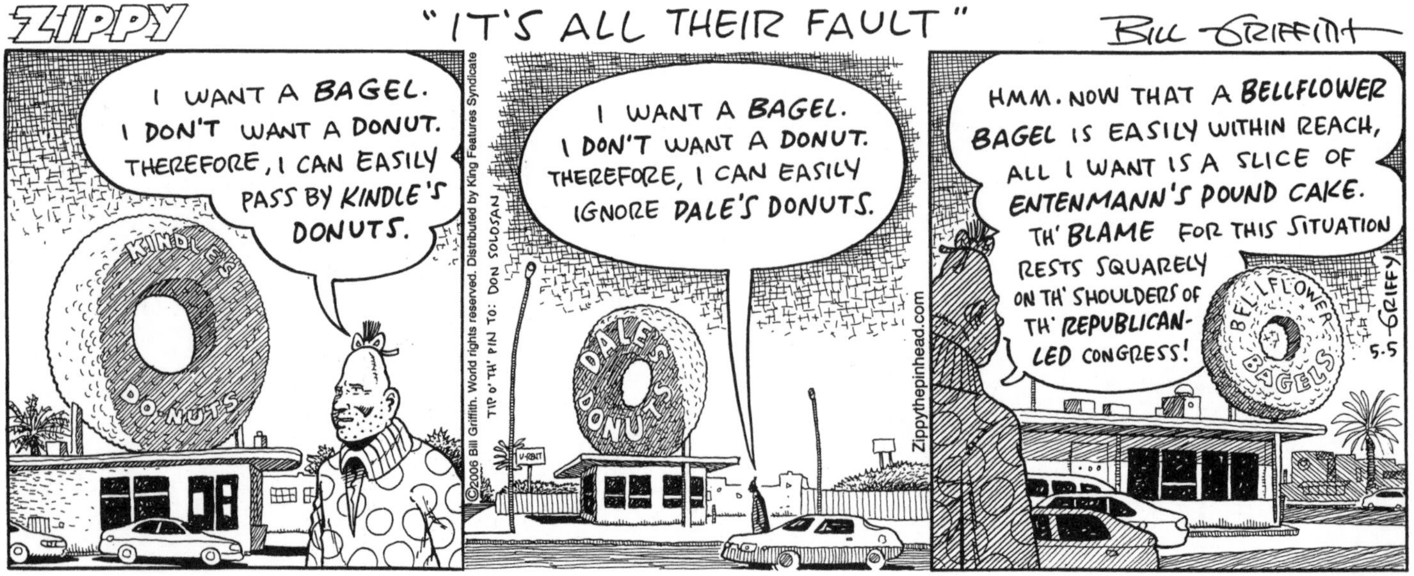
ZIPPY
"IT'S ALL THEIR FAULT"
BILL GRIFFITH
I WANT A BAGEL. I DON'T WANT A DONUT. THEREFORE, I CAN EASILY PASS BY KINDLE'S DONUTS.
KINDLE'S DO-NUTS
©2006 Bill Griffith. World rights reserved. Distributed by King Features Syndicate
TIP O' TH' PIN TO: DON SOLDOSAN
I WANT A BAGEL. I DON'T WANT A DONUT. THEREFORE, I CAN EASILY IGNORE DALE'S DONUTS.
DALE'S DONUTS
Zippythepinhead.com
HMM. NOW THAT A BELLFLOWER BAGEL IS EASILY WITHIN REACH, ALL I WANT IS A SLICE OF ENTENMANN'S POUND CAKE. TH' BLAME FOR THIS SITUATION RESTS SQUARELY ON TH' SHOULDERS OF TH' REPUBLICAN-LED CONGRESS!
BELLFLOWER BAGELS
GRIFFY 5·5

146

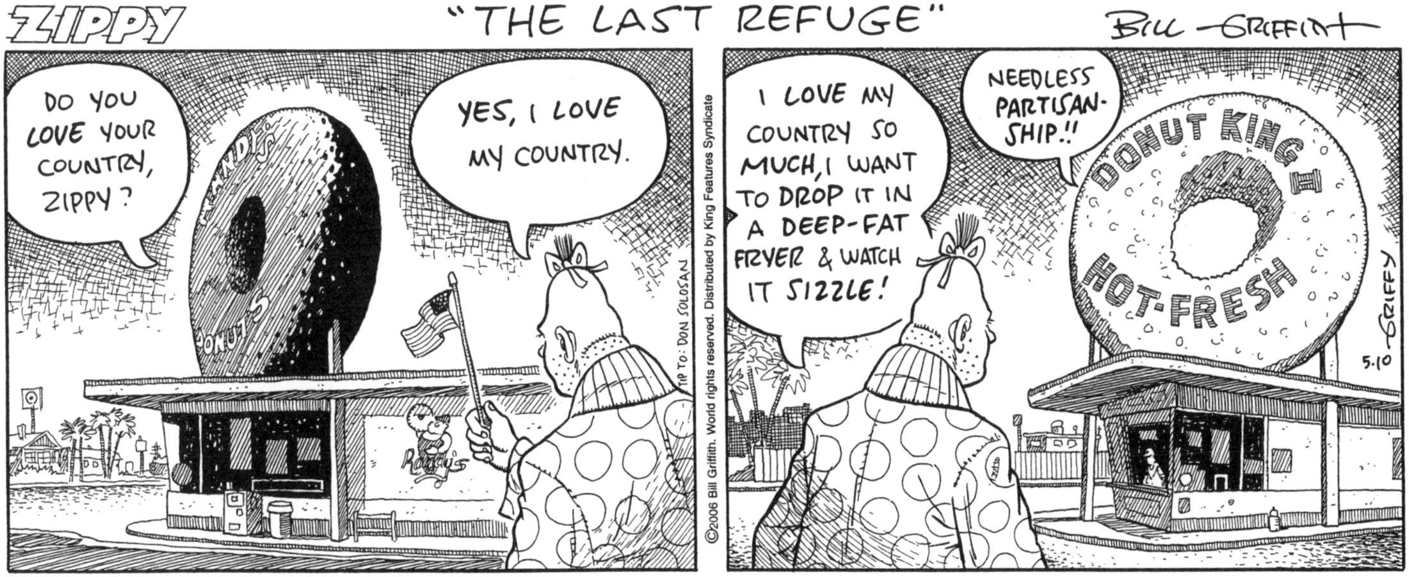
ZIPPY
"THE LAST REFUGE"
BILL GRIFFITH
DO YOU LOVE YOUR COUNTRY, ZIPPY?
YES, I LOVE MY COUNTRY.
TIP TO: DON SOLOSAN
©2006 Bill Griffith. World rights reserved. Distributed by King Features Syndicate
I LOVE MY COUNTRY SO MUCH, I WANT TO DROP IT IN A DEEP-FAT FRYER & WATCH IT SIZZLE!
NEEDLESS PARTISANSHIP!!
DONUT KING II
HOT-FRESH
GRIFFY
5.10

147

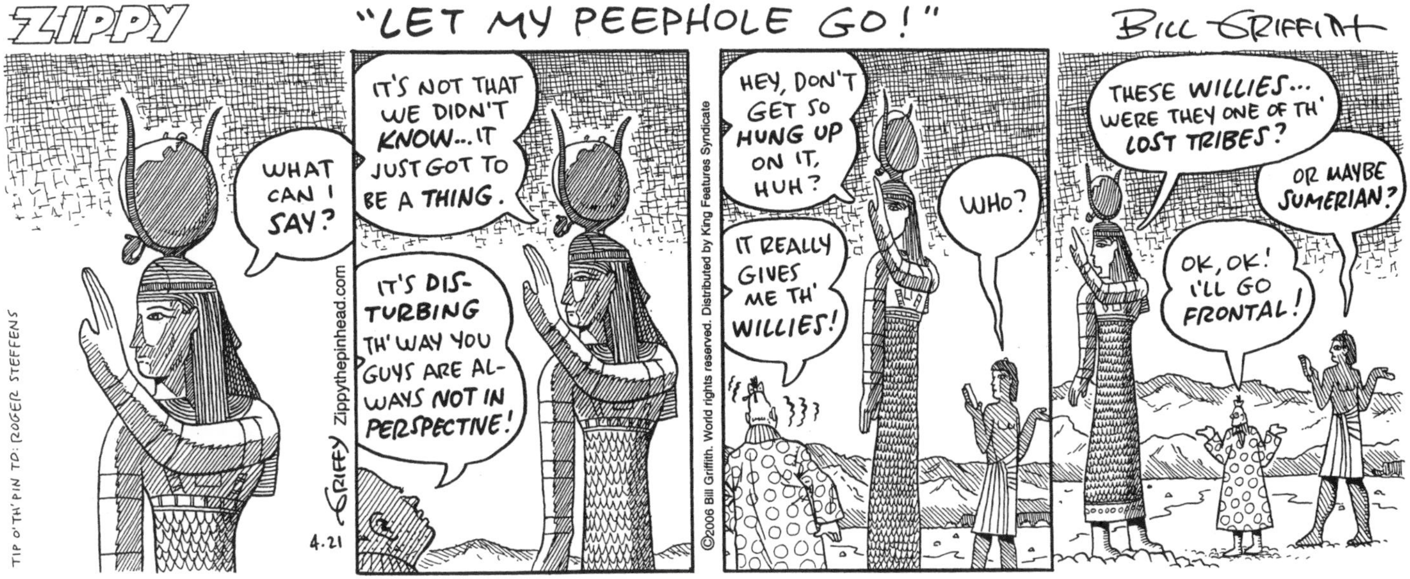
ZIPPY
"LET MY PEEPHOLE GO!"
BILL GRIFFITH
TIP O'TH' PIN TO: ROGER STEFFENS
WHAT CAN I SAY?
GRIFFY
4.21
Zippythepinhead.com
IT'S NOT THAT WE DIDN'T KNOW... IT JUST GOT TO BE A THING.
IT'S DISTURBING TH' WAY YOU GUYS ARE ALWAYS NOT IN PERSPECTIVE!
©2006 Bill Griffith. World rights reserved. Distributed by King Features Syndicate
HEY, DON'T GET SO HUNG UP ON IT, HUH?
IT REALLY GIVES ME TH' WILLIES!
WHO?
THESE WILLIES... WERE THEY ONE OF TH' LOST TRIBES?
OR MAYBE SUMERIAN?
OK, OK! I'LL GO FRONTAL!

148

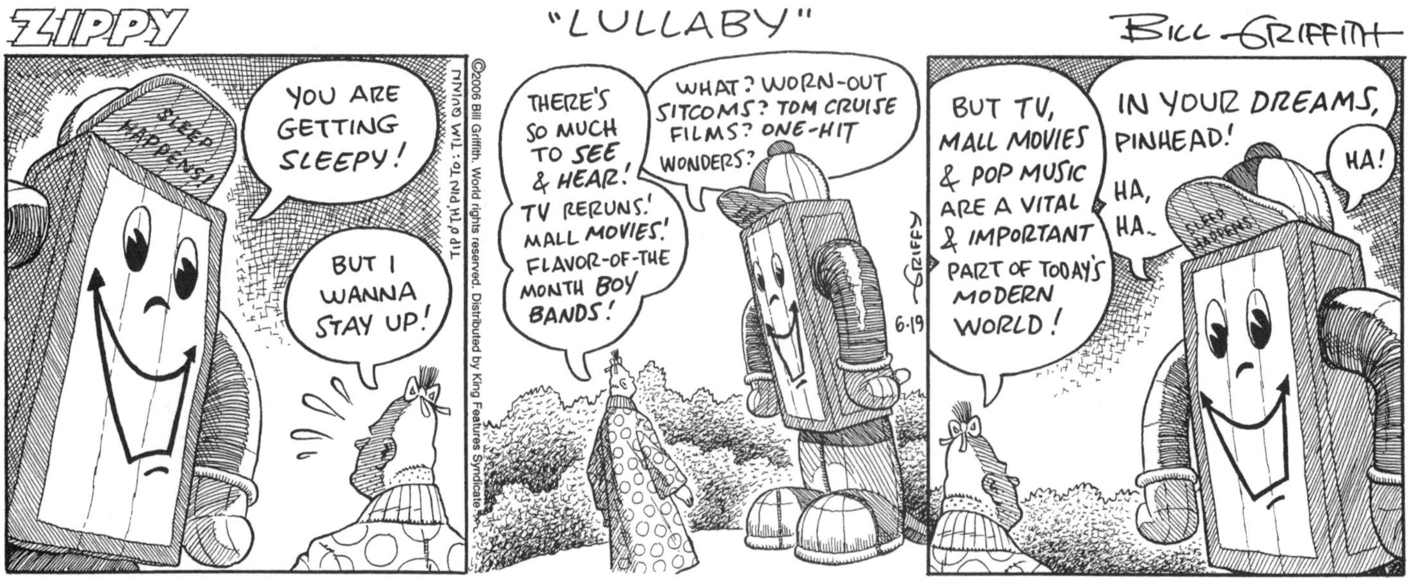
ZIPPY
"LULLABY"
BILL GRIFFITH
SLEEP HAPPENS!
YOU ARE GETTING SLEEPY!
BUT I WANNA STAY UP!
©2006 Bill Griffith. World rights reserved. Distributed by King Features Syndicate.
TIP'O'TH'PIN TO: TIM QUINN
THERE'S SO MUCH TO SEE & HEAR! TV RERUNS! MALL MOVIES! FLAVOR-OF-THE MONTH BOY BANDS!
WHAT? WORN-OUT SITCOMS? TOM CRUISE FILMS? ONE-HIT WONDERS?
GRIFFY 6·19
BUT TV, MALL MOVIES & POP MUSIC ARE A VITAL & IMPORTANT PART OF TODAY'S MODERN WORLD!
IN YOUR DREAMS, PINHEAD!
HA, HA..
HA!

149

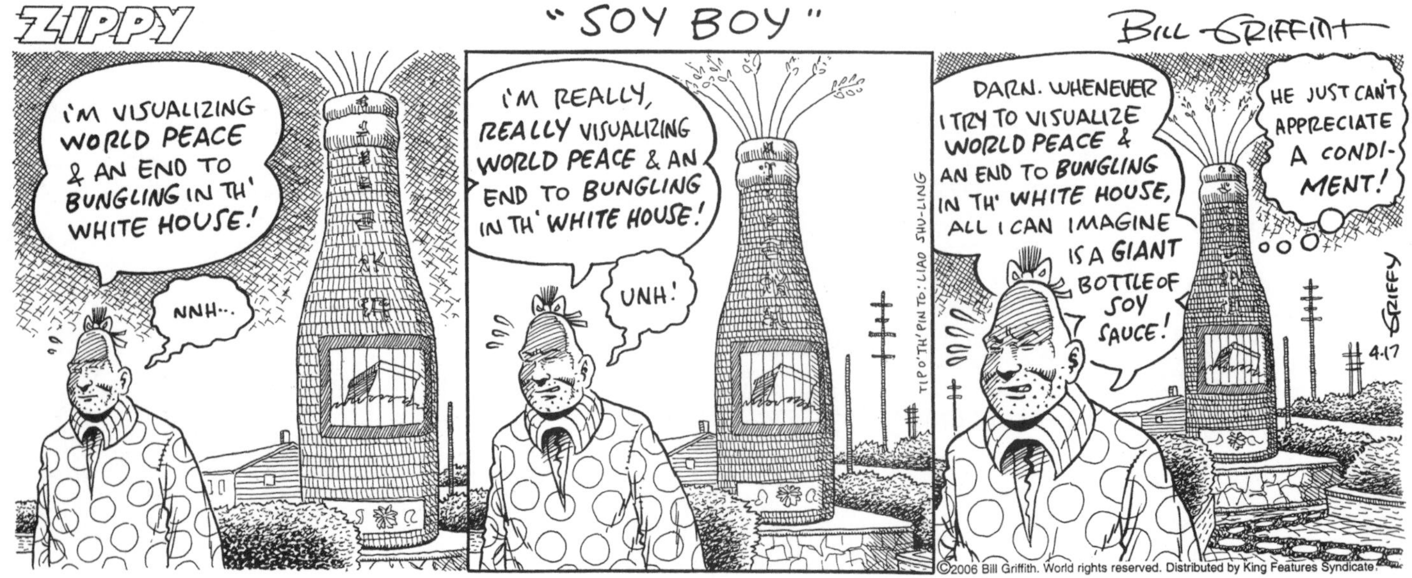
ZIPPY
"SOY BOY"
BILL GRIFFITH
I'M VISUALIZING WORLD PEACE & AN END TO BUNGLING IN TH' WHITE HOUSE!
NNH..
I'M REALLY, REALLY VISUALIZING WORLD PEACE & AN END TO BUNGLING IN TH' WHITE HOUSE!
UNH!
TIP'O'TH'PIN TO: LIAO SHU-LING
DARN. WHENEVER I TRY TO VISUALIZE WORLD PEACE & AN END TO BUNGLING IN TH' WHITE HOUSE, ALL I CAN IMAGINE IS A GIANT BOTTLE OF SOY SAUCE!
HE JUST CAN'T APPRECIATE A CONDI-MENT!
GRIFFY 4·17
©2006 Bill Griffith. World rights reserved. Distributed by King Features Syndicate.

150

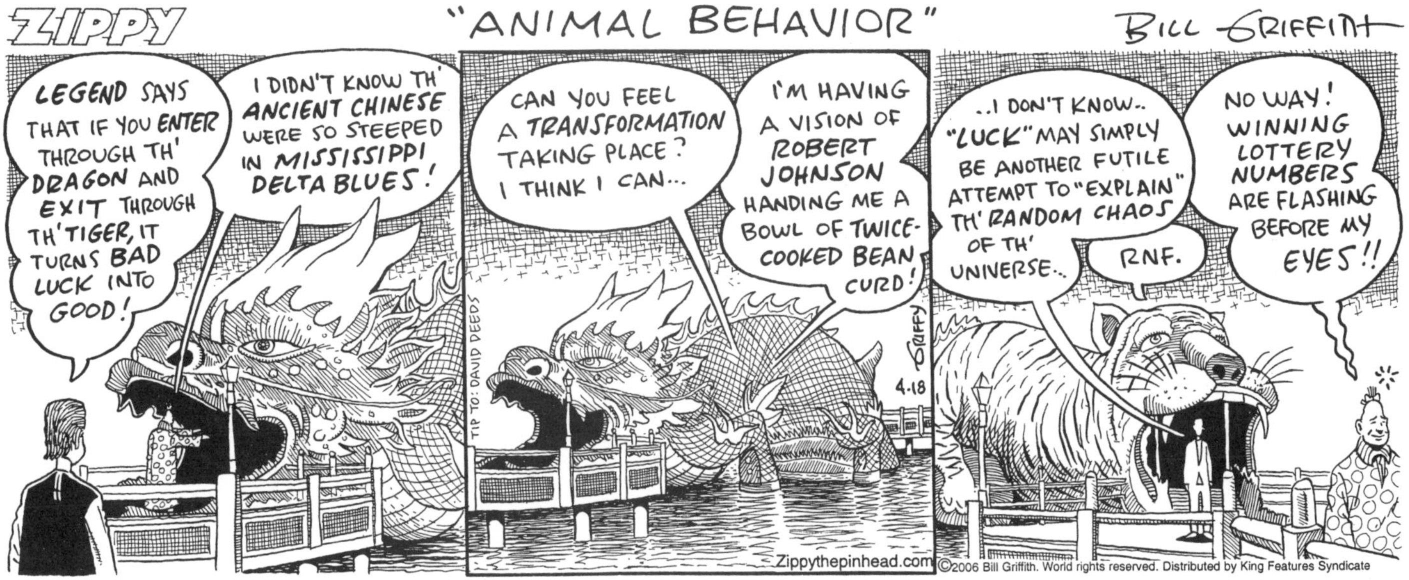
ZIPPY
"ANIMAL BEHAVIOR"
BILL GRIFFITH
LEGEND SAYS THAT IF YOU ENTER THROUGH TH' DRAGON AND EXIT THROUGH TH' TIGER, IT TURNS BAD LUCK INTO GOOD!
I DIDN'T KNOW TH' ANCIENT CHINESE WERE SO STEEPED IN MISSISSIPPI DELTA BLUES!
CAN YOU FEEL A TRANSFORMATION TAKING PLACE? I THINK I CAN...
I'M HAVING A VISION OF ROBERT JOHNSON HANDING ME A BOWL OF TWICE-COOKED BEAN CURD!
TIP TO: DAVID DEEDS
GRIFFY
4-18
..I DON'T KNOW.. "LUCK" MAY SIMPLY BE ANOTHER FUTILE ATTEMPT TO "EXPLAIN" TH' RANDOM CHAOS OF TH' UNIVERSE..
RNF.
NO WAY! WINNING LOTTERY NUMBERS ARE FLASHING BEFORE MY EYES!!
Zippythepinhead.com
©2006 Bill Griffith. World rights reserved. Distributed by King Features Syndicate

151

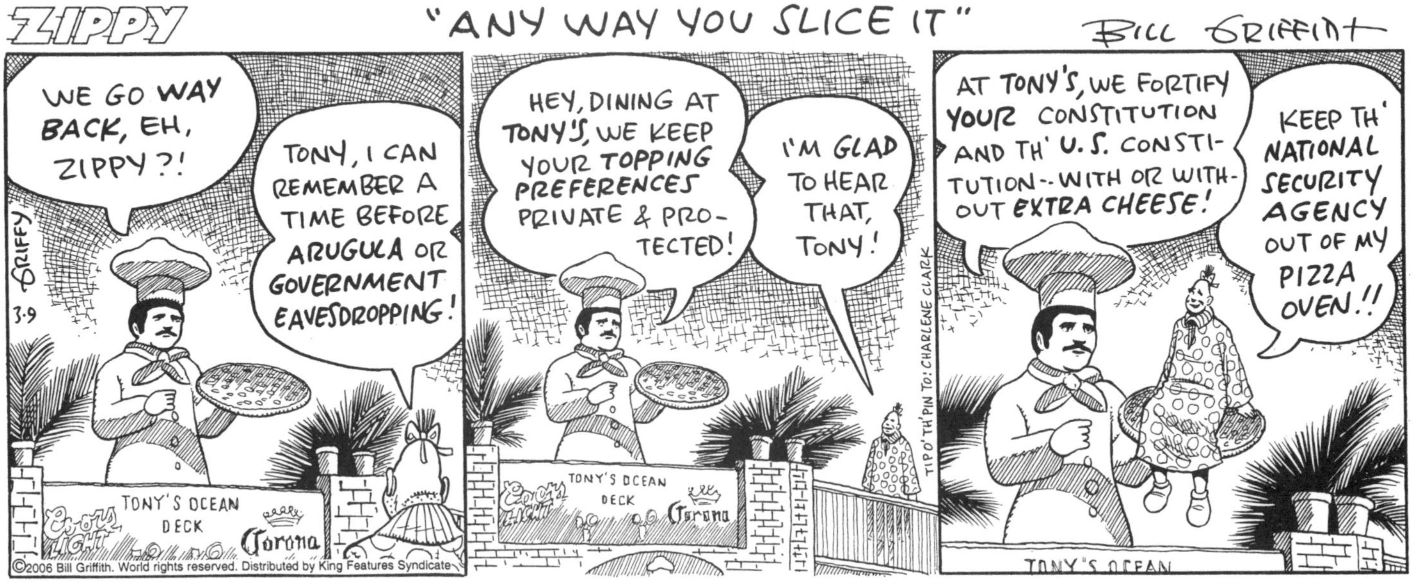
ZIPPY
"ANY WAY YOU SLICE IT"
BILL GRIFFITH
WE GO WAY BACK, EH, ZIPPY?!
TONY, I CAN REMEMBER A TIME BEFORE ARUGULA OR GOVERNMENT EAVESDROPPING!
GRIFFY
3-9
TONY'S OCEAN DECK
Corona
HEY, DINING AT TONY'S, WE KEEP YOUR TOPPING PREFERENCES PRIVATE & PRO-TECTED!
I'M GLAD TO HEAR THAT, TONY!
TIP O' TH' PIN TO: CHARLENE CLARK
AT TONY'S, WE FORTIFY YOUR CONSTITUTION AND TH' U.S. CONSTI-TUTION--WITH OR WITH-OUT EXTRA CHEESE!
KEEP TH' NATIONAL SECURITY AGENCY OUT OF MY PIZZA OVEN!!
TONY'S OCEAN
©2006 Bill Griffith. World rights reserved. Distributed by King Features Syndicate

152

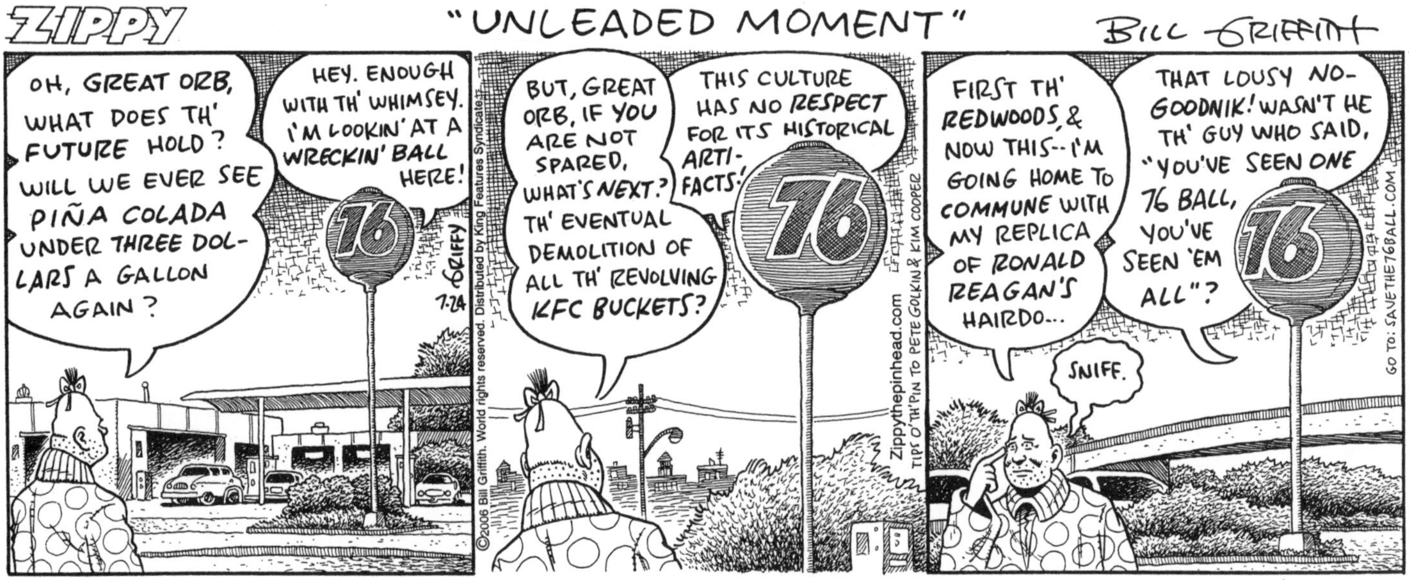
ZIPPY
"UNLEADED MOMENT"
BILL GRIFFITH
OH, GREAT ORB, WHAT DOES TH' FUTURE HOLD? WILL WE EVER SEE PIÑA COLADA UNDER THREE DOLLARS A GALLON AGAIN?
HEY. ENOUGH WITH TH' WHIMSEY. I'M LOOKIN' AT A WRECKIN' BALL HERE!
76
GRIFFY 7-24
©2006 Bill Griffith. World rights reserved. Distributed by King Features Syndicate.
BUT, GREAT ORB, IF YOU ARE NOT SPARED, WHAT'S NEXT? TH' EVENTUAL DEMOLITION OF ALL TH' REVOLVING KFC BUCKETS?
THIS CULTURE HAS NO RESPECT FOR ITS HISTORICAL ARTIFACTS!
76
Zippythepinhead.com
TIPS O' TH' PIN TO PETE GOLKIN & KIM COOPER
FIRST TH' REDWOODS, & NOW THIS--I'M GOING HOME TO COMMUNE WITH MY REPLICA OF RONALD REAGAN'S HAIRDO...
SNIFF.
THAT LOUSY NO-GOODNIK! WASN'T HE TH' GUY WHO SAID, "YOU'VE SEEN ONE 76 BALL, YOU'VE SEEN 'EM ALL"?
76
GO TO: SAVETHE76BALL.COM

153

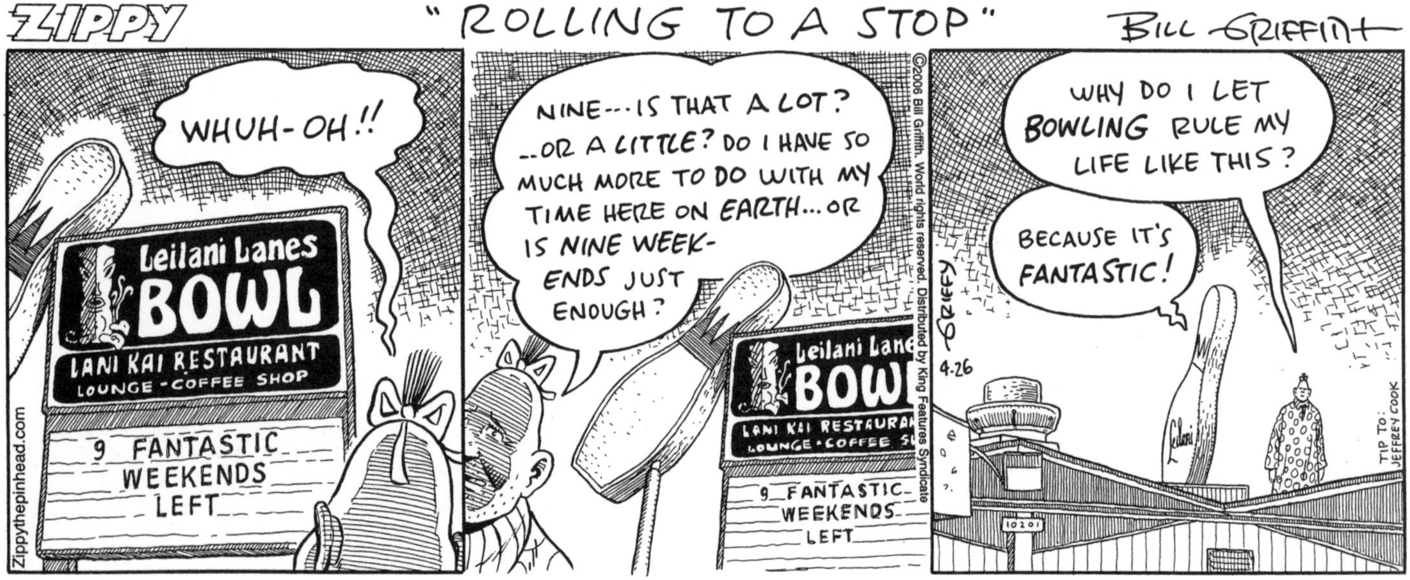
ZIPPY
"ROLLING TO A STOP"
BILL GRIFFITH
WHUH-OH!!
Leilani Lanes BOWL
LANI KAI RESTAURANT
LOUNGE - COFFEE SHOP
9 FANTASTIC WEEKENDS LEFT
Zippythepinhead.com
NINE---IS THAT A LOT? --OR A LITTLE? DO I HAVE SO MUCH MORE TO DO WITH MY TIME HERE ON EARTH...OR IS NINE WEEKENDS JUST ENOUGH?
9 FANTASTIC WEEKENDS LEFT
©2006 Bill Griffith. World rights reserved. Distributed by King Features Syndicate
GRIFFY 4-26
WHY DO I LET BOWLING RULE MY LIFE LIKE THIS?
BECAUSE IT'S FANTASTIC!
TIP TO: JEFFREY COOK

154

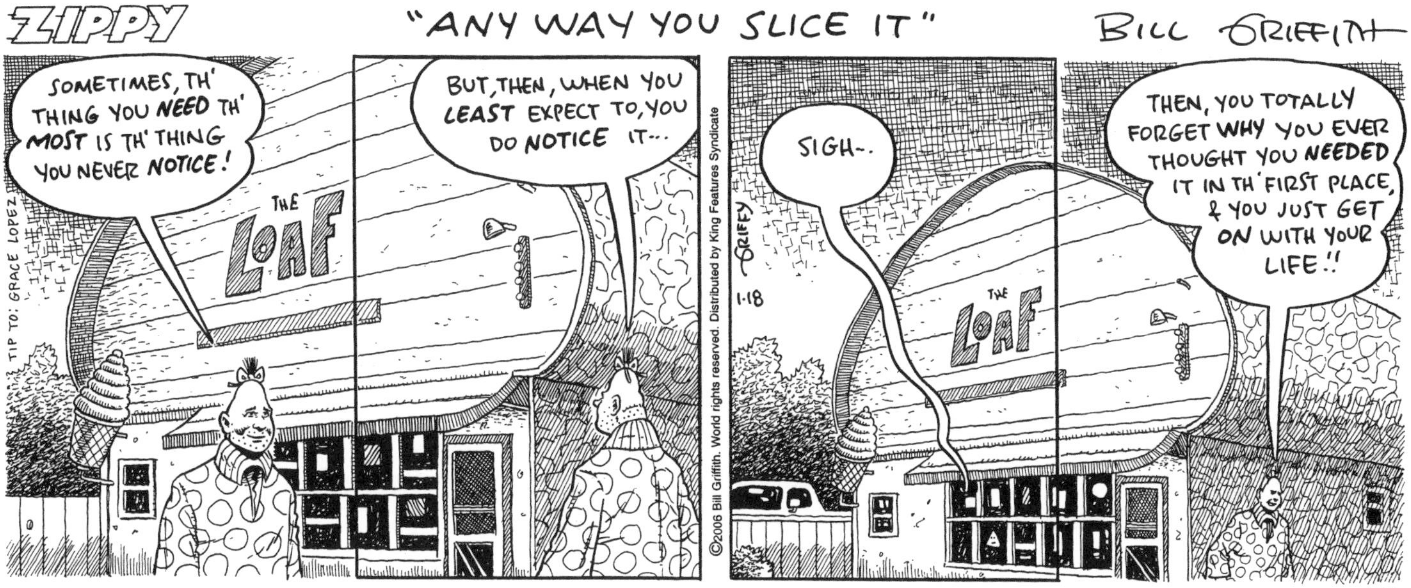
ZIPPY
"ANY WAY YOU SLICE IT"
BILL GRIFFITH
SOMETIMES, TH' THING YOU NEED TH' MOST IS TH' THING YOU NEVER NOTICE!
BUT, THEN, WHEN YOU LEAST EXPECT TO, YOU DO NOTICE IT...
SIGH..
THEN, YOU TOTALLY FORGET WHY YOU EVER THOUGHT YOU NEEDED IT IN TH' FIRST PLACE, & YOU JUST GET ON WITH YOUR LIFE!!
THE LOAF
TIP TO: GRACE LOPEZ
©2006 Bill Griffith. World rights reserved. Distributed by King Features Syndicate
GRIFFY 1-18

155

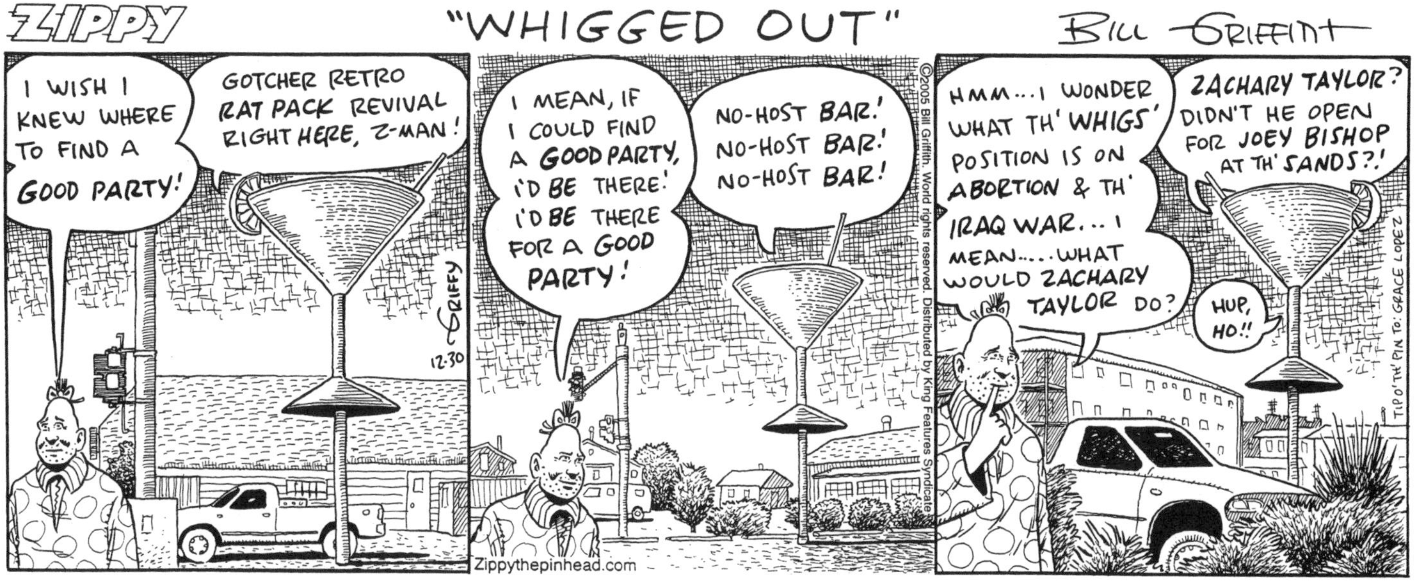
ZIPPY
"WHIGGED OUT"
BILL GRIFFITH
I WISH I KNEW WHERE TO FIND A GOOD PARTY!
GOTCHER RETRO RAT PACK REVIVAL RIGHT HERE, Z-MAN!
I MEAN, IF I COULD FIND A GOOD PARTY, I'D BE THERE! I'D BE THERE FOR A GOOD PARTY!
NO-HOST BAR! NO-HOST BAR! NO-HOST BAR!
HMM... I WONDER WHAT TH' WHIGS' POSITION IS ON ABORTION & TH' IRAQ WAR... I MEAN.... WHAT WOULD ZACHARY TAYLOR DO?
ZACHARY TAYLOR? DIDN'T HE OPEN FOR JOEY BISHOP AT TH' SANDS?!
HUP, HO!!
GRIFFY 12-30
©2005 Bill Griffith. World rights reserved. Distributed by King Features Syndicate
Zippythepinhead.com
TIP O' TH' PIN TO: GRACE LOPEZ

156

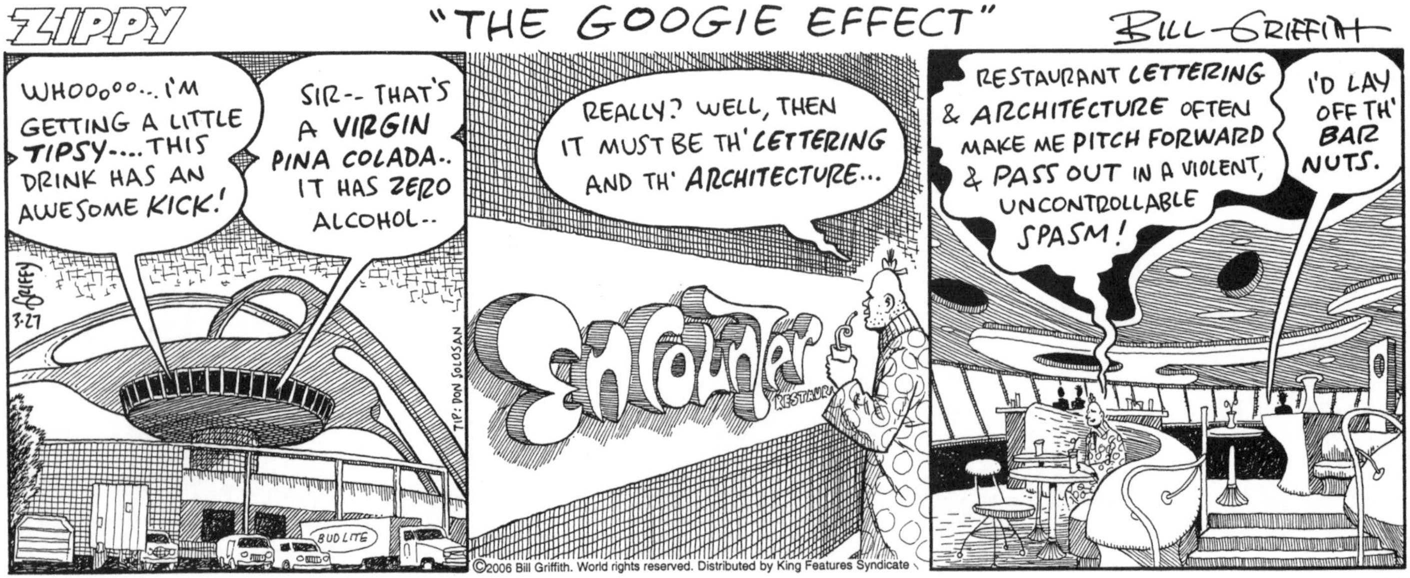
ZIPPY
"THE GOOGIE EFFECT"
BILL GRIFFITH
WHOOOOOO... I'M GETTING A LITTLE TIPSY.... THIS DRINK HAS AN AWESOME KICK!
SIR-- THAT'S A VIRGIN PINA COLADA.. IT HAS ZERO ALCOHOL--
GRIFFY 3-27
TIP: DON SOLOSAN
BUD LITE
REALLY? WELL, THEN IT MUST BE TH' LETTERING AND TH' ARCHITECTURE...
ENCOUNTER
RESTAURANT LETTERING & ARCHITECTURE OFTEN MAKE ME PITCH FORWARD & PASS OUT IN A VIOLENT, UNCONTROLLABLE SPASM!
I'D LAY OFF TH' BAR NUTS.
©2006 Bill Griffith. World rights reserved. Distributed by King Features Syndicate

157

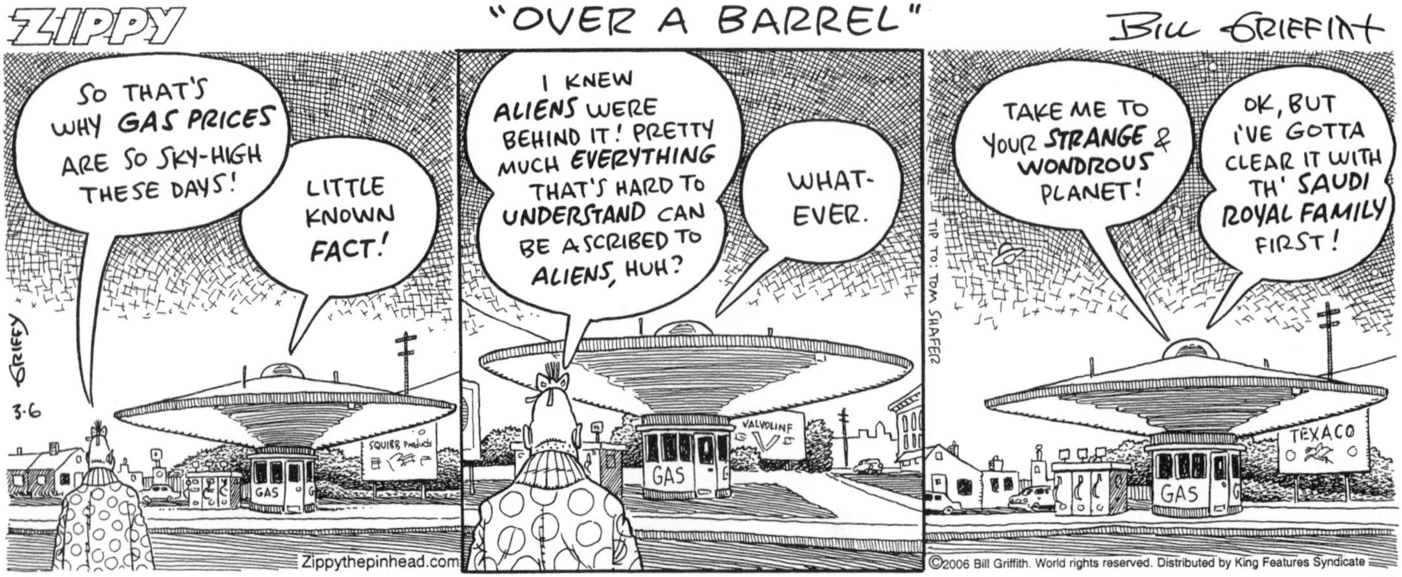
ZIPPY
"OVER A BARREL"
BILL GRIFFITH
SO THAT'S WHY GAS PRICES ARE SO SKY-HIGH THESE DAYS!
LITTLE KNOWN FACT!
GRIFFY 3-6
GAS
I KNEW ALIENS WERE BEHIND IT! PRETTY MUCH EVERYTHING THAT'S HARD TO UNDERSTAND CAN BE ASCRIBED TO ALIENS, HUH?
WHAT-EVER.
VALVOLINE
GAS
TIP TO: TOM SHAFER
TAKE ME TO YOUR STRANGE & WONDROUS PLANET!
OK, BUT I'VE GOTTA CLEAR IT WITH TH' SAUDI ROYAL FAMILY FIRST!
TEXACO
GAS
Zippythepinhead.com
©2006 Bill Griffith. World rights reserved. Distributed by King Features Syndicate

158

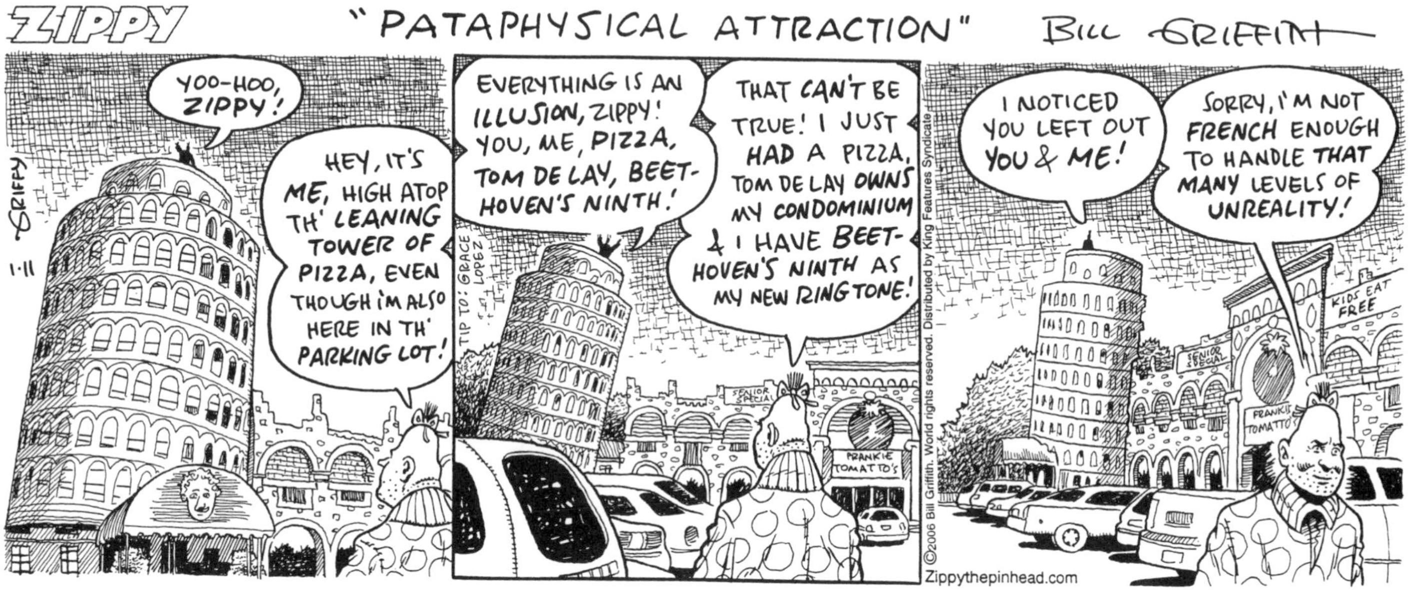
ZIPPY
"PATAPHYSICAL ATTRACTION"
BILL GRIFFITH
YOO-HOO, ZIPPY!
HEY, IT'S ME, HIGH ATOP TH' LEANING TOWER OF PIZZA, EVEN THOUGH I'M ALSO HERE IN TH' PARKING LOT!
GRIFFY
1·11
EVERYTHING IS AN ILLUSION, ZIPPY! YOU, ME, PIZZA, TOM DE LAY, BEETHOVEN'S NINTH!
TIP TO: GRACE LOPEZ
THAT CAN'T BE TRUE! I JUST HAD A PIZZA, TOM DE LAY OWNS MY CONDOMINIUM & I HAVE BEETHOVEN'S NINTH AS MY NEW RINGTONE!
SENIOR SPECIAL
FRANKIE TOMATTO'S
©2006 Bill Griffith. World rights reserved. Distributed by King Features Syndicate
I NOTICED YOU LEFT OUT YOU & ME!
SORRY, I'M NOT FRENCH ENOUGH TO HANDLE THAT MANY LEVELS OF UNREALITY!
KIDS EAT FREE
Zippythepinhead.com

159

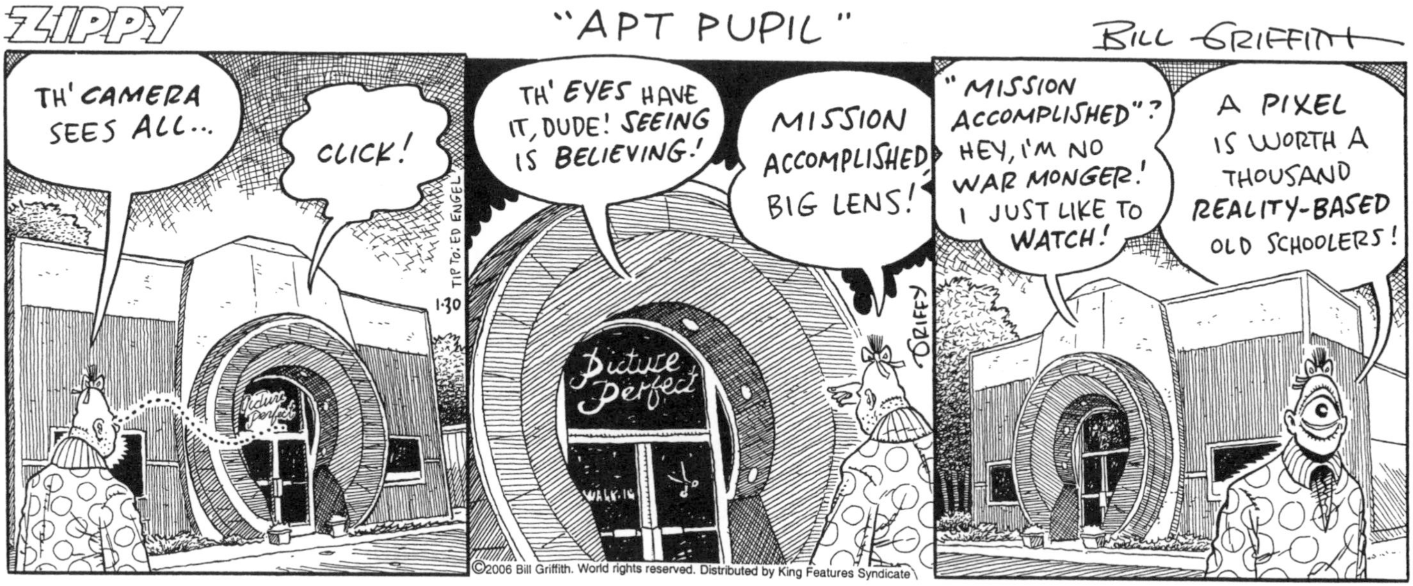
ZIPPY
"APT PUPIL"
BILL GRIFFITH
TH' CAMERA SEES ALL...
CLICK!
TIP TO: ED ENGEL
1·30
TH' EYES HAVE IT, DUDE! SEEING IS BELIEVING!
MISSION ACCOMPLISHED, BIG LENS!
Picture Perfect
WALK-IN
GRIFFY
©2006 Bill Griffith. World rights reserved. Distributed by King Features Syndicate
"MISSION ACCOMPLISHED"? HEY, I'M NO WAR MONGER! I JUST LIKE TO WATCH!
A PIXEL IS WORTH A THOUSAND REALITY-BASED OLD SCHOOLERS!

160

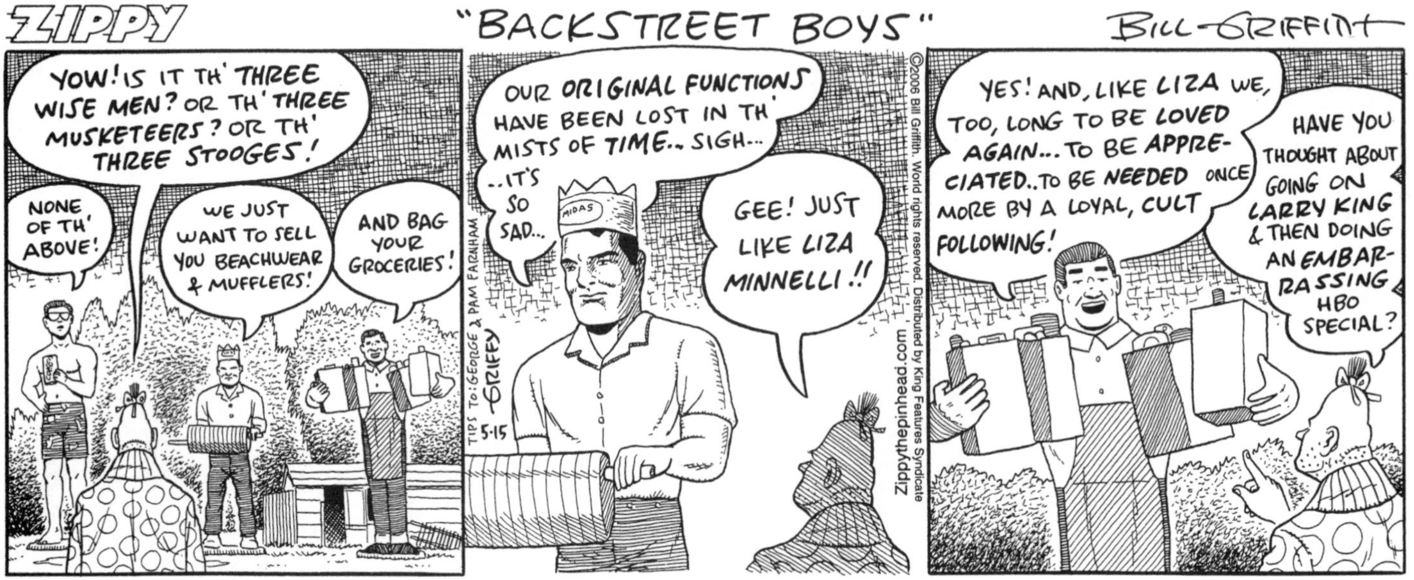
ZIPPY
"BACKSTREET BOYS"
BILL-GRIFFITH
YOW! IS IT TH' THREE WISE MEN? OR TH' THREE MUSKETEERS? OR TH' THREE STOOGES!
NONE OF TH' ABOVE!
WE JUST WANT TO SELL YOU BEACHWEAR & MUFFLERS!
AND BAG YOUR GROCERIES!
TIPS TO: GEORGE & PAM FARNHAM
GRIFFY 5-15
OUR ORIGINAL FUNCTIONS HAVE BEEN LOST IN TH' MISTS OF TIME.. SIGH...
..IT'S SO SAD...
MIDAS
GEE! JUST LIKE LIZA MINNELLI!!
©2006 Bill Griffith. World rights reserved. Distributed by King Features Syndicate
Zippythepinhead.com
YES! AND, LIKE LIZA WE, TOO, LONG TO BE LOVED AGAIN... TO BE APPRECIATED.. TO BE NEEDED ONCE MORE BY A LOYAL, CULT FOLLOWING!
HAVE YOU THOUGHT ABOUT GOING ON LARRY KING & THEN DOING AN EMBARRASSING HBO SPECIAL?
161

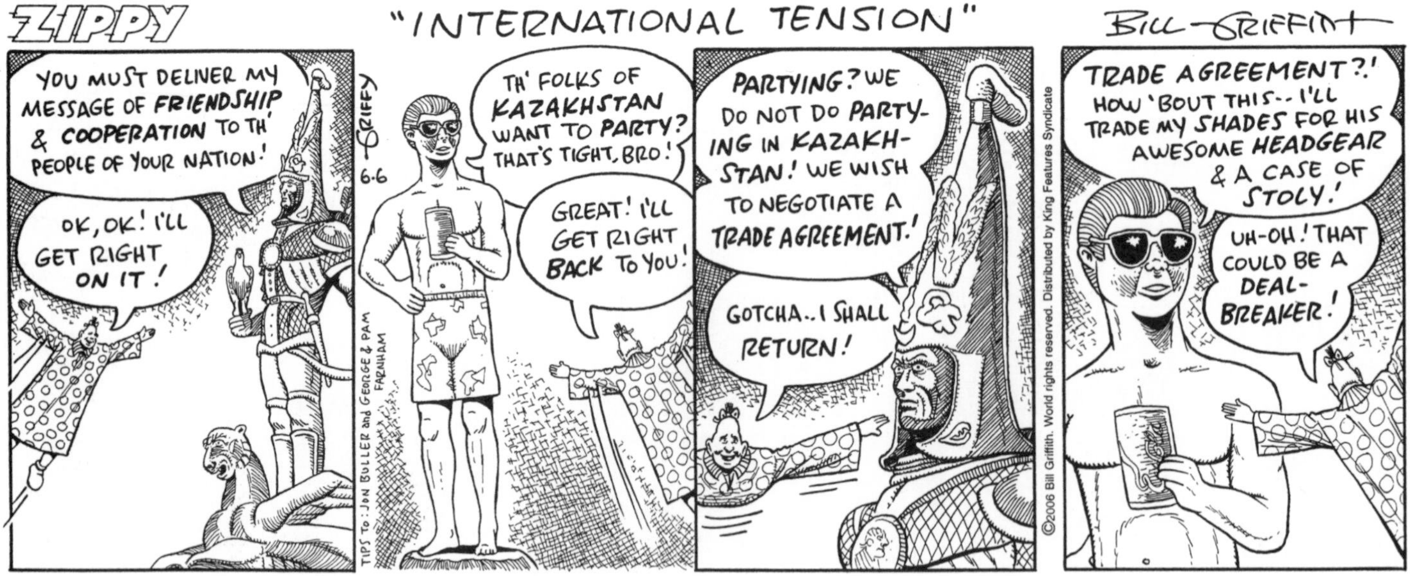
ZIPPY
"INTERNATIONAL TENSION"
BILL-GRIFFITH
YOU MUST DELIVER MY MESSAGE OF FRIENDSHIP & COOPERATION TO TH' PEOPLE OF YOUR NATION!
OK, OK! I'LL GET RIGHT ON IT!
GRIFFY 6-6
TIPS TO: JON BULLER and GEORGE & PAM FARNHAM
TH' FOLKS OF KAZAKHSTAN WANT TO PARTY? THAT'S TIGHT, BRO!
GREAT! I'LL GET RIGHT BACK TO YOU!
PARTYING? WE DO NOT DO PARTYING IN KAZAKHSTAN! WE WISH TO NEGOTIATE A TRADE AGREEMENT!
GOTCHA.. I SHALL RETURN!
©2006 Bill Griffith. World rights reserved. Distributed by King Features Syndicate
TRADE AGREEMENT?! HOW 'BOUT THIS-- I'LL TRADE MY SHADES FOR HIS AWESOME HEADGEAR & A CASE OF STOLY!
UH-OH! THAT COULD BE A DEAL-BREAKER!
162

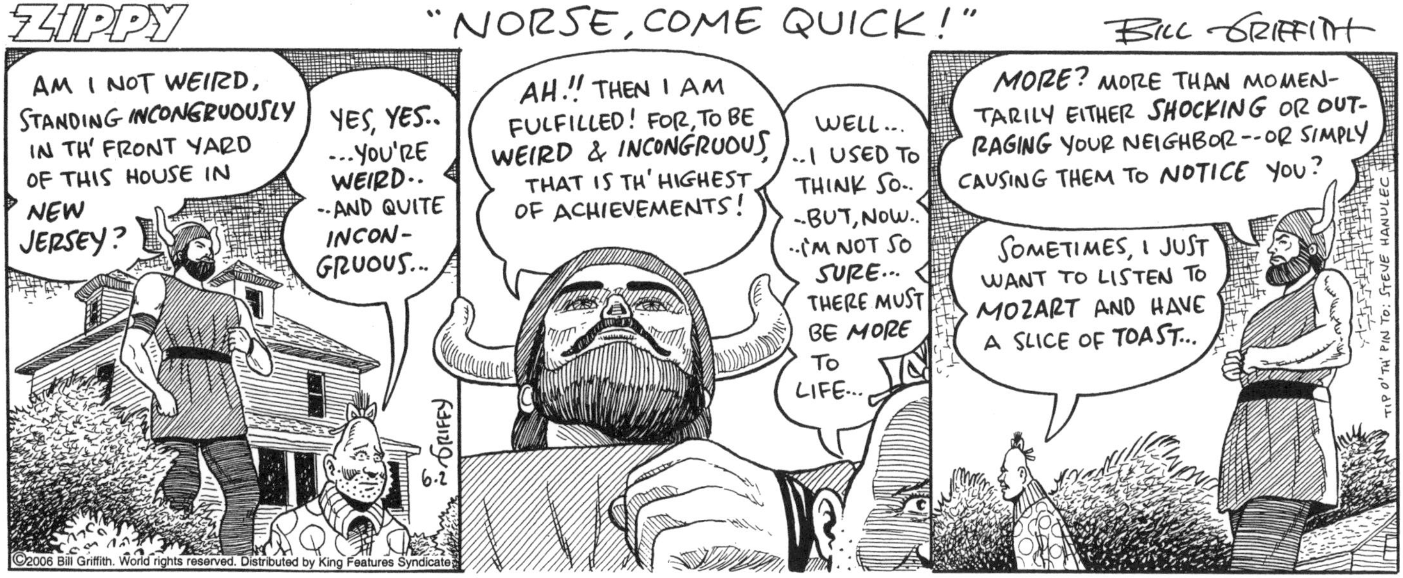
ZIPPY
"NORSE, COME QUICK!"
BILL GRIFFITH
AM I NOT WEIRD, STANDING INCONGRUOUSLY IN TH' FRONT YARD OF THIS HOUSE IN NEW JERSEY?
YES, YES.. ...YOU'RE WEIRD.. ..AND QUITE INCONGRUOUS...
GRIFFY 6-2
©2006 Bill Griffith. World rights reserved. Distributed by King Features Syndicate
AH!! THEN I AM FULFILLED! FOR, TO BE WEIRD & INCONGRUOUS, THAT IS TH' HIGHEST OF ACHIEVEMENTS!
WELL... ..I USED TO THINK SO.. ..BUT, NOW.. ..I'M NOT SO SURE... THERE MUST BE MORE TO LIFE...
MORE? MORE THAN MOMENTARILY EITHER SHOCKING OR OUTRAGING YOUR NEIGHBOR--OR SIMPLY CAUSING THEM TO NOTICE YOU?
SOMETIMES, I JUST WANT TO LISTEN TO MOZART AND HAVE A SLICE OF TOAST...
TIP O' TH' PIN TO: STEVE HANULEC

163

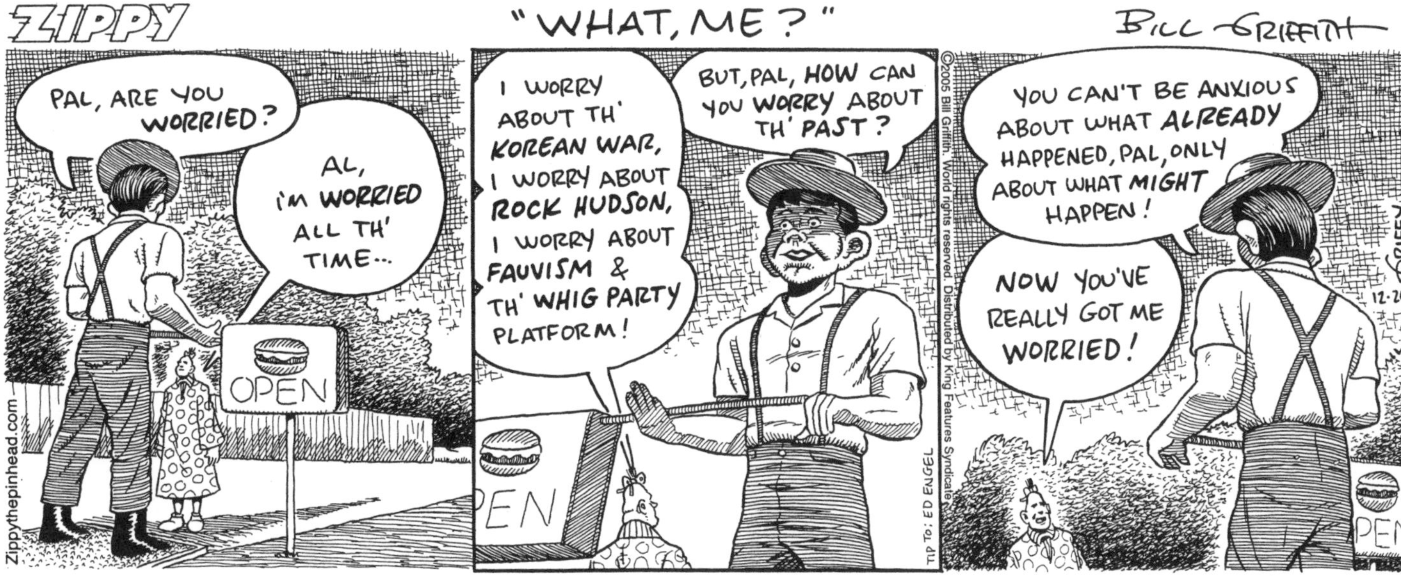
ZIPPY
"WHAT, ME?"
BILL GRIFFITH
PAL, ARE YOU WORRIED?
AL, I'M WORRIED ALL TH' TIME...
OPEN
Zippythepinhead.com
I WORRY ABOUT TH' KOREAN WAR, I WORRY ABOUT ROCK HUDSON, I WORRY ABOUT FAUVISM & TH' WHIG PARTY PLATFORM!
BUT, PAL, HOW CAN YOU WORRY ABOUT TH' PAST?
TIP TO: ED ENGEL
©2005 Bill Griffith. World rights reserved. Distributed by King Features Syndicate
YOU CAN'T BE ANXIOUS ABOUT WHAT ALREADY HAPPENED, PAL, ONLY ABOUT WHAT MIGHT HAPPEN!
NOW YOU'VE REALLY GOT ME WORRIED!
GRIFFY 12-26

164

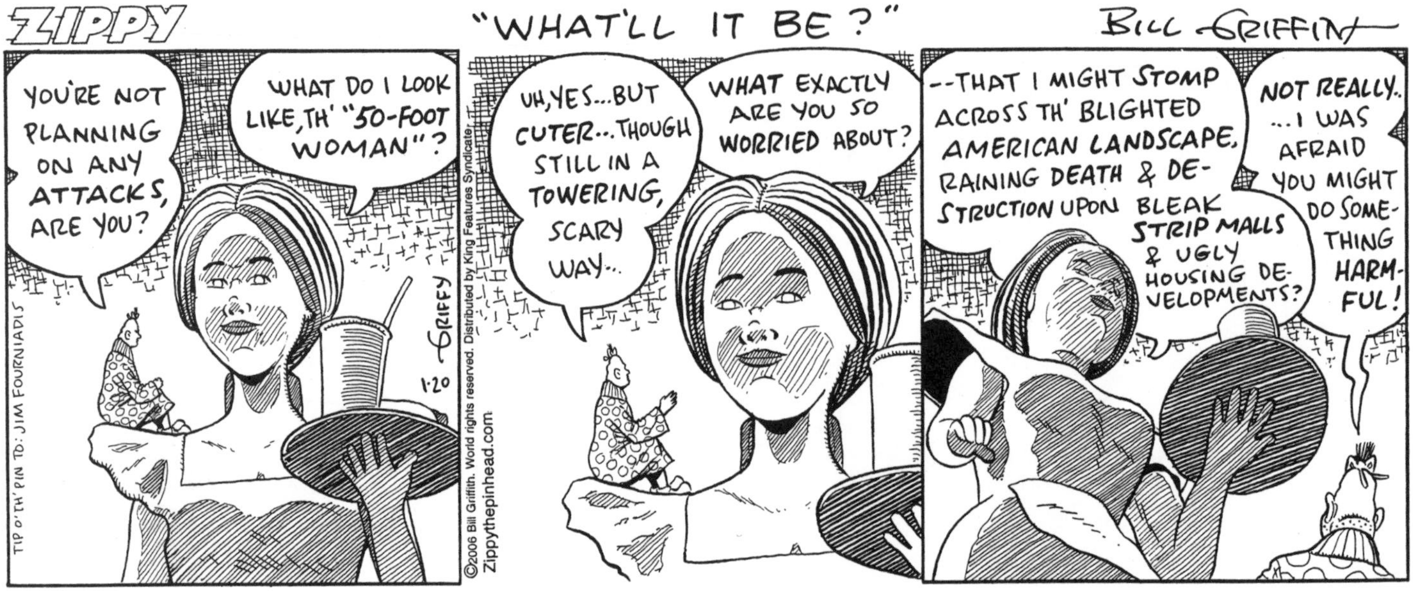
ZIPPY
"WHAT'LL IT BE?"
BILL GRIFFITH
YOU'RE NOT PLANNING ON ANY ATTACKS, ARE YOU?
WHAT DO I LOOK LIKE, TH' "50-FOOT WOMAN"?
TIP O' TH' PIN TO: JIM FOURNIADIS
GRIFFY 1·20
©2006 Bill Griffith. World rights reserved. Distributed by King Features Syndicate.
Zippythepinhead.com
UH, YES...BUT CUTER...THOUGH STILL IN A TOWERING, SCARY WAY...
WHAT EXACTLY ARE YOU SO WORRIED ABOUT?
--THAT I MIGHT STOMP ACROSS TH' BLIGHTED AMERICAN LANDSCAPE, RAINING DEATH & DESTRUCTION UPON BLEAK STRIP MALLS & UGLY HOUSING DEVELOPMENTS?
NOT REALLY.. ...I WAS AFRAID YOU MIGHT DO SOMETHING HARMFUL!

165

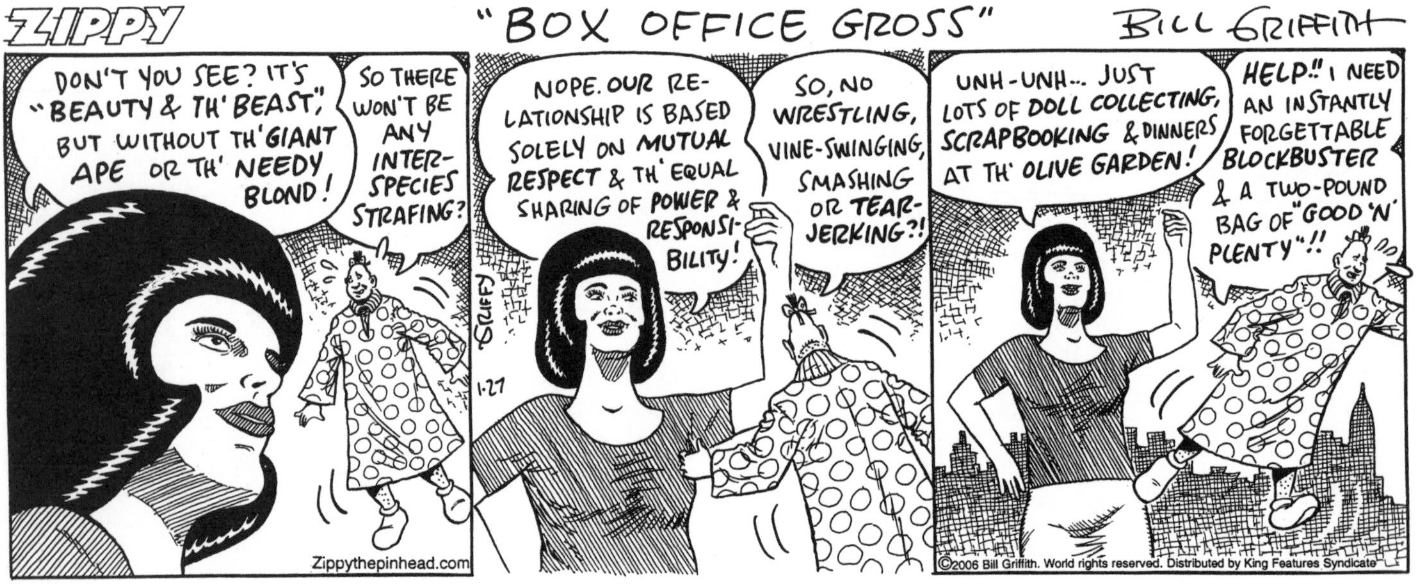
ZIPPY
"BOX OFFICE GROSS"
BILL GRIFFITH
DON'T YOU SEE? IT'S "BEAUTY & TH' BEAST", BUT WITHOUT TH' GIANT APE OR TH' NEEDY BLOND!
SO THERE WON'T BE ANY INTER-SPECIES STRAFING?
Zippythepinhead.com
NOPE. OUR RELATIONSHIP IS BASED SOLELY ON MUTUAL RESPECT & TH' EQUAL SHARING OF POWER & RESPONSIBILITY!
SO, NO WRESTLING, VINE-SWINGING, SMASHING OR TEAR-JERKING?!
GRIFFY 1·27
UNH-UNH... JUST LOTS OF DOLL COLLECTING, SCRAPBOOKING & DINNERS AT TH' OLIVE GARDEN!
HELP!! I NEED AN INSTANTLY FORGETTABLE BLOCKBUSTER & A TWO-POUND BAG OF "GOOD 'N' PLENTY"!!
©2006 Bill Griffith. World rights reserved. Distributed by King Features Syndicate

166

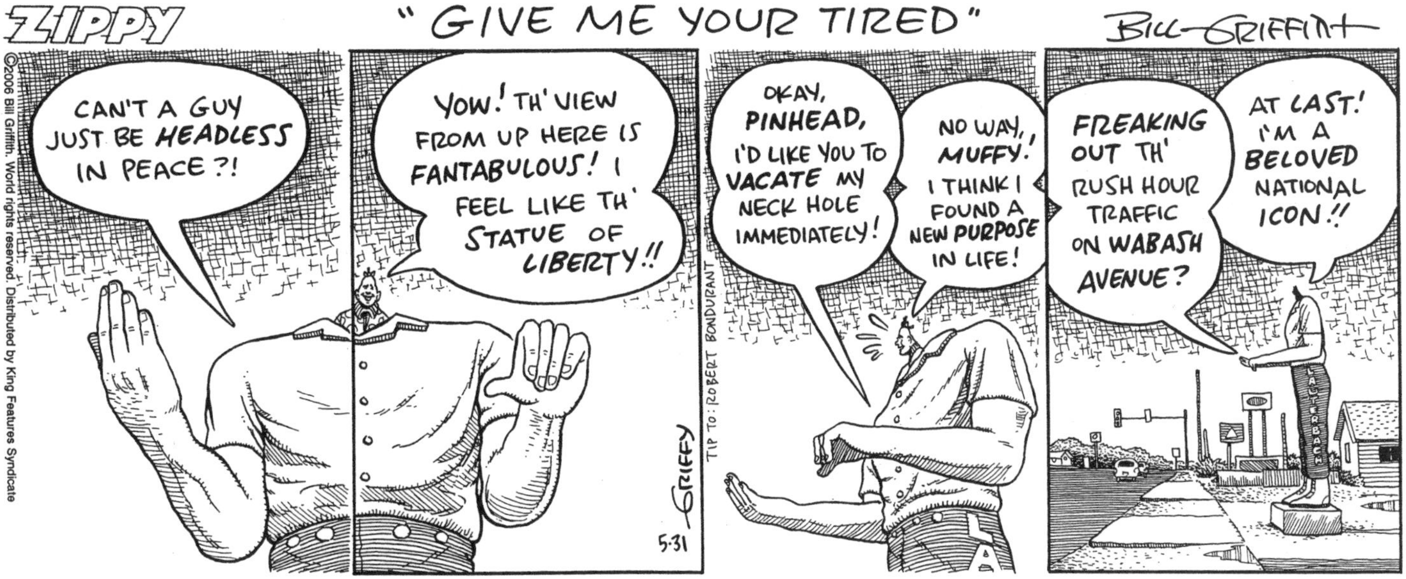
ZIPPY
"GIVE ME YOUR TIRED"
BILL GRIFFITH
©2006 Bill Griffith. World rights reserved. Distributed by King Features Syndicate
CAN'T A GUY JUST BE HEADLESS IN PEACE?!
YOW! TH' VIEW FROM UP HERE IS FANTABULOUS! I FEEL LIKE TH' STATUE OF LIBERTY!!
GRIFFY
5·31
TIP TO: ROBERT BONDURANT
OKAY, PINHEAD, I'D LIKE YOU TO VACATE MY NECK HOLE IMMEDIATELY!
NO WAY, MUFFY! I THINK I FOUND A NEW PURPOSE IN LIFE!
FREAKING OUT TH' RUSH HOUR TRAFFIC ON WABASH AVENUE?
AT LAST! I'M A BELOVED NATIONAL ICON!!
LAUTERBACH

167

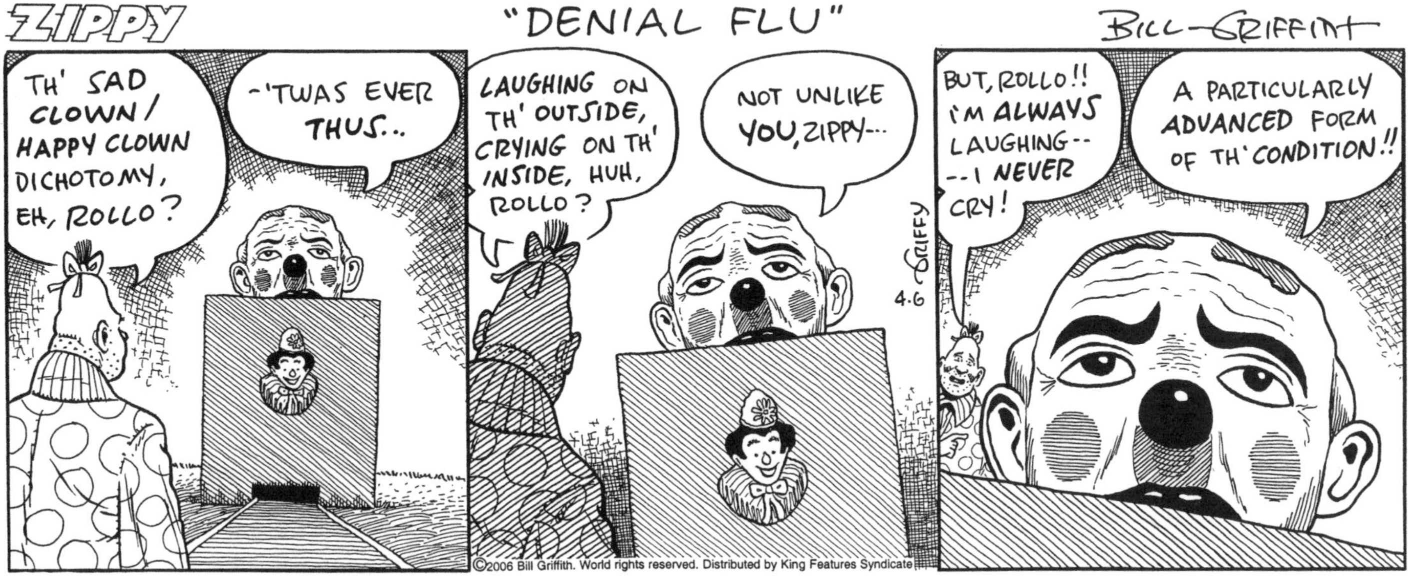
ZIPPY
"DENIAL FLU"
BILL GRIFFITH
TH' SAD CLOWN/HAPPY CLOWN DICHOTOMY, EH, ROLLO?
-'TWAS EVER THUS..
LAUGHING ON TH' OUTSIDE, CRYING ON TH' INSIDE, HUH, ROLLO?
NOT UNLIKE YOU, ZIPPY--
GRIFFY
4·6
BUT, ROLLO!! I'M ALWAYS LAUGHING-- --I NEVER CRY!
A PARTICULARLY ADVANCED FORM OF TH' CONDITION!!
©2006 Bill Griffith. World rights reserved. Distributed by King Features Syndicate

168

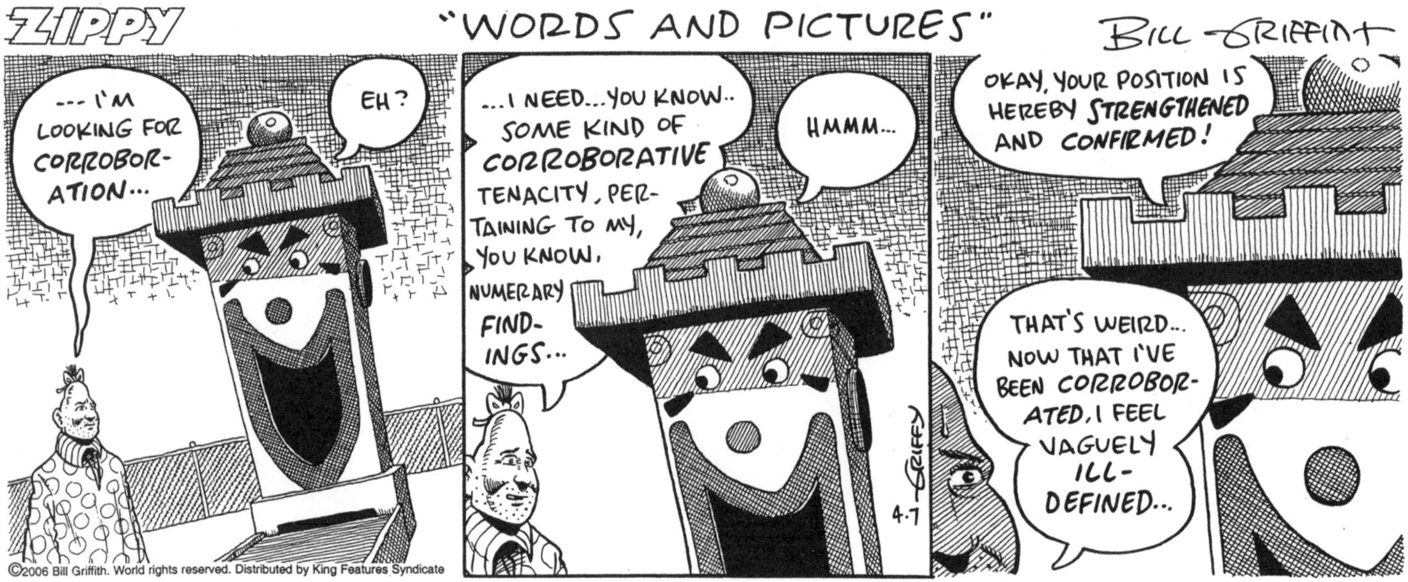
ZIPPY
"WORDS AND PICTURES"
BILL GRIFFITH
--- I'M LOOKING FOR CORROBOR-ATION...
EH?
...I NEED...YOU KNOW.. SOME KIND OF CORROBORATIVE TENACITY, PER-TAINING TO MY, YOU KNOW, NUMERARY FIND-INGS...
HMMM...
OKAY, YOUR POSITION IS HEREBY STRENGTHENED AND CONFIRMED!
THAT'S WEIRD... NOW THAT I'VE BEEN CORROBOR-ATED, I FEEL VAGUELY ILL-DEFINED...
GRIFFY
4-7
©2006 Bill Griffith. World rights reserved. Distributed by King Features Syndicate

169

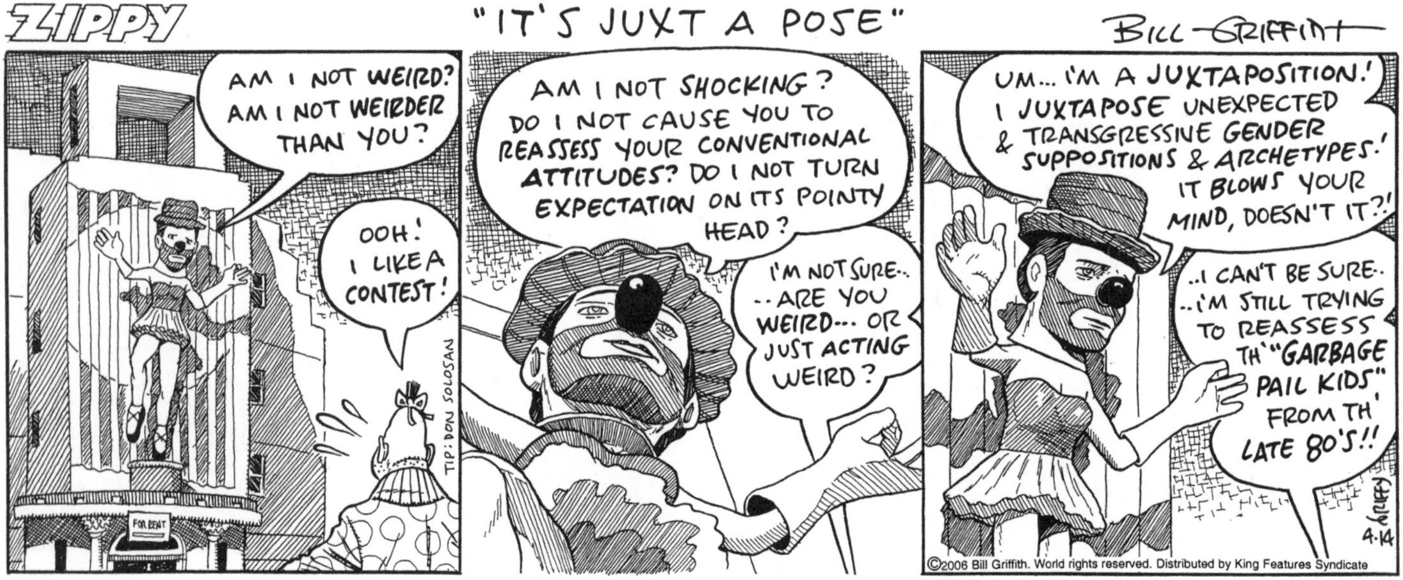
ZIPPY
"IT'S JUXT A POSE"
BILL GRIFFITH
AM I NOT WEIRD? AM I NOT WEIRDER THAN YOU?
OOH! I LIKE A CONTEST!
FOR RENT
TIP: DON SOLOSAN
AM I NOT SHOCKING? DO I NOT CAUSE YOU TO REASSESS YOUR CONVENTIONAL ATTITUDES? DO I NOT TURN EXPECTATION ON ITS POINTY HEAD?
I'M NOT SURE.. ..ARE YOU WEIRD... OR JUST ACTING WEIRD?
UM... I'M A JUXTAPOSITION! I JUXTAPOSE UNEXPECTED & TRANSGRESSIVE GENDER SUPPOSITIONS & ARCHETYPES! IT BLOWS YOUR MIND, DOESN'T IT?!
..I CAN'T BE SURE.. ..I'M STILL TRYING TO REASSESS TH' "GARBAGE PAIL KIDS" FROM TH' LATE 80'S!!
GRIFFY
4-14
©2006 Bill Griffith. World rights reserved. Distributed by King Features Syndicate

170

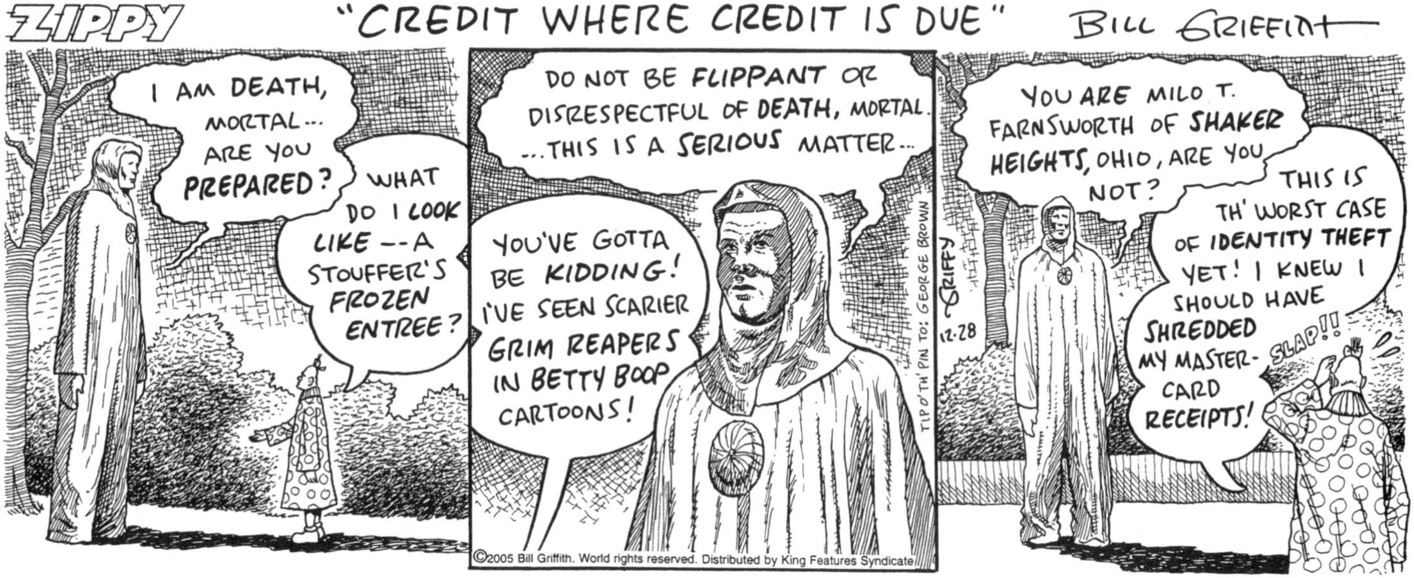
ZIPPY
"CREDIT WHERE CREDIT IS DUE"
BILL GRIFFITH
I AM DEATH, MORTAL... ARE YOU PREPARED?
WHAT DO I LOOK LIKE -- A STOUFFER'S FROZEN ENTREE?
DO NOT BE FLIPPANT OR DISRESPECTFUL OF DEATH, MORTAL ...THIS IS A SERIOUS MATTER...
YOU'VE GOTTA BE KIDDING! I'VE SEEN SCARIER GRIM REAPERS IN BETTY BOOP CARTOONS!
TIP O' TH' PIN TO: GEORGE BROWN
GRIFFY 12·28
YOU ARE MILO T. FARNSWORTH OF SHAKER HEIGHTS, OHIO, ARE YOU NOT?
THIS IS TH' WORST CASE OF IDENTITY THEFT YET! I KNEW I SHOULD HAVE SHREDDED MY MASTER-CARD RECEIPTS!
SLAP!!
©2005 Bill Griffith. World rights reserved. Distributed by King Features Syndicate

171

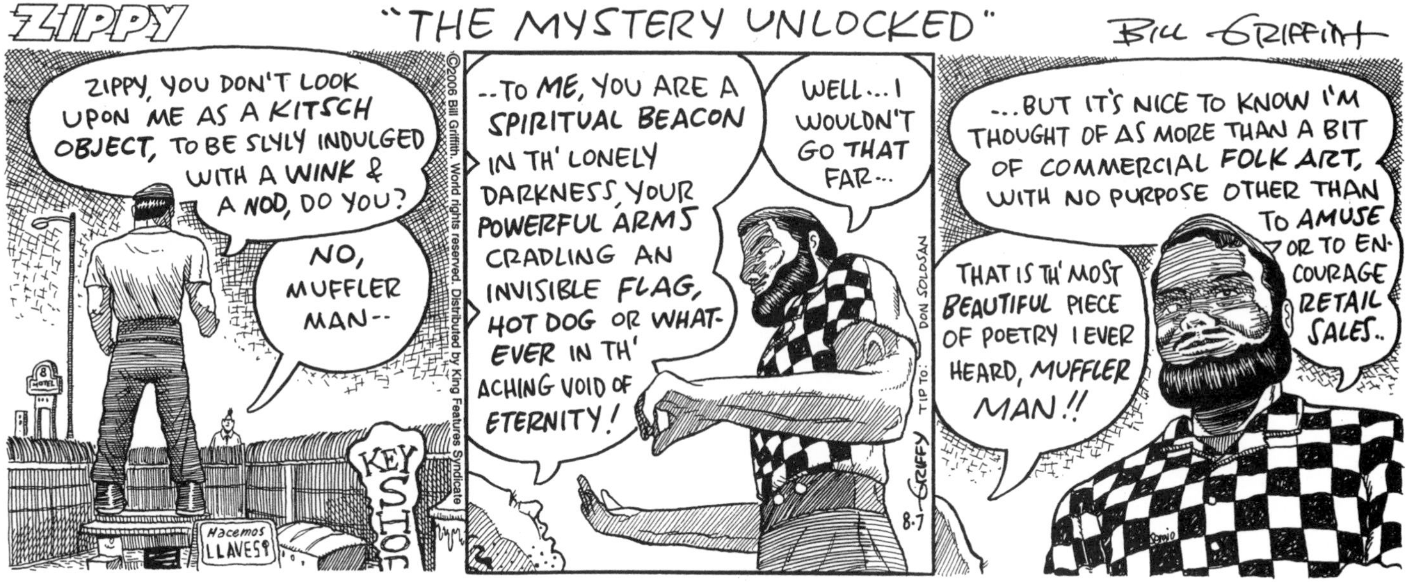
ZIPPY
"THE MYSTERY UNLOCKED"
BILL GRIFFITH
ZIPPY, YOU DON'T LOOK UPON ME AS A KITSCH OBJECT, TO BE SLYLY INDULGED WITH A WINK & A NOD, DO YOU?
NO, MUFFLER MAN--
8 MOTEL
KEY SHOP
Hacemos LLAVES!
©2006 Bill Griffith. World rights reserved. Distributed by King Features Syndicate
--TO ME, YOU ARE A SPIRITUAL BEACON IN TH' LONELY DARKNESS, YOUR POWERFUL ARMS CRADLING AN INVISIBLE FLAG, HOT DOG OR WHAT-EVER IN TH' ACHING VOID OF ETERNITY!
WELL...I WOULDN'T GO THAT FAR...
TIP TO: DON SOLOSAN
GRIFFY 8·7
...BUT IT'S NICE TO KNOW I'M THOUGHT OF AS MORE THAN A BIT OF COMMERCIAL FOLK ART, WITH NO PURPOSE OTHER THAN TO AMUSE OR TO EN-COURAGE RETAIL SALES..
THAT IS TH' MOST BEAUTIFUL PIECE OF POETRY I EVER HEARD, MUFFLER MAN!!

172

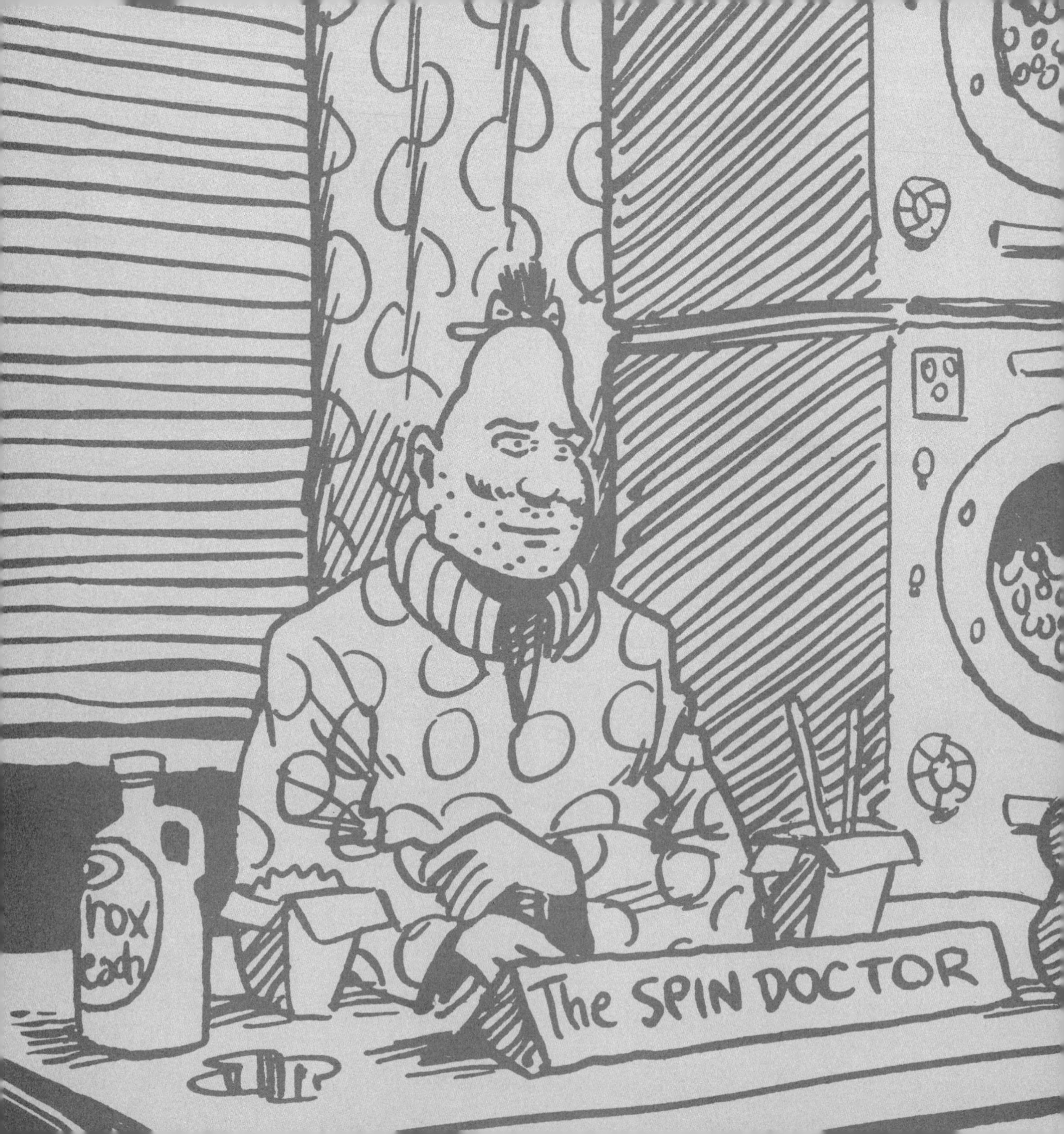
The SPIN DOCTOR

Selected Shorts

Encores from out-of-print books.

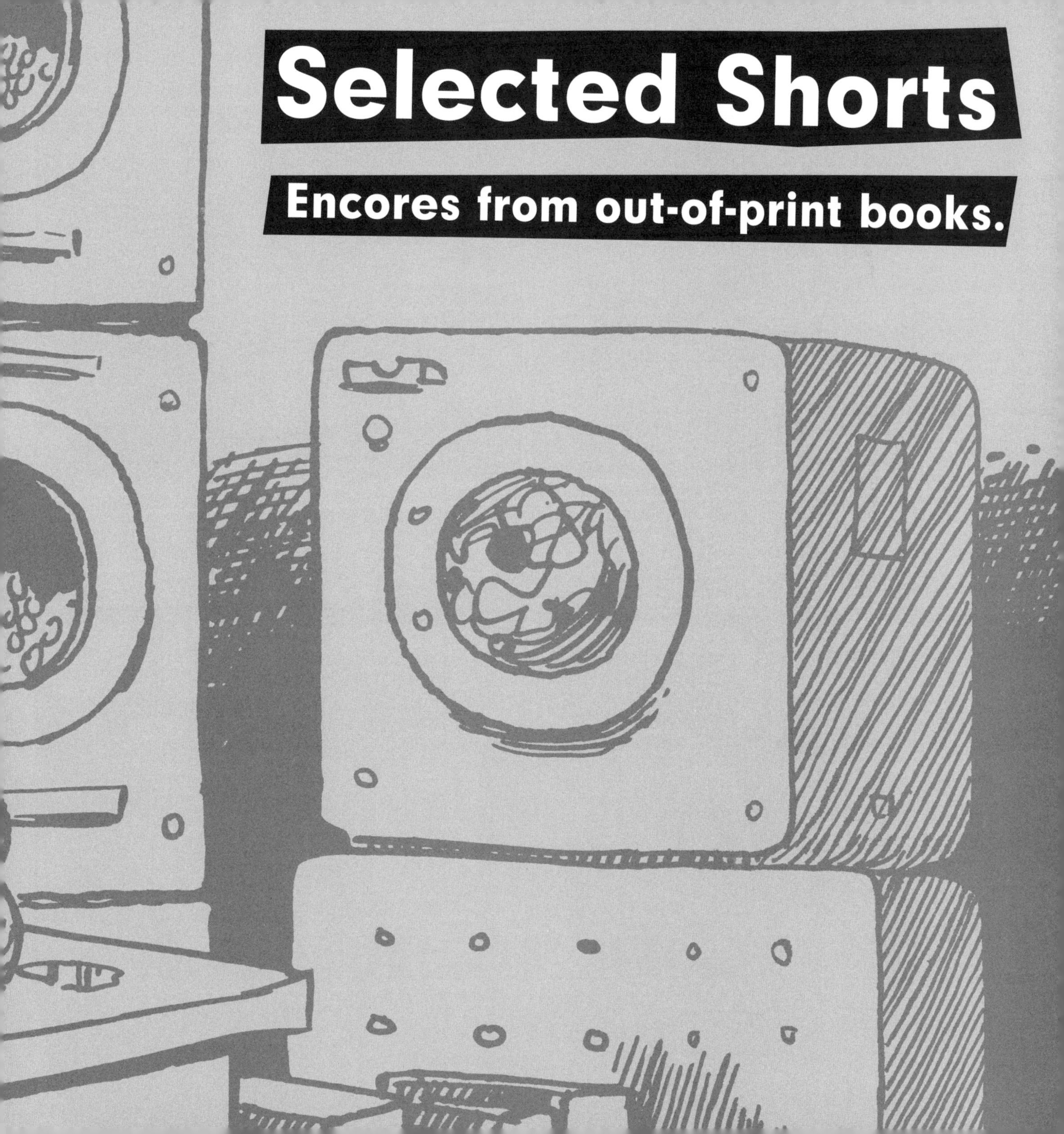

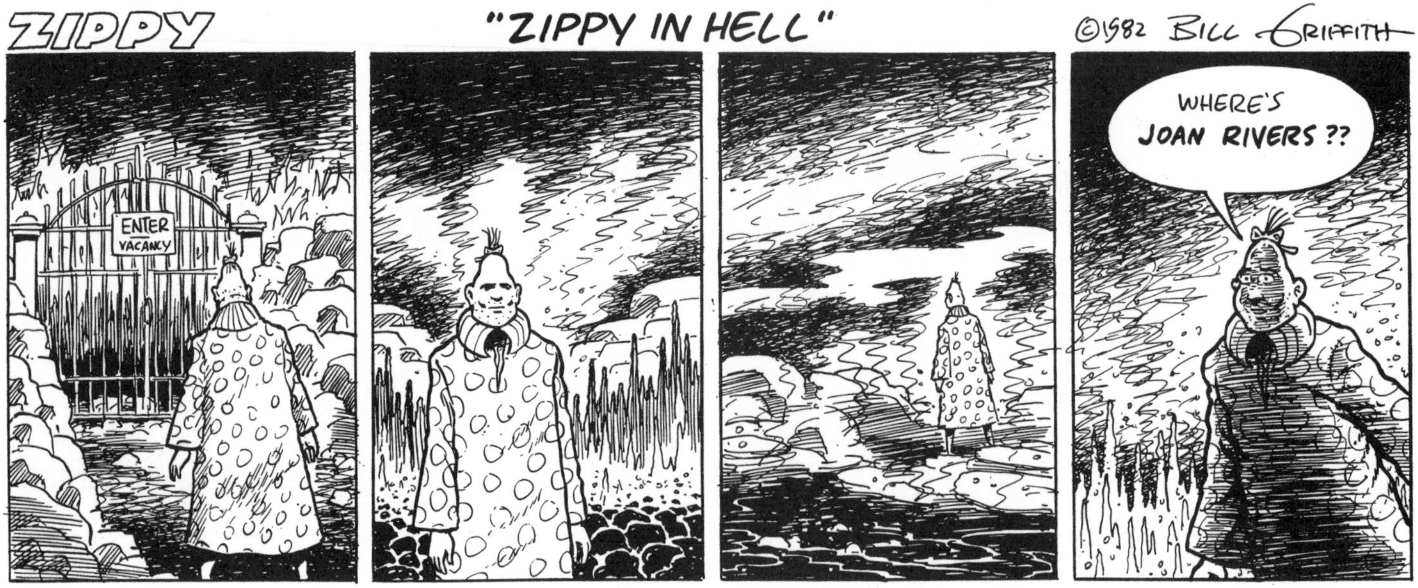
ZIPPY
"ZIPPY IN HELL"
©1982 BILL GRIFFITH
ENTER
VACANCY
WHERE'S JOAN RIVERS ??

173

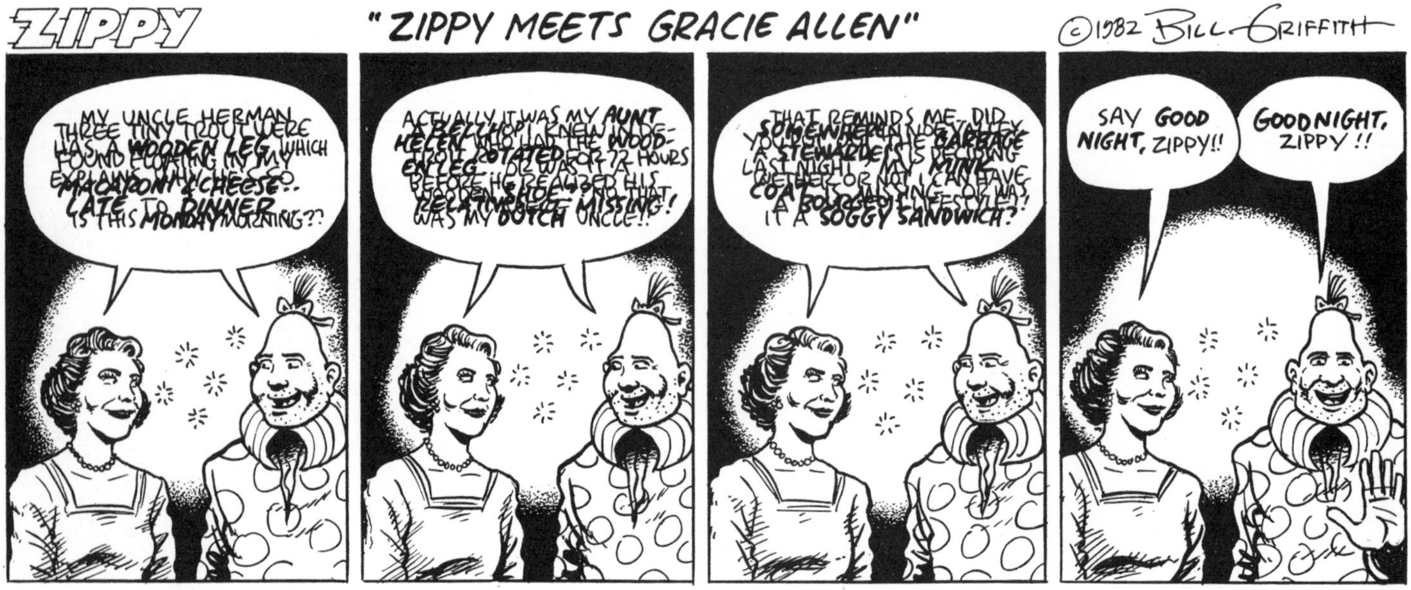
ZIPPY
"ZIPPY MEETS GRACIE ALLEN"
©1982 BILL GRIFFITH
MY UNCLE HERMAN HAS A WOODEN LEG WHICH EXPLAINS WHY HE'S SO LATE TO DINNER..
THREE TINY TROUT WERE FOUND FLOATING IN MY MACARONI & CHEESE.. IS THIS MONDAY MORNING??
ACTUALLY IT WAS MY AUNT HELEN WHO HAD THE WOODEN LEG.. OR WAS IT A WOODEN SHOE.. AND THAT WAS MY DUTCH UNCLE!!
A BELLHOP I KNEW IN DETROIT ROTATED FOR 72 HOURS BEFORE HE REALIZED HIS RELATIONSHIP WAS MISSING!
THAT REMINDS ME.. DID YOU PUT OUT THE GARBAGE LAST NIGHT? MY MINK COAT IS MISSING.. OR WAS IT A SOGGY SANDWICH?
SOMEWHERE IN NOE VALLEY, A STEWARDESS IS DECIDING WHETHER OR NOT I CAN HAVE A BOURGEOIS LIFESTYLE!
SAY GOOD NIGHT, ZIPPY!!
GOODNIGHT, ZIPPY!!

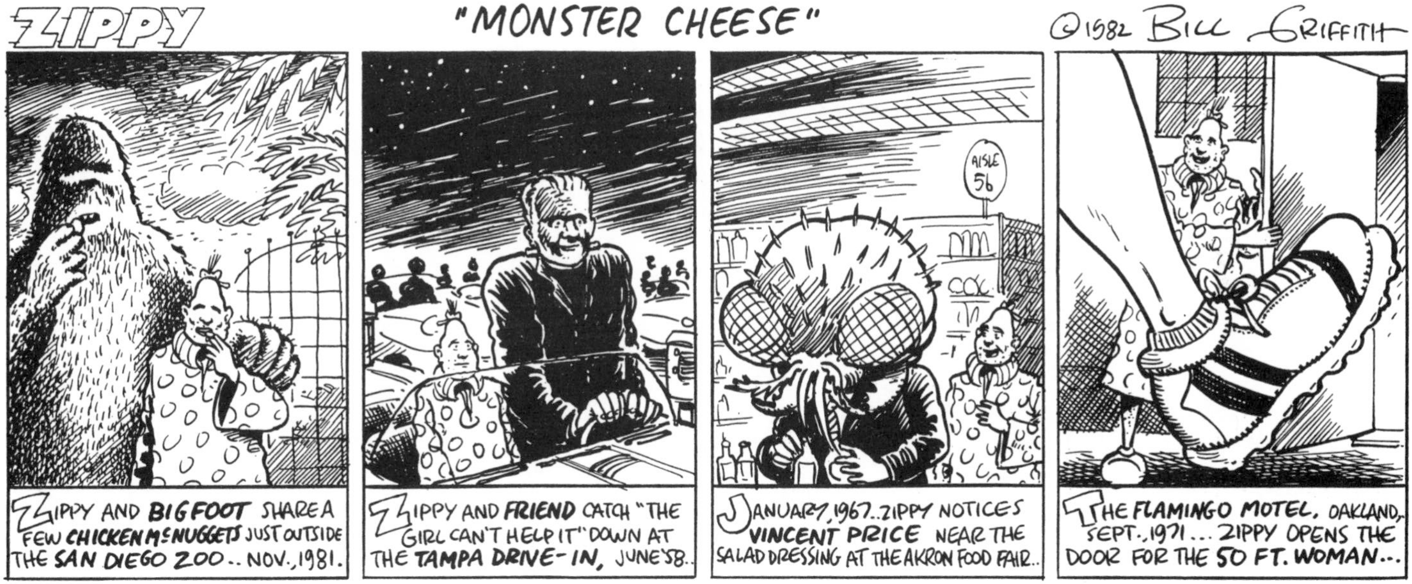
ZIPPY
"MONSTER CHEESE"
©1982 BILL GRIFFITH
ZIPPY AND BIGFOOT SHARE A FEW CHICKEN McNUGGETS JUST OUTSIDE THE SAN DIEGO ZOO.. NOV., 1981.
ZIPPY AND FRIEND CATCH "THE GIRL CAN'T HELP IT" DOWN AT THE TAMPA DRIVE-IN, JUNE '58..
AISLE 56
JANUARY, 1967.. ZIPPY NOTICES VINCENT PRICE NEAR THE SALAD DRESSING AT THE AKRON FOOD FAIR..
THE FLAMINGO MOTEL, OAKLAND, SEPT., 1971... ZIPPY OPENS THE DOOR FOR THE 50 FT. WOMAN...

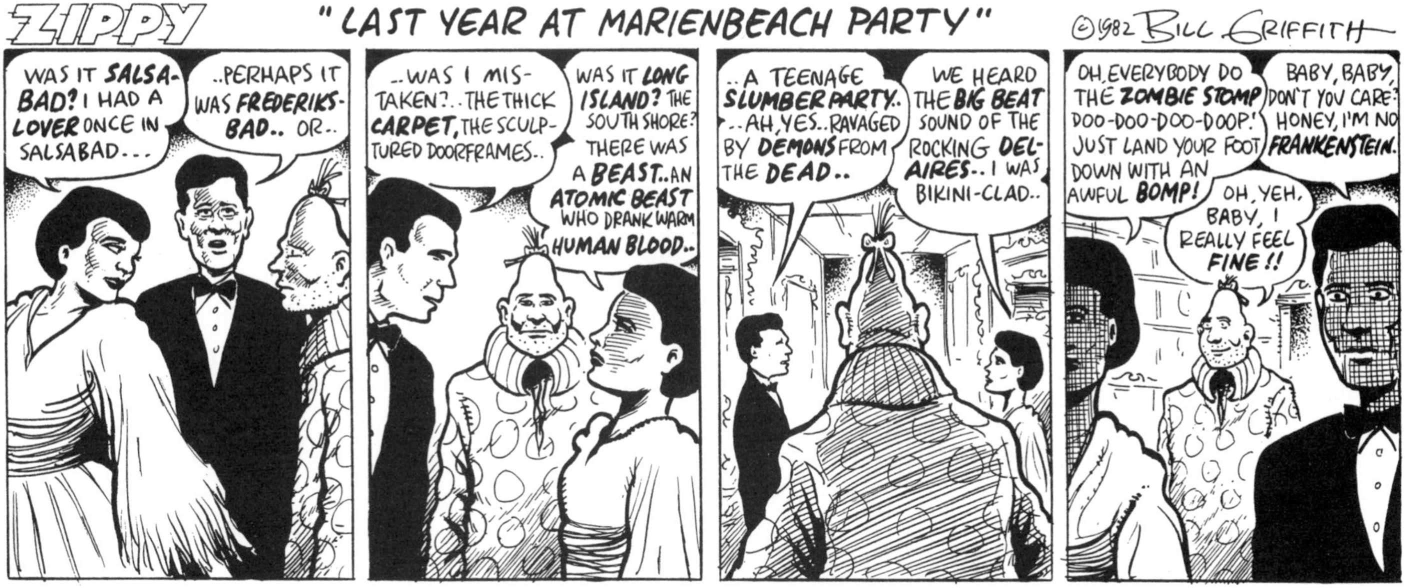
ZIPPY
"LAST YEAR AT MARIENBEACH PARTY"
©1982 BILL GRIFFITH
WAS IT SALSA-BAD? I HAD A LOVER ONCE IN SALSABAD...
..PERHAPS IT WAS FREDERIKS-BAD.. OR..
..WAS I MIS-TAKEN?.. THE THICK CARPET, THE SCULP-TURED DOORFRAMES..
WAS IT LONG ISLAND? THE SOUTH SHORE? THERE WAS A BEAST.. AN ATOMIC BEAST WHO DRANK WARM HUMAN BLOOD..
..A TEENAGE SLUMBER PARTY.. ..AH, YES.. RAVAGED BY DEMONS FROM THE DEAD..
WE HEARD THE BIG BEAT SOUND OF THE ROCKING DEL-AIRES.. I WAS BIKINI-CLAD..
OH, EVERYBODY DO THE ZOMBIE STOMP DOO-DOO-DOO-DOOP! JUST LAND YOUR FOOT DOWN WITH AN AWFUL BOMP!
BABY, BABY, DON'T YOU CARE? HONEY, I'M NO FRANKENSTEIN.
OH, YEH, BABY, I REALLY FEEL FINE!!

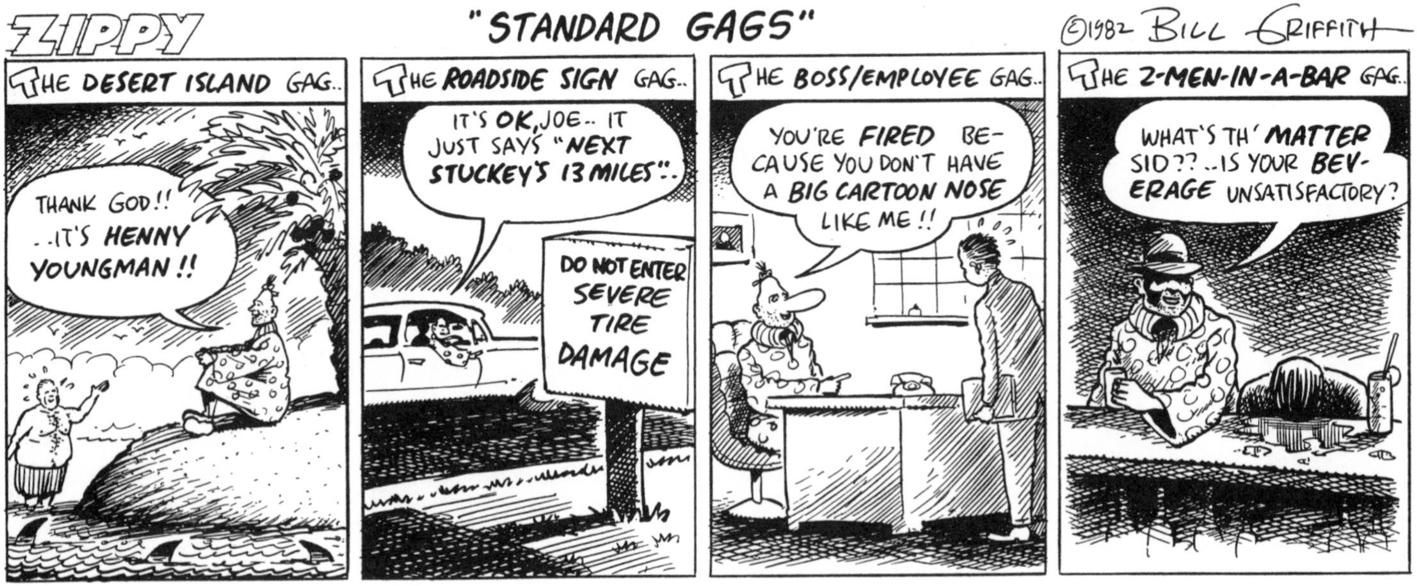
ZIPPY
"STANDARD GAGS"
©1982 BILL GRIFFITH
THE DESERT ISLAND GAG..
THANK GOD!! ..IT'S HENNY YOUNGMAN!!
THE ROADSIDE SIGN GAG..
IT'S OK, JOE.. IT JUST SAYS "NEXT STUCKEY'S 13 MILES"..
DO NOT ENTER SEVERE TIRE DAMAGE
THE BOSS/EMPLOYEE GAG..
YOU'RE FIRED BECAUSE YOU DON'T HAVE A BIG CARTOON NOSE LIKE ME!!
THE 2-MEN-IN-A-BAR GAG..
WHAT'S TH' MATTER SID?? ..IS YOUR BEVERAGE UNSATISFACTORY?

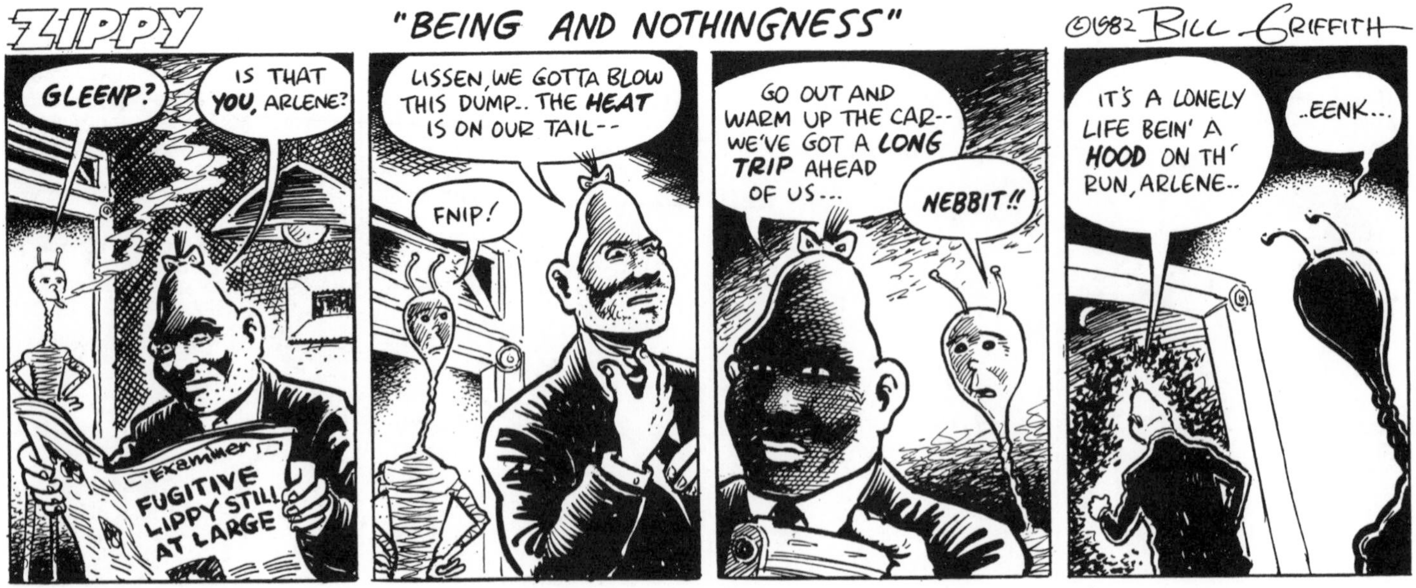
ZIPPY
"BEING AND NOTHINGNESS"
©1982 BILL GRIFFITH
GLEENP?
IS THAT YOU, ARLENE?
Examiner
FUGITIVE LIPPY STILL AT LARGE
LISSEN, WE GOTTA BLOW THIS DUMP.. THE HEAT IS ON OUR TAIL--
FNIP!
GO OUT AND WARM UP THE CAR-- WE'VE GOT A LONG TRIP AHEAD OF US...
NEBBIT!!
IT'S A LONELY LIFE BEIN' A HOOD ON TH' RUN, ARLENE..
..EENK...

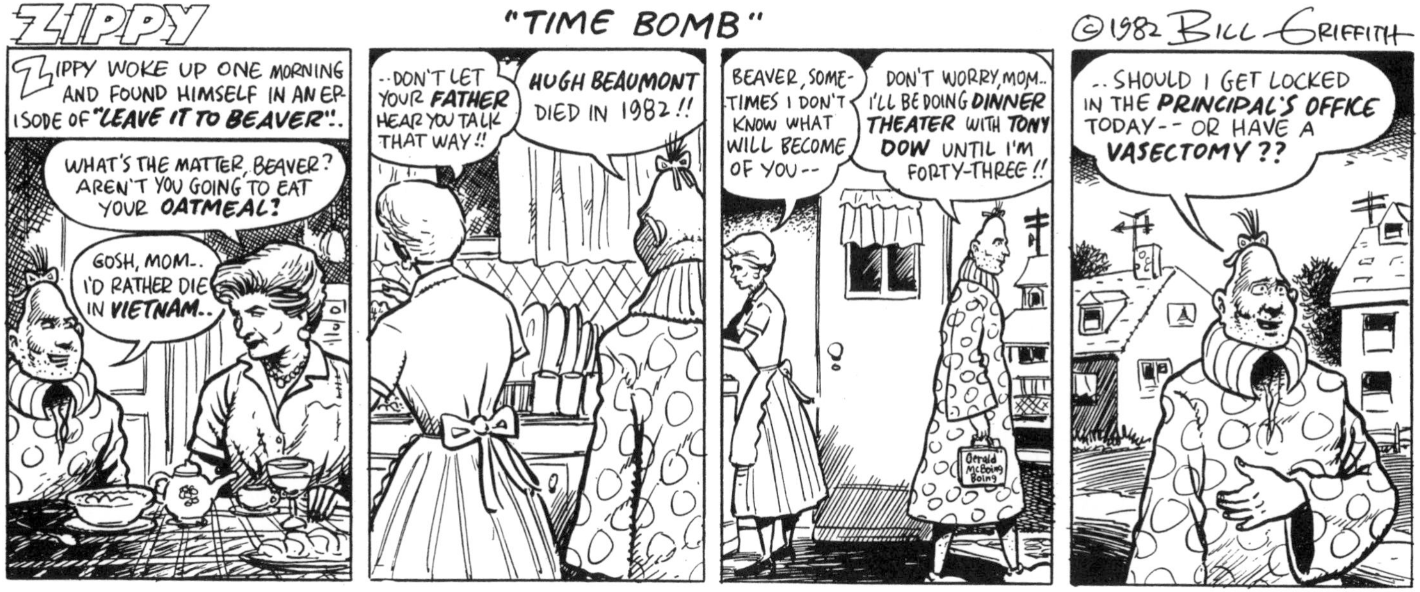
ZIPPY
"TIME BOMB"
©1982 BILL GRIFFITH
ZIPPY WOKE UP ONE MORNING AND FOUND HIMSELF IN AN EPISODE OF "LEAVE IT TO BEAVER"..
WHAT'S THE MATTER, BEAVER? AREN'T YOU GOING TO EAT YOUR OATMEAL?
GOSH, MOM.. I'D RATHER DIE IN VIETNAM..
..DON'T LET YOUR FATHER HEAR YOU TALK THAT WAY!!
HUGH BEAUMONT DIED IN 1982!!
BEAVER, SOMETIMES I DON'T KNOW WHAT WILL BECOME OF YOU--
DON'T WORRY, MOM.. I'LL BE DOING DINNER THEATER WITH TONY DOW UNTIL I'M FORTY-THREE!!
Gerald McBoing Boing
..SHOULD I GET LOCKED IN THE PRINCIPAL'S OFFICE TODAY-- OR HAVE A VASECTOMY??

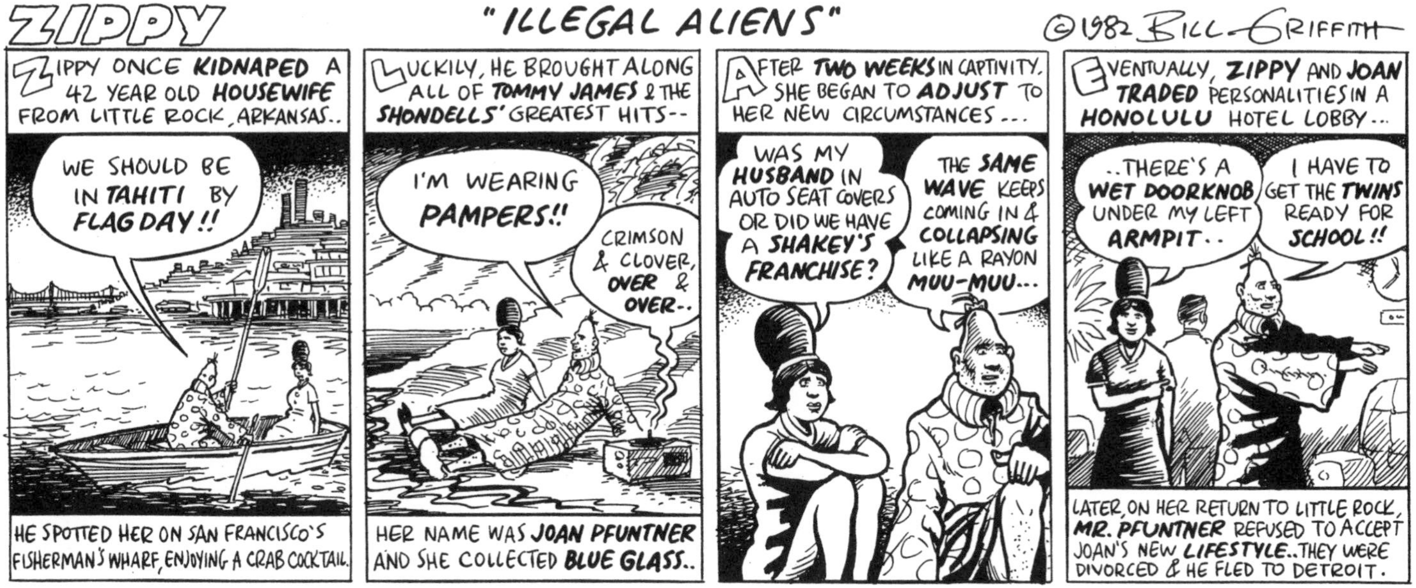
ZIPPY
"ILLEGAL ALIENS"
©1982 BILL GRIFFITH
ZIPPY ONCE KIDNAPED A 42 YEAR OLD HOUSEWIFE FROM LITTLE ROCK, ARKANSAS..
WE SHOULD BE IN TAHITI BY FLAG DAY!!
HE SPOTTED HER ON SAN FRANCISCO'S FISHERMAN'S WHARF, ENJOYING A CRAB COCKTAIL.
LUCKILY, HE BROUGHT ALONG ALL OF TOMMY JAMES & THE SHONDELLS' GREATEST HITS--
I'M WEARING PAMPERS!!
CRIMSON & CLOVER, OVER & OVER..
HER NAME WAS JOAN PFUNTNER AND SHE COLLECTED BLUE GLASS..
AFTER TWO WEEKS IN CAPTIVITY, SHE BEGAN TO ADJUST TO HER NEW CIRCUMSTANCES...
WAS MY HUSBAND IN AUTO SEAT COVERS OR DID WE HAVE A SHAKEY'S FRANCHISE?
THE SAME WAVE KEEPS COMING IN & COLLAPSING LIKE A RAYON MUU-MUU...
EVENTUALLY, ZIPPY AND JOAN TRADED PERSONALITIES IN A HONOLULU HOTEL LOBBY...
..THERE'S A WET DOORKNOB UNDER MY LEFT ARMPIT..
I HAVE TO GET THE TWINS READY FOR SCHOOL!!
LATER, ON HER RETURN TO LITTLE ROCK, MR. PFUNTNER REFUSED TO ACCEPT JOAN'S NEW LIFESTYLE.. THEY WERE DIVORCED & HE FLED TO DETROIT.

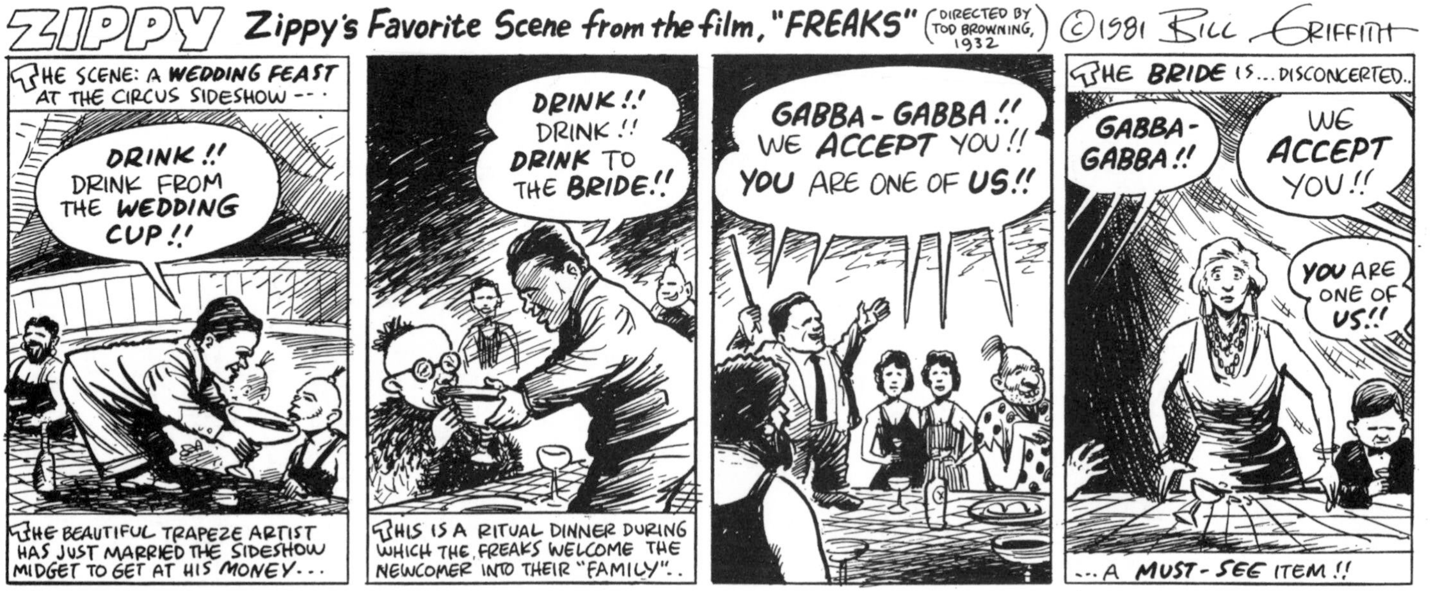
ZIPPY
Zippy's Favorite Scene from the film, "FREAKS" (DIRECTED BY TOD BROWNING, 1932)
©1981 BILL GRIFFITH
THE SCENE: A WEDDING FEAST AT THE CIRCUS SIDESHOW --
DRINK!! DRINK FROM THE WEDDING CUP!!
THE BEAUTIFUL TRAPEZE ARTIST HAS JUST MARRIED THE SIDESHOW MIDGET TO GET AT HIS MONEY...
DRINK!! DRINK!! DRINK TO THE BRIDE!!
THIS IS A RITUAL DINNER DURING WHICH THE FREAKS WELCOME THE NEWCOMER INTO THEIR "FAMILY"..
GABBA-GABBA!! WE ACCEPT YOU!! YOU ARE ONE OF US!!
THE BRIDE IS... DISCONCERTED..
GABBA-GABBA!!
WE ACCEPT YOU!!
YOU ARE ONE OF US!!
...A MUST-SEE ITEM!!

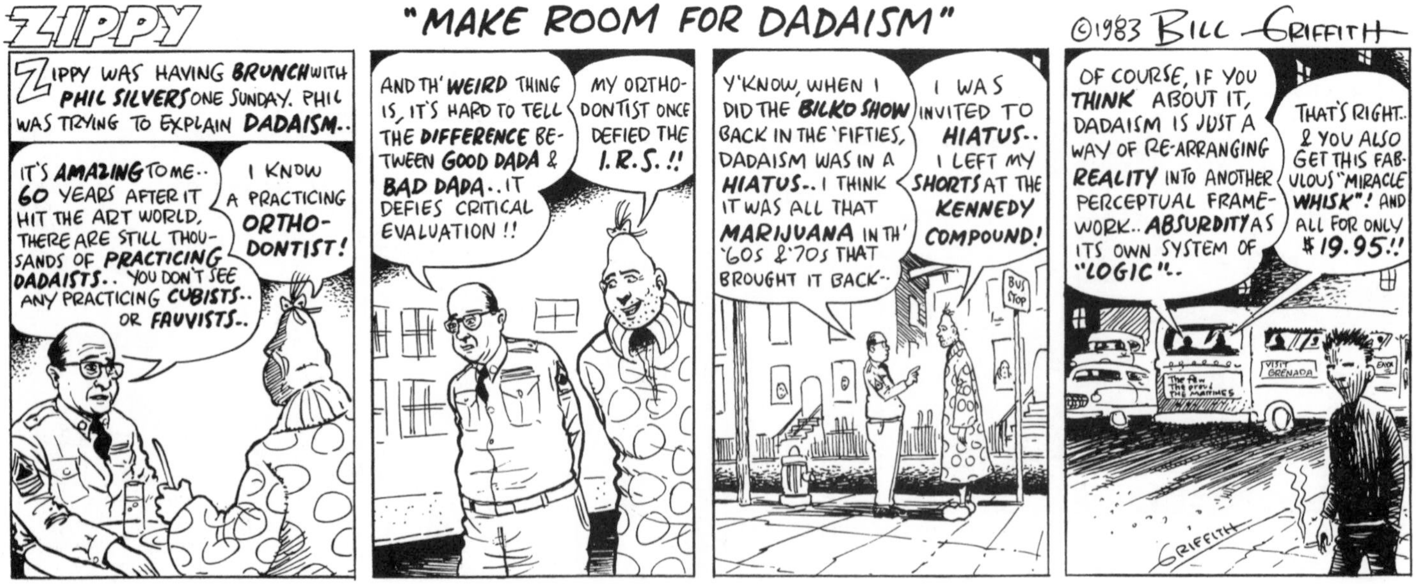
ZIPPY
"MAKE ROOM FOR DADAISM"
©1983 BILL GRIFFITH
ZIPPY WAS HAVING BRUNCH WITH PHIL SILVERS ONE SUNDAY. PHIL WAS TRYING TO EXPLAIN DADAISM..
IT'S AMAZING TO ME.. 60 YEARS AFTER IT HIT THE ART WORLD, THERE ARE STILL THOUSANDS OF PRACTICING DADAISTS.. YOU DON'T SEE ANY PRACTICING CUBISTS.. OR FAUVISTS..
I KNOW A PRACTICING ORTHODONTIST!
AND TH' WEIRD THING IS, IT'S HARD TO TELL THE DIFFERENCE BETWEEN GOOD DADA & BAD DADA.. IT DEFIES CRITICAL EVALUATION!!
MY ORTHODONTIST ONCE DEFIED THE I.R.S.!!
Y'KNOW, WHEN I DID THE BILKO SHOW BACK IN THE 'FIFTIES, DADAISM WAS IN A HIATUS.. I THINK IT WAS ALL THAT MARIJUANA IN TH' '60s & '70s THAT BROUGHT IT BACK..
I WAS INVITED TO HIATUS.. I LEFT MY SHORTS AT THE KENNEDY COMPOUND!
BUS STOP
OF COURSE, IF YOU THINK ABOUT IT, DADAISM IS JUST A WAY OF RE-ARRANGING REALITY INTO ANOTHER PERCEPTUAL FRAMEWORK.. ABSURDITY AS ITS OWN SYSTEM OF "LOGIC"..
THAT'S RIGHT.. & YOU ALSO GET THIS FABULOUS "MIRACLE WHISK"! AND ALL FOR ONLY $19.95!!
VISIT GRENADA
GRIFFITH

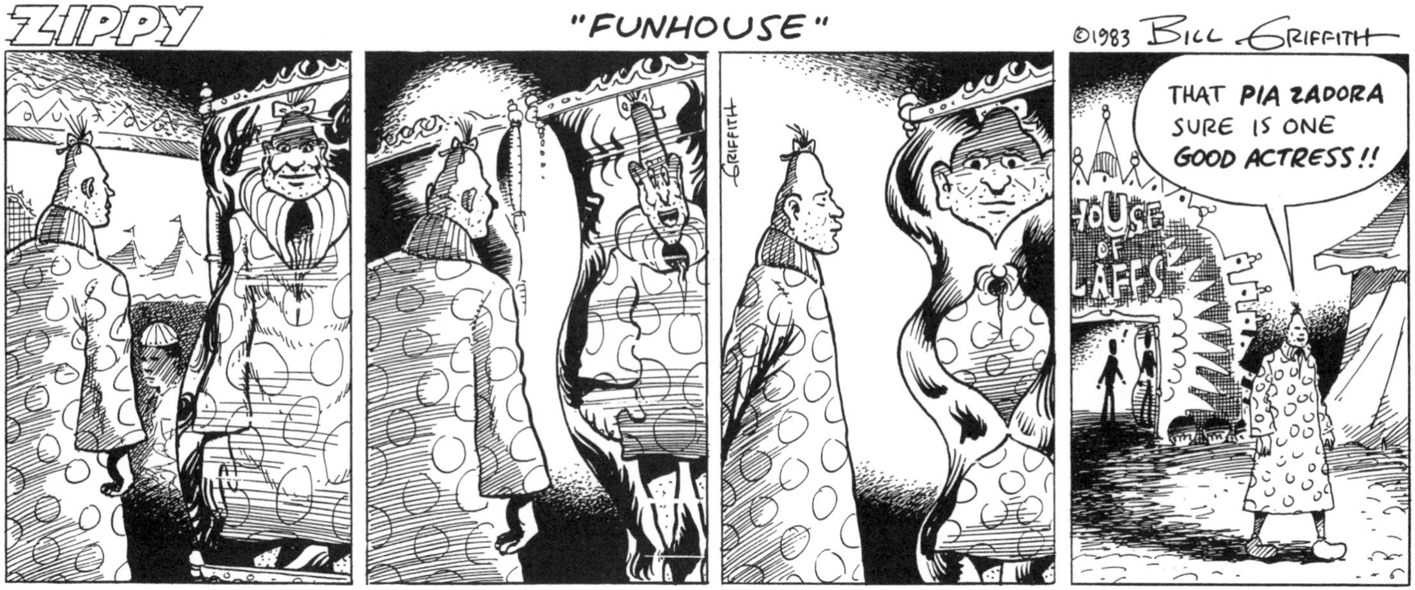
ZIPPY
"FUNHOUSE"
©1983 Bill Griffith
Griffith
THAT PIA ZADORA SURE IS ONE GOOD ACTRESS!!
HOUSE OF LAFFS

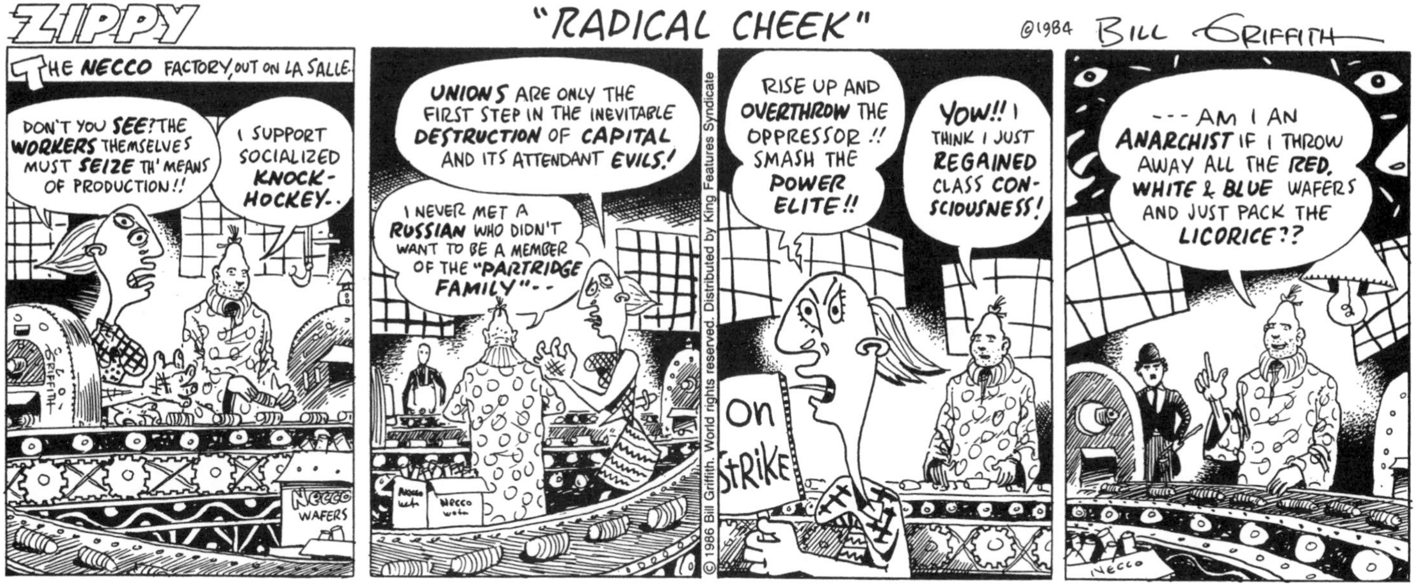
ZIPPY
"RADICAL CHEEK"
©1984 Bill Griffith
THE NECCO FACTORY, OUT ON LA SALLE.
DON'T YOU SEE? THE WORKERS THEMSELVES MUST SEIZE TH' MEANS OF PRODUCTION!!
I SUPPORT SOCIALIZED KNOCK-HOCKEY..
Griffith
NECCO WAFERS
UNIONS ARE ONLY THE FIRST STEP IN THE INEVITABLE DESTRUCTION OF CAPITAL AND ITS ATTENDANT EVILS!
I NEVER MET A RUSSIAN WHO DIDN'T WANT TO BE A MEMBER OF THE "PARTRIDGE FAMILY"--
© 1986 Bill Griffith. World rights reserved. Distributed by King Features Syndicate
RISE UP AND OVERTHROW THE OPPRESSOR!! SMASH THE POWER ELITE!!
YOW!! I THINK I JUST REGAINED CLASS CON-SCIOUSNESS!
On STRIKE
---AM I AN ANARCHIST IF I THROW AWAY ALL THE RED, WHITE & BLUE WAFERS AND JUST PACK THE LICORICE??
NECCO

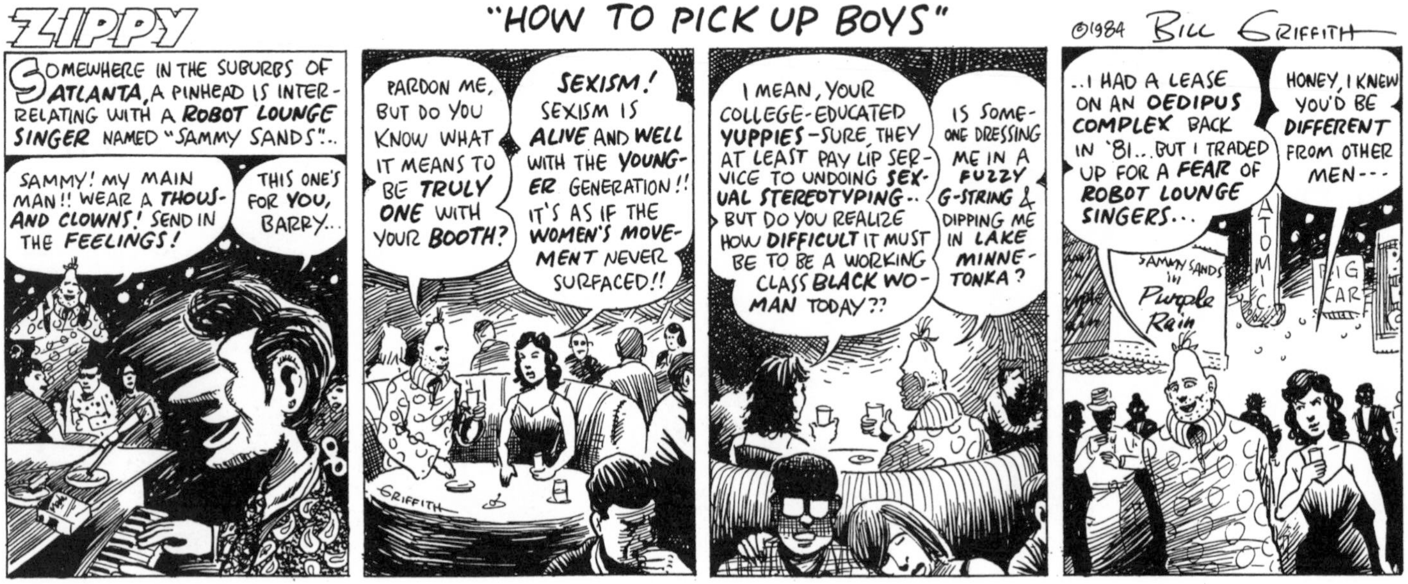
ZIPPY
"HOW TO PICK UP BOYS"
©1984 BILL GRIFFITH
SOMEWHERE IN THE SUBURBS OF ATLANTA, A PINHEAD IS INTER-RELATING WITH A ROBOT LOUNGE SINGER NAMED "SAMMY SANDS"..
SAMMY! MY MAIN MAN!! WEAR A THOUSAND CLOWNS! SEND IN THE FEELINGS!
THIS ONE'S FOR YOU, BARRY...
PARDON ME, BUT DO YOU KNOW WHAT IT MEANS TO BE TRULY ONE WITH YOUR BOOTH?
SEXISM! SEXISM IS ALIVE AND WELL WITH THE YOUNGER GENERATION!! IT'S AS IF THE WOMEN'S MOVEMENT NEVER SURFACED!!
GRIFFITH
I MEAN, YOUR COLLEGE-EDUCATED YUPPIES - SURE, THEY AT LEAST PAY LIP SERVICE TO UNDOING SEXUAL STEREOTYPING.. BUT DO YOU REALIZE HOW DIFFICULT IT MUST BE TO BE A WORKING CLASS BLACK WOMAN TODAY??
IS SOMEONE DRESSING ME IN A FUZZY G-STRING & DIPPING ME IN LAKE MINNETONKA?
..I HAD A LEASE ON AN OEDIPUS COMPLEX BACK IN '81... BUT I TRADED UP FOR A FEAR OF ROBOT LOUNGE SINGERS...
HONEY, I KNEW YOU'D BE DIFFERENT FROM OTHER MEN---
SAMMY SANDS in Purple Rain
ATOMIC
BIG CAR

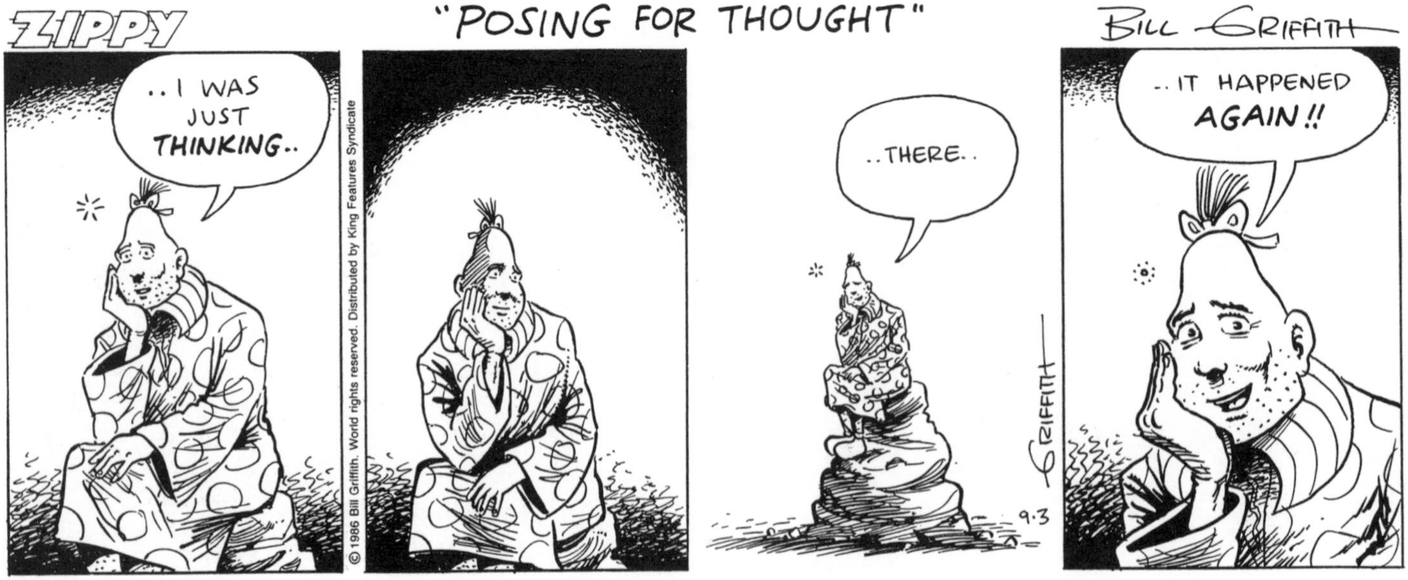
ZIPPY
"POSING FOR THOUGHT"
BILL GRIFFITH
..I WAS JUST THINKING..
© 1986 Bill Griffith. World rights reserved. Distributed by King Features Syndicate
..THERE..
GRIFFITH
9-3
..IT HAPPENED AGAIN!!

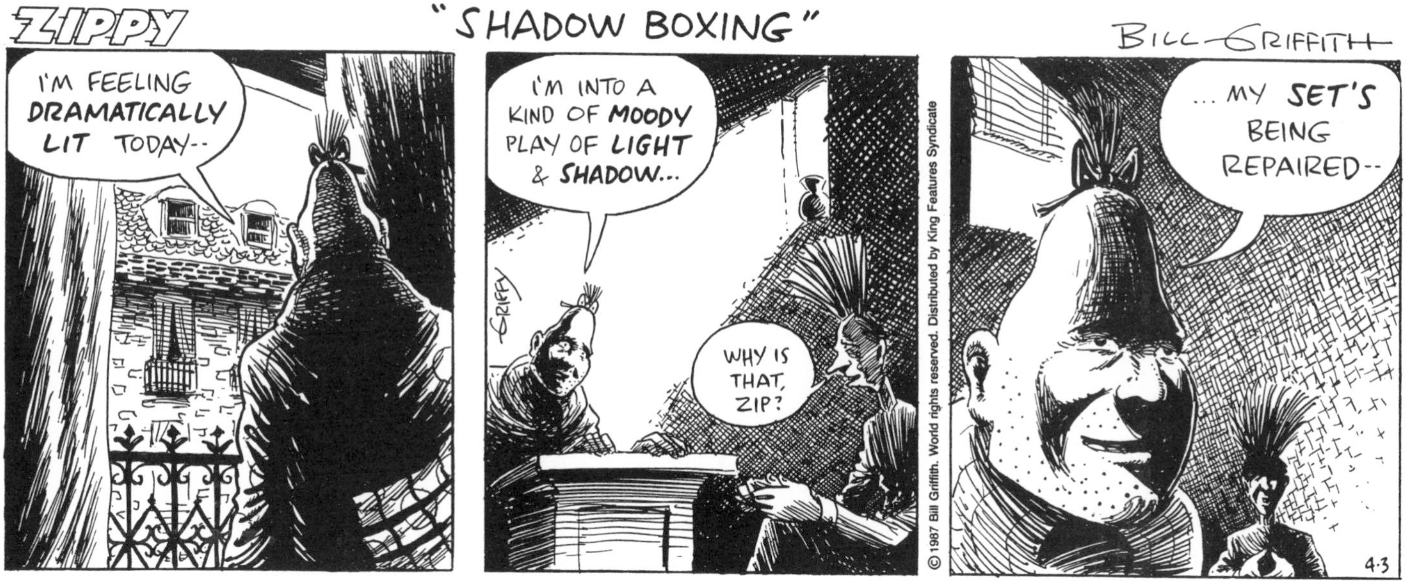
ZIPPY
"SHADOW BOXING"
BILL GRIFFITH
I'M FEELING DRAMATICALLY LIT TODAY--
I'M INTO A KIND OF MOODY PLAY OF LIGHT & SHADOW...
GRIFFY
WHY IS THAT, ZIP?
© 1987 Bill Griffith. World rights reserved. Distributed by King Features Syndicate
... MY SET'S BEING REPAIRED--
4·3

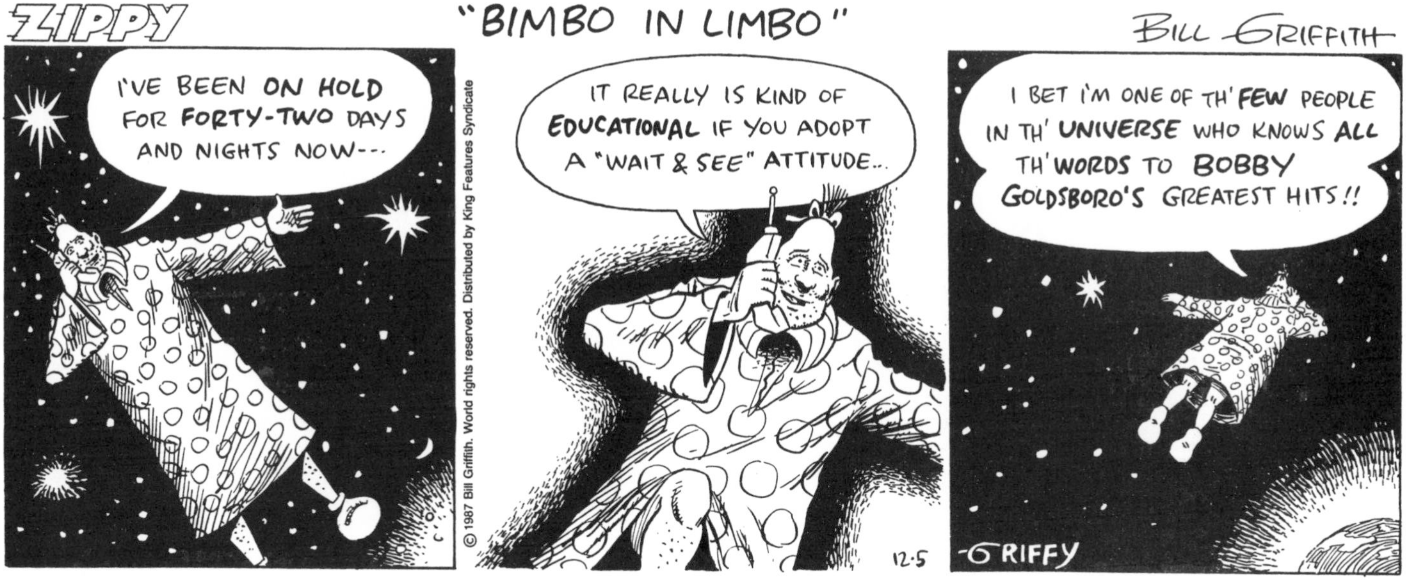
ZIPPY
"BIMBO IN LIMBO"
BILL GRIFFITH
I'VE BEEN ON HOLD FOR FORTY-TWO DAYS AND NIGHTS NOW---
© 1987 Bill Griffith. World rights reserved. Distributed by King Features Syndicate
IT REALLY IS KIND OF EDUCATIONAL IF YOU ADOPT A "WAIT & SEE" ATTITUDE..
12·5
I BET I'M ONE OF TH' FEW PEOPLE IN TH' UNIVERSE WHO KNOWS ALL TH' WORDS TO BOBBY GOLDSBORO'S GREATEST HITS!!
GRIFFY

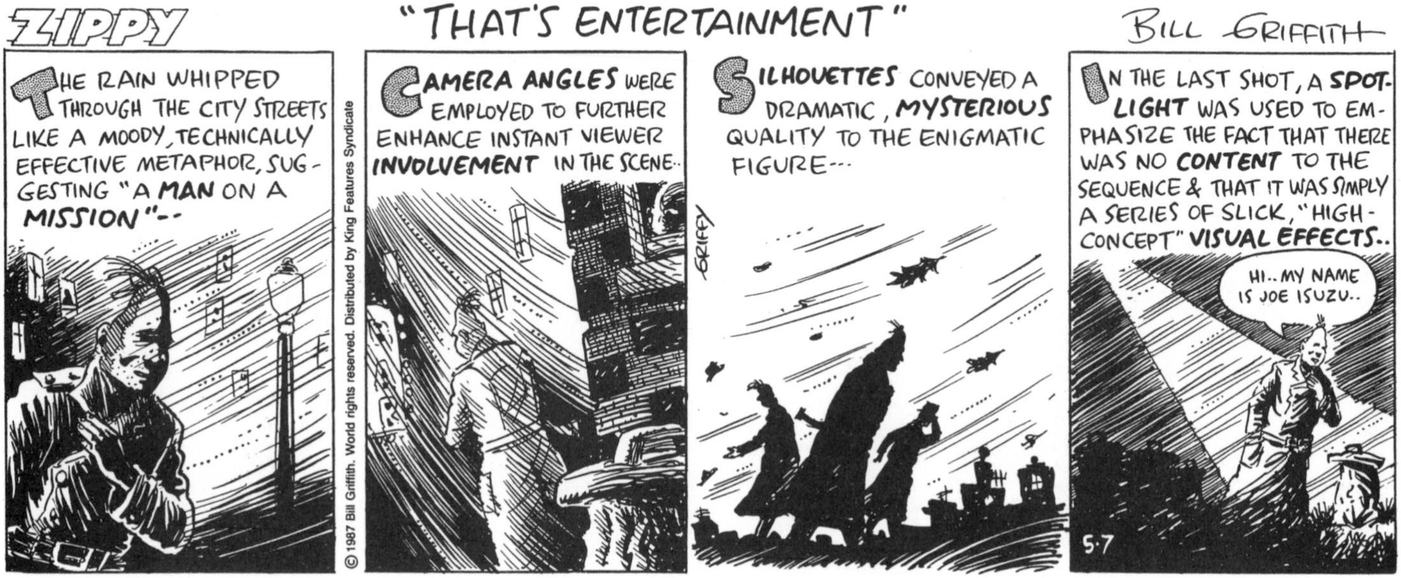
ZIPPY
"THAT'S ENTERTAINMENT"
BILL GRIFFITH
THE RAIN WHIPPED THROUGH THE CITY STREETS LIKE A MOODY, TECHNICALLY EFFECTIVE METAPHOR, SUGGESTING "A MAN ON A MISSION"--
© 1987 Bill Griffith. World rights reserved. Distributed by King Features Syndicate
CAMERA ANGLES WERE EMPLOYED TO FURTHER ENHANCE INSTANT VIEWER INVOLVEMENT IN THE SCENE..
GRIFFY
SILHOUETTES CONVEYED A DRAMATIC, MYSTERIOUS QUALITY TO THE ENIGMATIC FIGURE---
IN THE LAST SHOT, A SPOTLIGHT WAS USED TO EMPHASIZE THE FACT THAT THERE WAS NO CONTENT TO THE SEQUENCE & THAT IT WAS SIMPLY A SERIES OF SLICK, "HIGH-CONCEPT" VISUAL EFFECTS..
HI.. MY NAME IS JOE ISUZU..
5·7

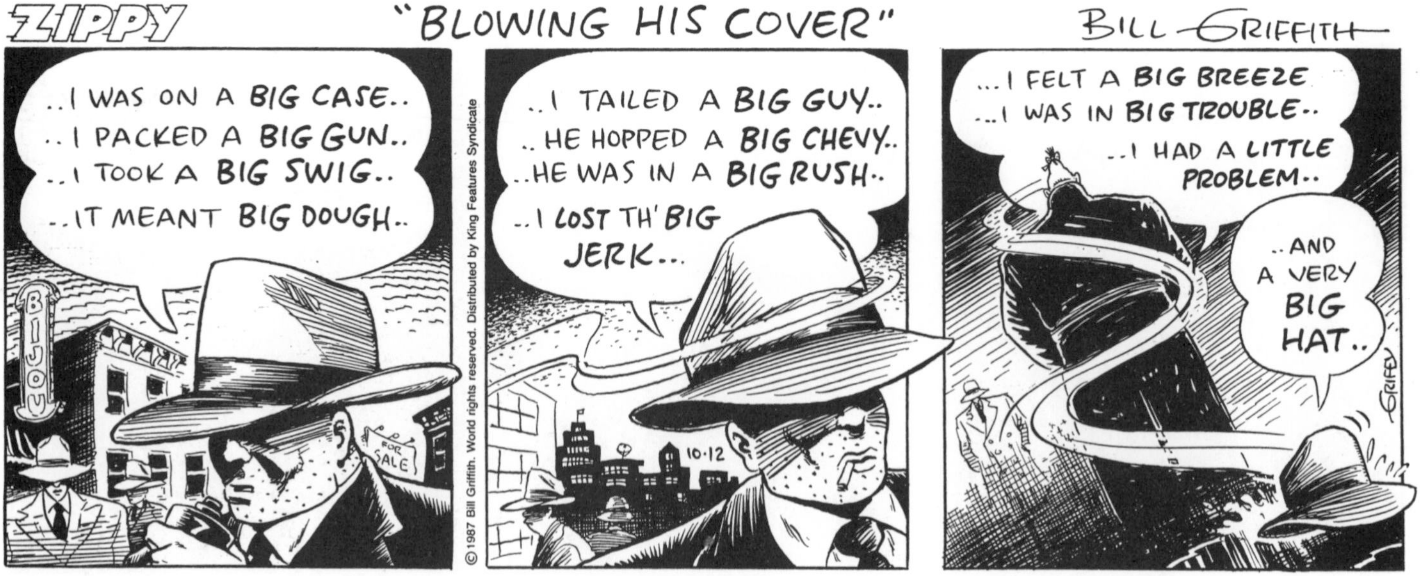
ZIPPY
"BLOWING HIS COVER"
BILL GRIFFITH
..I WAS ON A BIG CASE.. ..I PACKED A BIG GUN.. ..I TOOK A BIG SWIG.. ..IT MEANT BIG DOUGH..
BIJOU
FOR SALE
© 1987 Bill Griffith. World rights reserved. Distributed by King Features Syndicate
..I TAILED A BIG GUY.. ..HE HOPPED A BIG CHEVY.. ..HE WAS IN A BIG RUSH.. ..I LOST TH' BIG JERK...
10·12
...I FELT A BIG BREEZE ...I WAS IN BIG TROUBLE.. ..I HAD A LITTLE PROBLEM..
..AND A VERY BIG HAT..
GRIFFY

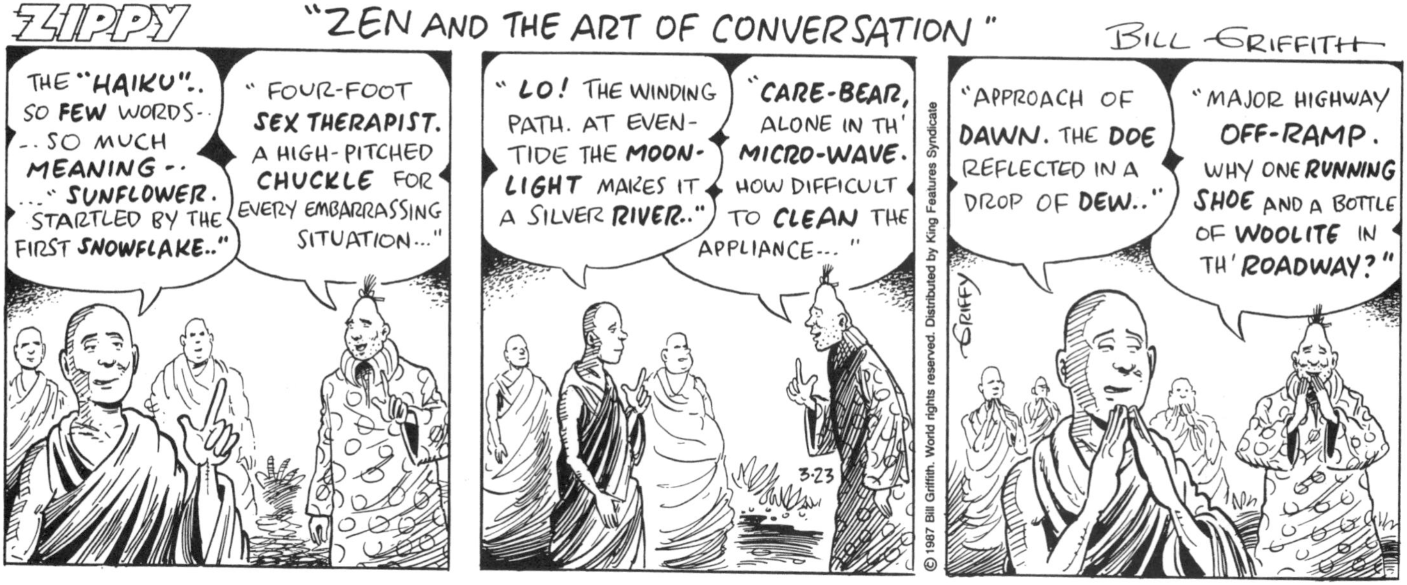
ZIPPY
"ZEN AND THE ART OF CONVERSATION"
BILL GRIFFITH
THE "HAIKU".. SO FEW WORDS-- -- SO MUCH MEANING-. ..." SUNFLOWER. STARTLED BY THE FIRST SNOWFLAKE.."
" FOUR-FOOT SEX THERAPIST. A HIGH-PITCHED CHUCKLE FOR EVERY EMBARRASSING SITUATION..."
" LO! THE WINDING PATH. AT EVEN-TIDE THE MOON-LIGHT MAKES IT A SILVER RIVER.."
"CARE-BEAR, ALONE IN TH' MICRO-WAVE. HOW DIFFICULT TO CLEAN THE APPLIANCE--- "
3·23
© 1987 Bill Griffith. World rights reserved. Distributed by King Features Syndicate
GRIFFY
"APPROACH OF DAWN. THE DOE REFLECTED IN A DROP OF DEW.."
" MAJOR HIGHWAY OFF-RAMP. WHY ONE RUNNING SHOE AND A BOTTLE OF WOOLITE IN TH' ROADWAY?"

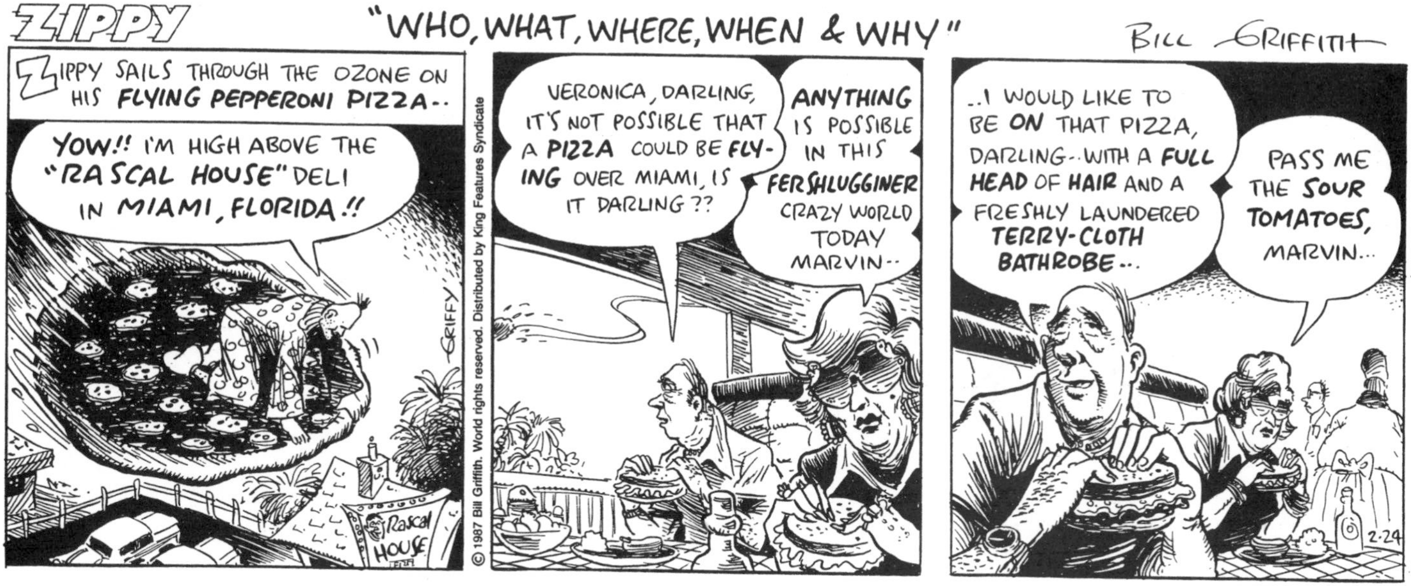
ZIPPY
"WHO, WHAT, WHERE, WHEN & WHY"
BILL GRIFFITH
ZIPPY SAILS THROUGH THE OZONE ON HIS FLYING PEPPERONI PIZZA--
YOW!! I'M HIGH ABOVE THE "RASCAL HOUSE" DELI IN MIAMI, FLORIDA!!
GRIFFY
RASCAL HOUSE
© 1987 Bill Griffith. World rights reserved. Distributed by King Features Syndicate
VERONICA, DARLING, IT'S NOT POSSIBLE THAT A PIZZA COULD BE FLY-ING OVER MIAMI, IS IT DARLING??
ANYTHING IS POSSIBLE IN THIS FERSHLUGGINER CRAZY WORLD TODAY MARVIN--
..I WOULD LIKE TO BE ON THAT PIZZA, DARLING--WITH A FULL HEAD OF HAIR AND A FRESHLY LAUNDERED TERRY-CLOTH BATHROBE--.
PASS ME THE SOUR TOMATOES, MARVIN...
2·24

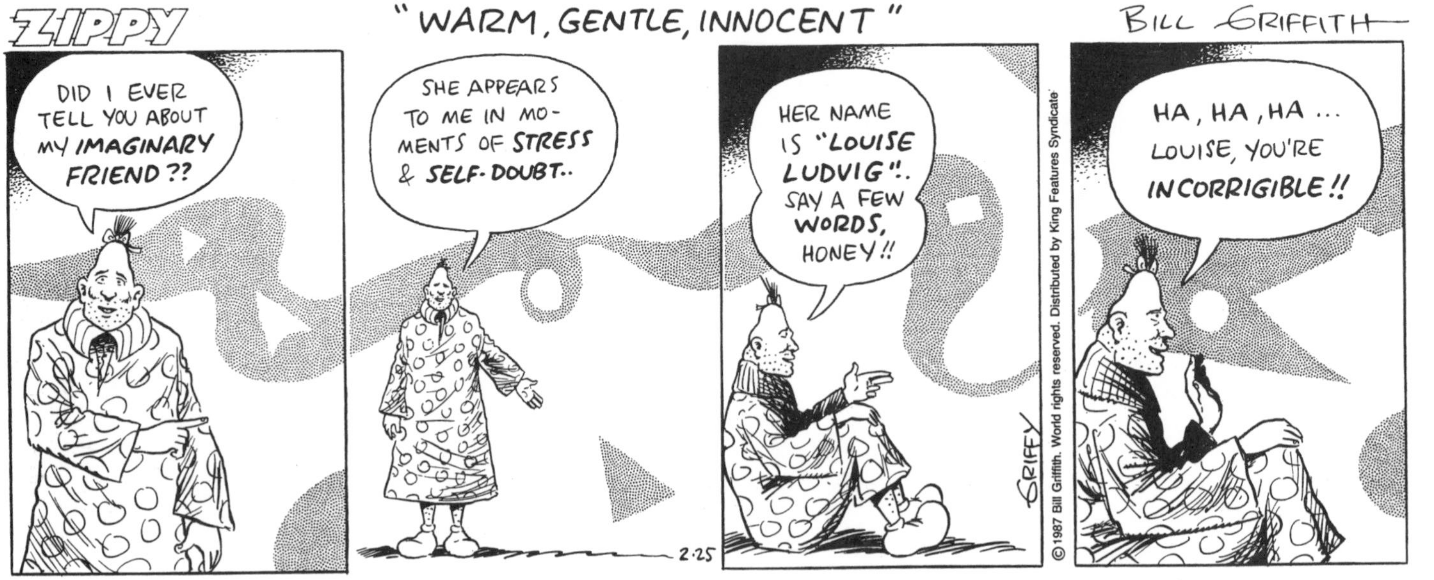
ZIPPY
"WARM, GENTLE, INNOCENT"
BILL GRIFFITH
DID I EVER TELL YOU ABOUT MY IMAGINARY FRIEND ??
SHE APPEARS TO ME IN MO-MENTS OF STRESS & SELF-DOUBT..
HER NAME IS "LOUISE LUDVIG".. SAY A FEW WORDS, HONEY !!
HA, HA, HA ... LOUISE, YOU'RE INCORRIGIBLE !!
GRIFFY
2·25
© 1987 Bill Griffith. World rights reserved. Distributed by King Features Syndicate

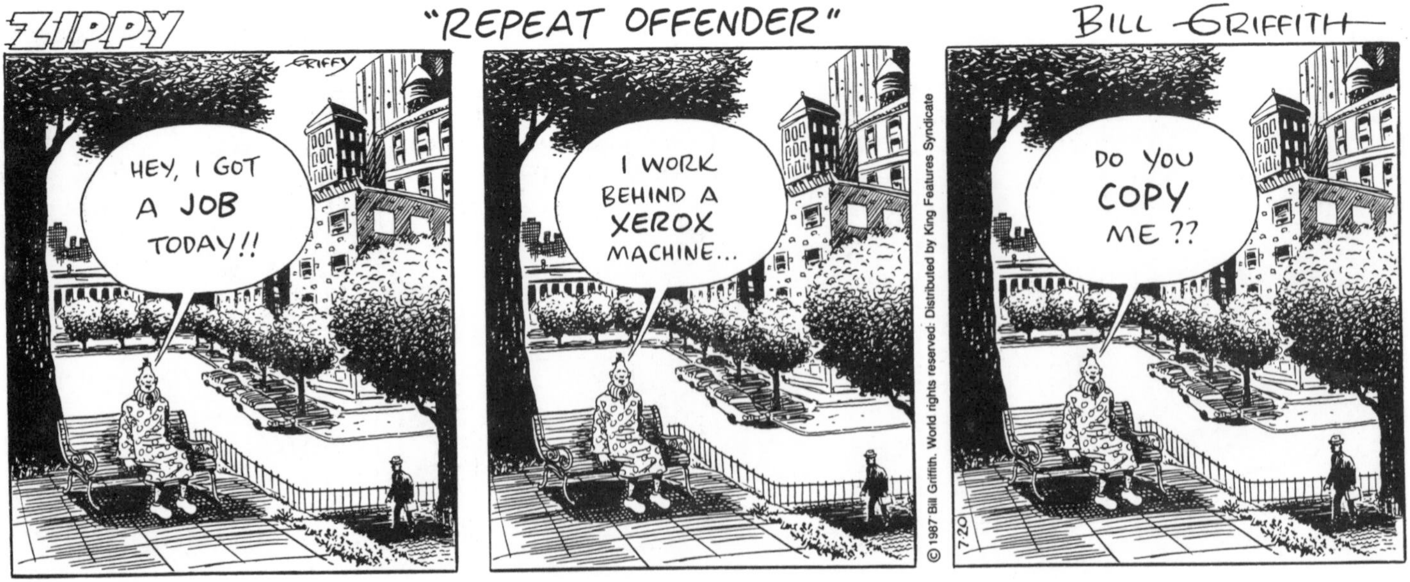
ZIPPY
"REPEAT OFFENDER"
BILL GRIFFITH
GRIFFY
HEY, I GOT A JOB TODAY !!
I WORK BEHIND A XEROX MACHINE...
DO YOU COPY ME ??
7·20
© 1987 Bill Griffith. World rights reserved. Distributed by King Features Syndicate

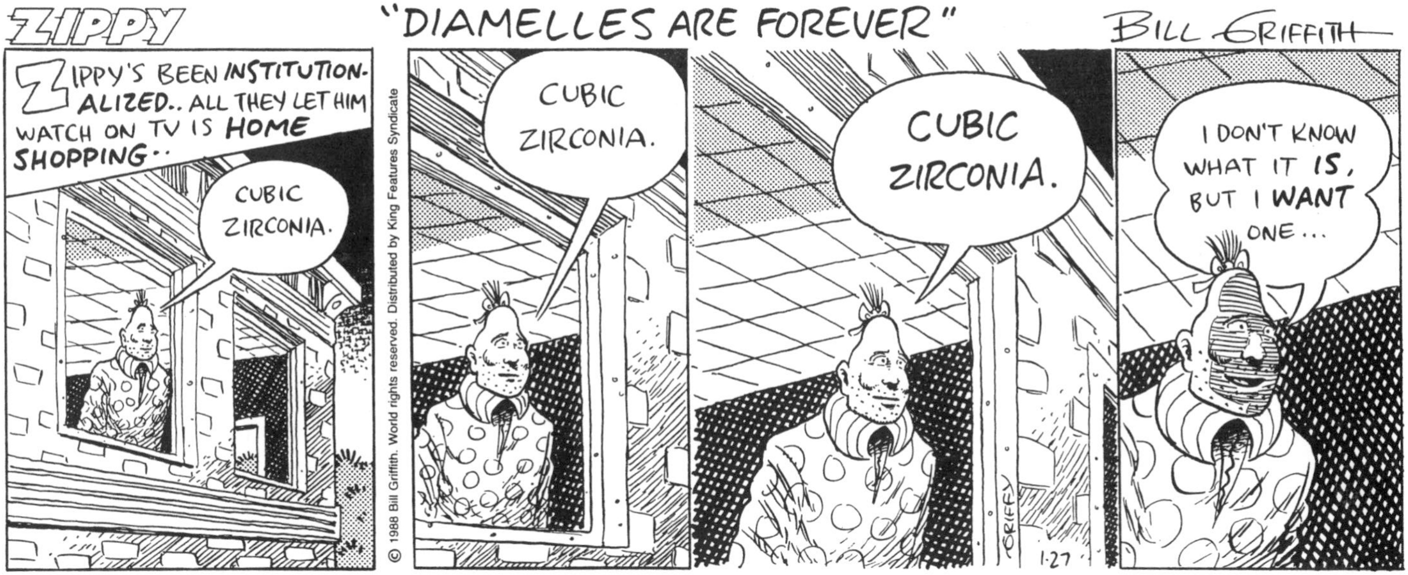
ZIPPY
"DIAMELLES ARE FOREVER"
BILL GRIFFITH
ZIPPY'S BEEN INSTITUTIONALIZED.. ALL THEY LET HIM WATCH ON TV IS HOME SHOPPING..
CUBIC ZIRCONIA.
CUBIC ZIRCONIA.
CUBIC ZIRCONIA.
I DON'T KNOW WHAT IT IS, BUT I WANT ONE...
GRIFFY
1·27
© 1988 Bill Griffith. World rights reserved. Distributed by King Features Syndicate

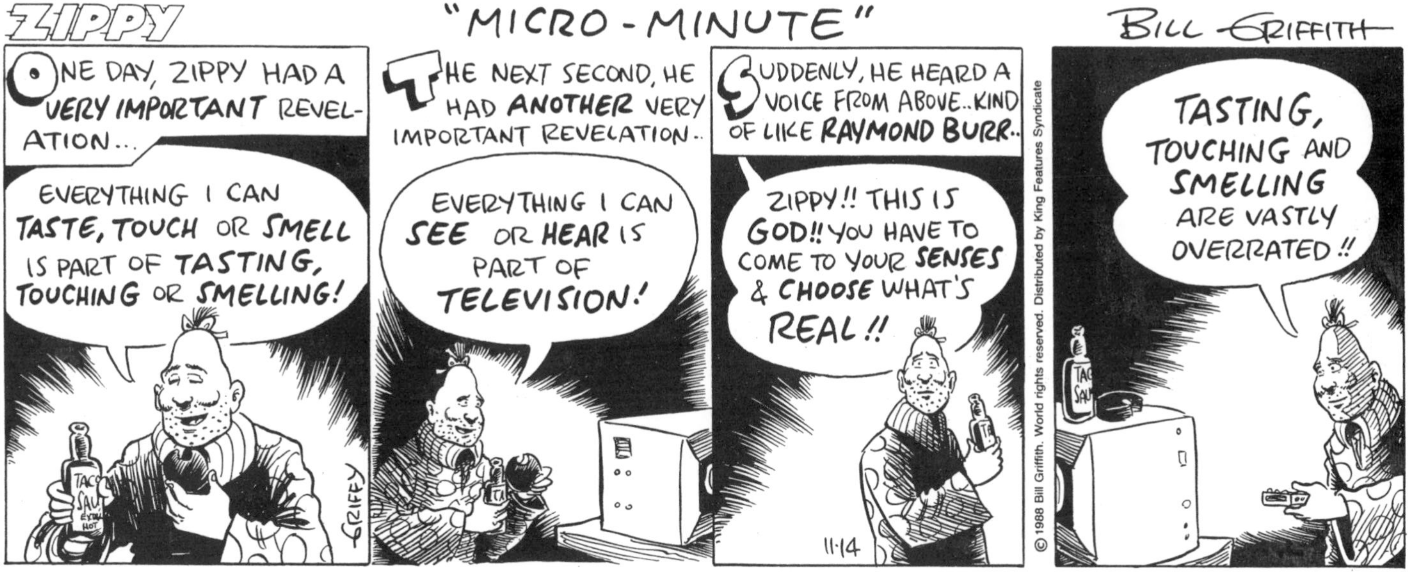
ZIPPY
"MICRO-MINUTE"
BILL GRIFFITH
ONE DAY, ZIPPY HAD A VERY IMPORTANT REVELATION...
EVERYTHING I CAN TASTE, TOUCH OR SMELL IS PART OF TASTING, TOUCHING OR SMELLING!
THE NEXT SECOND, HE HAD ANOTHER VERY IMPORTANT REVELATION..
EVERYTHING I CAN SEE OR HEAR IS PART OF TELEVISION!
SUDDENLY, HE HEARD A VOICE FROM ABOVE..KIND OF LIKE RAYMOND BURR..
ZIPPY!! THIS IS GOD!! YOU HAVE TO COME TO YOUR SENSES & CHOOSE WHAT'S REAL!!
TASTING, TOUCHING AND SMELLING ARE VASTLY OVERRATED!!
GRIFFY
11·14
© 1988 Bill Griffith. World rights reserved. Distributed by King Features Syndicate

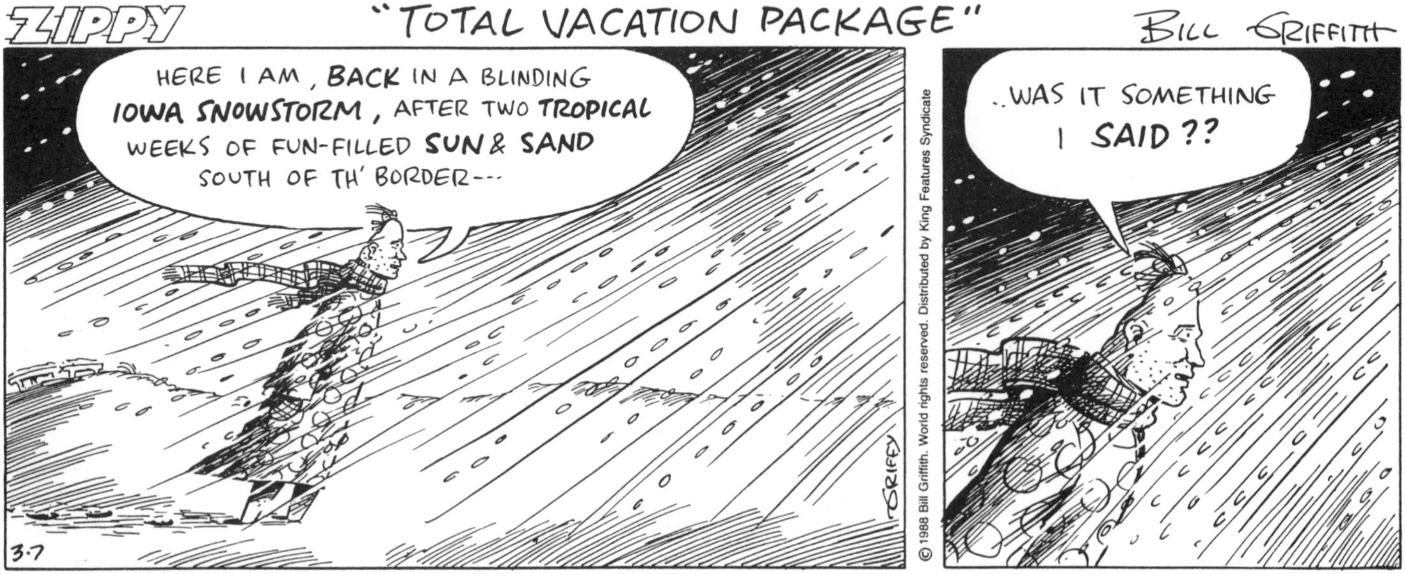
ZIPPY
"TOTAL VACATION PACKAGE"
BILL GRIFFITH
HERE I AM, BACK IN A BLINDING IOWA SNOWSTORM, AFTER TWO TROPICAL WEEKS OF FUN-FILLED SUN & SAND SOUTH OF TH' BORDER---
..WAS IT SOMETHING I SAID??
GRIFFY
3·7
© 1988 Bill Griffith. World rights reserved. Distributed by King Features Syndicate

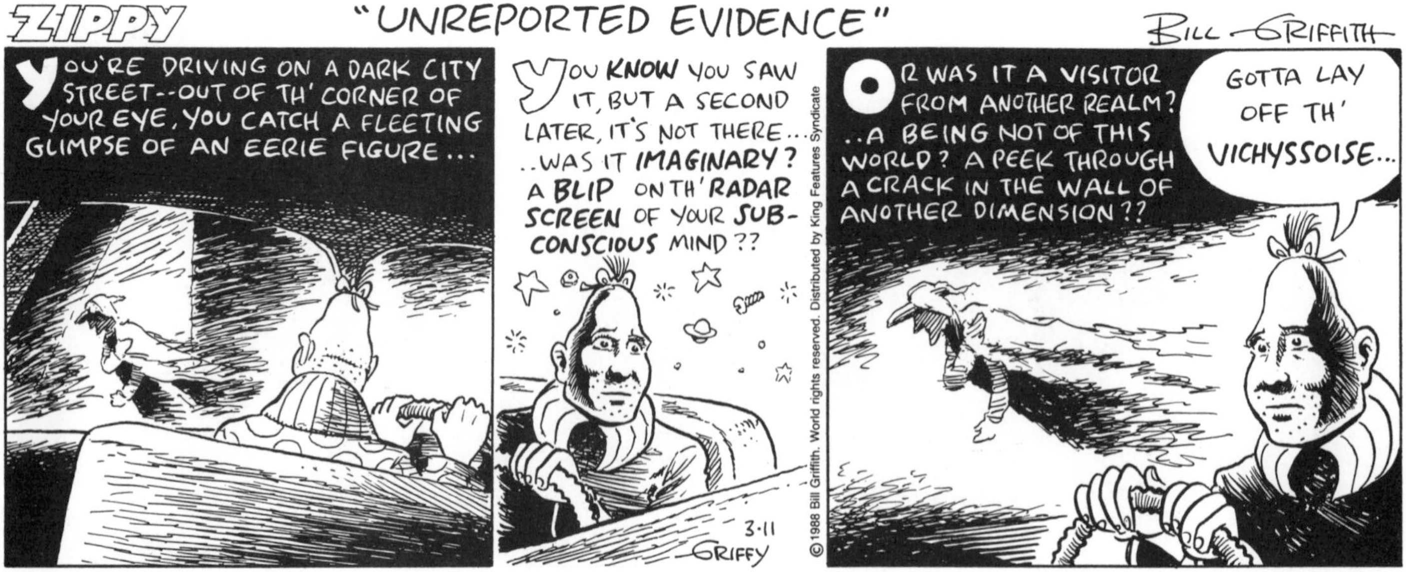
ZIPPY
"UNREPORTED EVIDENCE"
BILL GRIFFITH
YOU'RE DRIVING ON A DARK CITY STREET--OUT OF TH' CORNER OF YOUR EYE, YOU CATCH A FLEETING GLIMPSE OF AN EERIE FIGURE...
YOU KNOW YOU SAW IT, BUT A SECOND LATER, IT'S NOT THERE... ..WAS IT IMAGINARY? A BLIP ON TH' RADAR SCREEN OF YOUR SUB-CONSCIOUS MIND??
OR WAS IT A VISITOR FROM ANOTHER REALM? ..A BEING NOT OF THIS WORLD? A PEEK THROUGH A CRACK IN THE WALL OF ANOTHER DIMENSION??
GOTTA LAY OFF TH' VICHYSSOISE...
3·11
GRIFFY
© 1988 Bill Griffith. World rights reserved. Distributed by King Features Syndicate

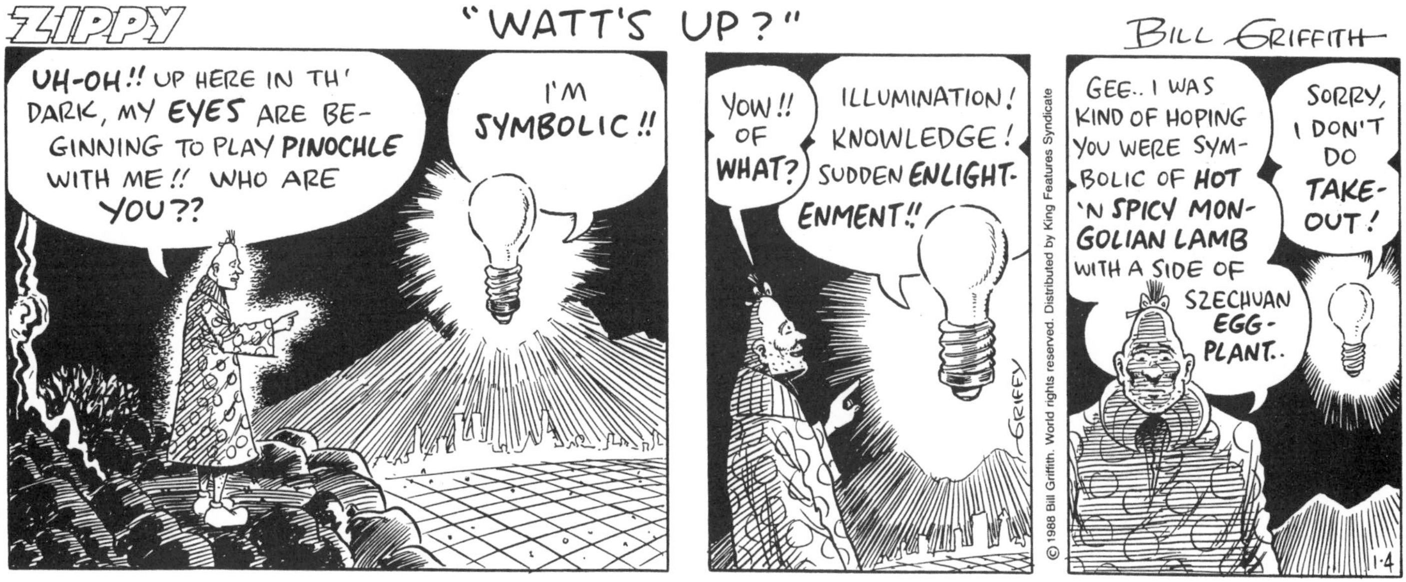
ZIPPY
"WATT'S UP?"
BILL GRIFFITH
UH-OH!! UP HERE IN TH' DARK, MY EYES ARE BEGINNING TO PLAY PINOCHLE WITH ME!! WHO ARE YOU??
I'M SYMBOLIC!!
YOW!! OF WHAT?
ILLUMINATION! KNOWLEDGE! SUDDEN ENLIGHTENMENT!!
GEE.. I WAS KIND OF HOPING YOU WERE SYMBOLIC OF HOT 'N SPICY MONGOLIAN LAMB WITH A SIDE OF SZECHUAN EGGPLANT..
SORRY, I DON'T DO TAKE-OUT!
GRIFFY
© 1988 Bill Griffith. World rights reserved. Distributed by King Features Syndicate
1·4

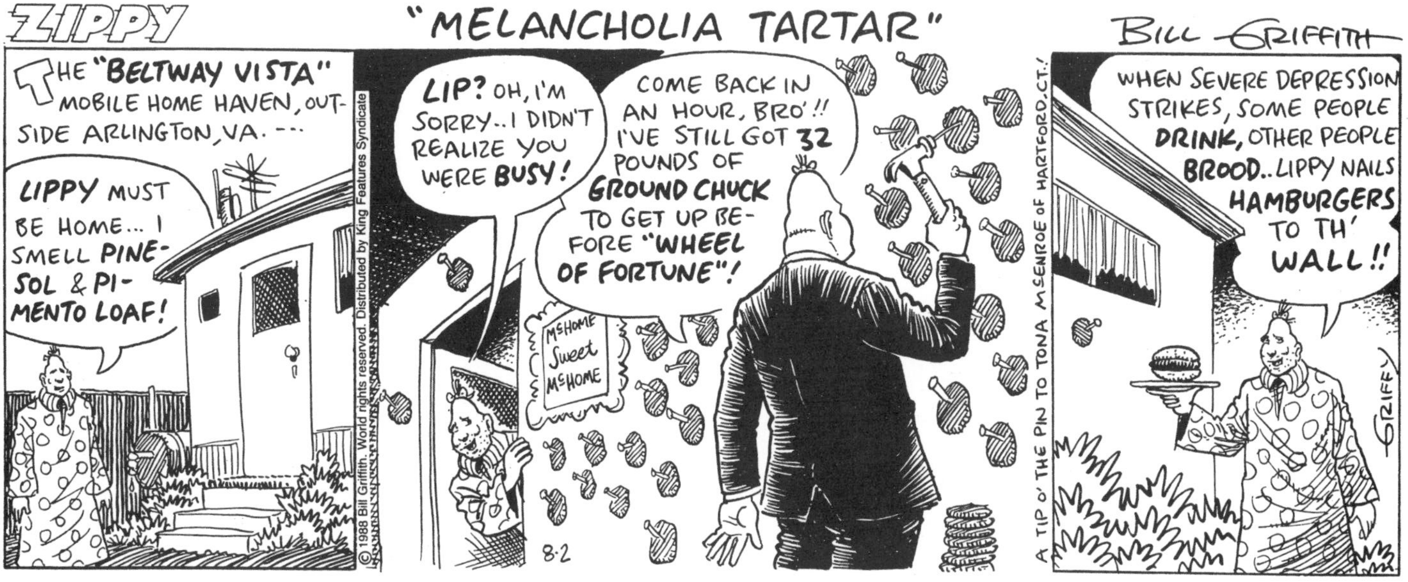
ZIPPY
"MELANCHOLIA TARTAR"
BILL GRIFFITH
THE "BELTWAY VISTA" MOBILE HOME HAVEN, OUTSIDE ARLINGTON, VA. --
LIPPY MUST BE HOME... I SMELL PINE-SOL & PIMENTO LOAF!
© 1988 Bill Griffith. World rights reserved. Distributed by King Features Syndicate
LIP? OH, I'M SORRY.. I DIDN'T REALIZE YOU WERE BUSY!
COME BACK IN AN HOUR, BRO'!! I'VE STILL GOT 32 POUNDS OF GROUND CHUCK TO GET UP BEFORE "WHEEL OF FORTUNE"!
McHOME Sweet McHOME
8·2
A TIP O' THE PIN TO TONA McENROE OF HARTFORD, CT.!
WHEN SEVERE DEPRESSION STRIKES, SOME PEOPLE DRINK, OTHER PEOPLE BROOD.. LIPPY NAILS HAMBURGERS TO TH' WALL!!
GRIFFY

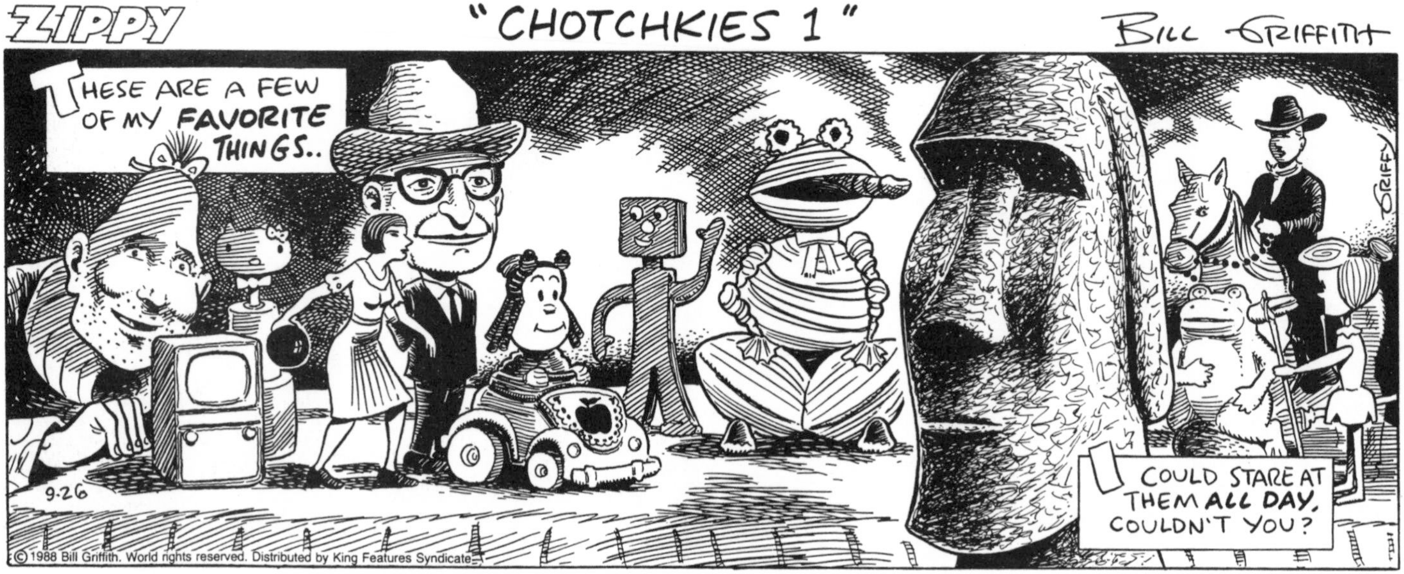
ZIPPY
"CHOTCHKIES 1"
BILL GRIFFITH
THESE ARE A FEW OF MY FAVORITE THINGS..
I COULD STARE AT THEM ALL DAY, COULDN'T YOU?
9·26
GRIFFY
© 1988 Bill Griffith. World rights reserved. Distributed by King Features Syndicate

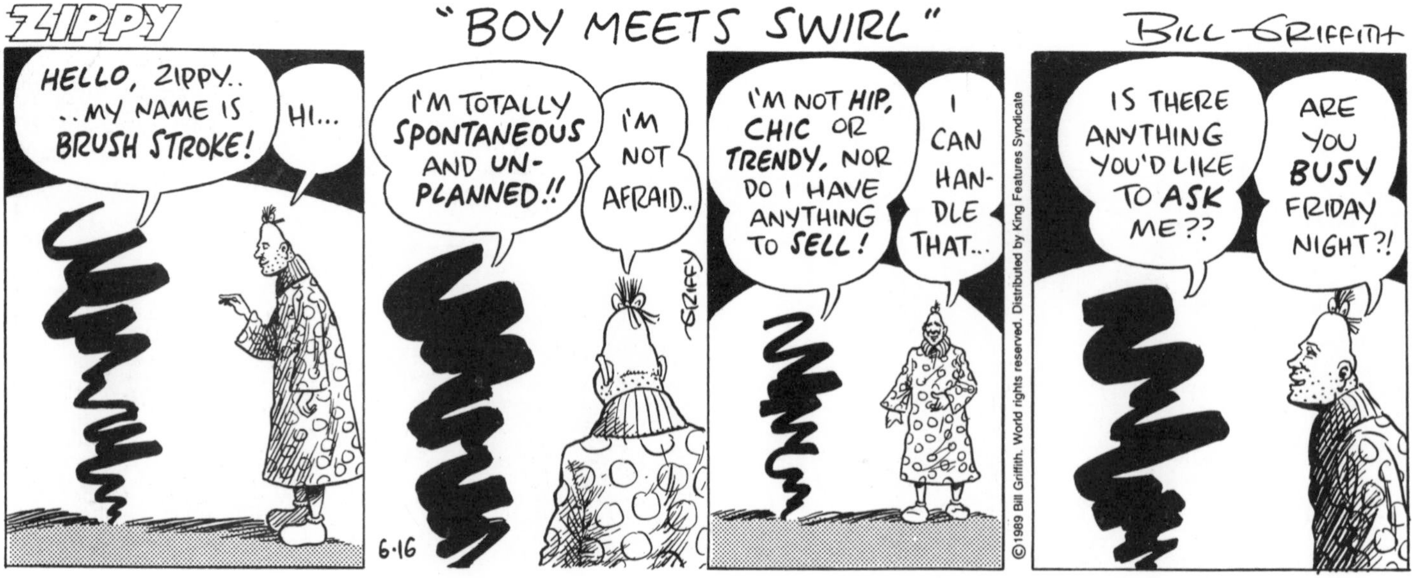
ZIPPY
"BOY MEETS SWIRL"
BILL GRIFFITH
HELLO, ZIPPY.. ..MY NAME IS BRUSH STROKE!
HI...
I'M TOTALLY SPONTANEOUS AND UN-PLANNED!!
I'M NOT AFRAID..
GRIFFY
6·16
I'M NOT HIP, CHIC OR TRENDY, NOR DO I HAVE ANYTHING TO SELL!
I CAN HAN-DLE THAT...
© 1989 Bill Griffith. World rights reserved. Distributed by King Features Syndicate
IS THERE ANYTHING YOU'D LIKE TO ASK ME??
ARE YOU BUSY FRIDAY NIGHT?!

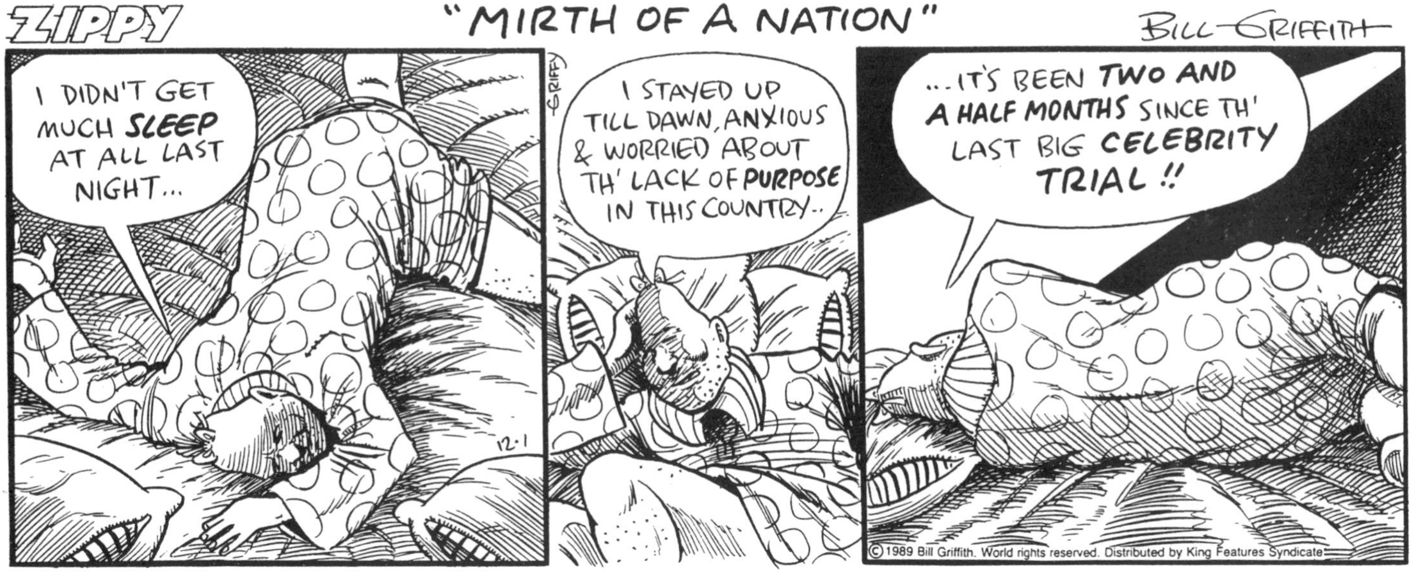
ZIPPY
"MIRTH OF A NATION"
BILL GRIFFITH
I DIDN'T GET MUCH SLEEP AT ALL LAST NIGHT...
I STAYED UP TILL DAWN, ANXIOUS & WORRIED ABOUT TH' LACK OF PURPOSE IN THIS COUNTRY..
...IT'S BEEN TWO AND A HALF MONTHS SINCE TH' LAST BIG CELEBRITY TRIAL!!
© 1989 Bill Griffith. World rights reserved. Distributed by King Features Syndicate

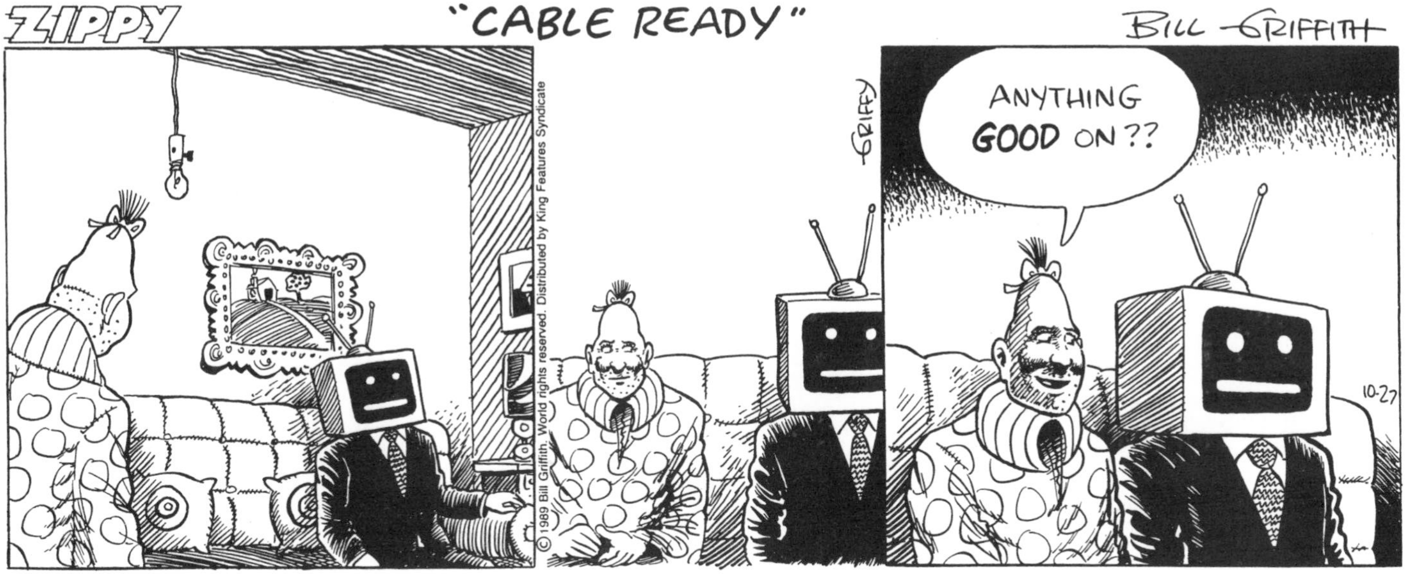
ZIPPY
"CABLE READY"
BILL GRIFFITH
© 1989 Bill Griffith. World rights reserved. Distributed by King Features Syndicate
ANYTHING GOOD ON??

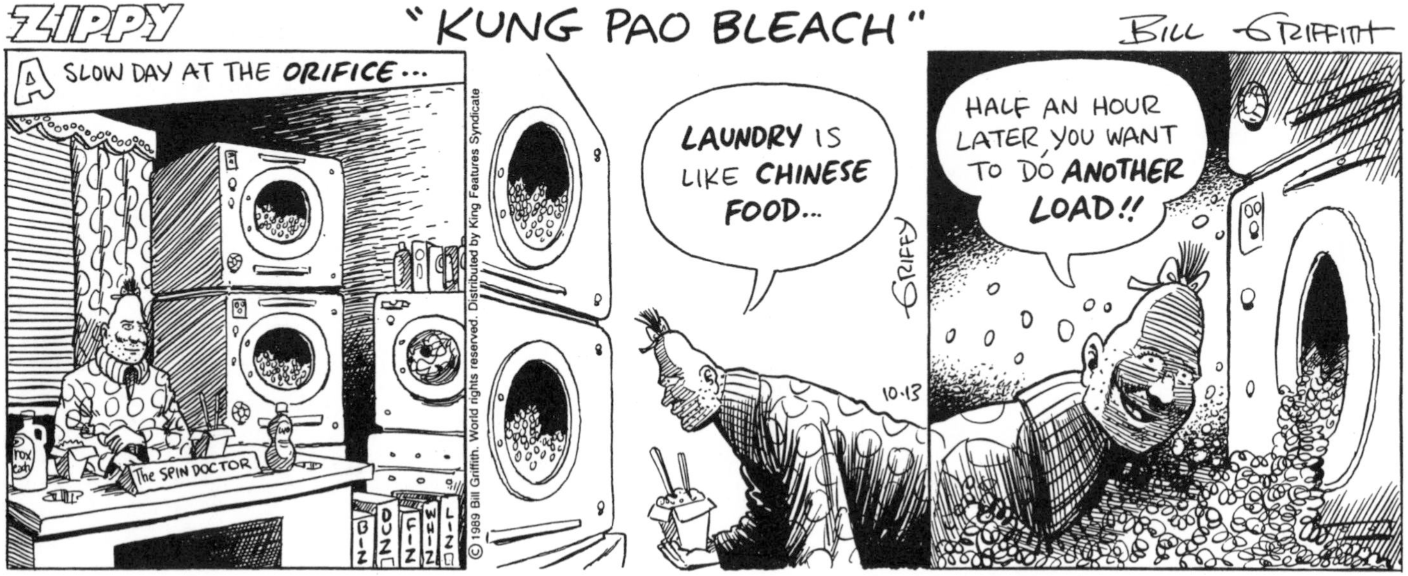
ZIPPY
"KUNG PAO BLEACH"
BILL GRIFFITH
A SLOW DAY AT THE ORIFICE...
The SPIN DOCTOR
BIZ DUZ FIZ WHIZ LIZ
© 1989 Bill Griffith. World rights reserved. Distributed by King Features Syndicate
LAUNDRY IS LIKE CHINESE FOOD...
GRIFFY
10-13
HALF AN HOUR LATER, YOU WANT TO DO ANOTHER LOAD!!

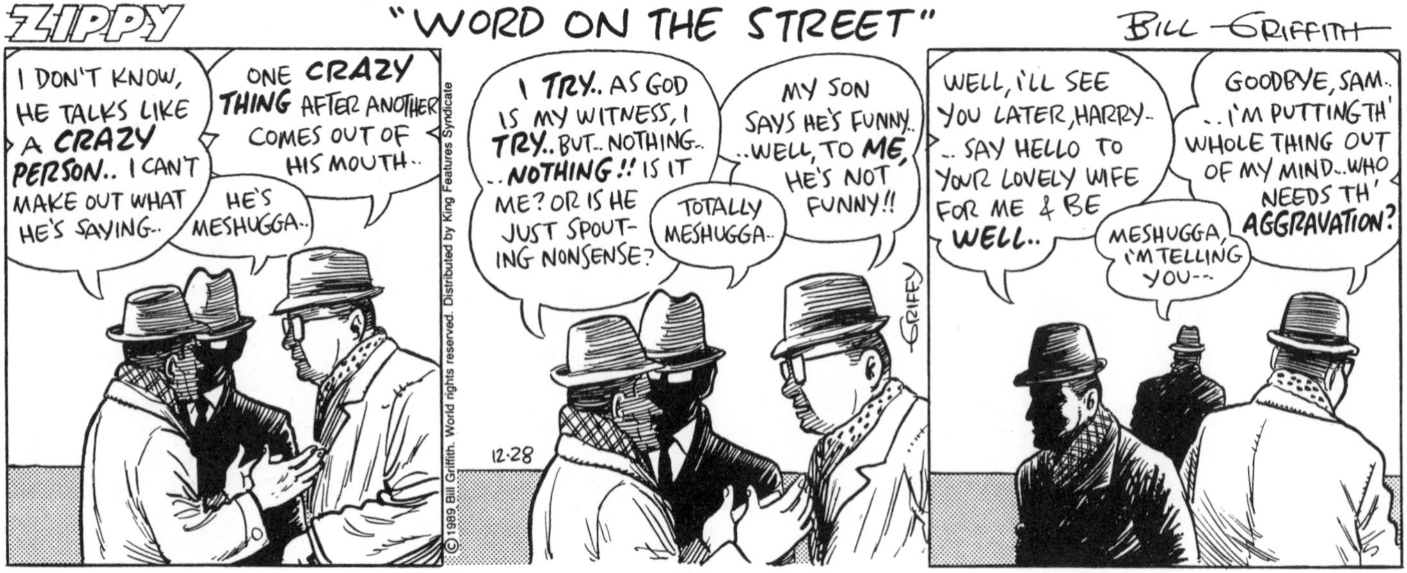
ZIPPY
"WORD ON THE STREET"
BILL GRIFFITH
I DON'T KNOW, HE TALKS LIKE A CRAZY PERSON.. I CAN'T MAKE OUT WHAT HE'S SAYING..
ONE CRAZY THING AFTER ANOTHER COMES OUT OF HIS MOUTH..
HE'S MESHUGGA..
© 1989 Bill Griffith. World rights reserved. Distributed by King Features Syndicate
I TRY.. AS GOD IS MY WITNESS, I TRY.. BUT.. NOTHING.. ..NOTHING!! IS IT ME? OR IS HE JUST SPOUTING NONSENSE?
MY SON SAYS HE'S FUNNY.. ..WELL, TO ME, HE'S NOT FUNNY!!
TOTALLY MESHUGGA..
GRIFFY
12-28
WELL, I'LL SEE YOU LATER, HARRY.. ..SAY HELLO TO YOUR LOVELY WIFE FOR ME & BE WELL..
GOODBYE, SAM.. ..I'M PUTTING TH' WHOLE THING OUT OF MY MIND..WHO NEEDS TH' AGGRAVATION?
MESHUGGA, I'M TELLING YOU--

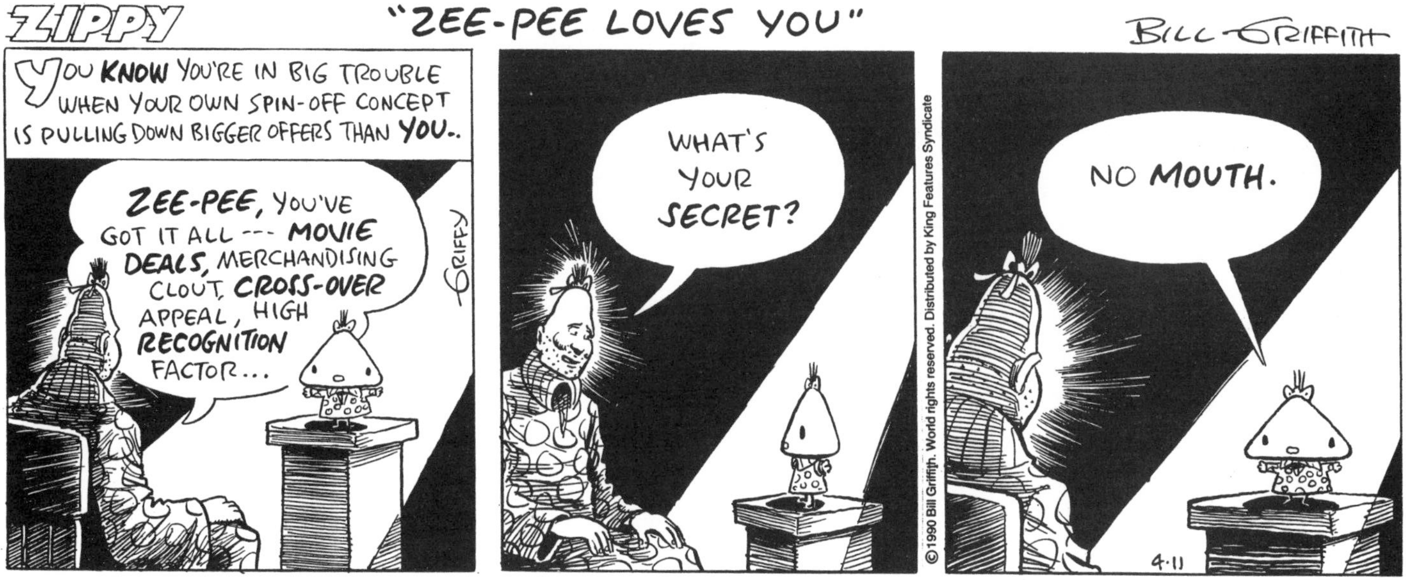
ZIPPY
"ZEE-PEE LOVES YOU"
BILL GRIFFITH
YOU KNOW YOU'RE IN BIG TROUBLE WHEN YOUR OWN SPIN-OFF CONCEPT IS PULLING DOWN BIGGER OFFERS THAN YOU..
ZEE-PEE, YOU'VE GOT IT ALL --- MOVIE DEALS, MERCHANDISING CLOUT, CROSS-OVER APPEAL, HIGH RECOGNITION FACTOR...
GRIFFY
WHAT'S YOUR SECRET?
© 1990 Bill Griffith. World rights reserved. Distributed by King Features Syndicate
NO MOUTH.
4·11

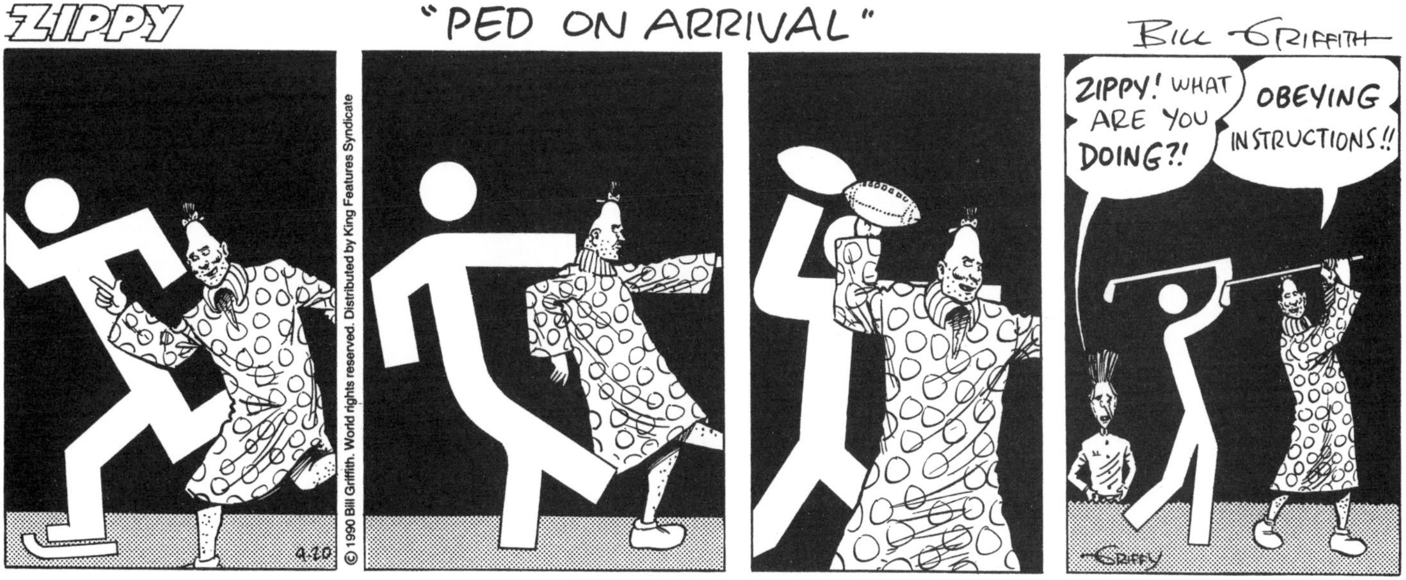
ZIPPY
"PED ON ARRIVAL"
BILL GRIFFITH
4·20
© 1990 Bill Griffith. World rights reserved. Distributed by King Features Syndicate
ZIPPY! WHAT ARE YOU DOING?!
OBEYING INSTRUCTIONS!!
GRIFFY

ZIPPY & GRIFFY Chapter 1

1. Santa Monica, CA. [pg. 8]

2. Universal Music Group building, Santa Monica, CA. [pg. 8]

3. Coca-Cola Bottling Plant, Los Angeles, CA. Rangoon is known as Yangon in Myanmar (formerly Burma), which is called Myanma Naingngandaw by Myanmarians. Yangon means "End of strife." [pg. 9]

4. National Car Wash, Los Angeles, CA. [pg. 9]

5. Charley's Beauty Salon, formerly Tamale House, Montebello, CA. [pg. 10]

6. 1) Huntington Park, CA 2) Alhambra, CA 3) West Los Angeles, CA. All buildings are formerly "Chili Bowl" restaurants, first built by Arthur Whizin in 1931. The last Chili Bowls were phased out in the mid 1940s. [pg. 10]

7. John Ronald Reuel Tolkien (1892-1973) was bitten by a tarantula as a child in South Africa. Smurfs are called Les Schtroumpfs in French, created in 1959 by Belgian cartoonist Peyo. In the animated Smurf TV series, Baby Smurf was voiced by ventriloquist Paul Winchell (1922-2005) whose two dummies were Jerry Mahoney and Knucklehead Smiff (1950s-60s). [pg. 11]

8. Clark's Elioak Farm, Ellicott City, MD. [pg. 11]

9. Houston, TX. [pg 12]

10. Pirate's Golf, Ocean City, NJ. "Up, up and away in my beautiful balloon" is a lyric from Up, Up And Away (1967) by The Fifth Dimension. In 1969, group member Florence La Rue married the band's manager, Marc Gordon, in a hot air balloon over Los Angeles. [pg. 12]

11. Wayne Junction Diner (defunct), N. Philadelphia, PA. Stanley Fafara (1949-2003) played Whitey Whitney on the Leave It To Beaver TV show (1957-1963). In the mid-60s, he moved in with the rock band Paul Revere and the Raiders, where he discovered hard drugs. He was arrested several times for burglarizing pharmacies and died living on Skid Row in Portland, OR in 2003. [pg. 13]

12. Greensboro, NC. The first blog (then called an online diary) was created in 1994 by Swarthmore student Justin Hall. The term "blog" (weblog) was coined in 1997. [pg. 13]

13. Golf course, Yamanashi Prefecture, Japan. [pg. 14]

14. Universal City, Los Angeles, CA. The Incredible Hulk was created for Marvel Comics in 1962 by Stan Lee and Jack Kirby. During a battle with his arch-enemy "Speedfreek," The Hulk was cut open with "adamantium" blades and had to hold his stomach to keep his intestines from spilling out. His alter ego, Bruce Banner, has brown eyes. [pg. 14]

15. 1) In 2005, Canadians were warned that Sealtest 1% Chocolate Milk was contaminated with a chemical sanitizer. 2) At the Hopalong Cassidy Cowboy Museum near Wichita, KS, you can buy an official Hopalong Cassidy cookie jar for $250.00. 3) Tang, the orange-flavored, powdered soft drink, was formulated by General Foods in 1959. Sales were poor until NASA began using it on Gemini space flights in 1965. [pg. 15]

16. Kentucky Center for the Performing Arts, Louisville, KY. Statue by Jean Dubuffet (1901-1985) who once said, "Personally, I believe very much in values of savagery; I mean, instinct, mood, passion, violence, madness." [pg. 15]

17. Conny's Creamy Cone, St. Paul, MN. According to the Boston Globe, George W. Bush has chosen to ignore over 750 laws passed by Congress in his "signing statements" made at the time of passage. [pg. 16]

18. Twistee Treat, St. Petersburg, FL. The Brady Bunch TV show ran from 1969 to 1974. It starred Robert Reed (b. 1932) as the father. He also had a role in the film Rocket Attack U.S.A. in 1961. He died of AIDS in 1992. Ann B. Davis (b. 1926), the housekeeper, Alice, in the series, retired from acting briefly in 1976 when she joined an Episcopalian commune. About the experience, she said, "I never heard a voice from the clouds saying get out of show business." Her most recent TV work was in a Swiffer commercial in 2004. [pg. 16]

19. Boardwalk, Santa Cruz, CA. The pop band Flock of Seagulls was formed in 1980 by two hairdresser brothers, Mike and Ali Score. Their one top-ten hit was "Wishing (If I Had a Photograph of You)" in 1983. Skeeball was invented in 1909 by J.D. Estes. The game is found in most franchises of the restaurant chain Chuck E. Cheese's. [pg. 17]

20. Roy's Grill, Rossville, GA. The Desperate Housewives series (2004-) stars Teri Hatcher (b. 1964), who began her TV career in 1985 on The Love Boat as "Amy, the Love Boat Mermaid." [pg. 17]

21. Downey, CA. McDonald's signature Big Mac (fat content: 21.5 grams) was first introduced in 1968. Their "Big Breakfast" has the highest fat content of any McDonald's product at 36 grams per serving. The "Mega Mac" (four patties and two slices of cheese) is now available only in Ireland. [pg. 18]

22. Patty's Place, Topeka, KS. The first Starbucks coffee shop opened in 1971 in Seattle WA. There are over 10,800 outlets worldwide, though not one in Italy as of 2006. Pat Robertson (b. 1930) claimed to direct the course of Hurricane Felix in 1995. [pg. 18]

23. The Deputy Dawg animated TV series ran from 1959 to 1972. Its star was voiced by Dayton Allen (1919-2004), also the voice of Phineas T. Bluster on the original Howdy Doody Show, 1947. It was directed by a young Ralph Bakshi (b. 1938), who went on to mangle Robert Crumb's Fritz the Cat in 1972. Doris Day (b. 1924) starred in numerous movie musicals in the 1950s. She's mentioned in Billy Joel's "We Didn't Start the Fire" (1989). In his 1945 film Fallen Angel, Dana Andrews (1909-1992) plays a con man who meets Linda Darnell (1923-1965) in a California diner, where much of the film takes place. Dell Comics published comics from 1929 to 1973. Among its many titles were Woody Woodpecker, Dick Tracy and Beach Blanket Bingo. Terrytoons animation studio was founded by Paul Terry in 1928 and lasted until 1968. Their most popular characters included Mighty Mouse, Gandy Goose, Deputy Dawg and Heckle and Jeckle. Cartoonist Kim Deitch's father, Gene Deitch (b. 1924), was put in control of the company in 1955 and introduced a number of new characters, including Tom Terrific and Sick Sick Sidney. [pg. 20]

24. Milwaukee Road train, observation and dining car, Union Station, Kansas City, MO. William Powell (1892-1984) was most famous for his Thin Man films, beginning in 1934. Myrna Loy (1905-1993), also noted for her Thin Man performances, was married four times, including to John Hertz of the famous rent-a-car company. Richard Gere (b. 1949) once said, "I know who I am. No one else knows who I am. If I was a giraffe, and someone said I was a snake, I'd think, no, actually, I'm a giraffe." The Dalai Lama (b. 1935) once said, "Sometimes in my dreams there are women. When such dreams happen, immediately I think, I am a monk." [pg. 20]

25. Zippy is driving a 1964 Chrysler Newport. [pg. 21]

26. Hearst Tower, 300 W. 57th St., New York, NY. Home of King Features (15th floor). The X-Men Marvel comic series was created by Stan Lee and Jack Kirby in 1963. X-Man Northstar, the first openly gay superhero (Superman still hasn't come out), is an accomplished trapeze artist and novelist. Billy DeBeck's Barney Google debuted in 1919. The strip introduced the word "heebie-jeebies" into the English language. [pg. 21]

27. Twiggy, the British supermodel, was born Leslie Hornby in 1949 and is one quarter Jewish. [pg. 22]

28. Whoopie Pies are found throughout Pennsylvania Dutch country in the U.S. They are made of two chocolate cake disks, sandwiching a sweet, creamy white frosting. In the Hindu religion, a chakra is the nexus of metaphysical and biophysical energy. [pg. 23]

29. Salisbury, MD. The Shmoo character was created by cartoonist Al Capp (1909-1979) for his comic strip Li'l Abner in 1948. Shmoos are so entertaining, people who watch them never have the urge to go to the movies or turn on the television. [pg. 23]

30. The iPod was introduced by Apple in 2001. 100 iPods were sold every minute in the first three months of 2006. The first Woolworth's five-and-ten-cent store was founded in 1878. It now survives as Foot Locker Inc. [pg. 24]

31. Chips Restaurant, Hawthorne, CA. See *Zippy Quarterly #9* (Fantagraphics, 1995) for the complete story of the "man behind the pinhead," Lazlo Crannick. [pg. 24]

32. Capitol Records building, Los Angeles, CA. "Sympathy For the Devil" was recorded by the Rolling Stones in 1968. It was also the title of a 1968 Jean-Luc Godard (b. 1930) film. Godard's favorite American writers are cartoonists Jules Feiffer and Charles Schulz. "Yummy, Yummy, Yummy" was recorded by the Ohio Express in 1968. Bobby Vinton was born Stanley Robert Vintula, Jr. in 1935. His son, Robbie, played him in the 1990 Martin Scorsese film Goodfellas. [pg. 25]

33. Fisherman's Village, Marina Del Rey, CA. [pg. 25]

ZIPPY SOLO Chapter 2

34. Clifton, NJ. [pg. 28]

35. KFC restaurant, Los Angeles, CA. Colonel Sanders (Harland David Sanders [1890-1980]) opened his first Kentucky Fried Chicken restaurant in 1952. He sold the company in 1964. In 1975, KFC sued Sanders for calling their gravy "wallpaper paste." [pg. 29]

36. Lee's Summit, MO. [pg. 29]

37. Zanzibar is the name of two East African spice islands off mainland Tanzania called Ungula and Pemba. The rock musician Freddie Mercury (Queen's lead singer) was born in Zanzibar in 1946 (died 1991). [pg. 30]

38. Carhenge, built by Jim Reinders in 1987 in Alliance, NB. [pg. 31]

39. La Boca Night Club, formerly Dark Room camera store, Los Angeles, CA. [pg. 31]

40. The Sears Coldspot refrigerator debuted in 1928, re-designed in 1934 by streamline genius Raymond Loewy. The Yoo-Hoo soft drink was famously pitched by New York Yankees catcher Yogi Berra in the 1950s-60s. Yogi once said, "I never said half the things I said." Ulysses (Odysseus in Latin) is the main character in Homer's epic poem, *The Odyssey*. The Sirens try to lure Odysseus's ship to destruction on the cliffs with their seductive singing, much like the effect of Yoo-Hoo on a sideshow pinhead. [pg. 32]

41. "Disco Duck" was a novelty disco song released by Rick Dees and His Cast of Idiots in 1976. Dees' next release, "Dis-Gorilla" (a King Kong parody), failed to repeat Disco Duck's wild success. [pg. 32]

42. Winston-Salem, NC. The Krispy Kreme donut chain was founded in Winston-Salem in 1937. The company went public in 2000, but by 2004, stock share fell precipitously due to over-rapid expansion and poor management. Bill Griffith wisely stayed out of the stock market, though Zippy readers often urged him to buy Krispy shares before the company was Kremed in 2005. [pg. 33]

43. Oklahoma City, OK. [pg. 33]

44. Beach City Chevrolet, Long Beach, CA. [pg. 34]

45. Springfield, IL. [pg. 34]

46. 1) Wein-O-Rama, Cranston, RI 2) Burg-O-Rama, Oxford, MA 3) Liquorama. Providence, RI [pg. 35]

47. Philip Grausman sculptures. Lyrics from "Witch Doctor," 1958, by David Seville, A.K.A. Ross Bagdasarian, who created The Chipmunks fictional music group later that same year. [pg. 36]

48. Philip Grausman sculpture (not the Zippy head). [pg. 36]

49. On April 11th, 2006 (the release date of this strip), the Jeopardy TV quiz show featured a category called "What's The Point?". One of the answers was a visual clue – a colorful cartoon portrait. The correct question was, "Who is Zippy the Pinhead?". The contestant with the correct response went on to win that day's game. [pg. 37]

50. 1&2) Jekyll Island Miniature Golf, Jekyll Island, GA 3) Putt-Putt Golf Course, Drayton Plains, MI 4) Panama City Beach, FL [pg. 38]

51. Stew Leonard's mega-market, Yonkers, NY. Tuxedo Sam is a Hello Kitty sidekick, created by Sanrio around 1980. His mottos are "Eternally Cool" and "He wants to help but is not needed." [pg. 40]

52. Corner of 6th Avenue and 3rd St., Park Slope, Brooklyn, NY. [pg. 40]

53. 5th Avenue, Park Slope, Brooklyn, NY, 1946. [pg. 41]

54. Park Slope, Brooklyn, NY, 1928. [pg. 41]

55. Team Zippy is a real bike club somewhere in the midwestern U.S. [pg. 42]

56. Zippy Removals (movers), Geelong, Victoria, Australia. [pg. 42]

57. Coney Island boardwalk, Brooklyn, NY. [pg. 43]

58. Frisch's, Cincinnati, OH [pg. 43]

ZIPPY & CO. Chapter 3

59. Tail O' The Pup hot dog stand, Los Angeles, CA (currently boarded up). Zippy and Zerbina don't know it, but they're discussing "Polyamory." a real group devoted to challenging the monogamous marriage model. Monogamous marriage model! Monogamous marriage model! Monogamous marriage model! [pg. 46]

60. Los Angeles, CA. [pg. 47]

61. Zurich, Switzerland. [pg. 47]

62. Santa Monica, CA. Eugene Pallette (1889-1954) appeared as a character actor in many American films, especially during the 1930s-40s. His best-known role may have been as Friar Tuck in The Adventures of Robin Hood (1938). [pg. 51]

63. Inami-cho, Wakayama Prefecture, Japan. Panel 1 Japanese translation: "Changing people and the town." [pg. 52]

64. Shoe Museum, Seattle, WA. Flock of Seagulls: see Pindex #19. The Garbage Pail Kids trading cards were released by the Topps Company in 1985. They were a parody of the popular Cabbage Patch Kids dolls and the brain-child of cartoonist Art Spiegelman, co-edited by cartoonist Mark Newgarden. In *The Garbage Pail Kids Movie* (1987), the role of Valerie Vomit was portrayed by Debbie Lee Carrington, who also made an uncredited appearance in the film *The Bonfire of the Vanities* (1990) as "a crying midget." [pg. 53.)

65. Myrtle Beach, SC. The original *King Kong* movie, directed by Merian C. Cooper, was released in 1933. In a 1971 episode of the BBC TV series, *The Goodies*, "Kitten Kong" terrorized London, destroying St. Paul's Cathedral. [pg. 53]

66. Cherokee, NC. Tinkerbell is the fictional fairy from J.M. Barrie's play and novel *Peter Pan* (1904). Disney's animated 1953 version popularized the character and she became a mascot for the company. Contrary to popular belief, Disney did not model her figure after the young Marilyn Monroe. [pg. 54]

67. 1) Manitou Springs, CO 2) Detroit, MI 3) Seattle, WA [pg. 54]

68. Oxford, MA. There really are "Snap Checkers" at French's Foods, overseeing every crunchy onion sliver for crispness at the manufacturing plant in Wolcott, NY. [pg. 55]

69. Wilmington, DE. *American Idol* winner (2002) Kelly Clarkson (b. 1982) really wanted to be a marine biologist. TV host Regis Philbin (b. 1931) has the world's record for Most Hours on Camera. He passed the 15,188 hour mark on 8/20/04. [pg. 55]

70. Tarzana, CA. [pg. 56]

71. Daytona, FL. [pg. 56]

72. Miner's Hat Realty, Kellogg, ID. [pg. 57]

DINERAMA Chapter 4

73. Risser's Diner, Stouchsburg, PA. [pg. 60]

74. L & S Diner, Harrisonburg VA. Pierce Brosnan (b. 1951) began his showbiz career as a fire eater on the streets of London. Phillip Seymour Hoffman (b. 1967) began his career as a defendant in a role on TV's *Law and Order* in 1990. *On The Waterfront* (1954) starred Marlon Brando and Eva Marie Saint. Brando's "I coulda been a contender" line in the film was voted by the American Film Institute as the third most memorable line in all of cinema. [pg. 61]

75. Cindy's Diner, N. Scituate, RI. [pg. 61]

76. Little Tavern, Wash. DC (out of business). Semiotics is the study of signs and how their meaning is understood. [pg. 62]

77. Charlie's Sandwich Shoppe, Boston, MA. [pg. 62]

78. Omar Diner, Meriden, CT. Oprah Winfrey (b. 1954) once seriously dated movie critic Roger Ebert. Warner Bros. animated cartoon character Elmer Fudd began his film career in 1937. His original name was Egghead and he was voiced by radio actor Arthur Q. Bryan (1899-1959). [pg. 63]

79. Miss Oxford Diner, Oxford, MA. [pg. 63]

80. Granby CT. Pop Tarts were introduced by Kelloggs in 1964 and took the toaster-pastry market by storm. Eventually, they developed a non-dislodging sugar sprinkle technology, revolutionizing the industry. [pg. 64]

81. West Shore Diner, Harrisburg, PA. The kazoo is a type of mirliton, modifying the voice by use of a vibrating membrane. African in origin, a kazoo was played by Mike Judge's Beavis and Butt-head characters in a Red Hot Chili Peppers music video. [pg. 64]

82. Wolfe's Diner, Harrisburg, PA. Yoo-Hoo: See Pindex #40. [pg. 65]

83. Peg's Diner, Whitinville, MA. The term "happy camper," an example of Valley Girl slang, first appeared in the early 1980s. [pg. 65]

84. Mel's Diner, Lebanon, PA. [pg. 66]

85. Chip's Restaurant, Hawthorne, CA. *Three's Company* ran on ABC TV from 1977 to 1984. Starring John Ritter (1948-2003), the show also featured Don Knotts (1924-2006) as landlord Ralph Furley, often seen wearing a wide variety of pure polyester leisure suits. [pg. 66]

86. Plum Crazy Diner, Westminster, MD. [pg. 67]

87. American Dream Diner, Harrisburg, PA. [pg. 67]

88. Bluebird Diner, Brooklyn, NY. Grinder is the term for a hero or submarine sandwich in the New England region. [pg. 68]

89. Dinah's Restaurant, Los Angeles, CA. Al Gore's IQ has been reported as 134 and George W. Bush's as 91. [pg. 68]

90. The New Ideal Diner, Aberdeen, MD. Condoleezza Rice's IQ is often reported as "genius" level (over 140). [pg. 69]

91. Miss Florence Diner, Florence, MA. The type font in the last panel is Brush Script. [pg. 69]

SUNDAY COLOR & MORE Chapter 5

92. Elsie the Cow is the advertising mascot of the Borden Company, first used in 1938. She made a live appearance at the New York World's Fair in 1939. [pg. 72]

93. 2 & 3) Houston, TX 4) Santa Monica Pier CA. Yoo-Hoo: See Pindex #40. [pg. 72]

94. Colletto Fava Mountain, near Artesina, Italy. Gelatin is the name of a Viennese art collective. [pg. 73]

95. 1 & 2) Marco Polo Motel, Seattle, WA 3) Bagdad (sic) Theatre, Portland OR [pg. 73]

96. Pok-A-Dot restaurant, Batavia, NY. [pg. 74]

97. Davies Chuck Wagon Diner, Lakewood, CO. Walter Winchell (1897-1972) invented the gossip column at the *New York Evening Graphic*. Among other words he introduced into the English language are "scram," "pushover" and "belly laugh." *The Katzenjammer Kids* by Rudolf Dirks (1877-1968) was one of the first daily comic strips, debuting in 1897. Katzenjammer (literally, cat howling) is a German term meaning "contrition after a failed endeavor." [pg. 75]

98. 1, 2 & 4) Four Sisters Owl Diner, Lowell, MA. 3) Puna, HI . [pg. 75]

99. Based on the author's accidental meeting with Arnold Stang in late 2005 in Boston MA. Mr. Stang was, in fact, extremely gracious and friendly. Stang (b. 1925) also voiced Shorty in the animated Popeye series as well as the Honey Nut Cheerios Bee in the 1980s. [pg. 76]

100. Overlea Diner, Overlea, MD. The HBO TV series *Big Love*, the story of a polygamous family in Salt Lake City, premiered in 2006. Polygamy has been banned by the Mormon Church in Utah since 1890. [pg. 76]

101. White Mana Diner, Jersey City, NJ. [pg. 77]

102. Teddy Bear Motel, Whittier, NC. The text of Revelation 14:02 in the Bible reads: "And I heard a voice from heaven, as the voice of many waters, and as the voice of a great thunder: and I heard the voice of harpers harping with their harps." [pg. 77]

103. Baby Huey is a large, naïve cartoon duck whose first appearance in Harvey Comics was in 1956. President Bill Clinton once said, "I'm a lot like Baby Huey. I'm fat. I'm ugly. But if you push me down, I keep coming back." [pg. 78]

104. Statue created by the Wellness Resource Center, University of Missouri at Columbia, to demonstrate Barbie's real-life anatomical equivalent. [pg. 78]

105. Film Noir actors mentioned were: Victor Mature (1913-199), Dana Andrews (1909-1982), Jack Palance (b. 1919 Vladimir Palahniuk), Scott Brady (1924-1985), Lloyd Nolan (1902-1985), Peter Lorre (1904-1964) and William Bendix (1906-1964). Zsa Zsa Gabor (b. 1917) starred in the sci-fi epic, *Queen of Outer Space* (1958). Zsa Zsa played the Queen of Venus on an all-female planet. [pg. 79]

106. Bill's Grill, Framingham, MA. [pg. 80]

107. Based on the author's visit to The Center for Cartoon Studies, White River Junction, VT, April 2006. The Polka Dot Restaurant's hours of operation are generally a mystery to the town's residents. The Hotel Coolidge, across the street, began life in 1849 as the Junction House, a railroad hotel. [pg. 80]

108. Al's Chickenette, Hays, KS. Jazz saxophonist Charlie Parker (1920-1955) was a founding exponent of bebop. Poet Allen Ginsberg (1927-1997) is best known as the author of *Howl* (1956), his first published work. The author once attended a reading of *Kaddish* by Ginsberg in 1960 and asked the poet to autograph his copy of *Howl*. Ginsberg obliged, asking the 16-year-old Griffith, "Man, like what year is this?" [pg. 81]

109. World's Largest Laundromat, Berwyn, IL. The 13,500 square foot facility runs entirely on solar power and features an aviary and "free pizza nights." as well as 301 washing machines. [pg. 81]

110. Clark's Elioak Farm, Ellicott City, MD. Structure originally from "Enchanted Forest" theme park, same city. [pg. 82]

111. Wilson's Carpet Outlet, Jersey City, NJ, as featured in the opening credits of the HBO TV series, *The Sopranos*. [pg. 82]

112. Burbank, CA. A lacto-vegetarian diet includes dairy products such as milk, cheese, butter and yogurt. It excludes eggs. Were he forced into lacto-vegetarianism, Zippy could never have the Big Boy Blockbuster Breakfast Special. [pg. 83]

113. Fukuoka, Japan. [pg. 83]

114. Crazy Joe's Furniture, Howell, NJ. [pg. 84]

115. Oakdale, WI. [pg. 84]

116. Fallen Dreamer sculpture by Tom Otterness, Sheldon Memorial Art Gallery, Lincoln, NB. Payday is a peanut caramel candy bar first introduced in 1932 by the Martoccio Macaroni Company. [pg. 85]

117. Philadelphia, PA. [pg. 85]

118. Stockholm, Sweden. [pg. 86]

119. Sculpture by Tom Otterness, Hudson River Park, New York, NY. [pg. 86]

120. Billy's Burg-O-Rama, Oxford, MA. [pg. 87]

121. Yin and Yang by Robert Arneson, San Francisco, CA. Leslie Gore was born Leslie Sue Goldstein in 1946. "Sunshine, Lollipops and Rainbows" hit the charts at #13 in 1965. [pg. 87]

122. Culver City, CA. [pg. 88]

123. In 1916, Albert Einstein expanded his Special Theory to include the effect of gravitation on the shape of space and the flow of time. This General Theory of Relativity proposes that matter causes space to curve, much in the way that the one pink sock falls into a black hole inside the dryer when you're not looking. [pg. 88]

124. That's Ernie Bushmiller's Nancy in the last panel. [pg. 89]

125. Carl Anderson's comic strip, *Henry*, debuted in 1932. Don Trachte began drawing the strip upon Anderson's death in 1948. Trachte became friends with illustrator Norman Rockwell (1894-1978) and bought a 1954 Rockwell *Saturday Evening Post* cover, "Breaking Home Ties." In 2002, the Trachte family asked that the Norman Rockwell Museum store the painting, but, in cleaning it, they began to suspect it was not original. In 2006, Trachte's sons decided the painting they thought was genuine

was a fake and searched Trachte's home for the original. It was found under a false upstairs wall. Trachte had painted a clever copy to avoid letting the painting fall into the hands of his wife years earlier in a bitter divorce settlement. [pg. 89]

126. "So You Want To Be A Nationally Syndicated Cartoonist": *The Comics Journal Special Edition 2001*[pg. 90], "Patriotic Duty": *The Comics Journal Special Edition 2002* [pg. 91], "Cartoonist Descending An Elevator": *The Comics Journal Special Edition 2003* [pg. 92], "She Asked Me To Stretch Her Canvas!": *The Comics Journal Special Edition 2005* [pg. 93]. [pgs. 90-93]

ROADSIDE ATTRACTIONS Chapter 6

127A-C. Bob's Big Boy, Burbank, CA. [pg. 96-97]

128. 1) Melrose Ave., Los Angeles, CA. 2 & 3) Boardwalk, Santa Cruz, CA. Laffing Sal, an automated, maniacally laughing fun house figure, was manufactured by the Philadelphia Toboggan Company in the early 1930s. Another example can be found in San Francisco's Musee Mecanique. Sal once had a chortling partner, Laffing Sam. [pg. 97]

129. Sollitto's Liquors, Providence, RI. [pg. 98]

130. Woodbury, NJ. [pg. 98]

131. Hollywood, CA. [pg. 99]

132. Topeka KS. Ward and June Cleaver, Beaver Cleaver's understanding parents, were played in the *Leave It To Beaver* TV show (1957-1963) by actors Hugh Beaumont (1909-1982) and Barbara Billingsley (b. 1915). After retiring from acting in the late 1960s, Beaumont had a successful career as a Christmas tree grower. Billingsley went on to do *Airplane!* in 1980. [pg. 99]

133. Saugerties, NY. [pg. 100]

134. New Haven, CT. The elephant statue depicted was placed on the sidewalk by the animal rights organization, PETA, to protest ill treatment of circus animals. [pg. 100]

135. South Pasadena, CA. [pg. 101]

136. Sculpture by Michael D. Stutz, South Pasadena, CA. [pg. 101]

137. Route 66, AZ. Franz Kafka (1883-1924) and William Burroughs (1914-1997) are among Zippy's favorite novelists. [pg. 102]

138. Mountaineer Inn, Asheville, NC. Constructivism began as an art movement in Russia in 1914. It dismissed "pure" art, advocating instead that art be used as an instrument for social purpose. It also influenced the Bauhaus movement in Germany in the 1930s. [pg. 102]

139. Zippy Cleaners, 149 Elizabeth St., New York, NY. *Being and Nothingness* (1943) is a treatise advocating freedom over determinism by Existentialist philosopher and novelist Jean-Paul Sartre (1905-1980). [pg. 103]

140. Fahrney's Pens, Washington DC. "The pen is mightier than the sword."– Benjamin Franklin (1706-1790), Sean Penn (b. 1960). Larry King (b. 1933). William Marcy "Boss" Tweed (1823-1878). [pg. 103]

141. Frozen Dairy Bar, Arlington, VA. [pg. 104]

142. Tropical Treat, Baltimore, MD. [pg. 104]

143. Felix Chevrolet, Los Angeles, CA. Felix the Cat was created by Otto Messmer in 1919. Cartoonist/animator Pat Sullivan also lays claim to Felix. Airplane pioneer Charles Lindbergh took a Felix doll with him on his first transatlantic flight in 1927. Robert Crumb's Fritz the Cat first appeared in print in 1965 (*Help* magazine #22). After his disgust with the commercialized *Fritz the Cat* movie in 1972, Crumb killed off Fritz in his solo title, *The People's Comics*, later that same year. [pg. 105]

144. Mary Sue Candy Company, Baltimore, MD. [pg. 105]

145. The Donut Hole, La Puente, CA. [pg. 106]

146. 1) Kindle's Donuts, Los Angeles, CA 2) Dale's Donuts, Compton, CA 3) Bellflower Bagels, Los Angeles, CA. Entenmann's Bakery started in Brooklyn, NY in 1898. [pg. 106]

147. 1) Randy's Donuts, Inglewood, CA 2) Donut King II, Gardena, CA [pg. 107]

148. Timna, Israel. [pg. 107]

149. Mattress Warehouse, Woodlawn, MD. [pg. 108]

150. Siluo Township, Taiwan. [pg. 108]

151. Kaohsiung, Taiwan. Bluesman Robert Johnson's (1911-1938) last words were, "I pray that my redeemer will come and take me from my grave."[pg. 109]

152. Tony's Ocean Deck, Ocean City, MD. [pg. 109]

153. Composite of Union 76 gas stations in N. Hollywood CA, Sacramento CA and San Marino CA. An effort is currently underway to convince the Union 76 company to stop dismantling their signature elevated orange balls. For more on how to help, go to: www.savethe76ball.com [pg. 110]

154. Leilani Lanes, Seattle, WA (demolished 2006). [pg. 110]

155. The Loaf, Elysburg, PA. [pg. 111]

156. Ocean City, MD. The Whig Party (1833-1860) was formed to oppose the policies of President Andrew Jackson and the Democratic Party he had founded. The Whigs supported the supremacy of the Congress over the Executive branch and elected two Presidents, William Henry Harrison (1773-1841) and Zachary Taylor (1784-1850). Comedian Joey Bishop's (b. 1918) catch phrase was "Son of a gun!" [pg. 111]

157. Encounter Restaurant, Los Angeles International Airport, Los Angeles, CA. [pg. 112]

158. Gas station, Ashtabula, OH (demolished). Under the rule of the Saud Royal Family in Saudi Arabia, lashing is often meted out for "sexual deviance." The lasher is required to hold a Koran under his armpit as he administers the whip, so as to "limit the force of the strike." [pg. 112]

159. Frankie Tomatto's, Markham, Ontario, Canada. The real Leaning tower of Pisa began to tilt shortly after its construction in 1173. Italian dictator Benito Mussolini (1883-1945) ordered the tower righted, but the concrete poured into its foundation only caused it to sink further into the soft soil. [pg. 113]

160. Picture Perfect Hair Salon, Asheville, NC. [pg. 113]

161. Backyard of George and Pam Farnham, Unger, WV. Left to right, the statues are: Brian the Surfer, The Midas Muffler Man and Big John of the Big John Supermarket chain. [pg. 114]

162. 1 & 3) Monument of Independence, Almaty, Kazakhstan. 2 & 4) Brian the Surfer (see Pindex #161). [pg. 114]

163. Upper Deerfield, NJ. [pg. 115]

164. Mr. Bill's, Winslow Township, NJ. One of several "Alfred E. Neuman" Muffler Men in existence. Doris Day once said she never knew her famous co-star Rock Hudson (1925-1985), was gay. Fauvism flourished in the late 19th Century in France (Les Fauves means "wild beasts" in French). Among its practitioners were painters Paul Gaugin and the young Henri Matisse. [pg. 115]

165. Atop the Colonial Diner, Flint, MI. *Attack of the 50 Foot Woman* was released in 1958, starring Allison Hayes (1930-1977). [pg. 116]

166. Uniroyal Tire Lady, Hilltop, NJ. The Olive Garden restaurant chain was founded in Orlando, FL in 1982. Every Fall, they feature a "Never Ending Pasta Bowl." [pg. 116]

167. Springfield, IL. Muffler Man decapitated in a severe windstorm, 2006. [pg. 117]

168. Jawor's Fun Golf, Roseville, MI. [pg. 117]

169. Royal Oak Miniature Golf, Royal Oak, MI. [pg. 118]

170. Sculpture by Jonathon Borofsky, Venice, CA. Garbage Pail Kids: see Pindex #64. [pg. 118]

171. Franconia Sculpture Park, Taylor Falls, MN. [pg. 119]

172. "Sergio" the Muffler Man, Los Angeles, CA [pg.119]

SELECTED SHORTS Chapter 7

173. The reprints in this chapter are selected from the following Zippy collections:
Nation of Pinheads, 1983, And/Or Press, Berkeley CA
Pointed Behavior, 1984, Last Gasp, Inc., San Francisco CA
Pindemonium, 1986, Last Gasp, Inc., San Francisco CA
King Pin, 1987, E.P. Dutton, New York NY
Pinhead's Progress, 1989, E.P. Dutton, New York NY
From A to Zippy, 1991, Penguin Books, New York NY
[pgs. 122- 139]

ALSO AVAILABLE FROM FANTAGRAPHICS

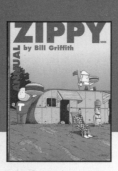

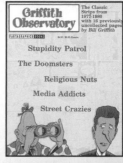